Tamil Nadu Human Development Report
2017

State Planning Commission
Government of Tamil Nadu

First published in 2017
by

ACADEMIC FOUNDATION
4772-73 / 23 Bharat Ram Road, (23 Ansari Road),
Darya Ganj, New Delhi - 110 002 (India).
Phones : 23245001 / 02.
Fax : +91-11-23245005.
E-mail : booksaf@gmail.com
www.academicfoundation.org

Tamil Nadu Human Development Report 2017

ISBN 9789332703513

Typeset by Italics India, New Delhi.

Printed and bound by The Book Mint, New Delhi.
www.thebookmint.in

Contents

List of Tables, Figures and Boxes

Tables

Figures

Boxes

Edappadi K. PALANISWAMI
Chief Minister

SECRETARIAT
Chennai - 600 009

Date 1.3.2017

FOREWORD

I am very happy that the second Tamil Nadu Human Development Report is being brought out by the State Planning Commission. Our Revered Leader the late Hon'ble Chief Minister Puratchi Thalaivi Amma had written the Foreword for the first Tamil Nadu Human Development Report which was brought out in 2003. It is well known that Tamil Nadu is one of the most progressive States in India. In the period since 1991, Tamil Nadu has witnessed the most rapid improvement in terms of social economic indicators amongst all the States in the country.

In 2012, our Revered Leader the late Hon'ble Chief Minister Puratchi Thalaivi Amma had launched the Tamil Nadu Vision 2023 with goals and themes which would have the most perceptible impact on the lives of common citizens including substantial increase in income through generation of fruitful employment, improving quality of life through the provision of high quality infrastructure and services, focused growth of sectors where the State has a competitive advantage and above all peace, prosperity and protection of the vulnerable. The goal of my Government is to enable the people of Tamil Nadu to realise their legitimate expectations of further enhancing the quality of their lives.

Documents like the Human Development Report help to measure the progress along the path that we had set for us. It also helps to compare Tamil Nadu's achievements in various social, economic sectors with other States, particularly comparator States.

Our Revered Leader the late Hon'ble Chief Minister Puratchi Thalaivi Amma did not believe in resting on laurels. In the Tamil Nadu Vision 2023 Document aspirational and ambitions targets have been set. The present Human Development Report while highlighting the achievements of Tamil Nadu along different dimensions of Human Development, also identifies the next order of challenges that lie ahead of us, thereby enabling the State to address them in a concerted fashion.

I am confident that this Report will contribute significantly in realising the development goals of Tamil Nadu and also to ensure that we are in line to implement the Sustainable Development Goals identified by the United Nations for achievement by 2030.

1/3/2017

K. PALANISWAMI

D. JAYAKUMAR
MINISTER FOR FISHERIES, FINANCE,
PERSONNEL AND ADMINISTRATIVE REFORMS

GOVERNMENT OF TAMIL NADU
TRUTH ALONE TRIUMPHS

SECRETARIAT
CHENNAI - 600 009.

Date 01.03.2017

FOREWORD

Tamil Nadu has been India's most progressive State and is amongst the top three on several economic and social indicators. Our visionary leader, the late Hon'ble Chief Minister Puratchi Thalaivi Amma, has vowed to make Tamil Nadu reach the status of developed countries in human development. With this commitment, the late Hon'ble Chief Minister Puratchi Thalaivi Amma has allocated Rs.2.11 lakh crore for the Twelfth Five Year Plan and designed special programmes for the empowerment of the poor and women like Solar Powered Green Houses, Maternity Assistance, Welfare kit for both the mother and New-born baby, Educational aids to children, Free bicycles and Laptops for students and Habitation Improvement scheme to improve infrastructure at the habitation level touching all walks of human life.

State's consistent investment with more than 60 per cent of the budget in social sectors has yielded significant results such as high income, low poverty levels, high enrolment and better nutrition level. The gross enrolment in tertiary education is very high when compared to other major Indian States.

The Tamil Nadu Human Development Report 2017 prepared by the State Planning Commission presents a detailed analysis on the different aspects of human well-being in a disaggregated manner. The report highlights achievements of the State and also the inter district disparities which require the attention of the State for correctional measures. This, I hope, will help to focus our attention on the relatively less developed districts. I appreciate the efforts made by the officials of the State Planning Commission and other development departments who contributed in the preparation of this report.

D. Jayakumar 1/3/17.

D. JAYAKUMAR

Acknowledgements

The preparation of the Tamil Nadu Human Development Report has been an initiative of the Government of Tamil Nadu supported by the United Nations Development Programme and the NITI Aayog.

The State Planning Commission has been assisted by Madras Institute of Development Studies (MIDS), Chennai, in the preparation of State Human Development Report.

Tmt. Santha Sheela Nair I.A.S., (Retd.), former Vice Chairman, State Planning Commission, Dr. Girija Vaidyanathan I.A.S., Chief Secretary to Government, and Thiru. S. Krishnan I.A.S., Principal Secretary, PD&SI Department guided the formulation of concepts towards preparation of the Human Development Report and provided critical review.

Thiru. Anil Meshram, I.A.S., Member Secretary, State Planning Commission, Thiru M.Balaji, I.A.S., former Member Secretary, Dr. Sugato Dutt, I.F.S., Head of Division (Land Use) and Thiru. P.Selvarajan, former Head of Division (Rural Development & District Planning) developed the report through their interactions and analytical feedback with the varied agencies of Government.

The State Planning Commission acknowledges with gratitude the Departments of Adi Dravidar & Tribal Welfare, Backward Classes and Minorities Welfare, Differently-abled, Economics & Statistics, Health & Family Welfare, Higher Education, Labour & Employment, Public Health & Preventive Medicine and School Education for providing necessary data towards the preparation of the report and validating the authenticity.

Thiru Tuhin Pandey, former Joint Secretary & National Project Coordinator–HDBI & SCDP Project, NITI Aayog, Thiru Vikram Singh Gaur, Joint Secretary & National Project Coordinator–HDBI & SCDP Project, Thiru Sharad Pant, Director (State Plans Coordination) and Dr. Sumeeta Bannerji, Assistant Resident Representative, UNDP, Ms. Ritu Mathur, Programme Analyst, UNDP, Dr. Swayamprabha Das, Project Manager, NITI Aayog (HDBI Project), provided technical support and funding for the preparation of the report.

The State Planning Commission also acknowledges the institutional support offered by MIDS in this venture, and is grateful to Prof. Shashanka Bhide, Director MIDS and Prof. R. Maria Saleth, former Director, MIDS in particular.

The Senior District Planning Officer, State Planning Commission Ms. S. Namagiri, and Planning Officer, (RD&DP) Division, Tmt. G.N. Krupa, liaisoned with all departments and institutions concerned and contributed richly towards the authentication of the contents.

Last, but not least, all the officials and staff of State Planning Commission contributed in making this work fruitful.

1

State Profile

While India has increased its per capita income in recent years through fairly sustained high growth rates in income, its human development indicators still trail those of some countries with similar incomes. An oft-cited example is Bangladesh which, despite lower per capita incomes, fares better than India in various human development parameters. It is in this regard that States like Tamil Nadu within the country have been hailed as a model in recent years for combining relatively high growth with high levels of human development. In fact, Tamil Nadu along with Kerala, is likely to rank at the top among South Asian countries, with regard to attainments in health and education. Dreze and Sen (2013), in their book, *India: An Uncertain Glory*, clearly highlight the progress that the State has made in various aspects of human development such as education, health and poverty reduction. The factors that drive this process and the continuing challenge to improve further therefore warrant attention.

The experience of a relatively advanced state like Tamil Nadu also offers lessons for other less developed ones in the country. Importantly, it also offers a window to observe some of the inadequacies in the path traversed this far and hopefully help such States avoid similar pitfalls. While the possible discordance between growth and development is now well recognised, there is a growing realisation of the importance of institutions that govern growth and distribution. In the context of India, Dreze and Sen (2013) cite literature to show how the institution of caste has inhibited growth. As Ambedkar has pointed out, caste is not a division of labour, but a division of labourers that poses barriers to mobility and access to resources. The process of rendering institutions more inclusive is therefore critical to ensure growth and more importantly to ensure that the fruits of growth are shared in a broad-based manner. This is particularly important in a context where investments in human capital are seen to be critical to sustain a virtuous cycle of growth and development. Tamil Nadu has been a State that is witness to a long history of social and political mobilisation against caste-determined hierarchies; and it has been pointed out that its relatively better performance in terms of growth, poverty reduction and human development can be attributed to such collective action (Kalaiyarasan, 2014).

Tamil Nadu is a State that continued to have poverty levels higher than the national average even until the 1980s. It is only since the early 1990s that we witness rapid reduction in poverty and improvement in per capita incomes. As Dreze and Sen (2013) point out, the State's investments in social infrastructure, such as the free Mid-day Meal Scheme (MDMS) for school children, driven by the emergence of concerted public action with its roots in social movements that sought to question and delegitimise social hierarchies and democratise public spheres have been critical to this shift. Further, the case of Tamil Nadu clearly demonstrates that investments made in social welfare need not undermine the growth imperative as it was believed that such investments dried up resources for productive growth-enhancing investments. In fact, it would appear that investments in social sectors driven by democratising collective action have led to translation of such inputs into growth increases. Importantly, the improvements in growth have allowed the State to mobilise resources that could be channelled back into social sectors.

There are, however, challenges for such high performing States in order to sustain and improve upon their achievements. As the latest *Global Human Development Report* (GHDR) fears, high attainments can easily be undermined by natural and economic shocks in an increasingly interdependent world. The Report highlights the various vulnerabilities that have emerged on account of environment, financial instability, political conflicts and unresponsive State institutions.

> Real progress on human development, then, is not only a matter of enlarging people's critical choices and their ability to be educated, be healthy, have a reasonable standard of living and feel safe. It is also a matter of how secure these achievements are and whether conditions are sufficient for sustained human development. An account of progress in human development is incomplete without exploring and assessing vulnerability (p.1).

The Report observes that since 2008, there has been a reduction in the rate at which improvements in human development have taken place globally. It introduces the concept of human vulnerability to refer to the sources through which people's capabilities and choices can be undermined. Women, for instance, are more vulnerable than men. Similarly, the aged, children, casually employed and marginal social groups are all subject to certain vulnerabilities in this regard. Then again, an inability to address capabilities at one node in the life cycle can have repercussions throughout one's life cycle. Lack of education as a child or of employment for youth, for example, will perpetuate long-term vulnerabilities. To address this, the Report calls for a targeted intervention aimed at specific vulnerable groups. In this context, the Report emphasises "*human resilience*—ensuring that people's choices are robust, now and in the future, and enabling people to cope and adjust to adverse events." Recognition of the multidimensional aspects of poverty is therefore essential to ensure such human resilience. It also highlights the importance of putting in place institutions that can insulate people from future vulnerabilities.

The Government of Tamil Nadu has set high standards for itself in its developmental endeavour. Premised on the idea of inclusive growth, the Vision 2023 document envisages six-fold increase in per capita incomes in real terms to reach the level of current median income of the upper middle income countries and also to attain a human development index comparable to that of the developed countries by 2023.[1] The document also anticipates a poverty-free Tamil Nadu to be achieved by focussing on inclusive growth policies that will assure productive employment for the marginalised and the vulnerable. Here it seeks to provide appropriate ecosystems for innovation and an institutional environment for skill formation. With regard to skill formation, the Statement envisions training and preparing 20 million persons over the next 11 years with attention to differences in schooling attainments and corresponding opportunities for skill development.

In terms of demand, the document places heavy emphasis on the manufacturing sector, given its employment absorption potential and availability of employment for labour market entrants with differential skill levels. In the domain of human development, it seeks to provide quality healthcare for all, universal secondary education, increase enrolment in colleges (including vocational education) to over 50 per cent, ensure hut free rural and slum-free urban Tamil Nadu, as well as an open, defecation-free and garbage-free environment.

The second TNHDR (Tamil Nadu Human Development Report) will therefore be a useful document to understand the progress that the State has made with regard to various parameters of human development and the implications and challenges entailed with attainment of the goals set out by the Vision 2023 document. The second TNHDR also pays attention to aspects of human vulnerability as highlighted in the Global HDR. Discussions of multidimensional poverty, social security policies and emerging vulnerabilities accompany an engagement with the challenges for sustaining and improving current attainments across various parameters of human development. The persistence of some important gaps and the need for special policy attention will be highlighted in discussions in each of the chapters.

Chapter 2 focuses on district-level disparities on various indices, such as the HDI (human development index), GII (gender inequality index), CDI (child development index) and MPI (multidimensional poverty index). The remaining chapters address specific aspects of human development, such as employment, poverty, health and nutrition, education, gender aspects and social security policies. The final chapter attempts to highlight the over-arching challenges through a summary of important observations made in each chapter. In the rest of this chapter, we provide an overview of trends in demographic, economic and social development of the State.

Some Trends in Tamil Nadu's Development Experience

Demography

Accounting for close to 6 per cent of the country's population, Tamil Nadu's population stood at 72.14 million as of March 2011, which has gone up to 74.32 million in 2013. The decadal growth rate of population for the period 2001-2011 was 15.6 per cent, which is higher than that of the previous decade (i.e., 11.19% during 1991-2001). Yet, the 2001-2011 decadal growth rate was lower, compared to that at the national level (i.e., 17.64%). The decadal change in rural population was 6.49 per cent and that of urban population was 27.16 per cent, for the period 2001-2011, indicating a growing urbanisation of the State's population. During the same period, the rural population grew at 12.3 per cent and the urban population grew at 31.8 per cent at all-India level. The State attracts a significant number of in-migrants from other parts of the country, even though there has been a large-scale out-migration from the State. In fact, according to Chandrasekhar and Sharma (2014: 11), Tamil Nadu and Kerala are the only two advanced States that have a negative net migration rate, i.e., more people out-migrate compared to those migrating into the State.

The population density is gradually increasing over a period of time. As per the Census 2011, the State has a population density of 555 persons per sq km, which is

1. "Over the next 11 years, Tamil Nadu, given its factor endowments and the combination of strengths and opportunities, will aim to grow its GSDP at 11% or more per annum—about 20% more than the expected growth rate of India's GDP over the same period. Given the expected increase in population of 15% over the next 11 years, the increase in per capita income would amount to 6 times over this period" (p.11), *Vision Tamil Nadu 2023: Strategic Plan for Infrastructure Development in Tamil Nadu*, Government of Tamil Nadu (2012).

much above the national average of 382 persons per sq km; the population density was 478 persons per sq km in 2001, 429 in 1991 and 372 in 1981. Increasing population density also produces negative externalities, such as sewage pollution and solid waste, affecting human well-being if it is not backed by adequate investments in appropriate urban infrastructure. Moreover, Tamil Nadu is the most urbanised large State in the country with 48.45 per cent of its population living in urban areas. Rapid urbanisation leads to enhanced human capital through access to better education and healthcare facilities, but it does also adversely affect the quality of life due to various environmental problems unique to urban areas, such as air pollution. Sex ratio has increased from 987 in 2001 to 995 in 2011, which is a good sign. While the sex ratio is favourable in 16 out of 32 districts, it is however unfavourable in the remaining 16 districts. In 15 districts, the sex ratio is below the State average of 995. The chapter on gender disparities in well-being discusses this aspect in greater detail.

Tamil Nadu's slum population was estimated to be 2.8 million in 2011, which constitutes approximately 8 per cent of its total urban population (i.e., 34.90 million). Around 18.88 per cent of Chennai's population live in slums out of which 50 per cent live in dense slum areas; in 1981, the slum population was 13.8 per cent, which increased to 15.3 per cent in 1991 and further to 19.6 per cent in 2001. The government has been concerned about improving welfare of the slum population by applying various measures, especially through housing schemes. For example, from 1971 until 2007, a total of 81,038 tenements have been constructed and handed over to slum households by the Tamil Nadu Slum Clearance Board (TSCB) (Raman, 2011), and by 2010-11, the total number of tenements went up to 1.05 lakh (in: *www.tnscb.org.in/*). Under the Jawaharlal Nehru National Urban Renewal Mission (JNNURM), 35,270 tenements are to be constructed as integrated townships in Chennai, Madurai and Coimbatore at a total cost of ₹15,024.80 million.

Economy

Tamil Nadu is an economic powerhouse in India. From 2010-11 to 2013-14, Tamil Nadu has constantly maintained its status as a State with the second largest economy in terms of the size of real GSDP (gross state domestic product). In 2013-14, the size of its GSDP was ₹480,618.00 crore in terms of constant prices (2004-05); in 2010-11, the real GSDP was estimated at ₹403,416.00 crore, which increased to ₹433,238.00 crore in 2011-12 and further to ₹447,944.00 crore in 2012-13. The real GSDP registered a growth rate of 14.64 per cent at current prices and 7.29 per cent at constant prices in 2013-14 (see Table 1.1).

The improved power situation and a good north-east monsoon in 2014 are expected to significantly enhance economic growth in the coming years. Although the decline in real GSDP growth rate in recent years can be attributed to the influence of overall global recession, Tamil Nadu economy is withstanding its impact better than many other Indian States.

During 2005-06 to 2013-14, Tamil Nadu economy's average growth rate of real GSDP was 9.20 per cent which is, relatively, a better growth rate, compared to India as a whole. During the above period, the primary sector grew at 4.38 per cent, the secondary sector registered a growth rate of 8.42 per cent and that of the tertiary sector was 10.48 per cent. Table 1.1 provides a comparative picture of Tamil Nadu's growth performance vis-à-vis other States.

A comparison of the nine-year (2005-06 to 2013-14) average growth rate of real GSDP of some of the major States in India reveals that Tamil Nadu has ranked 5th among all the Indian States in terms of income growth. Although the State ranked 9th in terms of agricultural growth and 6th in terms of industrial and service sector growth, the overall rank is higher than that of individual sectors (see Table 1.2). This is due to the consistent and strong growth performance of Tamil Nadu across sectors, which is a reflection of the diversified and resilient structure of its economy. The following sub-sections provide a sectoral overview.

Agriculture

Around 40 per cent of the State's population is still directly dependent on agriculture for its livelihood. The State has been divided into seven agro-climatic subzones for planning agricultural development. In 2004-05, agriculture and allied activities contributed 11.65 per cent to the NSDP (net state domestic product), which declined to 8.7 per cent in 2011-12. During 2005-06 to 2013-14, the primary sector grew, on an average, at 4.38 per cent (as against 3.96 per cent at all-India level). In the Eleventh Plan period (2007-2008 to 2011-12), this sector grew at 3.49 per cent as it recorded negative growth rate in the initial two years, especially due to bad monsoon. An important aspect of the State's agricultural sector is the predominance of marginal landholdings therein (Table 1.3).

Table 1.1

Growth Rate of Gross State Domestic Product at Constant Prices (Tamil Nadu)

Sector	2005-06	2006-07	2007-08	2008-09	2009-10	2010-11	2011-12	2012-13	2013-14
Agriculture	11.49	15.42	-4.69	-2.70	6.56	7.69	11.05	-13.04	8.22
Forestry and Logging	5.74	-0.54	2.82	-0.88	3.16	3.30	2.49	3.44	4.08
Fishing	43.04	1.95	-6.47	1.17	6.58	8.16	3.40	1.03	0.70
Agriculture and Allied Activities (1+2+3)	13.26	13.24	-4.41	-2.29	6.35	7.47	9.95	-11.11	7.33
Mining and Quarrying	-4.86	4.36	1.17	-1.78	9.30	3.13	13.15	5.96	6.01
Sub-total of Primary	12.12	12.76	-4.13	-2.27	6.51	7.23	10.12	-10.20	7.24
Manufacturing (5.1+5.2)	15.11	18.75	0.59	-1.31	29.18	12.31	1.42	1.12	4.58
Registered	22.07	24.06	-1.96	-2.44	41.31	14.26	0.75	0.90	4.58
Unregistered	4.37	9.18	5.82	0.82	6.91	7.59	3.13	1.68	4.58
Construction	16.19	4.45	18.61	5.31	5.18	22.49	9.24	-2.18	1.22
Electricity, Gas and Water Supply	2.06	3.62	-27.81	-74.31	22.36	38.71	13.75	151.04	-9.98
Sub-total of Secondary	14.54	13.62	3.90	-2.06	21.14	15.52	3.96	2.06	3.07
Industry (b+4)	14.08	13.44	3.86	-2.06	20.93	15.32	4.09	2.12	3.11
Transport, Storage and Communication (8.1+8.2+8.3+8.4)	12.40	13.56	9.35	15.49	13.87	14.13	7.53	4.41	6.73
Railways	4.22	7.44	11.47	17.62	14.19	-1.71	-14.13	0.46	0.46
Transport by Other Means (including storage)	10.57	11.31	7.14	7.57	8.23	8.99	10.97	2.86	7.55
Storage	4.60	22.09	9.35	5.28	22.73	10.38	13.19	-1.51	5.97
Communication	20.76	21.21	13.90	32.49	23.80	25.93	6.78	7.22	6.50
Trade, Hotel and Restaurants	16.28	20.58	4.30	3.66	4.50	13.22	7.68	2.76	7.33
Banking and Insurance	17.55	19.09	17.11	10.18	2.97	14.65	9.73	12.65	12.65
Real Estate, Ownership of Dwellings and Business Services	15.17	16.50	16.75	13.40	6.82	10.03	14.16	12.79	14.99
Public Administration	3.48	12.53	1.01	24.50	0.53	8.85	0.83	-4.46	5.76
Other Services	12.18	11.48	7.34	10.31	10.69	14.26	7.46	2.35	5.08
Sub-total of Tertiary (8+9+10+11+12+13)	14.02	16.57	9.33	10.56	6.90	12.80	8.77	6.05	9.31
Growth Rate of GSDP	13.96	15.21	6.13	5.45	10.83	13.12	7.39	3.39	7.29

Source: Computed from CSO data.

Table 1.2

Nine Year Average Annual Growth of GSDP and Sectors of Major States (2005-06 to 2013-14) at 2004-05 Prices

States	Agriculture and Allied		Industry		Services		GSDP	
	Growth (%)	Rank	Growth (%)	Rank	Growth (%)	Rank	Growth (%)	Rank
Andhra Pradesh	5.11	7	7.88	10	9.73	10	8.21	8
Gujarat	5.36	4	9.58	3	11.45	3	9.75	3
Karnataka	3.43	13	6.13	15	9.08	14	7.25	15
Kerala	-0.52	20	8.98	5	9.63	11	8.07	9
Maharashtra	5.34	5	9.16	4	10.07	7	9.31	4
Tamil Nadu	4.54	9	8.79	6	10.17	6	9.15	5
India	3.96		6.91		9.08		7.62	

Source: Shanmugam, 2014.

Table 1.3

Number of Operational Holdings in Tamil Nadu (2010-11)

Category	Number of Operational Holdings	Percentage
Marginal (up to 1 ha.)	6266372	77.18
Small (1ha.-2 ha)	1181797	14.55
Semi-Medium (2 ha.-4 ha.)	502332	06.18
Medium (4 ha-0 ha.)	150570	01.85
Large (10 ha. and above)	17365	0.21
ALL SIZE CLASSES	8118436	100.00

Source: *Statistical Handbook of Tamil Nadu, 2013.*

Approximately, 92 per cent of the farmers in the State belong to marginal and small farmer category (Table 1.3). Fragmentation of land, despite increased production and productivity in the agriculture sector, poses a major challenge for achieving a 'second green revolution' in the State. Declining returns to agriculture has been a disconcerting feature of agricultural development in the State, with cost-price differentials being one of the highest in the country. Since large-scale or cooperative farming has the potential to increase production and productivity in the farm sector and establish better economic linkages in terms of processing and marketing in the coming years, identifying and implementing appropriate institutional arrangements are critical to not only sustain or increase production and productivity in the agricultural sector, but also to ensure better returns for farmers in the State and thereby ensure better economic resilience in the long term.

Another area of concern has been the decline in net sown area in the State. The net area sown had witnessed a gradual decline from 56.38 lakh ha. in 1950s to 50.43 lakh ha. in 2008-09, and further to 49.85 lakh ha. in 2011-12. Due to a boom in the real estate sector and land-use pattern changes taking place in rural areas, the proportion of land put under non-agricultural uses had expanded from 21.69 lakh ha. in 2007-08 to 21.73 lakh ha. in 2008-09 and to 21.80 lakh ha. in 2011-12. Although the net sown area had declined, interestingly the latest estimates suggest that the State had achieved 10.33 million metric tonnes of food grain output during 2013-14, registering an increase by 0.18 million metric tonnes over the state's output in 2011-12. This is due to increased productivity of certain principal crops being cultivated in the State (see Table 1.4). The productivity of both cereal crops as well as pulses has increased by approximately 49 per cent between 2007-08 and 2011-12.

Table 1.4

Trend in Productivity of Principal Crops (kg/ha.)

Crops	2007-2008	2010 -2011	2011-2012
Cereal Crops	2571	3039	3848.72
Pulses	2125	2393	3163.86

Source: *Statistical Handbook of Tamil Nadu*, various years.

Policy measures to address vulnerabilities emanating within the agricultural sector will be therefore critical for sustaining human development as well as facilitating more balanced growth in the State. In order to promote a second green revolution, the State government has proposed to initiate the following measures, as mentioned in its Vision 2023 document: improving soil healthcare and increasing productivity per unit area; providing access to quality inputs; bringing fallow lands under cultivation; increasing the cropping and irrigation intensity; promoting micro-irrigation to increase water use efficiency; massive farm mechanisation to meet labour shortage; speedy transfer of information through ICT (information and communication technology) enabled extension; strengthening and improving agriculture infrastructure including market infrastructure and paving way for market-led agriculture; and, raising the income of farmers.

Industry

Tamil Nadu is the second most industrialised State after Maharashtra, accounting for around 11 per cent industrial output of the country (2011-12). The government is the major investor with 51 per cent of total investment, while that made by private Indian investors stands at 29.9 per cent and by foreign investors at 14.9 per cent (Kathuria, 2014). However, in recent years, most investments have been from the private sector. The major industries are automobiles, auto-components, light and heavy engineering, machinery, cotton, textiles, rubber, food products, transport equipment, chemicals, and leather and leather goods. The manufacturing sector has a unique diversity consisting of both modern (e.g., automobiles and power-driven pumps) as well as traditional industries (e.g., leather and textiles). Compared to other States, the industries in Tamil Nadu are more spatially distributed across all its regions (there are 27 clusters in 13 districts), with several of them being export-oriented in nature. The industry sector contributed 27.91 per cent to the NDP (net domestic product) of the State, with the manufacturing sector alone accounting for nearly 17.5 per cent of NDP in 2011-12. However, this share has been virtually stagnant between 2004-05 and 2011-12, with the construction sector increasing its share in industry from 9.69 per cent to 10.09 per cent. Clearly, the decline in the share of agricultural sector and stagnation in the secondary sector has been compensated by growth in the services/tertiary sector.

In terms of FDI (foreign direct investments), Tamil Nadu ranks third at the national level. Between April 2010 and May 2014, the Chennai region received FDI of about ₹67,964 crore, accounting for 6.32 per cent of the total FDIs made in India during this period. Tamil Nadu has been a leader in attracting foreign investment into the ICT and automobile sectors. The contribution of ICT to the economy of Tamil Nadu in recent years is worth mentioning. Export earnings from the sector increased from ₹5,223 crore in 2001-02 to ₹46,791 crore in 2011-12, employing about 145,000 professionals directly. Tamil Nadu accounts for 23 per cent of the country's total export earnings (Rajeev, 2014).

Per Capita Income

The real per capita income (2004-05 prices) of Tamil Nadu rose to ₹62,361 in 2013-14 (advanced estimates) from ₹46,692 in 2009-10 and from ₹30,062 in 2004-05. In other words, per capita income has doubled during the last nine years. The State government aims to increase the nominal per capita income by six fold from 2010-11 level to ₹450,000 (US$ 10,000) in 2023 in line with per capita income of UMI (upper middle income) countries. Although the growth of per capita NSDP is relatively high in comparison to many other Indian States and is also escalating fast over a period of time, wide disparity in per capita income between districts has become a serious developmental concern. For example, the per capita income of Kanyakumari district is four times greater than that of Perambalur district. Out of 32 districts, 18 districts have per capita income lower than the State's average per capita income (State Planning Commission, 2012). The reassessment of per capita consumption expenditure at district level may, however, be a more revealing measure of welfare-level disparities. Unfortunately, district level data is not available.

Importantly, this growth in the state's income has been accompanied by investments in the social sector that has led to considerable improvements in poverty reductions and improvements in other aspects of human development. In fact, in terms of per capita development expenditure comprising of expenditure on both social and economic services, the state ranked second highest among all states in 2011-12 and well above the all India average.[2]

Poverty Levels

In 2011-12, 15.8 per cent of the rural and 6.6 per cent of the urban population in Tamil Nadu lived at BPL (below the poverty line). In fact, it is one of the larger States with relatively low poverty levels. As far as poverty reduction is concerned, the state has thus performed very well especially given its high levels until the late 1980s and early 1990s. Through various public policies and welfare schemes, the poverty reduction strategies in Tamil Nadu have yielded pay-offs. For

2. Finance Accounts of the State Governments, Comptroller and Auditor General, Government of India, cited in Panagariya et al. (2014: 86).

example, in 1993-94, the proportion of poor people in rural areas was 51.2 per cent, which has declined to 15.8 per cent in 2011-12. Indeed, the State gained 34 percentage point reduction in rural poverty during the past two decades.[3] Among social groups, the poverty reduction is significant. The rate of decline in poverty among SCs/STs (scheduled castes/scheduled tribes) was 2.3 percentage points per annum during 1993-1994 and 2011-12. During the period 1993-94 to 2011-12, the incidence of urban poverty also lowered from 33.8 to 6.6 per cent in Tamil Nadu, with a reduction of 1.5 percentage points per annum. The chapter on employment, income and poverty addresses this issue in greater detail. The Government of Tamil Nadu in its Vision 2023 document clearly lays out strategies for facilitating inclusive growth with a major aim to reduce poverty and inequality.

Health

Tamil Nadu has been often highlighted for its strong public intervention in the domain of healthcare, leading to substantial achievements on the health front. The LEB (life expectancy at birth) in the State was 67 for males and 71 for females in 2005-06. The IMR (infant mortality rate) stood at 68 in Tamil Nadu in 1992-93, coming down to 48 in 1998-99, to 30 in 2005-06 and to 22 by 2011. The MMR (maternal mortality ratio) too has declined significantly. The MMR was 111 per 100,000 live births during 2004-2006 and declined to 97 during 2007-2009. The IMR in 2013 was 24 in 1000 deliveries, as against 48 at the all-India level. The U5MR (under-5 mortality rate) was 95 in the State in 1992-93 and declined significantly to 25 by 2011.

The National Family Health Survey (NFHS) 3 (2005-06) reveals that the fertility level was 1.8 children per woman, which was comparatively lower than the all-India level at 2.7 children per woman. Indeed, the fertility level in Tamil Nadu was the lowest among all Indian States, except Andhra Pradesh (AP) and Goa which also achieved fertility level at 1.8 children per women. Fertility rate decreased by 0.3 children per mother between NFHS-1 (1992-93) and NFHS-2 (1998-99) and by 0.4 children per mother between NFHS-2 and NFHS-3. The fertility rate in rural areas (1.9 children per woman) was slightly higher than in urban areas (1.7 children per woman). The CBR (crude birth rate) for the State declined from 31.4 in 1971 to 19.3 in 2000 and to 15.9 in 2011. The CDR (crude death rate) declined from 14.4 in 1971 to 7.9 in 2000 and to 7.4 in 2011. The TFR (total fertility rate) for Tamil Nadu has shown a sharp decline from 3.9 in 1971 to 2.0 in 1997 and to 1.7 in 2007-2009 (SRS).

Literacy and Education

Tamil Nadu's human development achievements include substantial improvements in educational attainments over a long period, backed with investments made by both public and private actors (chapter on Literacy and Education). The achievements on the education front are reflected in terms of significant improvements in human development in the State. The literacy rate of the State has been increasing progressively over the years. As per the 2011 Census, the literacy rate in Tamil Nadu stands at 80.33 per cent, next only to Kerala (with 93.91%) and Maharashtra (with 82.91%), and much higher than the all-India level, i.e., 74.04 per cent. The literacy rates in rural and urban areas are 73.8 per cent and 87.24 per cent, respectively.

The State government in its endeavour for Universalisation of Primary Education has invested considerably in education infrastructure, especially in rural areas. This is partly reflected in the GER (gross enrolment ratio) which has gone up from 95.73 per cent in 2001-02 to 112 per cent in 2010-11. At the primary level, the gross enrolment of boys is 111.8 per cent and that of girls is 112.2 per cent for year 2010-11. In the case of NER (net enrolment ratio) in 2010-11, it stands at 99.60 per cent for all students; 99.57 per cent for boys; and 99.63 per cent for girls.

Table 1.5

Gross Enrolment Ratio in Tamil Nadu, 2010-11

Classes	*Gross Enrolment Ratio (Total)*	
	ST	*All Categories*
Class I-V (6-10 years)	137	116
Class VI-VIII (11-13 years)	88.9	85.5
Class I-VIII (6-13 years)	119.7	104.3
Classes IX-X (14-15 Years)	53.3	65
Classes I-X (6-15 Years)	106.8	96.2
Classes XI-XII (16-17 Years)	28.8	39.3
Classes IX-XII (14-17 Years)	41.5	52.1
Classes I-XII (6-17 Years)	94.8	86.5

Source: Statistics of School Education, 2010-11.

In the domain of adult education, Tamil Nadu became the only State in the country to have achieved its target in the 'Saakshar Bharat' scheme, by educating over

3. The information used in this section is drawn largely from: Kalaiyarasan (2014).

17.25 lakh adults. The State also has done very well in terms of enrolment in higher education. According to the provisional results of All India Survey on Higher Education (AISHE) 2014-15 conducted by the Ministry of Human Resource Department (MHRD), the GER in higher education of those in the age group of 18-23 is 46.9 in 2014-5 for the state and highest among all major states.

Tamil Nadu has been very active in terms of ensuring greater social inclusion and quality of education, through various innovative programmes, such as implementing nutritious meal scheme, introducing and strengthening ICT in the education sector, introducing ABL (activity-based learning) and ALM (active learning methodology), providing free bicycles for schoolchildren, providing free laptops to school and college students and so on.[4]

Infrastructure

Sustaining and improving human development, and minimising vulnerabilities also require robust and inclusive economic growth. The relationship between economic growth and investments in infrastructure is well known. The power sector in the State has an installed capacity of 22,474.7 MW in 2015, as against 13,084.75 MW in 2007-08. Another essential feature is that the transmission and distribution loss is comparatively lower at 18 per cent. Tamil Nadu is also a leader in renewable energy in the country with an installed capacity of 8,533 MW which accounts for nearly 37 per cent of installed capacity in the state and 23.29 per cent of the country's installed capacity for renewable energy. Efforts are also underway to strengthen distribution and improve quality of supply to rural areas (*http://cms.tn.gov.in/sites/default/files/documents/energy_e_pn_2015_16.pdf*). As per the Vision 2023 document, the energy demand-supply gap in Tamil Nadu is fairly high. The energy deficit of the State in FY (financial year) 2013 was around 17.5 per cent as compared to 2.8 per cent in FY 2008, and peak deficit in FY 2013 was over 13 per cent. This energy demand gap poses an important challenge to sustained growth of the State, which in turn could affect its human development. The State government, having realised the potential negative impact of energy demand gap on the growth, proposed to initiate certain long-term measures, such as setting up of an additional 20,000 MW of power generating capacity including two ultra-mega power projects of 4,000 MW each; thrust for green power by maximising investments in wind power and solar energy so as to create incremental renewable generation capacity of 10,000 MW; and significant investment in the transmission sector to create the required evacuation capacity with buffers for higher power generation capacity.[5]

The total length of major roads in the State stands at 62,017 km at present. It includes 4,974 km national highways, 10,764 km State highways, 11,247 km major district roads and 35,032 other district and sugarcane roads[6]. Including the rural roads, total length of the road networks in Tamil Nadu is 272,252.61 km. The length of the total surfaced roads was 216,352.37 km and that of the un-surfaced road was 55,900.242 km. Tamil Nadu has therefore well-established road networks with a road density that is 2.5 times that of all-India and hence contributes to a number of social and economic benefits. However, one of the negative externalities of improved road networks is road accidents. In 2011, a total number of 65,873 road accidents occurred in the State, where 74,245 persons were injured and 15,422 persons were killed.

As for financial infrastructure, as of 2012-13, the total number of bank branches in Tamil Nadu was 7,830, which constitutes about 7.5 per cent of the total number of bank branches in India. During this period, the population served per branch stood at 9,946, which is lower than the all-India level of 12,598. The aggregate bank deposit was ₹401,182.00 and the gross bank credit was ₹466,031.00. The credit-deposit ratio at the State level was 116.20, which was higher than the all-India figure of 78.10.

The water supply and sanitation situation in Tamil Nadu is in a relatively better position compared to the all-India status. Out of 94,614 rural habitations, 84,003 habitations (88.90%) have been fully covered with a water supply of 40 LPCD (litres per capita per day) or more and the remaining 10,611 (i.e., 11.10%) habitations have been covered partially. At present, there is no uncovered habitation in the State. However, a lower proportion of the households have access to drinking water source, latrine and a bathroom within their homes. Further in terms of sanitation, Tamil Nadu has been noted for relatively high levels of open defecation (45.7% in 2011), which is higher than States like Kerala, Maharashtra and Gujarat.

4. For further details on various schemes on education, please see chapter on Literacy and Education.

5. *http://agritech.tnau.ac.in/pdf/2012/TN%20VISION%202023_Volume%20II.pdf.*

6. *www.tnhighways.gov.in/about.html*

In the case of urban water supply, Chennai region needs special mention. The total water demand in the Chennai metropolitan area was estimated at 848 MLD (million litres per day), but the supply was 765 MLD in 2010. The supply-demand gap was supposed to come primarily from groundwater sources. Around 6,530 deep bore wells have been dug at different locations in the city to supplement the supply from surface sources. In addition, Chennai Metro Water hires private tanker trucks regularly to deliver water to areas with less coverage, greater scarcity and more slum population. For instance, about 6,000 tanker trucks (with a capacity of between 10,000 and 20,000 litres each) were used to deliver 120 MLD of water to different locations of the metropolitan area in 2004. At present, private trucks make around 700 trips to deliver an estimated 125 MLD of water, purely on a commercial basis (Venkatachalam, 2014). In rest of the urban areas, over a third of the Corporations (12) and Municipalities (125) are provided with more than 110 LPCD of water (*www.spc.tn.gov.in/12plan_english/6.%20 WATER_SUPPLY.pdf*). In recent years, rapid growth of the private water markets is observed in almost all regions of the State. Even though the private markets fulfil water requirements of the consumers to a certain extent, quality of the water supplied is reported to be poor. Tapping into alternate and more sustainable sources and regulating the current system of water supply therefore require the state's attention.

Environment and Natural Resources

The natural capital stock consisting of various environmental and natural resources is important for enhancing and sustaining wellbeing, health and livelihoods. Tamil Nadu is endowed with abundant environmental and natural resources. The natural capital stock of the State generates four different types of ecosystem services namely, provisioning services (e.g., food, freshwater, etc.); regulating services (e.g., climate regulation, water purification, etc.); cultural services (e.g., spiritual, recreational, aesthetic, etc.); and supporting services (e.g., nutrient recycling, soil formation, etc.). Changes in the ecosystem services do significantly affect human wellbeing in the State, even though the causal relationship between ecosystem services and its impact on human wellbeing has not yet been adequately quantified. Since the estimation of GSDP is silent about changes in numerous non-market ecosystem services and their impact on economic welfare, human development of the State measured by using the variant of GSDP may deviate from properly reflecting real human welfare. In other words, if people of the State are enjoying a greater amount of non-market benefits from nature, then the current wellbeing measured by applying conventional GSDP becomes underestimated; on the other hand, if people are experiencing more environmental problems, then the currently measured wellbeing becomes overestimated.

The State has 28,343 sq km of forest and tree cover, occupying 18 per cent of its total geographical area (130,058 sq. km). The State harbours rich flora and fauna, contributing to human welfare in many different ways. The State is endowed with 5,640 species of flowering plants—the highest number of plant species among all States in the country. The plant species include 533 endemic species, 230 red-listed species, 1,559 species of medicinal plants and 260 species of wild relatives of cultivated plants. In addition, the State is endowed with 165 species of fresh water fishes, 76 species of amphibians, 177 species of reptiles, 454 species of birds and 187 species of mammals. The Western Ghats with abundant flora and fauna acts as a global biodiversity hotspot. The State has demonstrated its commitment to protect the environment and biodiversity resources by way of creating 10 wildlife sanctuaries, 13 bird sanctuaries, a bird conservation reserve, 3 biosphere reserves, 4 elephant reserves and 3 tiger reserves. There are 1,175 ecologically important wetlands with a total water spread area of 1,615.12 sq km. Mangrove forests in three locations—namely, Muthupet in Thiruvarur district, Pichavaram in Cuddalore district and Kazhiveli in Villurpuram district, and coral reef formations in the Gulf of Mannar provide support to the unique biodiversity in the State. The State accounts for 30 per cent of total bio-resources in India and has a larger potential for promoting biodiversity-based industry. Apart from biotechnology industry, nature-based tourism has greater potential to improve conditions of the people in such regions—especially—if proper institutional arrangements are explored to promote eco-tourism. The total length of the coast line is 1,076 km, which constitutes about 13 per cent of the country's coast line as a whole; apart from being endowed with biological and ecological resources, the coast line supports a large fishing population and generated 61.15 million tonnes of protein in the year 2011-12. The State faces certain environmental challenges which need to be addressed in the coming years. The State's important water sources (rivers, lakes and wetlands) that generate various types of ecosystem benefits are to be protected from several negative externalities, such as dumping of solid and liquid waste and encroachment.

Water Resources

Water has become a key factor in determining growth and sustainability of Tamil Nadu economy—especially, its agricultural and livestock economy. The State is endowed with 3 per cent of water resources of the country. The average annual rainfall is 945 mm; the South-West monsoon (June–September) brings an average of 322 mm rainfall, the North-East monsoon (October–December) fetches 470 mm, and the remaining 153 mm of rainfall occurs during other periods. The average rainfall varies from 865 to 3,127 mm among sub-regions, making water availability and distribution naturally unequal. There are 17 major river basins in the State, acting both as a strong life support system and as a waste sink. The water potential of the State is 46,540 MCM (million cubic metres) per annum, of which 22,423 MCM accounts for groundwater and 19,525 MCM for surface water. Intensive agriculture, rapid urbanisation and growth of industries heightened the demand for water in the State, which is expected to increase to 57,725 MCM in 2050 from the current level of 54,395 MCM. Around 80 per cent of the utilisable water is being diverted for agricultural purposes. There are 2,239 irrigation canals with a length of 9,747 km, 81 reservoirs, 41,127 irrigation tanks, 315,000 tube wells and 1,505,844 open wells—dug especially for irrigation purposes. Erratic monsoons, declining storage capacity of the surface sources (such as, rivers and irrigation tanks), over-exploitation of groundwater in certain parts and industrial and sewage pollution in industrial and urban areas caused potential threat to the supply of good quality water. In fact, ground water in 138 out of 385 blocks is found to have been over-exploited with another 100 blocks in critical or semi-critical stages. Ensuring adequate water supply to meet growing demands as well as regeneration of water sources remains a critical challenge in the years to come. On the other hand, factors such as conversion of agricultural land for non-agricultural purpose, farmers abandoning agricultural practices and general decline in net area irrigated suggest that surface water previously used for irrigation purpose is now available for other beneficial uses. Reforming the pollution control policies with a greater role for incentive-based economic instruments is expected to generate significant marginal benefits in the economy. The government's high priority to protect water resources and to utilise available water resources more efficiently are reflected in the State's water policy, which includes promoting rainwater harvesting, encouraging the farmers to utilise micro-irrigation technology and strictly implementing pollution control measures in the industry sector.

Other Resources

The State is endowed with a limited number of mineral resources. Lignite, oil, bauxite, limestone, magnesite, mica and quartz are some of the mineral resources that are found in different parts of Tamil Nadu. In recent years, sand, especially from the river beds, is being mined and is supplied to the booming construction industry in the State. Sand mining leads to various kinds of environmental problems and therefore, regulation of sand mining has been made more effective. However, a prerequisite for optimum utilisation of sand available in the State is to prepare a sand accounting system, which would indicate the amount exploited every year, amount replenished and the final stock available. Based on the above information, sand mining activity can be regulated in an environmentally sustainable manner in the future.

The above discussion has highlighted the State's achievements in terms of growth, even while hinting at some critical environmental and resource constraints to sustaining the growth process. Such constraints are also likely to negatively impinge upon securing improvements in human development. The next chapter addresses the State's performance in various aspects of human development and spatial differences in this regard.

References

Chandrasekhar, S. and Ajay Sharma (2014). "Urbanization and Spatial Patterns of Internal Migration in India", *IGIDR Working Paper* No. WP-2014-016

Drèze, J. and A. Sen (2013). *An Uncertain Glory: India and its Contradictions*. Princeton University Press.

Government of Tamil Nadu (n.d.). *Vision 2023*.

Kalaiyarasan, A. (2014). "A Comparison of Developmental Outcomes in Gujarat and Tamil Nadu", *Economic and Political Weekly* 49(15): 55-63.

Kathuria, Vinish (2014). "Industrial Development in Tamil Nadu", in V.K. Natraj and A. Vaidyanathan (eds.), *Development Narratives: The Political Economy of Tamil Nadu*. New Delhi: Academic Foundation.

Panagariya A., P. Chakraborty and M. Govinda Rao (2014). *State Level Reforms, Growth and Development in Indian States*. New Delhi: Oxford University Press.

Rajeev, Meenakshi (2014). "IT Industry in Tamil Nadu", in V.K. Natraj and A. Vaidyanathan (eds.), *Development Narratives: The Political Economy of Tamil Nadu*. New Delhi: Academic Foundation.

Raman, Nithya (2011). "The Board and the Bank: Changing Policies towards Slums in Chennai", *Economic and Political Weekly* 46(31): 74-80.

Shanmugam, K.R. (2014). "Finances of Tamil Nadu Government". Madras School of Economics. *Mimeo*.

Venkatachalam, L. (2014). "Informal Water Markets and Willingness to Pay for Water: A Case Study of the Urban Poor in Chennai City, India", in *International Journal of Water Resources Development* 31(1): 134-45.

2

Status of Human Development

Human development paradigm, based on Sen's capability approach, has been recognised as a necessary corrective to growth-centric approaches to development, in view of limited trickle-down powers of market forces to spread benefits of growth and alleviate poverty. The capability approach provides a conceptual foundation for privileging the domain of human development, defined as a process of enlarging people's choices and enhancing human capabilities and freedoms, enabling them to live a long and healthy life, have access to knowledge and a decent standard of living, and participate in community life and decisions that affect their lives. Therefore, development is about removing obstacles to attaining such freedoms, such as illiteracy, ill health, lack of access to resources, or lack of civil and political freedoms.

The State is responsible for ensuring that access to entitlements is equitable, sufficient and universal. The HDI (human development index) is a composite index encompassing three core dimensions of human development—health, education and income—and it is used for measuring achievements in these areas. Human development provides insights for prioritising investment of public resources for improvement of overall human well-being and enhancing people's capabilities and opportunities. An implication of this emphasis is that the State has to focus not merely on economic growth but assume responsibility for investments in education, health and social security, protecting citizens' rights and ensuring equality before law. Simultaneously, it also means paying attention to, and investing in basic amenities that help promote better livelihoods, enhance efficiency, and create more socially or public owned facilities to be accessed by all. It is assumed that once the core dimensions of human development and capabilities to attain them are achieved, peoples' economic opportunities will automatically get widened in the development process. Subsequently, United Nations Development Programme (UNDP) enlarged the understanding of human development by incorporating aspects, such as use of more comprehensive measures of poverty (MPI or Multi Poverty Index), gender inequality (GII or Gender Inequality Index), food security (FSI or Food Security Index) and child development (CDI or Child Development Index). Although the dimensions have remained the same, the measurement of human development is now broad based and considers several additional indicators.

In Tamil Nadu, seen from the above perspective of development, several social security programmes have been implemented under different sectors and for different marginalised population groups, which had and are expected to have far-reaching implications for human development. In order to understand the status and regional variations in human development and its related aspects across districts in the State, different indices such as HDI, GII, CDI, FSI and MPI have been computed and discussed in this chapter.[1]

Human Development Index

Following the UNDP methodology, the index captures achievements across the three basic capabilities of health, education and living standards. The indicators that are used for deriving HDI at the district level are as follows:

Figure 2.1

Human Development Index: Components

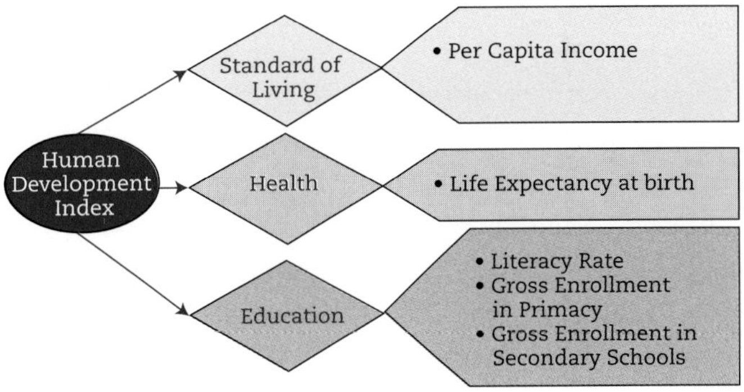

Human Development Index: Inter-district Variations

The HDI has been calculated for all the districts using PCI (per capita income) as a determinant of the standard of living. Health indicator is measured using the life expectancy at birth, and access to knowledge is assessed by considering the literacy rate and GER (gross enrolment ratios) at the primary and secondary levels. Table 2.1 provides a list of the five best and five worst performing districts across the various indicators mentioned above.

Table 2.1 indicates inter-district variations in the three basic indicators of human development. Kanyakumari district is in the top five districts with respect to PCI, life expectancy at birth and literacy rate. Kancheepuram, which also has a high PCI, does not fall in the top-five category in health and gross enrolment

1. Detailed discussion of the computation of all the indices and the values for all districts are provided in the annexures to this chapter.

Table 2.1

Top and Bottom Five Districts in Human Development Indicators

Table Indicators	*Top 5*	*Bottom 5 (from lowest to higher)*
Standard of living: Per Capita Income	Kanyakumari Kancheepuram Tiruppur Virudhunagar Tiruvallur	Ariyalur Perambalur Thiruvarur Villupuram Theni
Life Expectancy at Birth	Chennai Kanyakumari Coimbatore Thoothukudi Krishnagiri	Tiruppur The Nilgiris Theni Nagapattinam Madurai
Literacy Rate	Kanyakumari Chennai Thoothukudi The Nilgiris Kancheepuram	Dharmapuri Ariyalur Villupuram Erode Salem
GER- Primary	The Nilgiris Ramanathapuram Perambalur Pudukottai Tiruvarur	Tiruppur Ariyalur Chennai Tiruvanamalai Cuddalore
GER – Secondary	Dharmapuri Nagapattinam Perambalur Thanjavur Krishnagiri	Erode Karur Villupuram Chennai Tiruvanamalai

Source: Calculated from data provided by the Departments, Government of Tamil Nadu, 2013-14.

indicators. Tiruppur district, despite ranking high in PCI, performs poorly in health and education. While such anomalies across these dimensions exist in some districts, there are districts, like Ariyalur, which ranks among the bottom five districts in most parameters, such as PCI, literacy rate and GER for primary school. Clearly, interventions in such districts need to be more broad-based, as opposed to designing sector-specific interventions in districts such as Tiruppur that have high living standards but without comparable attainments in health or education.

Computation of the district level human development indices reveal the following pattern of ranking presented in Table 2.2.

Kanyakumari is the district with the highest HDI and Ariyalur has the lowest HDI. Thoothukudi, with high life expectancy at birth and high literacy rate, finds itself in the top five districts. Ariyalur and Perambalur, due to its PCI being so low, are placed in the bottom five districts. Coimbatore, in spite of its high degree of industrialisation and PCI, does not figure in the top five districts with high HDI. It goes on to show that high PCI does not necessarily translate into high human development indices, unless accompanied by investments made in the education, health and other social sectors.

Table 2.2

HDI Index Top and Bottom Five Districts

	HDI Index	
District	*Index*	*Rank*
Top 5 Districts		
Kanyakumari	0.944	1
Virudhunagar	0.855	2
Thoothukudi	0.852	3
Chennai	0.847	4
Kancheepuram	0.845	5
Bottom 5 Districts		
Thiruvarur	0.568	28
Villupuram	0.561	29
Theni	0.539	30
Perambalur	0.447	31
Ariyalur	0.282	32

Source: Calculated from data provided from the Departments, Government of Tamil Nadu, 2013-14.

Comparison with State Human Development Report-2003

The previous *Human Development Report (HDR)-2003* indicated that Chennai, Kancheepuram, Kanyakumari, Thoothukudi and Coimbatore were the top five districts. Though the two sets of indices are not strictly comparable given the bifurcation of some districts between the two time points, some comparative observations are made here. The latest HDR reveals that Kanyakumari has achieved the top position, while Coimbatore does not even figure in the top five. The new entrant in the top five district category is Virudhunagar in the latest HDR. Virudhunagar's rise to the top has been primarily due to its relatively higher per capita income which in turn can be attributed to the spread of small scale industries such as printing and fireworks, and also a vibrant agricultural marketing economy. The bottom five districts in the previous HDR are Perambalur, Villupuram, Dharmapuri, Tirunelveli and Pudukottai. Many of these districts have been bifurcated, but Perambalur and Villupuram continue to be at the bottom. Theni has newly entered into the bottom five. This indicates that investments made for improving livelihoods and also in education and health sectors must be increased in these districts so as to move them out of their low indices.

Figure 2.2

HDI Index

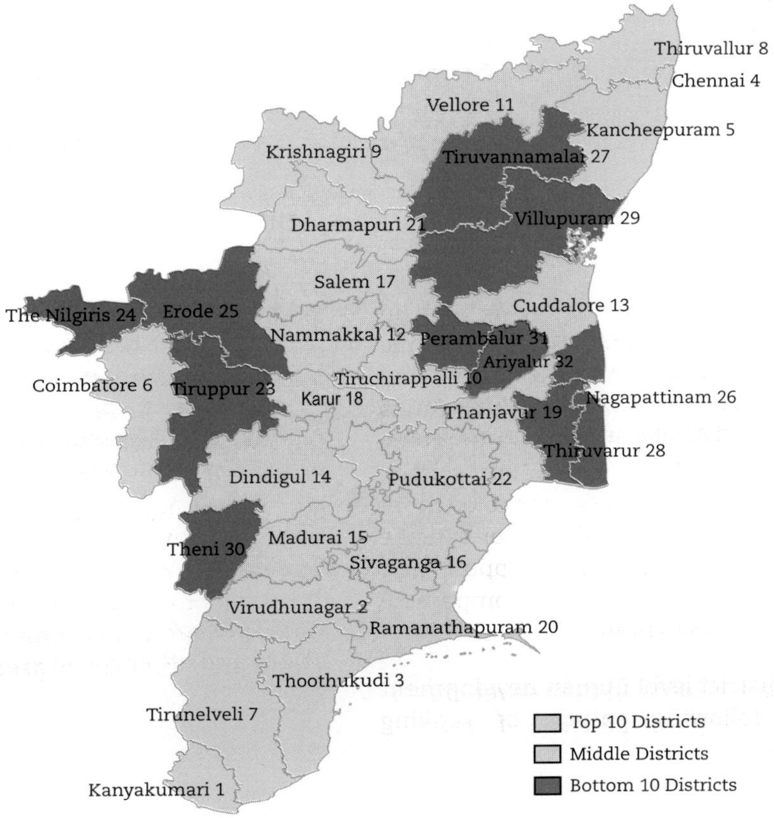

Source: Calculated from data provided from the Departments, Government of Tamil Nadu, 2013-14.

Gender Inequality Index

Disadvantages and discrimination faced by women and girls in the domains of access to health, education and the labour market foster gender inequalities in human development achievement. Equality between men and women exists, when both sexes have equal share in the distribution of power and influence; have equal possibilities for financial resources through businesses opportunities; enjoy equal access to education and the opportunity to develop personal ambitions, interests and talents; share responsibility for the home and children; and are completely free from coercion, intimidation and gender-based violence at work and at home (Engelman, 2009). Addressing the issue of gender inequality in the above-said domains therefore, is critical to accelerate human development.

Gender equality in health, education and labour market directly contributes towards increased access to employment and income earnings, and also a greater participation in decision-making process, thereby leading to human development. In turn, increased human development may also help in reducing gender inequality. Therefore, policies focusing on women's empowerment and aiming to bring them at par with men have become most prominent in the developing economies. This is diagrammatically represented in Figure 2.3.

Figure 2.3

Linkages between Gender Equality and Human Development

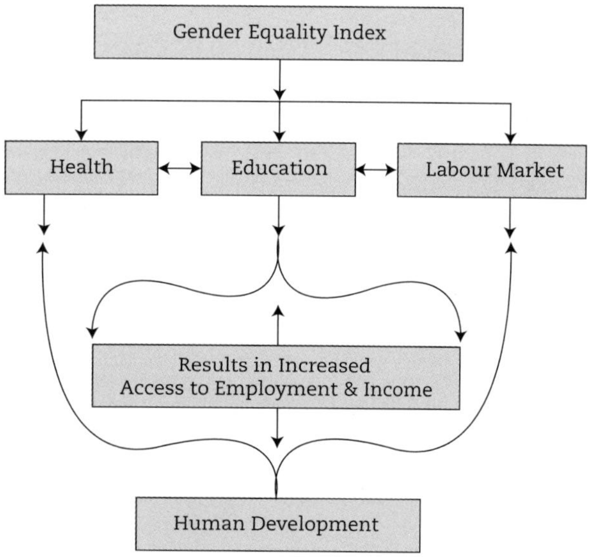

Source: District Human Development Report, Haveri, 2015.

GII measures the loss in potential of human development due to inequality between female and male achievements. As it reflects inequality, a value of zero represents no inequality and that of one represents the highest level of inequality in a society. The UNDP report of 2010 has brought out the GII index for all countries. For measuring GII, three dimensions are considered by the report. They are:

1. Reproductive health
2. Empowerment
3. Labour market

In the present exercise, the following indicators are used for computing gender inequality across districts in the State.

The health dimension is measured by three indicators: child sex ratio, MMR (maternal mortality ratio) and the percentage of institutional deliveries. The empowerment dimension is also measured by an indicator for political participation through differentials in the male-female share of elected representatives. In the domain of literacy, differentials in male-female literacy rates are used. The labour dimension is measured by male and female participation in the workforce and also the corresponding wage rates. The GII is designed to derive the extent to which achievements in these aspects of human development are eroded by gender inequality, and to provide empirical foundations for policy analysis and advocacy efforts. The following table identifies the top ranking and low ranking districts in terms of GII (Table 2.3). The spatial spread of these districts is depicted in Figure 2.5.

The GII of the State is the best in Nilgiris district where gender inequality is closest to zero (0.036), and inequality is the most in Ariyalur district which registers an index value of 0.118. In Ariyalur district, most of the gender-related indicators—female literacy rates and female agricultural wage rates—are low. A lower score in terms of indicators relating to capabilities, livelihood and empowerment has widened gender inequality in the district. Importantly, it should be noted that Ariyalur ranks low in overall human development indices as well, thus indicating an overlap of deprivations among women in the district. Kanyakumari has the highest health indicators in terms of low MMR and high institutional deliveries, but due to other factors, its position has moved to the middle level at rank 12. Kanyakumari's inequality is more in the livelihood indicator as one

Table 2.3

GII Index

District	Index	Rank	District	Index	Rank	District	Index	Rank
Top 5 Districts			*Middle 5 Districts*			*Bottom 5 Districts*		
The Nilgiris	0.036	1	Erode	0.065	11	Chennai	0.111	28
Virudhunagar	0.048	2	Kanyakumari	0.066	12	Madurai	0.112	29
Vellore	0.051	3	Karur	0.07	13	Villupuram	0.113	30
Nammakkal	0.054	4	Tiruppur	0.07	14	Sivaganga	0.114	31
Perambalur	0.057	5	Dharmapuri	0.074	15	Ariyalur	0.118	32

Source: Calculated from data provided by the Departments, Government of Tamil Nadu, 2014-15.

Figure 2.4

Components of Gender Inequality Index

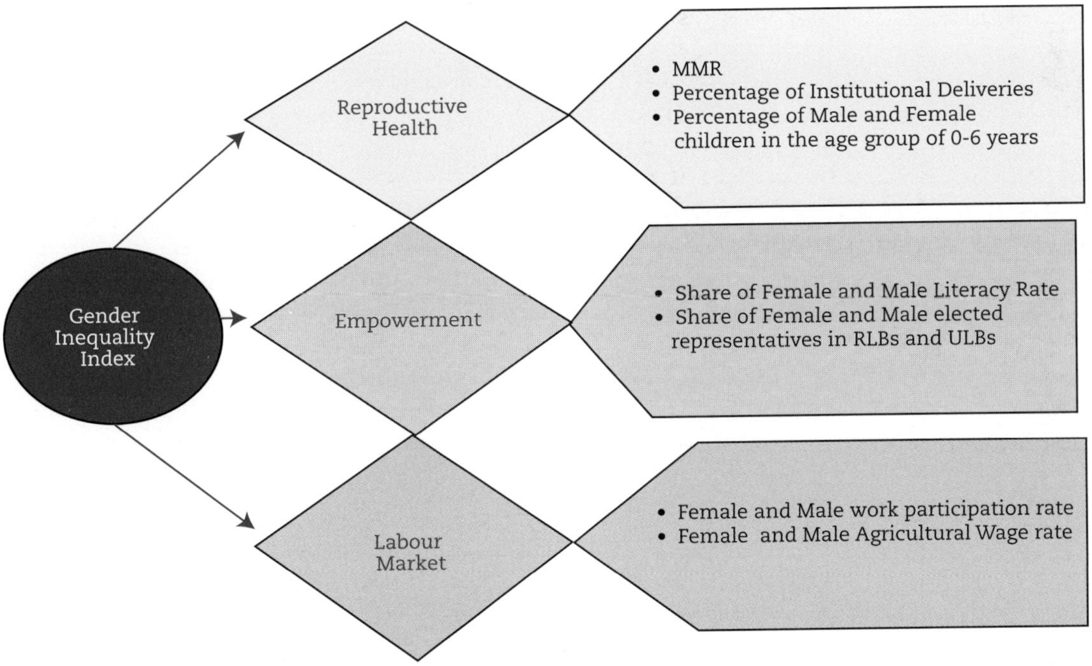

finds that female wage rate is only half of the male and their workforce participation rate is also much lower. Although participation rates may not actually indicate loss of economic power as revealed by micro-level studies (Jeyaranjan 2011), it is a conventionally used indicator. Madurai is one of the districts with high MMR and so it is placed within the bottom five districts in GII. Virudhunagar has the highest female political representation, while Nilgiris registers the lowest. Female agricultural wage was the highest in Salem (₹258.11) and lowest in Villupuram (₹74.88). The latter is a contributing factor for Villupuram district in order to be featured among districts with the highest levels of gender inequality. Female workforce participation rate is the highest in Perambalur and lowest in Kancheepuram (16.4).

Comparison of HDI and GII

This section attempts to compare the ranks of districts in terms of HDI and GII. It was found that in three districts—Virudhunagar, Pudukottai and Ariyalur—

Table 2.4

Comparison of HDI and GII

HDI Index			*GII Index*		
District	*Index*	*Rank*	*District*	*Index*	*Rank*
Top 10 Districts			*Top 10 Districts*		
Kanyakumari	0.944	1	The Nilgiris	0.036	1
Virudhunagar	0.855	2	Virudhunagar	0.048	2
Thoothukudi	0.852	3	Vellore	0.051	3
Chennai	0.847	4	Nammakkal	0.054	4
Kancheepuram	0.845	5	Perambalur	0.057	5
Coimbatore	0.844	6	Salem	0.058	6
Tirunelveli	0.802	7	Thanjavur	0.058	7
Thiruvallur	0.801	8	Dindigul	0.063	8
Krishnagiri	0.788	9	Thiruvallur	0.064	9
Trichy	0.774	10	Kancheepuram	0.064	10
Middle Districts			*Middle Districts*		
Vellore	0.742	11	Erode	0.065	11
Nammakkal	0.738	12	Kanyakumari	0.066	12
Cuddalore	0.719	13	Karur	0.07	13
Dindigul	0.691	14	Tiruppur	0.07	14
Madurai	0.689	15	Dharmapuri	0.074	15
Sivaganga	0.671	16	Ramanathapuram	0.075	16
Salem	0.669	17	Theni	0.075	17
Karur	0.668	18	Trichy	0.082	18
Thanjavur	0.655	19	Thoothukudi	0.083	19
Ramanathapuram	0.653	20	Cuddalore	0.083	20
Dharmapuri	0.644	21	Tirunelveli	0.084	21
Pudukottai	0.631	22	Pudukottai	0.085	22
Bottom 10 Districts			*Bottom 10 Districts*		
Tiruppur	0.627	23	Coimbatore	0.088	23
The Nilgiris	0.624	24	Krishnagiri	0.091	24
Erode	0.616	25	Thiruvarur	0.1	25
Nagapattiam	0.601	26	Tiruvannamalai	0.101	26
Tiruvannamalai	0.596	27	Nagapattiam	0.104	27
Thiruvarur	0.568	28	Chennai	0.111	28
Villupuram	0.561	29	Madurai	0.112	29
Theni	0.539	30	Villupuram	0.113	30
Perambalur	0.447	31	Sivaganga	0.114	31
Ariyalur	0.282	32	Ariyalur	0.118	32

Source: Calculated from data provided by the Departments, Government of Tamil Nadu, 2013-14.

Figure 2.5

GII Index

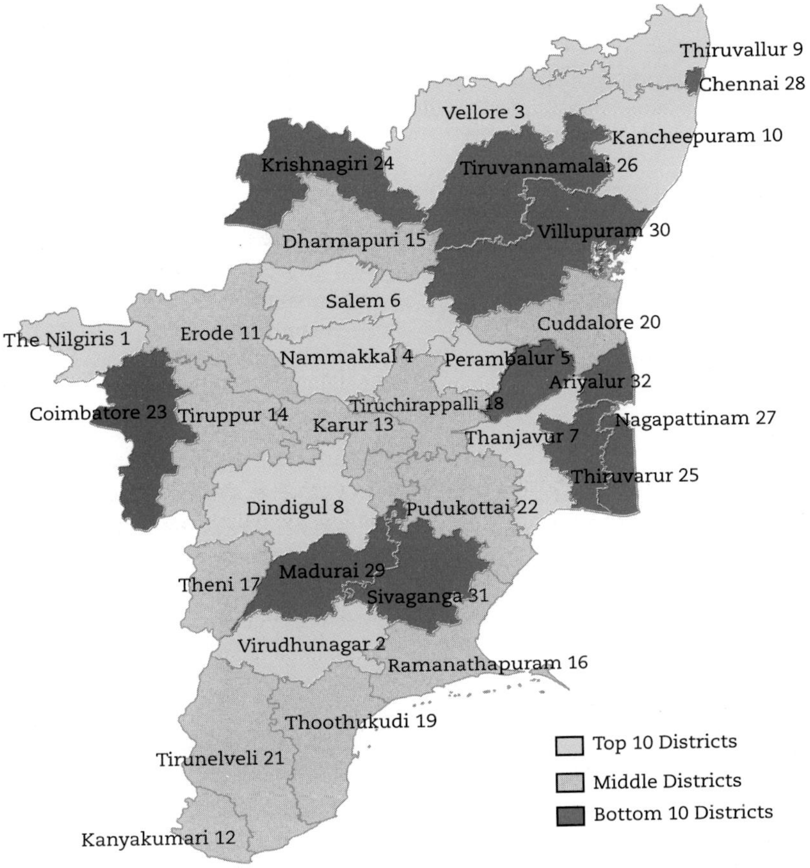

Source: Calculated from data provided by the Departments, Government of Tamil Nadu, 2014-15.

ranks were the same for both the indicators. Poor reproductive health services are a major contributor to differences noticed in gender inequality. Table 2.4 gives the top 10, middle 10 and bottom 10 districts for the two indices.

A closer look at both the indices reveals a few indices where HDI rank is greater than the GII, and some in which the scenario is vice-versa (see Table 2.5).

Sivaganga and Madurai have GII ranks close to the bottom, while their human development indices are on the higher side. In Perambalur, the Nilgiris, Erode, Theni and Thoothukudi, the GII is on lower side and the HDI also shows a corresponding low rank.

Child Development Index

Children are the potential assets of a nation. Integrated development is quite important during

Table 2.5

Rank Comparison of the Districts' HDI and GII

Parameters	*Districts*
Districts with HDI rank greater than the GII rank	Chennai
	Thoothukudi
	Krishnagiri
	Sivaganga
	Madurai
Districts with HDI rank lower than the GII rank	Perambalur
	The Nilgiris
	Erode
	Theni
Districts with HDI and GII of same rank	Virudhunagar
	Pudukottai
	Ariyalur

Source: Calculated from data provided by the Departments, Government of Tamil Nadu, 2013-14

their childhood, the period during which most of their cognitive, emotional and social skills and physical development as individuals, takes place. Computation of CDI helps policy makers to promote and develop public policies dedicated towards development of children. The CDI was developed by the "Save the Children" campaign in the United Kingdom (UK), in 2008, with the contributions of Terry McKinley, Director of the Centre for Development Policy and Research at the School of Oriental and African Studies (SOAS), University of London, with support from Katerina Kyrili. The indicators of CDI conventionally used are related to health, nutrition and education. The selected indicators are chosen because they are easily available, commonly understood, and clearly indicative of children's well-being. At the international level, the three indicators used for measuring CDI are:

- *Health*: Under-five mortality rate (the probability of dying between birth and five years of age, expressed as a percentage on a scale of 0 to 340 deaths per 1,000 live births). This means that a zero score in this component equals an under-five mortality rate of 0 deaths per 1,000 live births, and a score of 100 implies upper bound of 340 deaths per 1,000 live births.
- *Nutrition*: The percentage of children below five years who are moderately or severely under-weight. The common definition of moderately or severely under-weight, which has been used, is being below two standard deviations of the median weight for age of the reference population.
- *Education*: The percentage of primary school-aged children who are not enrolled in school.

The set of indicators used for computing the CDI in Tamil Nadu are given in Figure 2.6. It may be observed that the indicators used for computing CDI across the districts are different from the ones suggested above for the reason that the State has taken significant steps in the education and health sectors over past few decades, and these need to be captured in the measurement of CDI.

The child development index indicated above is a variant of the Achievements of Babies and Children (ABC) index and is calculated in the same manner as the HDI index, using the following indicators: probability of surviving until age five; proportion of children malnourished in the age group of 12-23 months; enrolment in primary and secondary levels'; transition rates from primary to upper primary and upper primary to secondary;children never enrolled; and juvenile sex ratio. Each indicator captures an important aspect of the well-being of children: survival until age five, adequate nourishment, educational attainment, and sex ratio respectively. The last indicator focuses on girls specifically, to impart some gender sensitivity to the index.

Dreze and Khera point to Tamil Nadu's lead in the field of child development (2012). They highlight that while Kerala's achievements in this regard are well known, Tamil Nadu is not far behind, and the fact that all districts of Tamil Nadu are doing well in this respect is quite remarkable. They state that this

Figure 2.6

Parameters for CDI

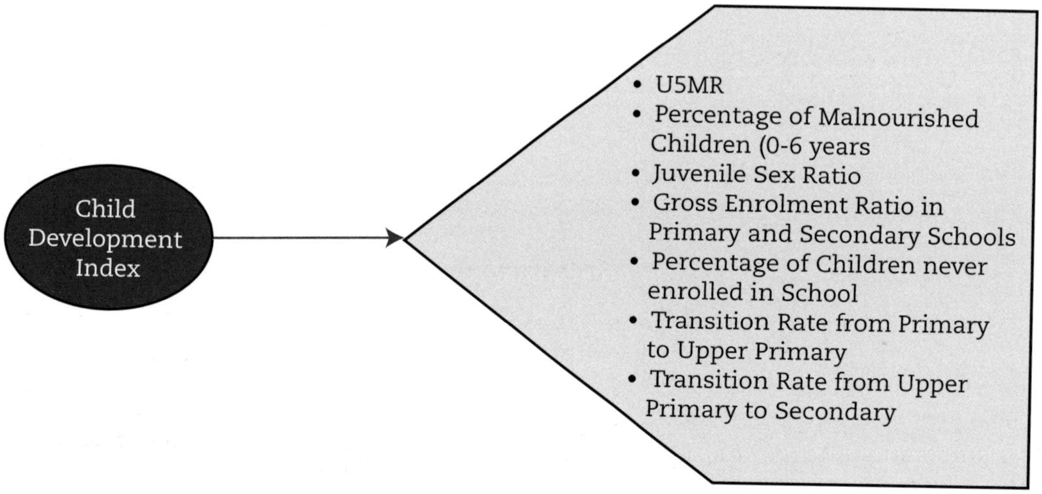

claim is consistent with recent evidence available on rapid improvements in child nutrition, healthcare and elementary education in Tamil Nadu, integrated with active social policies including free and universal provision of essential public services. Table 2.6 gives the five best and worst performing districts in the State in terms of CDI.

Table 2.6

CDI Index

District	Index	Rank
Top 5 Districts		
Kanyakumari	0.872	1
Coimbatore	0.745	2
Thoothukudi	0.712	3
Thanjavur	0.71	4
Sivaganga	0.706	5
Bottom 5 Districts		
Ramanathapuram	0.528	28
Vellore	0.523	29
Krishnagiri	0.474	30
Tiruvannamalai	0.426	31
Ariyalur	0.41	32

Source: Calculated from data provided by the Departments, Government of Tamil Nadu, 2013-14.

Kanyakumari district (0.872) stands first with respect to CDI, while Ariyalur (0.41) has the worst CDI. Kanyakumari and Thoothukudi also have high HDI values. Tiruvanamalai, Krishnagiri, Vellore and Ramanathapuram fare poorly with regard to child development indicators. Ariyalur has poor HDI too. Besides that, Tiruvanamalai and Vellore have tribal belts where malnourishment and gross access ratios are relatively low. Coimbatore, Thuthukoodi, Thanjavur and Sivaganga have high child development indices. Children in these districts are better off, in terms of survival rates, nutrition and educational attainment. The relative performance and ranks of the districts are spatially captured in Figure 2.8.

Multidimensional Poverty Index

The MPI (multidimensional poverty index) measures indicate not only proportion of people deprived that is, the incidence of poverty,but also the degree or intensity of deprivation for each poor household, thus providing us with a better understanding of the dimensions of deprivation. Both the incidence and intensity of these deprivations provide critical information for understanding and intervening in poverty alleviation. Economic growth that does not generate sufficient decent employment is unlikely to foster human development. In addition to money metric measures, efforts have been underway since 2010 so as to come up with additional measures for understanding ways in which the poor face overlapping deprivations across several dimensions, such as health, education and living standards. Such an understanding can help to better address poverty reduction and achievement of millennium development goals (MDGs).

Figure 2.7

Multidimensional Poverty Index

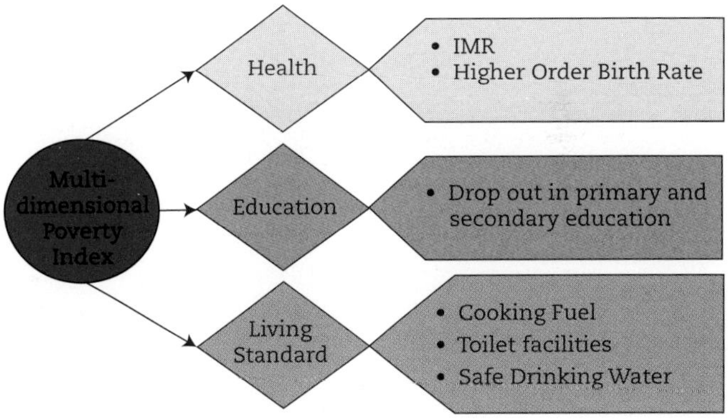

The MPI has seven indicators—two for health, two for education and three for standard of living. The three standard MDG indicators that are related to health and living standards, and which particularly affect women are access to clean drinking water, access to improved sanitation and use of clean cooking fuel. A person has access to clean drinking water, if the water source is any of the following types: piped water, public tap, borehole or pump, protected well, protected spring or rainwater. Also, the source must be within a distance of 30-minutes walk (round trip). A person is considered to have access to improved sanitation if the household has some type of flush toilet or latrine, or ventilated improved pit, or composting toilet, provided that they are not shared. If a household does not satisfy these conditions, then it is considered to be deprived in sanitation.

All standard of living indicators actually refer to the means to achieve better standards and are not direct measures of its functioning. Further, most indicators are related to MDGs, which provide stronger grounds for their inclusion. MPI can thus help in designing

Figure 2.8

CDI Index

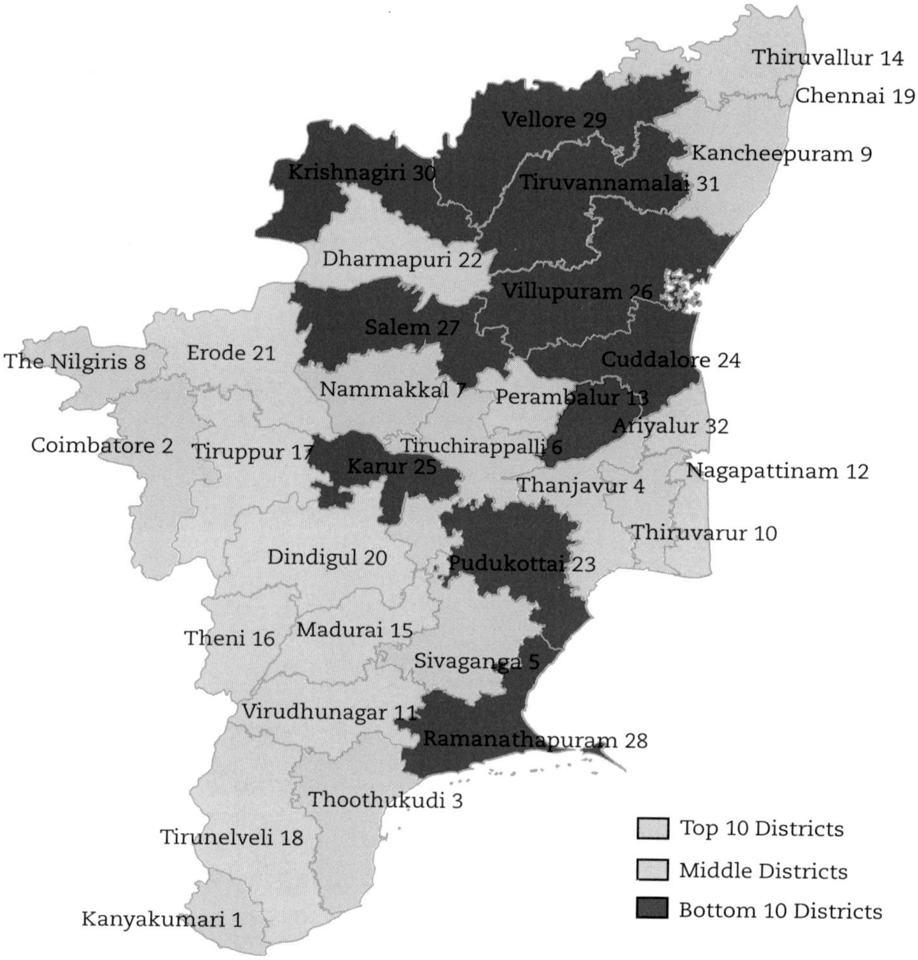

Source: Calculated from data provided by the Departments, Government of Tamil Nadu, 2013-14.

and formulating policies that are more effective in addressing poverty by identifying interconnections, monitoring impacts and allocations of resources effectively. The performance of districts on these parameters is given in Table 2.7 and spatially illustrated in Figure 2.9.

It is evident from the above table that Dharmapuri has the highest multidimensional poverty index and Kancheepuram ranks the lowest. The table also indicates that Dharmapuri, Perambalur, Virudhunagar and Ariyalur are the districts with the largest proportion of population in severe poverty, requiring targeted interventions. Dharmapuri has poor health, education and also standard of living indicators, high infant mortality rate (IMR) and low sanitation coverage. Perambalur, Virudhunagar and Ariyalur are also districts which have multiple deprivations in terms of health, education and standard of living. Kancheepuram and Chennai have the least level of deprivations, and both of them appear to be highly urbanised, well connected and have greater access to education and health facilities. The table on MPI values indicates that they are not highly divergent and many of the districts' values lie close together, indicating that even in the district with the lowest multidimensional poverty, there is scope for improving the values.

Table 2.7

MPI Index

District	*Index*	*Rank*
Top 5 Districts		
Kancheepuram	0.34	1
Chennai	0.34	2
Cuddalore	0.38	3
Coimbatore	0.41	4
Nagapattiam	0.41	5
Bottom 5 Districts		
Ariyalur	0.62	28
Virudhunagar	0.62	29
Ramanathapuram	0.63	30
Perambalur	0.63	31
Dharmapuri	0.7	32

Source: Calculated from data provided by the Departments, Government of Tamil Nadu, 2013-14.

Figure 2.9

MPI Index

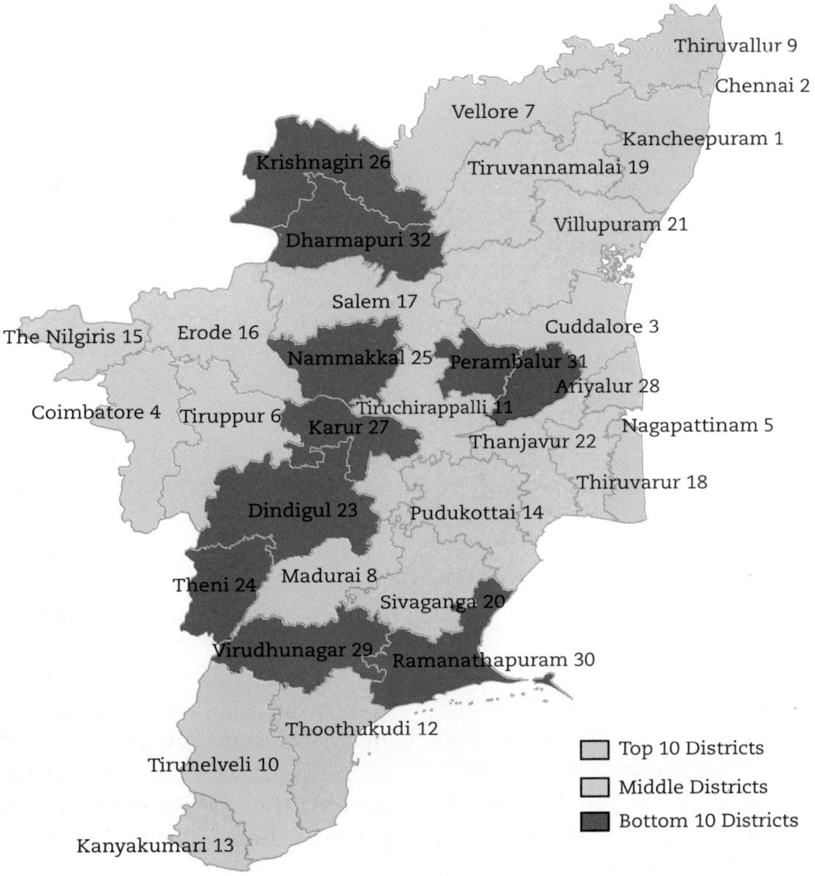

Source: Calculated from data provided by the Departments, Government of Tami Nadu, 2013-14.

Food Security Index

In India, the dimension of food security is important despite attaining self-sufficiency in food production. Though there has been a considerable improvement in productivity and production of rice and wheat, we have not been able to eliminate chronic hunger and poverty. Understanding of the different dimensions of food security, therefore, is of critical importance. The concept of food security in the Indian context has been increasingly refined during the last 50 years. After World War II, food security meant building emergency grain reserves and ensuring the physical availability of food in the market. After the onset of green revolution in the late 1960s, it became obvious that economic access to food is equally important to ensure food security at the household level. During the 1980s, the principle of social access was emphasised, with special reference to marginalised communities and gender discrimination. After the United Nations Conference on Environment and Development (UNCED) conference in Rio de Janeiro, there has been an increasing recognition of the role of environmental factors in food security. The ecological foundations essential for sustained agricultural progress are increasingly under stress due to human activities. One of the early initiatives in assessing the food security scenario in the country was the release of a series of Atlases by M.S. Swaminathan Research Foundation (MSSRF) that looked into the food security in rural and urban areas and also the Sustainability of Food Security atlas of India.

Ensuring food security is an overall objective of development programmes in most developing economies like India. Several problems, such as hunger, malnutrition, under-nutrition and poverty, arise due to food insecurity. Food security and poverty are inextricably linked as Figure 2.10 indicates.

The data given in Figure 2.11 indicates that, at the global level, there has been a positive association between food security and human development. Countries with high status of food security, such as the USA, UK and China, have fared better in the attainment of human development as compared to those ones with low status of food security, such as India, Pakistan, Bangladesh and Nepal. This implies that food security plays an important role in achieving better human development outcomes.

Figure 2.10

Association between Food Insecurity and Poverty

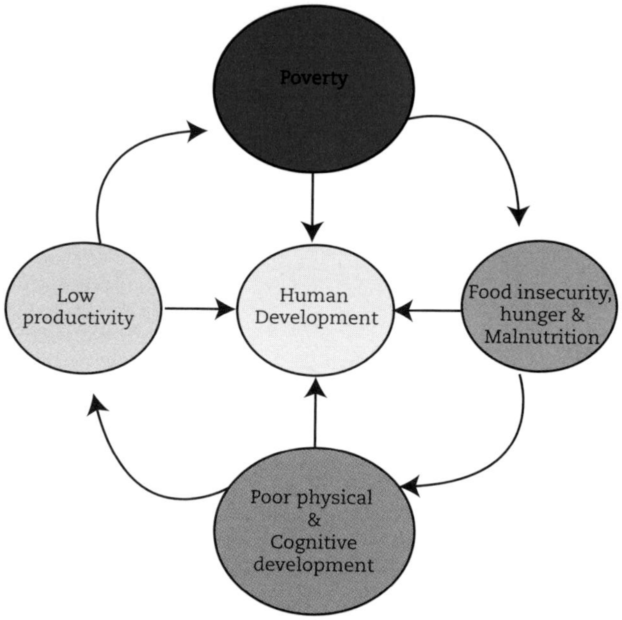

Figure 2.11

Association between Global Food Security Index and HDI of Selected Countries: 2013

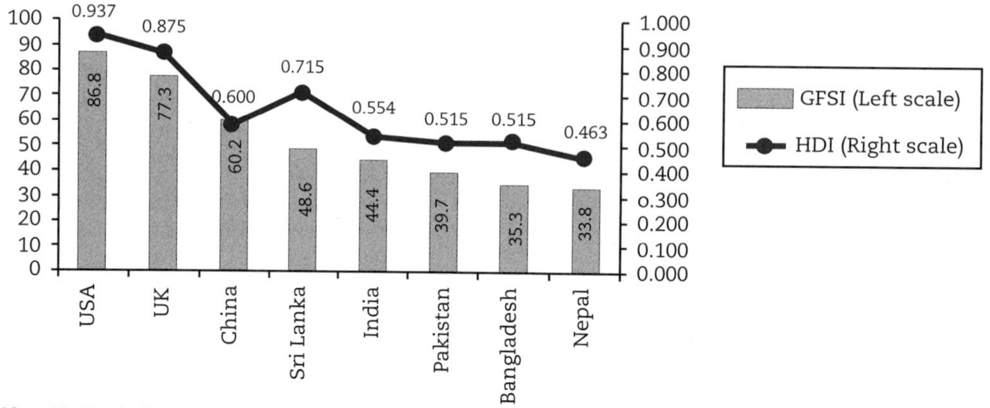

Source: UNDP *HDR 2013* and DuPont's *Global Food Security Index 2013*.

Figure 2.12

Indicators Used to Compute FSI

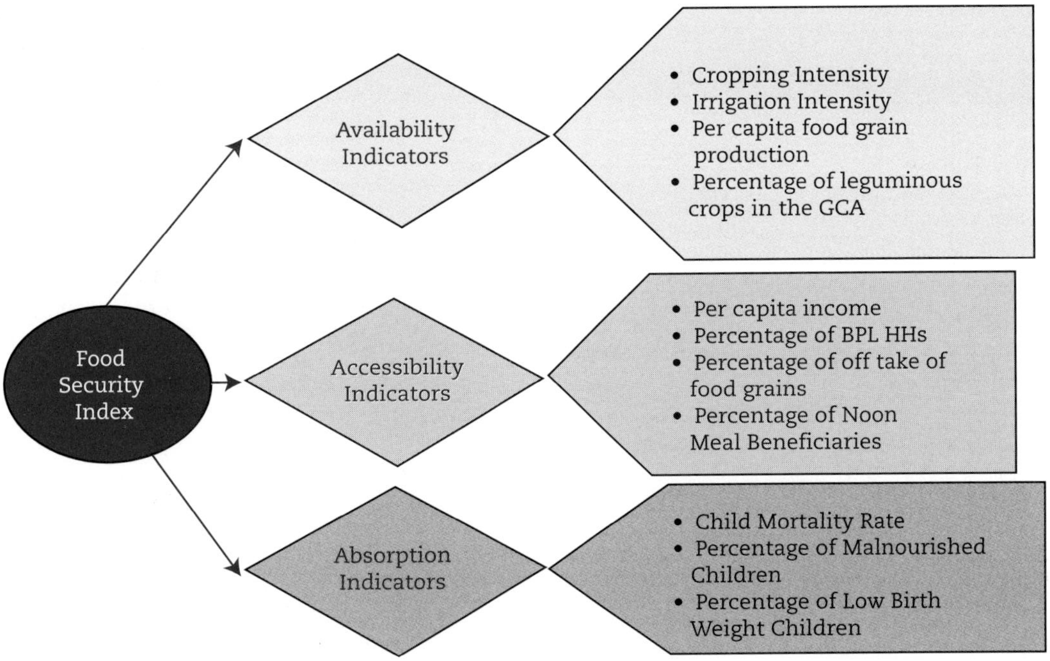

Despite a significant reduction in the incidence of poverty, chronic food insecurity persists in a significant proportion of the population. It has been possible to resolve the problem of food security by offering universal PDS and maintaining sufficient buffer stocks. Yet, there are areas that are food insecure and undernourished. The limitation is not food supply, but food distribution. Careful consideration of food security requires moving beyond food availability and recognising low incomes of the poor. It is also important to identify the choices that households and regions face, including exploitation of natural resources when incomes fall short. Substantial human resources are wasted due to malnutrition-related diseases.

The set of indicators (Figure 2.12) used for computing the FSI are as follows:

Food Security has three components—availability, accessibility and absorption. Availability of food indicates the physical presence of food or domestic production of Foodgrain from agriculture or allied sector in a particular region or place in certain duration and with given technology inventory levels. Accessibility of food refers to acquiring adequate amounts of food through production and stocks, in turn interlinking with the ability of people to obtain food, either through production, purchase or transfers. These components of food security are directly linked with economic ability of the population to afford the sufficient food for their survival. Last component of food security, absorption of food, is defined as a household's ability to absorb and metabolise the nutrients and appropriate nutritional content of the food consumed; and ability of the body to use it effectively. The average per capita availability of rice, from the State's own harvests in the 1980-81 to 1989-90 period, was 98.6 kg but has since then dropped to an average of 84.6 kg for the period 2000-01 to 2006-07.[2]

Looking at district-wise food security, there are clear differences in the levels of FSI across districts (Table 2.8).[3]

Table 2.8 on FSI indicates the presence of variations with reference to availability, access and absorption. The Delta districts and granaries of Tamil Nadu are

2. *http://infochangeindia.org/agriculture/analysis/the-hunger-index.html downloaded on june 25, 2015.*

3. This discussion on FSI does not take into account the district of Chennai, which is entirely an urban district.

Figure 2.13

FSI Index

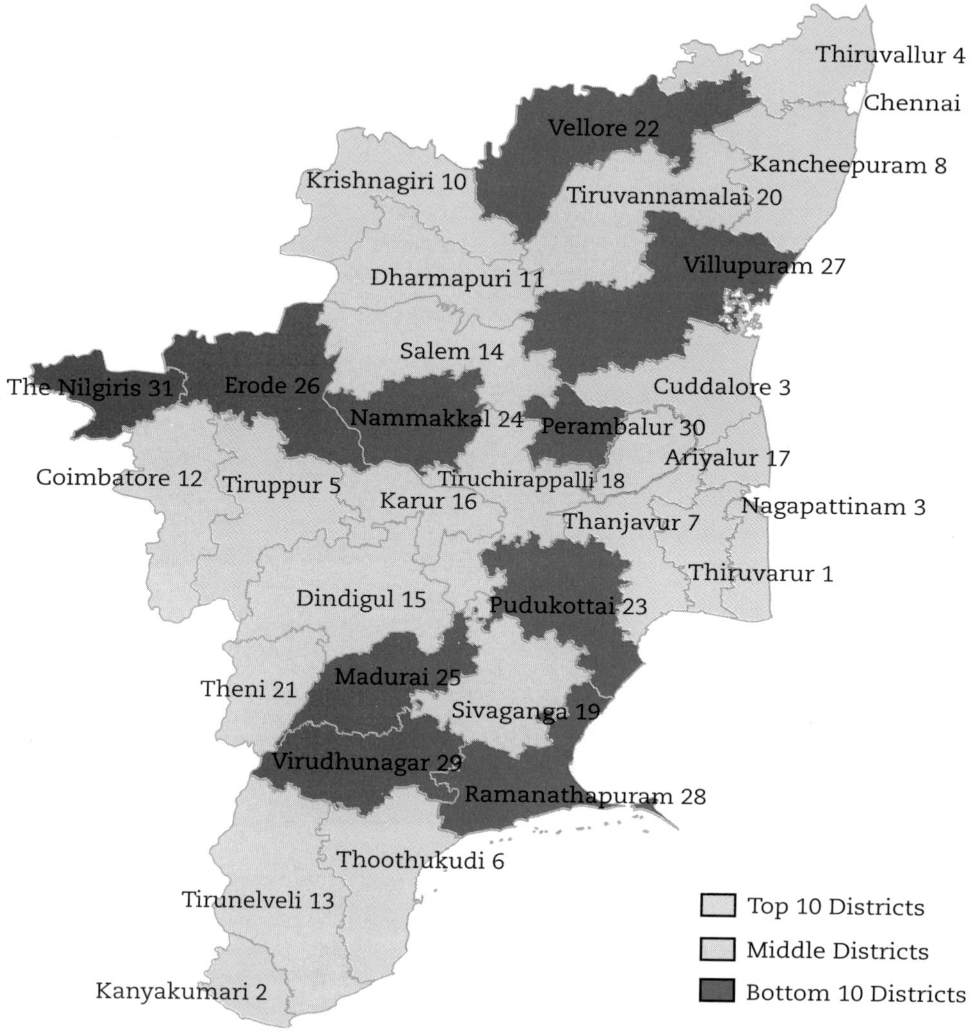

Source: Calculated from data provided by the Departments, Government of Tamil Nadu, 2013-14.

high on the availability indicators, but rank low on access and absorption indicators (details in appendix). The variations in FSI are between 0.58 in Tiruvarur to 0.23 in the Nilgiris. Figure 2.13 highlights the inter-district variations spatially.

In terms of accessibility, Karur has the highest rank, with the lowest rank accorded to Perambalur. This is because Perambalur has poor purchasing power. Kanyakumari has the highest rank in absorption levels as the district has high health indicators, while Tiruvanamalai has the lowest rank given the high levels of malnourishment.

Tiruvarur, Kanyakumari, Nagapatinam, Tiruvallur and Tiruppur are districts with the top five ranks in FSI. Kanyakumari, despite low availability, has high degree of access and absorption levels. The district of Tiruvallur has more or less equal levels of availability, access and absorption. Tiruppur has high absorption levels, although access and availability remain low. The bottom five districts in FSI are: the Nilgiris, Perambalur, Virudhunagar, Ramanathapuram and Villupuram. These districts have problems with respect to availability, access and absorption. Except the Nilgiris, the other districts are mostly dry in nature

Table 2.8

FSI Index

District	*Index*	*Rank*
Top 5 Districts		
Thiruvarur	0.58	1
Kanyakumari	0.562	2
Nagapattiam	0.524	3
Thiruvallur	0.511	4
Tiruppur	0.487	5
Bottom 5 Districts		
Villupuram	0.333	27
Ramanathapuram	0.286	28
Virudhunagar	0.268	29
Perambalur	0.267	30
The Nilgiris	0.226	31

Source: Calculated from data provided by the Departments, Government of Tamil Nadu, 2013-14.

where cultivation is rainfed, and they face problems related to availability of Foodgrains, along with poor access and low consumption levels. The Nilgiris has low availability because it mostly falls in the hilly terrain and cultivation in the region is mostly plantation type and involves high value horticultural crops.

The Food Insecurity Atlas of urban India brought out by MSSRF in 2006 points out that the urban poor are not significantly better off than their rural counterparts. It also highlights that urban calorie intake tends to be lower than that in the rural zones, with absorption levels influenced by sanitation levels and other environmental factors.

Conclusion

Progress made in the State has been accompanied by demographic changes, along with improvements in literacy levels and reductions in total fertility rate. In addition to core human development parameters, this chapter has sought to highlight inter-district variations across other critical parameters for ensuring sustained improvements in overall well-being such as gender inequality, child development, multidimensional poverty and food security indices. Districts like Kanyakumari, Thoothukudi and Coimbatore seem to be faring well in many of the indices, while those like Ariyalur, Perambalur and Villupuram perform poorly. Although some marginal changes are observed over time with the inclusion of Virudhunagar district in the top five districts, regional variations have more or less persisted over the decade. Despite sustained overall improvements, the chapter observes sharp inter-district differences across various dimensions of human development. Some of the districts with low levels of human development also rank low across other indices. Gender inequalities in well-being persist in the State across all three dimensions. Despite being one of the better performing states in terms of human development, there are significant inter-district and intra-district disparities even in the high HDI districts. As regards to the inter-relationship of different components of the HDI, many districts had varying levels of correlation. Indicators of CDI show scope for improvement and this is particularly relevant as it will have an impact on the next generation of Tamil Nadu. The multidimensional poverty index highlights not only inter-district variations that partially overlap with those in levels of human development, but along with indicators of food absorption, it also puts the spotlight on the relatively lower levels of sanitation that the State must take into account to formulate appropriate policy intervention.

Annexures

Methods for Computation of Indices: HDI

Method of Estimating HDI

For the estimation of HDI, the following steps have been followed:

- As a first step, a minimum and maximum value has to be set for each of the above indicators to transform them into indices lying between zero and one. For this purpose, the observed minimum and maximum figures for each of the indicators will be taken. Since the geometric mean has to be calculated, in the case of a positive indicator, the minimum value would be taken as 10 per cent less than the observed minimum value in the district. Similarly, in the case of a negative indicator, the maximum value would be taken as 10 per cent more than the observed maximum value.

- The index value (in the case of a positive indicator) is calculated using the formula:

  Index Value = (Actual Value – Min. Value) / (Max.Value – Min.Value)

  Example: Calculations will be based on highest values being assigned the highest ranks

- The index value (in the case of a negative indicator) is calculated by using the formula:

  Index Value = (Max. Value – Actual Value) / (Max.Value – Min.Value)

  However, for per capita income, first convert the actual per capita income, the minimum per capita income and maximum per capita income into natural log values, before converting into the index.

- For computing sectoral indices (health, education and standard of living), geometric mean is used and the method of calculation is as below. Thus, there will be three indices; one for standard of living, another for health and the last one for education.

  Sectoral Index = If I_1. I_2..... I_n are the n indices for a particular sector, then the geometric mean for the sector = $(I_1 \times . I_2 \times ..... I_n)^{(1/n)}$.

- To compute HDI, aggregate the three sectoral indices using geometric mean with the following formula-

  HDI= $(SI_l \times SI_h \times SI_e)^{(1/3)}$; where SI_l is the sectoral index for living standard, SI_h is the sectoral index for health and SI_e is the sectoral index for education.

Method

GII calculation method has been presented below:

1. Aggregating across dimensions within each gender group using geometric mean.

2. Aggregating across gender group using a harmonic mean.

$$HARM(G_F, G_M) = \left[\frac{(G_F)^{-1} + (G_M)^{-1}}{2}\right]^{-1}$$

3. Calculating the geometric mean of the arithmetic means of the each indicator.

$$G_{\bar{F},\bar{M}} = \sqrt[3]{\overline{health}.\overline{empowerment}.\overline{LFPR}}$$

4. Calculating the GII by comparing the equally distributed gender index to the reference standard. The GII value ranges from zero (no gender inequality across dimensions) to one (total inequality across dimensions).

$$GII = 1 - \frac{HARM(G_F, G_M)}{G_{\bar{F},\bar{M}}}$$

Computation of Child Development Index

- The set of indicators used are both positive and negative in nature.

- The index value (in the case of a positive indicator) is calculated using the formula:

  Index Value = (Actual Value – Min. Value) / (Max.Value – Min.Value)

- The index values for negative indicators is calculated using the following formula:

  Index Value = (Max. Value – Actual Value) / (Max.Value – Min.Value)

- The index values for each of the indicators would range between 0 and 1—0 indicating the lowest ranking for the district and 1 indicating the highest.

In the context of CDI, higher value indicates better child development.

Computation of Food Security Index

- The indicators are broadly categorised under the three parameters: availability, accessibility and absorption.
- The data collected for the above indicators are used for calculating the index values. This helps in making the values unit-less and would allow summation of the index values of all indicators.
- The index values are calculated for each of the indicators, after identifying whether they are positive or negative. This is done to make the index values unidirectional.
- The index value (in the case of a positive indicator) is calculated using the formula:

  Index Value = (Actual Value – Min. Value) / (Max.Value – Min.Value)

  Example: calculations are based on highest values being assigned the highest ranks.
- The index value (in the case of a negative indicator) is calculated by using the formula:

  Index Value = (Max. Value – Actual Value) / (Max.Value – Min.Value)
- The index value for each of the indicators ranges between 0 and 1—0 indicating the lowest and 1 implying the highest ranking of the district.
- The consolidated index for each of the parameters/sectors/dimensions is the average index value of all the indicators.
- The composite index is average of the indicators of all three parameters—availability, accessibility and absorption. This is used to assign ranks for the districts.

Annexure Table A-2.1

Data for Indicators of GII Index

Indicators	MMR	Institutional Deliveries	Male Literacy	Female Literacy	Male Worker Participation Rate	Female Worker Participation Rate	Male Agri. Wage Rate	Female Agri. Wage Rate	Male Elected Represent-tatves	Female Elected Body Representative	% of Male 0-6 Age Group	% of Female 0-6 Age Group
Source	Health Dept.	Health Dept.	Census	Census	Census	Census	SEA report of Agri Dept.	SEA report of Agri Dept	RD&PR Dept.	RD&PR Dept.	Census	Census
Unit	Rate	%	%	%	%	%	₹	₹	%	%	%	%
Year	2013-14	2013-14	2011	2011	2011	2011	2011-12	2011-12	2011	2011	2011	2011
Ariyalur	61	100	81.2	61.7	56.7	38.7	328.68	90.76	77	33	52.7	47.3
Chennai	33	100	93.7	86.6	58.6	19.4			64.81	35.19	51.3	48.7
Coimbatore	58	99.6	89.1	78.9	62.6	28	324.24	116.86	64.95	35.05	51.1	48.9
Cuddalore	89	100	85.9	70.1	57.1	32.5	238.93	105.26	61.55	38.45	52.7	47.3
Dharmapuri	65	99.8	76.9	59.8	57.6	41.7	244.58	96.17	66.7	33.3	52.3	47.7
Dindigul	81	100	84.2	68.3	61.6	40.8	204.97	115.17	63	37	51.7	48.3
Erode	64	100	80.4	64.7	64.8	41.3	283.65	124.24	63.33	36.67	51.2	48.8
Kancheepuram	79	100	89.9	79	58.7	16.4	188.54	87.80	41.45	58.55	51.1	48.9
Kanyakumari	30	100	93.6	89.9	56.6	16.42	562.96	215.17	63.79	36.21	50.9	49.1
Karur	98	99.9	84.5	66.9	62.3	40	199.94	115.62	58.93	41.07	51.6	48.4
Krishnagiri	76	99.3	78.7	63.9	58.5	34.38	280.61	103.71	63	37	51.9	48.1
Madurai	120	100	89.7	77.2	59.1	29.9	247.33	103.41	65.22	34.78	51.8	48.2
Nagapattiam	88	100	89.8	77.6	57.8	25.8	262.08	101.66	63.69	36.31	51	49
Nammakkal	63	100	82.6	66.6	61.1	42.8	245.18	124.34	62	38	52.3	47.7
Perambalur	73	100	82.9	65.9	57.6	48.4	263.49	155.94	61	39	52.3	47.7
Pudukottai	82	100	85.6	69	58.7	35.6	315.57	130.14	64.06	35.94	51.51	49
Ramanathapuram	100	99.6	87.8	73.5	57.5	31.3	198.71	140.92	63.82	36.18	51	49
Salem	67	99.9	80.2	65.2	60.8	35.9	305.05	258.11	68.3	31.7	52.2	47.8
Sivaganga	80	100	87.9	71.9	58.5	34.14	464.86	122.11	58.51	41.49	51	49
Thanjavur	49	100	89	76.5	57.6	24	251.79	114.85	63	37	51.1	48.9
The Nilgiris	39	99.9	91.7	79	58.9	36.7	197.75	93.26	70	30	50.4	49.6
Theni	78	99.8	85	69.5	59	35.91	307.44	132.43	59.17	40.83	51.7	48.3
Thiruvallur	80	100	89.7	78.3	58.8	23.5	189.13	93.75	62	38	51.4	48.6
Thiruvarur	110	99.8	89.1	76.7	59.9	26.7	260.94	117.42	60	40	51.1	48.9
Tiruvannamalai	60	99.5	83.1	65.3	59.8	40.6	267.85	85.12	66.5	33.5	51.8	48.2
Thoothukudi	100	99.9	91.1	81.3	58.2	27.6	248.36	134.90	65	35	50.9	49.1
Tirunelveli	91	100	89.2	76	57.6	36	340.06	149.47	63.1	36.9	51	49
Tiruppur	73	99.9	85.5	71.8	65.8	36.2	248.36	114.02	63.12	36.88	51.2	48.8
Trichy	89	99.9	89.7	76.9	58.4	31	247.36	113.81	63	37	51.4	48.6
Vellore	66	99.8	86.5	74.9	57.3	28.6	187.90	95.16	61.21	38.79	51.4	48.6
Villupuram	56	100	80.5	63.2	58.4	39.9	230.07	74.88	63	37	51.5	48.5
[illegible]	[illegible]	[illegible]	[illegible]	[illegible]	[illegible]	[illegible]	[illegible]	[illegible]	[illegible]	[illegible]	[illegible]	[illegible]

Annexure Table A-2.2

a. HDI Index: Data

Indicators	Per Capita Income	Life Expectancy at Birth	Literacy Rate	Gross Enrolment in Primary	Gross Enrolment in Secondary
Source	DOES	SPC	Census	Education Department	Education Department
Unit	Rs.	Age	%	Rate	Rate
Year	2011-12	2011	2011	2013-14	2013-14
Ariyalur	19467	72.6	71.3	99.14	95.64
Chennai	66240	78.6	90.2	101.35	88.39
Coimbatore	77975	76.6	84	102.45	92.44
Cuddalore	56315	74	78	102.04	98.76
Dharmapuri	56262	72.6	68.5	102.09	107.7
Dindigul	56376	73.6	76.3	102.5	92.52
Erode	75670	73.7	72.6	102.37	70.08
Kancheepuram	92713	75.2	84.5	102.58	90.63
Kanyakumari	96070	77.7	91.7	102.52	95.53
Karur	71795	71.7	75.6	102.32	84.9
Krishnagiri	69318	76.5	74.5	102.26	99.56
Madurai	67258	70.12	83.5	102.57	97.22
Nagapattiam	41208	70	83.6	102.54	103.52
Nammakkal	68213	74.2	74.6	102.6	95.92
Perambalur	24256	72.6	74.3	102.9	102.52
Pudukottai	43890	72.5	77.2	102.84	95.75
Ramanathapuram	44707	72.7	80.7	102.93	95.54
Salem	58623	73.3	72.9	102.29	91.45
Sivaganga	50466	72.3	79.9	102.44	97.73
Thanjavur	48284	71.2	82.6	102.69	99.91
The Nilgiris	51738	68.95	85.2	103.13	99.47
Theni	39856	69	77.3	102.16	98.38
Thiruvallur	83594	74.1	84	102.66	89.83
Thiruvarur	34727	71	82.9	102.79	97.86
Tiruvannamalai	41569	73.3	74.2	101.72	88.78
Thoothukudi	74933	76.6	86.2	102.58	94.35
Tirunelveli	61899	76.2	82.5	102.55	98.39
Tiruppur	88549	68.1	78.8	98.79	95.31
Trichy	75393	72.7	83.2	102.44	99.01
Vellore	63185	74.8	79.2	102.51	89.95
Villupuram	35295	74.5	71.9	102.27	87.88
Virudhunagar	87361	76	80.2	102.53	98.92

Annexure Table A-2.2

b. HDI Index: Rank

District	HDI Index				Rank
	Living Standard Index	Health Index	Education Index	Overall Index	
Ariyalur	0.062	0.653	0.552	0.282	32
Chennai	0.782	1.000	0.778	0.847	4
Coimbatore	0.877	0.884	0.775	0.844	6
Cuddalore	0.686	0.734	0.738	0.719	13
Dharmapuri	0.686	0.653	0.596	0.644	21
Dindigul	0.687	0.711	0.675	0.691	14
Erode	0.860	0.717	0.378	0.616	25
Kancheepuram	0.979	0.804	0.767	0.845	5
Kanyakumari	1.000	0.948	0.886	0.944	1
Karur	0.829	0.601	0.598	0.668	18
Krishnagiri	0.808	0.879	0.690	0.788	9
Madurai	0.790	0.510	0.812	0.689	15
Nagapattiam	0.503	0.503	0.859	0.601	26
Nammakkal	0.799	0.746	0.673	0.738	12
Perambalur	0.191	0.653	0.715	0.447	31
Pudukottai	0.540	0.648	0.719	0.631	22
Ramanathapuram	0.550	0.659	0.769	0.653	20
Salem	0.710	0.694	0.607	0.669	17
Sivaganga	0.622	0.636	0.766	0.671	16
Thanjavur	0.596	0.573	0.823	0.655	19
The Nilgiris	0.636	0.443	0.861	0.624	24
Theni	0.483	0.445	0.727	0.539	30
Thiruvallur	0.918	0.740	0.755	0.801	8
Thiruvarur	0.402	0.561	0.813	0.568	28
Tiruvannamalai	0.508	0.694	0.601	0.596	27
Thoothukudi	0.854	0.884	0.820	0.852	3
Tirunelveli	0.742	0.861	0.808	0.802	7
Tiruppur	0.952	0.393	0.659	0.627	23
Trichy	0.858	0.659	0.819	0.774	10
Vellore	0.754	0.780	0.695	0.742	11
Villupuram	0.412	0.763	0.563	0.561	29
Virudhunagar	0.944	0.850	0.780	0.855	2

Annexure Table A-2.3

a. Gender Inequality Index: Data

Indicators	MMR	Institutional Deliveries	Male Literacy	Female Literacy	Male Worker Participation Rate	Female Worker Participation Rate	Male Agriculture Wage Rate	Female Agriculture Wage Rate	Male Elected Representatives	Female Elected Body Representative	% of Male 0-6 Age Group	% of Female 0-6 Age Group
Source	Health Dept	Health Dept	Census	Census	Census	Census	SEA report of Agriculture Dept	SEA report of Agriculture Dept	RD&PR Dept	RD&PR Dept	Census	Census
Unit	Rate	%	%	%	%	%	Rs	Rs	%	%	%	%
Year	2013-14	2013-14	2011	2011	2011	2011	2011-12	2011-12	2011	2011	2011	2011
Ariyalur	61	100	81.2	61.7	56.7	38.7	328.68	90.76	77	33	52.7	47.3
Chennai	33	100	93.7	86.6	58.6	19.4			64.81	35.19	51.3	48.7
Coimbatore	58	99.6	89.1	78.9	62.6	28	324.24	116.86	64.95	35.05	51.1	48.9
Cuddalore	89	100	85.9	70.1	57.1	32.5	238.93	105.26	61.55	38.45	52.7	47.3
Dharmapuri	65	99.8	76.9	59.8	57.6	41.7	244.58	96.17	66.7	33.3	52.3	47.7
Dindigul	81	100	84.2	68.3	61.6	40.8	204.97	115.17	63	37	51.7	48.3
Erode	64	100	80.4	64.7	64.8	41.3	283.65	124.24	63.33	36.67	51.2	48.8
Kancheepuram	79	100	89.9	79	58.7	16.4	188.54	87.80	41.45	58.55	51.1	48.9
Kanyakumari	30	100	93.6	89.9	56.6	16.42	562.96	215.17	63.79	36.21	50.9	49.1
Karur	98	99.9	84.5	66.9	62.3	40	199.94	115.62	58.93	41.07	51.6	48.4
Krishnagiri	76	99.3	78.7	63.9	58.5	34.38	280.61	103.71	63	37	51.9	48.1
Madurai	120	100	89.7	77.2	59.1	29.9	247.33	103.41	65.22	34.78	51.8	48.2
Nagapattiam	88	100	89.8	77.6	57.8	25.8	262.08	101.66	63.69	36.31	51	49
Nammakkal	63	100	82.6	66.6	61.1	42.8	245.18	124.34	62	38	52.3	47.7
Perambalur	73	100	82.9	65.9	57.6	48.4	263.49	155.94	61	39	52.3	47.7
Pudukottai	82	100	85.6	69	58.7	35.6	315.57	130.14	64.06	35.94	51.51	49
Ramanathapuram	100	99.6	87.8	73.5	57.5	31.3	198.71	140.92	63.82	36.18	51	49
Salem	67	99.9	80.2	65.2	60.8	35.9	305.05	258.11	68.3	31.7	52.2	47.8
Sivaganga	80	100	87.9	71.9	58.5	34.14	464.86	122.11	58.51	41.49	51	49
Thanjavur	49	100	89	76.5	57.6	24	251.79	114.85	63	37	51.1	48.9
The Nilgiris	39	99.9	91.7	79	58.9	36.7	197.75	93.26	70	30	50.4	49.6
Theni	78	99.8	85	69.5	59	35.91	307.44	132.43	59.17	40.83	51.7	48.3
Thiruvallur	80	100	89.7	78.3	58.8	23.5	189.13	93.75	62	38	51.4	48.6
Thiruvarur	110	99.8	89.1	76.7	59.9	26.7	260.94	117.42	60	40	51.1	48.9
Tiruvannamalai	60	99.5	83.1	65.3	59.8	40.6	267.85	85.12	66.5	33.5	51.8	48.2
Thoothukudi	100	99.9	91.1	81.3	58.2	27.6	248.36	134.90	65	35	50.9	49.1
Tirunelveli	91	100	89.2	76	57.6	36	340.06	149.47	63.1	36.9	51	49
Tiruppur	73	99.9	85.5	71.8	65.8	36.2	248.36	114.02	63.12	36.88	51.2	48.8
Trichy	89	99.9	89.7	76.9	58.4	31	247.36	113.81	63	37	51.4	48.6
Vellore	66	99.8	86.5	74.9	57.3	28.6	187.90	95.16	61.21	38.79	51.4	48.6
Villupuram	56	100	80.5	63.2	58.4	39.9	230.07	74.88	63	37	51.5	48.5
Virudhunagar	63	99.9	87.7	72.7	59.8	38.1	244.23	106.46	34	66	51.1	48.9

Annexure Table A-2.3

b. Gender Inequality Index: Rank

District	Fhlt_ ind	Mhlt_ ind	Femp_ ind	Memp_ ind	Flf_ ind	Mlf_ ind	GF	GM	GFM	Health Bar	Emp Bar	LF BAR	GFM Bar
Ariyalur	0.405	1	0.458	0.691	0.218	0.479	0.343	0.692	0.459	0.702	0.6	0.349	0.520
Chennai	0.550	1	0.529	0.678	0.194	0.586	0.384	0.735	0.504	0.775	0.6	0.390	0.567
Coimbatore	0.414	1	0.513	0.666	0.269	0.497	0.386	0.692	0.495	0.707	0.6	0.383	0.543
Cuddalore	0.335	1	0.503	0.653	0.254	0.318	0.350	0.592	0.440	0.668	0.6	0.286	0.480
Dharmapuri	0.392	1	0.456	0.645	0.251	0.332	0.355	0.598	0.446	0.696	0.6	0.292	0.482
Dindigul	0.351	1	0.496	0.650	0.320	0.237	0.382	0.536	0.446	0.676	0.6	0.278	0.476
Erode	0.395	1	0.487	0.639	0.351	0.434	0.407	0.652	0.501	0.698	0.6	0.392	0.536
Kancheepuram	0.356	1	0.609	0.575	0.132	0.170	0.306	0.461	0.368	0.678	0.6	0.151	0.393
Kanyakumari	0.577	1	0.543	0.672	0.357	0.752	0.482	0.797	0.600	0.789	0.6	0.555	0.643
Karur	0.319	1	0.510	0.636	0.318	0.221	0.373	0.520	0.434	0.660	0.6	0.269	0.467
Krishnagiri	0.361	1	0.484	0.636	0.256	0.407	0.355	0.637	0.456	0.681	0.6	0.331	0.502
Madurai	0.289	1	0.506	0.672	0.238	0.343	0.326	0.613	0.426	0.644	0.6	0.290	0.479
Nagapattiam	0.337	1	0.517	0.663	0.215	0.369	0.335	0.626	0.436	0.669	0.6	0.292	0.487
Nammakkal	0.398	1	0.494	0.645	0.357	0.344	0.413	0.605	0.491	0.699	0.6	0.351	0.519
Perambalur	0.370	1	0.497	0.642	0.474	0.372	0.443	0.620	0.517	0.685	0.6	0.423	0.548
Pudukottai	0.349	1	0.495	0.656	0.342	0.467	0.390	0.674	0.494	0.675	0.6	0.405	0.540
Ramanathapuram	0.316	1	0.507	0.659	0.347	0.208	0.382	0.515	0.439	0.658	0.6	0.278	0.474
Salem	0.386	1	0.462	0.659	0.599	0.458	0.475	0.671	0.556	0.693	0.6	0.529	0.590
Sivaganga	0.354	1	0.527	0.640	0.313	0.663	0.388	0.751	0.512	0.677	0.6	0.488	0.578
Thanjavur	0.452	1	0.517	0.659	0.244	0.348	0.385	0.612	0.473	0.726	0.6	0.296	0.502
The Nilgiris	0.506	1	0.490	0.686	0.223	0.207	0.381	0.522	0.440	0.753	0.6	0.215	0.457
Theni	0.358	1	0.516	0.638	0.350	0.455	0.401	0.662	0.500	0.679	0.6	0.403	0.540
Thiruvallur	0.354	1	0.525	0.659	0.180	0.173	0.322	0.485	0.387	0.677	0.6	0.177	0.414
Thiruvarur	0.301	1	0.531	0.649	0.265	0.374	0.349	0.624	0.447	0.651	0.6	0.319	0.497
Tiruvannamalai	0.407	1	0.472	0.659	0.194	0.387	0.334	0.634	0.438	0.704	0.6	0.291	0.487
Thoothukudi	0.316	1	0.519	0.670	0.313	0.342	0.371	0.612	0.462	0.658	0.6	0.327	0.504
Tirunelveli	0.331	1	0.516	0.660	0.394	0.500	0.407	0.691	0.512	0.666	0.6	0.447	0.559
Tiruppur	0.370	1	0.506	0.651	0.297	0.364	0.382	0.619	0.472	0.685	0.6	0.331	0.508
Trichy	0.335	1	0.517	0.662	0.275	0.341	0.362	0.609	0.454	0.668	0.6	0.308	0.495
Vellore	0.389	1	0.521	0.648	0.204	0.165	0.346	0.475	0.400	0.694	0.6	0.185	0.422
Villupuram	0.423	1	0.484	0.639	0.125	0.301	0.295	0.577	0.390	0.711	0.6	0.213	0.440
Virudhunagar	0.398	1	0.617	0.534	0.279	0.338	0.409	0.565	0.475	0.699	0.6	0.309	0.499

Annexure Table A-2.4

a. CDI Index: Data

Indicators	Under 5MR	Malnourish-ment	Enrolment in Primary	Enrolment in Secondary	Juvenile Sex Ratio	Percentage of Children Never Enrolled in Schools	Transition Rate from Primary to Upper Primary	Transition Rate from Upper Primary to Secondary
	Negative	Negative	Positive	Positive	Positive	Negative	Positive	Positive
Source	Health Dept	CDPO	Education Dept	Education Dept	Census	Education Dept	Education Dept	Education Dept
Unit	Rate	Rate	No.	No.	No.	%	Rate	Rate
Year	2012	2013	2013-14	2013-14	2011	2013-14	2013-14	2013-14
Ariyalur	24.28	18.91	99.14	95.64	897	0	97.82	98.44
Chennai	16.1	11.64	101.35	88.39	950	0	99.85	88.14
Coimbatore	17.6	11.48	102.45	92.44	956	0.04	99.83	97.3
Cuddalore	22.8	27.06	102.04	98.76	896	0.01	99.83	95.72
Dharmapuri	26.8	25.04	102.09	107.7	913	0.08	99.83	95.99
Dindigul	22.6	19.54	102.5	92.52	934	0.02	99.85	90.07
Erode	19.5	17.48	102.37	70.08	953	0.01	99.85	94.33
Kancheepuram	20.8	10.93	102.58	90.63	959	0.4	99.8	99.67
Kanyakumari	7	1.95	102.52	95.53	964	0	99.8	99.87
Karur	25.9	17.78	102.32	84.9	939	0.47	99.8	98.31
Krishnagiri	27.5	23.13	102.26	99.56	926	0.8	99.85	91.21
Madurai	28.3	15.89	102.57	97.22	932	0	99.83	94.29
Nagapattiam	27	25.24	102.54	103.52	959	0	99.78	91.46
Nammakkal	24.5	10.99	102.6	95.92	914	0.04	99.78	101.17
Perambalur	26.1	20.87	102.9	102.52	913	0	99.73	97.06
Pudukottai	23.3	26.31	102.84	95.75	960	0.3	99.78	92.8
Ramanathapuram	24	32.08	102.93	95.54	961	0.52	99.8	88.45
Salem	29.5	22.03	102.29	91.45	916	0.09	99.78	91.54
Sivaganga	26.9	10.68	102.44	97.73	960	0	99.83	92.31
Thanjavur	21.5	21.58	102.69	99.91	957	0	99.83	94.87
The Nilgiris	18.1	23.08	103.13	99.47	985	0.51	99.8	96.39
Theni	31.1	10.89	102.16	98.38	934	0	99.8	93.52
Thiruvallur	20.9	12.5	102.66	89.83	946	0.36	99.85	96.46
Thiruvarur	21.7	21.48	102.79	97.86	958	0.1	99.8	92.41
Tiruvannamalai	29.4	29.58	101.72	88.78	930	0.7	99.83	93.86
Thoothukudi	21.5	13.75	102.58	94.35	963	0.01	99.78	93
Tirunelveli	26.1	19.21	102.55	98.39	960	0.01	99.78	87.96
Tiruppur	0	10.44	98.79	95.31	952	0.2	99.48	94.15
Trichy	26.2	21.01	102.44	99.01	947	0	99.8	100.27
Vellore	30.8	23.11	102.51	89.95	944	0.01	99.78	82.77
Villupuram	26.7	31.04	102.27	87.88	941	0.008	99.75	92.49
Virudhunagar	26.7	29.1	102.53	98.92	955	0	99.85	98.27

Annexure Table A-2.4

b. CDI Indices

Districts	CDI Indices							
	Under 5MR	Malnourish-ment	Enrolment in Primary	Enrolment in Secondary	Juvenile Sex Ratio	Percentage of Children Never Enrolled in Schools	Transition Rate from Primary to Upper Primacy	Transition Rate from Upper Primary to Secondary
Ariyalur	0.219	0.437	0.081	0.679	0.011	1.000	0.000	0.852
Chennai	0.482	0.678	0.590	0.487	0.607	1.000	1.000	0.292
Coimbatore	0.434	0.684	0.843	0.594	0.674	0.950	0.990	0.790
Cuddalore	0.267	0.167	0.749	0.762	0.000	0.988	0.990	0.704
Dharmapuri	0.138	0.234	0.760	1.000	0.191	0.900	0.990	0.718
Dindigul	0.273	0.416	0.855	0.596	0.427	0.975	1.000	0.397
Erode	0.373	0.485	0.825	0.000	0.640	0.988	1.000	0.628
Kancheepuram	0.331	0.702	0.873	0.546	0.708	0.500	0.975	0.918
Kanyakumari	0.775	1.000	0.859	0.677	0.764	1.000	0.975	0.929
Karur	0.167	0.475	0.813	0.394	0.483	0.413	0.975	0.845
Krishnagiri	0.116	0.297	0.800	0.784	0.337	0.000	1.000	0.459
Madurai	0.090	0.537	0.871	0.721	0.404	1.000	0.990	0.626
Nagapattiam	0.132	0.227	0.864	0.889	0.708	1.000	0.966	0.472
Nammakkal	0.212	0.700	0.878	0.687	0.202	0.950	0.966	1.000
Perambalur	0.161	0.372	0.947	0.862	0.191	1.000	0.941	0.777
Pudukottai	0.251	0.192	0.933	0.682	0.719	0.625	0.966	0.545
Ramanathapuram	0.228	0.000	0.954	0.677	0.730	0.350	0.975	0.309
Salem	0.051	0.334	0.806	0.568	0.225	0.888	0.966	0.477
Sivaganga	0.135	0.710	0.841	0.735	0.719	1.000	0.990	0.518
Thanjavur	0.309	0.348	0.899	0.793	0.685	1.000	0.990	0.658
The Nilgiris	0.418	0.299	1.000	0.781	1.000	0.363	0.975	0.740
Theni	0.000	0.703	0.776	0.752	0.427	1.000	0.975	0.584
Thiruvallur	0.328	0.650	0.892	0.525	0.562	0.550	1.000	0.744
Thiruvarur	0.302	0.352	0.922	0.738	0.697	0.875	0.975	0.524
Tiruvannamalai	0.055	0.083	0.675	0.497	0.382	0.125	0.990	0.603
Thoothukudi	0.309	0.608	0.873	0.645	0.753	0.988	0.966	0.556
Tirunelveli	0.161	0.427	0.866	0.753	0.719	0.988	0.966	0.282
Tiruppur	1.000	0.718	0.000	0.671	0.629	0.750	0.818	0.618
Trichy	0.158	0.367	0.841	0.769	0.573	1.000	0.975	0.951
Vellore	0.010	0.298	0.857	0.528	0.539	0.988	0.966	0.000
Villupuram	0.141	0.035	0.802	0.473	0.506	0.990	0.951	0.528
Virudhunagar	0.141	0.099	0.862	0.767	0.663	1.000	1.000	0.842

Annexure Table A-2.4

c. CDI Values and Ranks District-Wise

District	*CDI Value*	*CDI Rank*
Kanyakumari	0.872	1
Coimbatore	0.745	2
Thoothukudi	0.712	3
Thanjavur	0.71	4
Sivaganga	0.706	5
Trichy	0.704	6
Nammakkal	0.699	7
The Nilgiris	0.697	8
Kancheepuram	0.694	9
Thiruvarur	0.673	10
Virudhunagar	0.672	11
Nagapattiam	0.657	12
Perambalur	0.656	13
Thiruvallur	0.656	14
Madurai	0.655	15
Theni	0.652	16
Tiruppur	0.651	17
Tirunelveli	0.645	18
Chennai	0.642	19
Dindigul	0.617	20
Erode	0.617	21
Dharmapuri	0.616	22
Pudukottai	0.614	23
Cuddalore	0.578	24
Karur	0.571	25
Villupuram	0.553	26
Salem	0.539	27
Ramanathapuram	0.528	28
Vellore	0.523	29
Krishnagiri	0.474	30
Tiruvannamalai	0.426	31
Ariyalur	0.41	32

Annexure Table A-2.5

a. MPI Index and Rank: District-wise

District	*MPI Index*	*MPI Rank*
Kancheepuram	0.34	1
Chennai	0.34	2
Cuddalore	0.38	3
Coimbatore	0.41	4
Nagapattiam	0.41	5
Tiruppur	0.42	6
Vellore	0.43	7
Madurai	0.45	8
Thiruvallur	0.46	9
Tirunelveli	0.46	10
Trichy	0.47	11
Thoothukudi	0.49	12
Kanyakumari	0.5	13
Pudukottai	0.51	14
The Nilgiris	0.52	15
Erode	0.52	16
Salem	0.53	17
Thiruvarur	0.53	18
Tiruvannamalai	0.53	19
Sivaganga	0.55	20
Villupuram	0.58	21
Thanjavur	0.59	22
Dindigul	0.59	23
Theni	0.6	24
Nammakkal	0.6	25
Krishnagiri	0.6	26
Karur	0.61	27
Ariyalur	0.62	28
Virudhunagar	0.62	29
Ramanathapuram	0.63	30
Perambalur	0.63	31
Dharmapuri	0.7	32

Annexure Table A-2.5

b. MPI Index: Data

Indicators	IMR	Higher Order Birth Rate	Dropout in Primary	Dropout in Secondary	Cooking Fuel (LPG, Kerosene, Electric and Biogas)	Access to Safe Drinking Water within Premises	Access to Toilet within Premises
	Negative	Positive	Negative	Negative	Positive	Positive	Positive
Source	Health Dept	Health Dept	Education Dept	Education Dept	Census of India	Census of India	Census of India
Unit	%		Rate	Rate	%	%	%
Year	2013-14	2013-14	2013-14	2013-14	2011	2011	2011
Ariyalur	9	13.40	1.07	8.33	20.80	66.43	18.10
Chennai	7	2.60	1.02	8.53	96.60	97.57	95.60
Coimbatore	6	3.20	1.22	8.22	81.00	95.67	66.70
Cuddalore	12	10.60	0.40	6.75	41.00	81.07	36.10
Dharmapuri	20	13.40	1.86	7.65	30.90	76.69	19.00
Dindigul	13	8.60	1.28	7.92	43.10	80.22	33.30
Erode	7	3.70	1.18	8.51	66.30	88.21	49.00
Kancheepuram	10	6.20	0.43	7.48	72.50	86.22	65.50
Kanyakumari	9	3.40	0.44	8.74	43.40	77.32	87.50
Karur	18	9.00	1.23	8.14	54.80	79.64	41.20
Krishnagiri	17	12.00	1.45	7.93	38.00	83.97	33.00
Madurai	12	7.20	0.73	8.40	63.70	91.21	59.20
Nagapattiam	14	11.30	0.43	7.10	36.90	84.34	39.50
Nammakkal	14	7.70	1.54	8.41	63.30	84.63	40.70
Perambalur	15	12.80	1.23	7.69	35.90	61.44	22.20
Pudukottai	12	12.40	0.70	7.64	23.60	77.48	28.00
Ramanathapuram	13	10.30	0.90	8.14	34.70	59.08	36.60
Salem	12	10.40	1.55	7.94	56.60	89.09	35.00
Sivaganga	13	9.00	0.48	8.39	37.40	76.74	40.70
Thanjavur	10	9.90	1.03	7.92	40.10	55.36	45.10
The Nilgiris	11	5.90	1.05	8.02	52.50	84.94	51.90
Theni	17	6.80	1.15	8.09	53.50	87.27	39.30
Thiruvallur	12	6.50	1.21	7.82	75.90	81.97	67.90
Thiruvarur	11	8.20	0.50	7.42	34.80	62.89	39.70
Tiruvannamalai	15	14.50	0.98	7.09	33.00	66.88	22.80
Thoothukudi	11	10.30	0.93	8.60	49.90	88.75	50.00
Tirunelveli	14	9.40	0.35	8.36	51.80	88.84	47.60
Tiruppur	7	3.70	0.82	8.30	77.60	93.09	57.20
Trichy	12	9.60	0.55	8.56	55.70	87.34	48.50
Vellore	11	13.40	0.89	7.42	48.90	75.84	41.10
Villupuram	17	13.50	0.98	7.34	31.30	69.97	21.10
Virudhunagar	12	6.70	0.94	8.62	53.50	74.49	30.90

Annexure Table A-2.5

c. MPI Indices

Districts	MPI Indices						
	IMR	Higher Order Birth Rate	Dropout in Primary	Dropout in Secondary	Cooking Fuel (LPG, Kerosene, Electric and Biogas)	Access to Safe Drinking Water	Access to Toilet within Premises
Ariyalur	0.786	0.908	0.523	0.206	0.000	0.262	0.000
Chennai	0.929	0.000	0.556	0.106	1.000	1.000	1.000
Coimbatore	1.000	0.050	0.424	0.261	0.794	0.955	0.627
Cuddalore	0.571	0.672	0.967	1.000	0.266	0.609	0.232
Dharmapuri	0.000	0.908	0.000	0.548	0.133	0.505	0.012
Dindigul	0.500	0.504	0.384	0.412	0.294	0.589	0.196
Erode	0.929	0.092	0.450	0.116	0.600	0.778	0.399
Kancheepuram	0.714	0.303	0.947	0.633	0.682	0.731	0.612
Kanyakumari	0.786	0.067	0.940	0.000	0.298	0.520	0.895
Karur	0.143	0.538	0.417	0.302	0.449	0.575	0.298
Krishnagiri	0.214	0.790	0.272	0.407	0.227	0.678	0.192
Madurai	0.571	0.387	0.748	0.171	0.566	0.849	0.530
Nagapattiam	0.429	0.731	0.947	0.824	0.212	0.687	0.276
Nammakkal	0.429	0.429	0.212	0.166	0.561	0.693	0.292
Perambalur	0.357	0.857	0.417	0.528	0.199	0.144	0.053
Pudukottai	0.571	0.824	0.768	0.553	0.037	0.524	0.128
Ramanathapuram	0.500	0.647	0.636	0.302	0.183	0.088	0.239
Salem	0.571	0.655	0.205	0.402	0.472	0.799	0.218
Sivaganga	0.500	0.538	0.914	0.176	0.219	0.506	0.292
Thanjavur	0.714	0.613	0.550	0.412	0.255	0.000	0.348
The Nilgiris	0.643	0.277	0.536	0.362	0.418	0.701	0.436
Theni	0.214	0.353	0.470	0.327	0.431	0.756	0.274
Thiruvallur	0.571	0.328	0.430	0.462	0.727	0.630	0.643
Thiruvarur	0.643	0.471	0.901	0.663	0.185	0.179	0.279
Tiruvannamalai	0.357	1.000	0.583	0.829	0.161	0.273	0.061
Thoothukudi	0.643	0.647	0.616	0.070	0.384	0.791	0.412
Tirunelveli	0.429	0.571	1.000	0.191	0.409	0.793	0.381
Tiruppur	0.929	0.092	0.689	0.221	0.749	0.894	0.505
Trichy	0.571	0.588	0.868	0.090	0.460	0.758	0.392
Vellore	0.643	0.908	0.642	0.663	0.371	0.485	0.297
Villupuram	0.214	0.916	0.583	0.704	0.139	0.346	0.039
Virudhunagar	0.571	0.345	0.609	0.060	0.431	0.453	0.165

Annexure Table A-2.6

a. Food Security Index: Data

Indicators	Per Capita Foodgrain Production	Leguminous Crop (Pulses) in GCA	Cropping Intensity	Irrigation Intensity	Percentage of BPL Families	U5MR	Malnourishment	Per Capita Income	% Noon-meal Beneficiaries	Offtake of Foodgrains in Districts	Percentage of Low Birth Weight (Less than 2.5 kg)	Foodgrains Allotment to Districts	Percentage of Offtake of Foodgrains to Total Allotment
Source	Agri. Dept	Agri. Dept	Dept of Eco. and Statistics	Dept of Eco. and Statistics	RD&PR Dept	Health Dept	CDPO	DOES	SW Dept	TNCS	Health Dept	TNCS	TNCS
Unit	MT	% Area			%	Rate	%	₹	%	MT	%	MT	MT
Year	2011-12	2011-12	2011-12	2011-12	2003	2012	2013	2011-12	2013-14	2013	2013-14	2013	2013
Ariyalur	0.22	3.61	1.04	1.05	37	24.28	18.91	19467	80	55265	6.7	58049	95.20
Coimbatore	0.02	22.53	1.38	1.14	39.31	17.6	11.48	77975	61	165181	7.1	238130	69.37
Cuddalore	0.12	28.47	1.38	1.14	30.97	22.8	27.06	56315	78	152042	9.8	173751	87.51
Dharmapuri	0.17	26.68	1.27	1.11	44.5	26.8	25.04	56262	90	92318	13.2	103621	89.09
Dindigul	0.20	20.01	1.02	1.22	37.15	22.6	19.54	56376	71	120991	6.2	149615	80.87
Erode	0.10	11.06	1.08	1.11	30.97	19.5	17.48	75670	70	102280	13.2	155613	65.73
Kancheepuram	0.10	1.1	1.14	1	43.05	20.8	10.93	92713	75	138956	8.1	156104	89.02
Kanyakumari	0.05	3.86	1.12	1.25	28.84	7	1.95	96070	69	133088	6.8	138078	96.39
Karur	0.09	14.98	1.08	1.19	38	25.9	17.78	71795	79	55785	9.3	70289	79.37
Krishnagiri	0.13	27.77	1.14	1.07	39	27.5	23.13	69318	90	114500	15.5	122254	93.66
Madurai	0.12	8.97	1.06	1.17	33	28.3	15.89	67258	69	150613	9.8	196202	76.76
Nagapattiam	0.37	34.98	1.81	1.34	27.08	27	25.24	41208	81	108619	11	115071	94.39
Nammakkal	0.05	14.85	1.21	1.14	44	24.5	10.99	68213	74	78078	12.3	114767	68.03
Perambalur	0.52	1.11	1.04	0	39	26.1	20.87	24256	60	38615	13.4	42265	91.36
Pudukottai	0.23	2.63	1.04	1	45.54	23.3	26.31	43890	83	94090	9.1	104469	90.06
Ramanathapuram	0.33	2.95	1	0	43.82	24	32.08	44707	78	87360	10.4	95974	91.02
Salem	0.11	24.75	1.44	1.01	22	29.5	22.03	58623	76	165069	10	219372	75.25
Sivaganga	0.23	1.23	1.01	0	30	26.9	10.68	50466	75	88969	9.9	96422	92.27
Thanjavur	0.31	15.77	1.43	1.31	35	21.5	21.58	48284	78	155551	10.3	164114	94.78
The Nilgiris	0.00	0.47	1	0	34.79	18.1	23.08	51738	72	57993	25	66020	87.84
Theni	0.16	16.52	1.12	1	29.68	31.1	10.89	39856	71	86119	14.4	96503	89.24

Indicators	Per Capita Foodgrain Production	Leguminous Crop (Pulses) in GCA	Cropping Intensity	Irrigation Intensity	Percentage of BPL Families	U5MR	Malnourishment	Per Capita Income	% Noon-meal Beneficiaries	Offtake of Foodgrains in Districts	Percentage of Low Birth Weight (Less than 2.5 kg)	Foodgrains Allotment to Districts	Percentage of Offtake of Foodgrains to Total Allotment
Source	Agri. Dept	Agri. Dept	Dept of Eco. and Statistics	Dept of Eco. and Statistics	RD&PR Dept	Health Dept	CDPO	DOES	SW Dept	TNCS	Health Dept	TNCS	TNCS
Unit	MT	% Area			%	Rate	%	₹	%	MT	%	MT	MT
Year	2011-12	2011-12	2011-12	2011-12	2003	2012	2013	2011-12	2013-14	2013	2013-14	2013	2013
Thiruvallur	0.09	8.26	1.25	2.36	27.02	20.9	12.5	83594	76	116556	11.1	129942	89.70
Thiruvarur	0.65	33	1.82	1.31	35	21.7	21.48	34727	78	84435	6.3	89448	94.40
Tiruvannamalai	0.16	8.3	1.25	1.03	32.67	29.4	29.58	41569	85	155196	11.6	166643	93.13
Thoothukudi	0.16	54.95	1.02	1.27	23.41	21.5	13.75	74933	65	91531	8	116173	78.79
Tirunelveli	0.18	15.99	1.16	1.57	28.6	26.1	19.21	61899	66	176401	10.5	203764	86.57
Tiruppur	0.12	26.85	1.02	1.02	35.66	0	10.44	88549	72	113292	9.5	161903	69.98
Trichy	0.13	8.97	1.08	1.17	35	26.2	21.01	75393	80	147807	10.4	182899	80.81
Vellore	0.05	22.63	1.12	1	42	30.8	23.11	63185	80	232183	14.7	245699	94.50
Villupuram	0.16	11.53	1.07	1	42	26.7	31.04	35295	86	216968	10.6	233417	92.95
Virudhunagar	0.13	20.63	1.03	0	45	26.7	29.1	87361	68	103711	12.4	130183	79.67

Annexure Table A-2.6

b. FSI Index: Rank

District	Availability Index	Rank	Accessibility Index	Rank	Absorption Index	Rank	FSI	Rank
Ariyalur	0.222	23	0.454	18	0.454	11	0.377	17
Coimbatore	0.346	10	0.263	30	0.597	3	0.402	12
Cuddalore	0.411	5	0.528	12	0.344	20	0.428	9
Dharmapuri	0.386	8	0.566	7	0.277	24	0.409	11
Dindigul	0.302	12	0.382	27	0.472	7	0.385	15
Erode	0.229	21	0.347	28	0.433	12	0.336	26
Kancheepuram	0.190	27	0.568	6	0.555	4	0.438	8
Kanyakumari	0.204	26	0.667	2	0.814	1	0.562	2
Karur	0.252	18	0.482	15	0.414	13	0.382	16
Krishnagiri	0.331	11	0.676	1	0.258	26	0.422	10
Madurai	0.227	22	0.390	26	0.401	15	0.339	25
Nagapattiam	0.690	2	0.581	4	0.302	23	0.524	3
Nammakkal	0.270	16	0.303	29	0.459	10	0.344	24
Perambalur	0.215	25	0.261	31	0.325	21	0.267	30
Pudukottai	0.217	24	0.470	16	0.356	19	0.347	23
Ramanathapuram	0.138	29	0.448	21	0.271	25	0.286	28
Salem	0.395	7	0.468	17	0.322	22	0.395	14
Sivaganga	0.095	30	0.528	11	0.469	8	0.364	19
Thanjavur	0.459	3	0.539	9	0.408	14	0.469	7
The Nilgiris	0.000	31	0.445	22	0.233	30	0.226	31
Theni	0.278	15	0.437	23	0.362	18	0.359	21
Thiruvallur	0.397	6	0.640	3	0.498	6	0.511	4
Thiruvarur	0.788	1	0.491	14	0.460	9	0.580	1
Tiruvannamalai	0.283	13	0.575	5	0.223	31	0.360	20
Thoothukudi	0.452	4	0.451	20	0.520	5	0.474	6
Tirunelveli	0.356	9	0.451	19	0.381	16	0.396	13
Tiruppur	0.281	14	0.414	24	0.765	2	0.487	5
Trichy	0.237	20	0.530	10	0.362	17	0.377	18
Vellore	0.263	17	0.563	8	0.234	29	0.354	22
Villupuram	0.240	19	0.510	13	0.250	27	0.333	27
Virudhunagar	0.152	28	0.405	25	0.246	28	0.268	29

References

Drèze, Jean and Reetika Khera (2012)."Regional Patterns of Human and Child Deprivation in India", *Economic and Political Weekly* 47(39): 42-49.

Engelman, R. (2009). *The State of World Population 2009—Facing a Changing World: Women, Population and Climate*. UNFPA.

Jeyaranjan, J. (2011). "Women and Pro-poor Policies in Rural Tamil Nadu: An Examination of Practices and Responses", *Economic and Political Weekly* 46(43): 64-74.

3

Income, Employment and Poverty

Tamil Nadu is seen as a State that has been able to combine high levels of economic growth with high levels of social development in recent years (Dreze and Sen, 2013). Apart from investments in health and education, a key dimension of inclusive development is the relationship between growth and employment. If growth does not generate adequate employment, poverty levels are likely to remain high even as levels of inequality increase. Jobless growth has been found to be a key aspect of the recent growth process. However, mere employment generation does not ensure inclusive growth. The category, 'working poor' essentially captures this phenomenon. People continue to work for incomes that do not allow them to escape from poverty. Apart from the quantum of employment, the quality of employment too is therefore important in ensuring that benefits of the growth in income are shared equally between capital and labour, and between different segments of labour. It is the growing recognition of this phenomenon that has made decent work one of the key developmental goals of the International Labour Organization (ILO) over the last decade and a half. Importantly, it is now well-recognised that growth does not trickle down automatically, but is made possible through strong public action and a set of appropriate institutional interventions.

This chapter will profile the employment and income dimensions of human development and the extent of poverty reduction across social and economic groups in the State over the last decade or so. Following this introduction, the chapter maps the changing composition of sectoral income and employment shares in the State in a comparative perspective. Comparison will be done across six States that include the four south Indian States, Maharashtra and Gujarat. The choice has been guided partly by convention and partly by the fact that Maharashtra and Gujarat, along with Tamil Nadu, are among the major industrialised States in the country. Differences and discrepancies in income and employment growth across sectors will be identified. This will be followed by an examination of income levels across districts in the State. Subsequent sections will focus on changes in absolute and relative poverty as captured by income inequality. Changes across social (across SC [scheduled caste], ST [scheduled tribe], OBC [other backward class] and minorities) and economic groups (as categorised by the National Sample Survey Organisation [NSSO]) will be mapped. Apart from absolute poverty, relative poverty has been identified as a major concern in fast growing developing economies with implications for social exclusion. Income inequality can capture this dimension to an extent. Rural and urban differences across social and economic groups in consumption inequality will also be depicted, patterns summarised and implications drawn. In addition to NSSO estimates on MPCE (monthly per capita expenditure) with regard to district-level poverty, the chapter also uses the MPI (multidimensional poverty index) to analyse inter-district variations.

At the district level, differences in work participation rates, share of agricultural labour and share of marginal workers will be charted and analysed. Relationships between agricultural productivity, wage levels and poverty, composition of employment and poverty will be examined to identify possible means of public intervention. In the final section, the chapter identifies the key challenges emerging in the State across the three dimensions—employment, income and poverty—based on the analyses carried out in the previous sections. The chapter concludes by highlighting some possible directions for public intervention.

Growth in Sectoral Income

Tamil Nadu has the fourth highest PCI (per capita income) of ₹57,131 among the major States in 2011-12 after Maharashtra, Haryana and only slightly less than Gujarat (₹57,508) in 2004-05 prices.

Table 3.1

Per Capita Income (Rupees)

State	2004-05	2011-12
Tamil Nadu	30062	57131
Andhra Pradesh	25321	42119
Karnataka	26882	41959
Kerala	31871	53877
Maharashtra	36077	62457
Gujarat	32021	57508
India	24143	38037

Source: Ministry of Statistics and Programme Implementation (MOSPI), Government of India, (GoI).

In fact, the State's PCI has become higher than that of Kerala and has almost caught up with Gujarat over the 7-year period as indicated in Table 3.1. While the decline in fertility rates may have contributed to this growth, economic factors cannot be discounted. Looking at sectoral shifts in income generation, though an all-India phenomenon, the declining share of agriculture in the state's income is particularly acute in Tamil Nadu as Table 3.2 illustrates.

Table 3.2

Sector-wise Shares of Income (% NDP)

State	*Sector*	*2004-05*	*2011-12*
Tamil Nadu	Agriculture and Allied	11.65	8.71
	Industry	28.68	27.91
	a. Registered	9.29	11.81
	b. Unregistered	7.66	5.45
	c. Construction	9.69	10.09
	Services	59.67	63.38
Andhra Pradesh	Agriculture and Allied	28.84	22.58
	Industry	18.82	18.75
	a. Registered	6.84	6.92
	b. Unregistered	3.43	2.8
	c. Construction	7.25	7.8
	Services	52.34	58.67
Karnataka	Agriculture and Allied	19.51	16.63
	Industry	27.98	25.07
	a. Registered	11.96	9.94
	b. Unregistered	3.78	3.46
	c. Construction	9.17	9.61
	Services	53.12	58.3
Kerala	Agriculture and Allied	16.47	8.5
	Industry	22.31	19.46
	a. Registered	3.32	2.76
	b. Unregistered	4.4	3.7
	c. Construction	13.29	12.22
	Services	61.23	72.04
Maharashtra	Agriculture and Allied	11.17	8.76
	Industry	26.74	26.76
	a. Registered	11.67	11.94
	b. Unregistered	6.53	5.6
	c. Construction	6.79	7.63
	Services	62.09	64.47
Gujarat	Agriculture and Allied	17.71	13.49
	Industry	35.57	36.93
	a. Registered	17.13	19.23
	b. Unregistered	6.24	5.43
	c. Construction	7.27	7.93
	Services	46.71	49.58
India	Agriculture and Allied	19.89	14.65*
	Industry	25.24	24.18*
	a. Registered	7.76	8.44*
	b. Unregistered	5.3	4.73*
	c. Construction	8.24	8.29*
	Services	54.87	61.17*

Notes: i. All percentages to Net Domestic Product; ii. Constant prices with base-year 2004-05.

*: First revised estimates

Source: MOSPI, CSO, National Accounts Reports/Publication.

Even among comparable States, we find that it has the lowest share along with Kerala. Importantly, within the 8.7 per cent contribution of agriculture to the State's income in 2011-12, it has been pointed out that bulk of the growth in the sector in the last decade has emanated from fisheries, livestock, horticulture and floriculture. There has been a considerable shift in land under cultivation towards horticulture and floriculture in this period. The implications of this shift for improvements in rural poverty and employment are however not clear.

In the non-agricultural segment, we observe that the State has increased its share of income originating from the registered manufacturing sector in the past seven years, and in fact it is the only State, other than Gujarat, where the share has increased by more than two percentage points. This is definitely a positive sign in terms of quality of employment if the registered sector is able to also increase its share of manufacturing employment. The other striking aspect is the increasing share of the construction and the services sector. In the case of services sector, however, the increase in its contribution to income has not been to the extent noted in other States, except Maharashtra.

Trends in Work Participation Rate and Workforce Composition

The emphasis on 'demographic dividend' makes it important to understand additions made to the workforce. Table 3.3 maps the additions made to workforce and the changes in the share of workers in the total population.

Looking at the workforce, there has been a steady rise in the supply of workers with an addition of more than 5 million workers over the last decade, leading to a total workforce of 32.88 million (Table 3.3). This increase in absolute number is considerably more than that in the previous decade (1991-2001) and has also been driven by a rise in the share of workforce in the total population from 44.76 per cent in 2001 to 45.58 per cent in 2011. In terms of the distinction between marginal and main workers, the share of marginal workers, i.e., workers who are employed for less than six months in a year, has increased slightly from 6.63 per cent in 2001 to 6.85 per cent in 2011. This increase is lesser than that in the previous decade, which saw a hike in the share of marginal workers by more than 2 per cent. However, the fact that nearly 5 million workers are marginally employed does not augur well for a fast-growing economy.

The work participation rate for both male and female workers continues to be high in the State relative to the all-India level (Table 3.4). Importantly, it has marginally increased by almost a percentage point to 45.6 per cent (from 44.7% in 2001). This increase, however, seems to be driven primarily by that in urban workers' participation as Table 3.4 shows.

Table 3.3

State-level Workforce Trends (1981-2011)

Category	1981		1991		2001		2011	
	Absolute	*Per cent*	*Absolute*	*Per cent*	*Absolute*	*Per cent*	*Absolute*	*Per cent*
Total Workers	20.2	41.7	24.2	43.3	27.88	44.76	32.88	45.58
Main Workers	19	39.3	22.8	40.8	23.76	38	27.94	38.73
Marginal Workers	1.2	2.42	1.4	2.5	4.12	6.63	4.94	6.85
Marginal (3-6 months)	---	---	---	---	---	---	4.22	5.85
Marginal (0-3 months)	---	---	---	---	---	---	0.72	1
Non-workers	28.21	58.27	31.7	56.7	34.53	55.06	39.26	54.42
Total Population	48.5	100	55.9	100	62.41	100	72.15	100

Notes: 1) Absolute values are in millions.
2) Percentage values are in terms of total population.
3) Missing data correspond to census years in which the question(s) were not enumerated.

Source: Census of India, 1981, 1991, 2001 and 2011.

Table 3.4

State-level Worker Population and Work Participation Rate by Region and Gender (1981-2011)

	1981	1991	2001	2011
	Number of Workers (million)			
	Rural			
Male	9.67	10.82	10.4	11.21
Female	5.41	7.01	7.18	7.65
Persons	15.08	17.83	17.58	18.86
	Urban			
Male	4.18	5.14	7.76	10.22
Female	0.93	1.22	2.48	3.80
Persons	5.11	6.36	10.24	14.02
	Total			
Male	13.85	15.96	18.16	21.43
Female	6.34	8.24	9.66	11.45
Persons	20.19	24.19	27.88	32.88
	Work Participation Rate			
	Rural			
Male	59.24	58.28	59.1	60
Female	33.55	38.5	41.4	41.2
Persons	46.48	48.49	50.3	50.7
	Urban			
Male	51.25	52.78	55.8	58.5
Female	11.97	13.1	18.9	21.8
Persons	32.05	33.34	37.5	40.2
	Total			
Male	56.58	56.39	57.6	59.3
Female	26.52	29.89	31.5	31.8
Persons	41.73	43.31	44.7	45.6

Source: Census of India, 1981, 1991, 2001 and 2011.

Disaggregating the worker population by gender and across rural and urban areas, an increase in the rural working population is noticed in the last decade, unlike in the previous decade, when there was an absolute decline in the number of male workers in rural Tamil Nadu (Table 3.4). Rural work participation rate has, however, remained almost stagnant with women's participation actually decreasing by 0.2 per cent and that of men increasing by only 0.9 per cent. This is suggestive of a tendency towards urbanisation of employment in the State. The stagnation of rural women's participation in work goes against the trend in the previous decades when work participation has increased. Overall, the share of women workers almost remained the same over the previous decade and has increased only by 0.1 per cent, unlike previously when the share of women workers increased by more than 3 percentage points. The reduction in work participation rate for women in rural areas can be explained by withdrawal of women workers from the labour force with increasing income levels of the households, as pointed out in micro-level studies (Jeyaranjan, 2011). In the case of urban Tamil Nadu, male and female workers' participation has increased from 55.8 to 58.5 per cent, and from 18.9 to 21.8 per cent respectively over the decade.

The next section maps the shifts in employment across sectors.

Shifts in Sectoral Employment

The dramatic decline in the share of agricultural sector income has not been matched by shifts in labour force

Table 3.5

Share of Employment across Sectors 2004-05 and 2009-10

States	2004-05 Agri.	2004-05 Manufac.	2004-05 Non-Manu.	2004-05 Industry	2004-05 Service	2009-10 Agri.	2009-10 Manufac.	2009-10 Non-Manu.	2009-10 Industry	2009-10 Service
AP	52.8	11.9	7	18.9	28.1	51.2	11	13.5	24.5	24.3
Gujarat	62.1	12.6	5.1	17.7	20.2	52.2	13.7	7.3	21	26.8
Karnataka	64.4	9.4	4.4	13.8	21.7	57.3	9.9	7.7	17.6	25.1
Kerala	40.1	13.5	11.6	25.1	34.8	32.1	12.4	16.3	28.7	39.2
MH	45.7	14.8	6.2	21	34.3	52.9	10.8	6.5	17.3	29.8
TN	46.4	19.6	7	26.6	27.1	41.8	17.2	14	31.2	27

Source: Planning Commission, GoI.

Table 3.6

Composition of Workforce by Industrial Classification (1981-2011)

Category	1981 Absolute	1981 Per cent	1991 Absolute	1991 Per cent	2001 Absolute	2001 Per cent	2011 Absolute	2011 Per cent
Cultivators	5.82	28.8	6.04	25	5.11	18.4	4.25	12.92
Agricultural Labourers	6.77	33.5	8.76	36.2	8.67	31.1	9.61	29.21
Household Industry and Manufacturing	0.97	4.8	0.87	3.6	1.46	5.3	1.36	4.15
Other Workers	6.64	32.9	8.53	35.2	12.57	45.2	17.66	53.72
Total Workers	20.2	100	24.19	100	27.81	100	32.88	100

Notes: 1) Absolute values are in millions.
2) Percentage values are in terms of total worker population.
Sources: Census of India, 1981, 1991, 2001 and 2011.

out of agriculture despite a decline in the share of agricultural employment as Table 3.5 illustrates.

The employment share has declined by 5 percentage points albeit from a high level (46.4%). The quantum of decline is much more than the decline in the share of agricultural income indicating a possible improvement in the returns of those dependent on agriculture. In terms of comparison across states, State's share of employment in agriculture is the lowest after Kerala.

Looking at the composition of the workforce within agriculture (Table 3.6), while the share of agricultural labour in the total workforce has declined by almost 2 percentage points, in absolute terms, the segment has increased unlike in the previous decade when there was an absolute fall in the workforce. While there was steady increase from 1961 to 1991 from 18.4 per cent to 36.2 per cent in 1991, over the last two decades there has been a fall in the share to 29.21 per cent in 2011.

However unlike in the previous decade (1991-2001), there has been an increase in the absolute numbers of agricultural workers in the period 2001-2011. This rise can be attributed to either the growth in agricultural sector, or an inability of the modern sector to absorb the growing workforce, or proletarianisation of the peasantry in the State, a phenomenon that has been noticed earlier. In the case of cultivators, we find a continuing decline in their share over the decades from 18.4 per cent in 2001 to 12.92 per cent in 2011. Between 2001 and 2011, while the number of cultivators declined by 0.86 million, that of agricultural workers increased by 0.94 million. It therefore appears to be a combination of all the factors.

In the non-agricultural segments, among those engaged in household industry and manufacturing, there has again been a fall in both the share and absolute numbers. In the case of household industry and manufacturing, regardless of an increase in

Table 3.7

Statement Showing State-wise Employment in the Organised Sector (in lakhs), 2011

Organised emp	*TN*	*Maharashtra*	*Gujarat*	*Karnataka*	*AP*	*Kerala*	*India*
Public Sector	14.4	21.43	7.93	10.62	12.77	5.77	175.48
Share	8.2	12.21	4.52	6.05	7.28	3.29	100
Private Sector	8.87	25.34	13.07	12.33	7.82	5.11	114.52
Share	7.74	22.13	11.41	10.77	6.83	4.47	100
Total	23.27	46.78	21	22.95	20.6	10.88	289.99

Source: Employment Review 2013, Directorate General of Employment & Training, Ministry of Labour and Employment, Governemnt of India.

the decade 1991-2001, we find that there has been a marginal decline from 5.3 to 4.15 per cent in the last decade. In other words, the share of employment has fallen in the last decade for all categories, except the 'other workers' category which accounts for more than 53 per cent of all workers in 2011, compared to just 45.2 per cent in 2001. While this can be interpreted as a shift away from traditional to modern employment, the fact that the share of marginal workers continues to be high highlights the need to focus on the quality of employment in the modern sector.

The disaggregate picture of employment in the non-agricultural sector (Table 3.5) shows that despite an increase in the share of industrial employment, the rising share has happened primarily due to a tremendous increase in the share of 'non-manufacturing', which includes the construction sector. The construction sector, it appears, has absorbed bulk of the workforce exiting agriculture. Though there is a fall in the share of manufacturing employment between the two time periods by more than two percentage points, the state continues to rank the highest in terms of its share of employment in manufacturing. The decline seems to have been compensated solely by an increase in employment in non-manufacturing as the services share in employment has increased only marginally.

A more disaggregate picture of employment across the six states is given in Annexure A-3.1. In line with the aggregate data, it also shows: a) the relatively lower share of employment in agriculture; b) the importance of construction to employment generation, with the State having the largest share of employment in this sector, after Kerala; c) the relatively higher share of manufacturing employment as a whole; and d) wholesale trade, automobile repair, transportation and storage, and accommodation and food service activities accounting for the bulk of service sector employment. Given the not so high value additions in such services, it is all the more important to focus on enhancing employment in manufacturing, in addition to improving the returns to labour by appropriate investments. The information and communication sector is, however, absorbing a larger workforce among all the States, except Karnataka.

Next, we compare the extent of organised sector employment available in Tamil Nadu *vis-à-vis* other States (Table 3.7).

More than 23 lakh workers are employed in the organised sector in the State, which is the highest in the country after Maharashtra. However, in terms of the share of organised employment in the country, it is not high, with the State accounting for 7.74 per cent of private organised sector employment, which is low compared to all States, except Kerala. Within organised manufacturing, however, the State continues to account for the largest number of factories and also the highest number of workers employed in the factories sector (organised manufacturing) in the entire country. In 2010-11, according to the Annual Survey of Industries (ASI) data, the State housed 36,848 factories employing 1,943,319 workers, which accounts for 17.4 per cent of total factories and 15.3 per cent of the total organised manufacturing employment in the country. In fact, since 2000-01, the share of employment has increased by 1 per cent from 14.2 per cent and the share in the number of factories by close to 2 per cent. This indicates that despite the increasing share in the number of factories, that of employment has not increased as much, thereby implying a possible decline in employment absorption in the manufacturing sector. Also importantly, the State accounted for only 10.36 per cent of the gross value added in manufacturing, regardless of its higher share in employment indicative of lower labour productivity. Importantly, the fixed capital per factory at ₹56,300,000 is close to only half that of Maharashtra and one-third of Gujarat. Apart from being indicative of the smaller size of firms in the State, it also goes to show that relative to the other highly industrialised States, capital intensity is lower with possible implications for labour productivity. The decline in share of manufacturing employment accompanied by lower labour productivity clearly demands policy attention. Next, we look at the quality of employment and changes in unemployment patterns in the State.

Trends in Unemployment and Modes of Employment

The NSSO reports on employment and unemployment trends are used to map the changes in quality of employment as expressed through regularity of employment. Considering distribution of the workforce between 2000 and 2011-12, the State has the highest share of casual labour and the lowest share of self-employment among the six States (Tables 3.8 and 3.9). Only 278 out of 1000 are self-employed in the State, which is lower than most States and much lower than the national average of 593. Interestingly, it is also a State that has a relatively higher share of people employed in regular salaried employment and a large share of population employed in casual work. In both the latter categories, the rates are not only higher than the all-India average (95 as compared to 56 at all-India level for regular employment and 628 as opposed to 351 for casual employment), but also exceeds that of most major States, other than Kerala and West Bengal, for regular employment and highest among major States for casual employment. These figures by and large hold good for both rural and urban employment.

Importantly, casualisation of the workforce in Tamil Nadu has increased relative to other States over the last decade, as Andhra Pradesh and Kerala had the same or more number of casual workers in 2000. The increase in casualisation of employment seems to have happened through reductions in self-employment as well as regular wage/salaried work. While the decline in self-employed may be due to small and marginal farmers exiting agriculture, the fall in share of the regular-waged workers is an aspect that needs to be taken into consideration. This is particularly important when the earlier observations on the share of income from registered manufacturing are taken into account. While the share of registered manufacturing has increased, it has not been accompanied by a corresponding rise in that of the regular wage/salaried employment.

Moving from the quality of employment to the quantum of employment and levels of unemployment in the State, it can be seen (Tables 3.10 and 3.11) that Tamil Nadu continued to have high levels of unemployment

Table 3.8

Distribution (per 1000) of Workers According to Usual Status (PS+SS) by Broad Employment Status 2011-12

				Total Workers				
No		*TN*	*AP*	*Gujarat*	*Karnataka*	*Kerala*	*Maharashtra*	*AI*
1	Self-employed	317	444	514	478	377	469	522
2	Regular Wage/Salaried	255	179	247	225	225	265	179
3	Casual Labour	428	377	239	297	398	266	299
4	Total	1000	1000	1000	1000	1000	1000	1000

Source: Key Indicators of Employment and Unemployment in India, NSS 68th Round.

Table 3.9

Per 1000 Distribution of Usually Employed by Category of Employment Across States, 2000

				Total Workers				
No		*TN*	*AP*	*Gujarat*	*Karnataka*	*Kerala*	*Maharashtra*	*AI*
1	Self-employed	345	403	456	436	359	381	469
2	Regular Wage/Salaried	286	228	210	229	238	301	244
3	Casual Labour	369	369	334	335	403	318	287
4	Total	1000	1000	1000	1000	1000	1000	1000

Source: Employment and Unemployment Situation in India, NSS 55th Round.

Table 3.10

Current Daily Status Unemployment Rates Across Key States, 2011-12

		AP	Gujarat	Karnataka	Kerala	Maharashtra	TN	AI
Rural	Male	50	26	37	130	44	111	57
	Female	46	35	33	293	42	119	63
	Person	48	28	35	180	43	114	59
Urban	Male	54	14	39	89	30	63	50
	Female	102	23	56	220	68	84	82
	Person	65	17	42	126	37	69	55

Source: Employment and Unemployment Situation in India, NSS 68th Round.

Table 3.11

Current Daily Status Unemployment Rates Across Key States, 2000

		AP	Gujarat	Karnataka	Kerala	Maharashtra	TN	AI
Rural	Male	81	51	44	200	63	143	72
	Female	81	42	40	261	69	123	70
	Person	81	48	43	217	65	135	71
Urban	Male	72	40	53	155	77	90	73
	Female	89	54	59	282	100	86	94
	Person	76	42	54	191	81	89	77

Source: Key Indicators of Employment and Unemployment in India, NSS 55th Round.

relative to other States (except Kerala), even though the levels have declined between the 2000 and 2011-2012.[1]

As Tables 3.10 and 3.11 suggest, unemployment levels have declined over the decade despite remaining relatively high in the state during both time points. Also, across all categories, male and female in rural and urban Tamil Nadu, the rate of unemployment is higher than all States except Kerala. However in the case of urban women, Andhra Pradesh has witnessed an increase in unemployment compared to the State. In fact, the NSSO report on youth employment also shows that among all the major metropolitan cities, the levels of unemployment are the highest for Chennai city. Although the factors driving this scenario are not clearly defined, an explanation based on micro-level observations can shed some light.

Rising aspirations for higher education have broad-based entry into tertiary education. According to the Annual Survey of Higher Education undertaken by the Ministry of Human Resources Development (MHRD), the State has the highest gross enrolment ratio at 38.2 per cent for the population in the age group of 18-23 among all major states in 2012-13.[2] If the increase in proportion of formally educated labour pool is not matched by adequate increases in employment, it can lead to the phenomenon of the educated unemployed. This has been observed in the context of Kerala in an earlier period, where despite labour shortages in the agricultural sector, there was a simultaneous presence of educated unemployed.

Trends in Wages and Salaries

This section will focus on wage levels across employment categories and across States, followed by

1. The unemployment rate based on current daily status has been used as it is the most inclusive measurement of unemployment.

2. *http://www.newindianexpress.com/states/tamil_nadu/TN-Tops-Higher-Education-Charts/2014/07/18/article2335713.ece* downloaded on June 15, 2015.

Table 3.12

Average Wage/Salary Earnings (₹) Per Day Received by Casual Labours of Age 15-59 Years, 2011-12

	TN	AP	Gujarat	Karnataka	Kerala	Maharashtra	AI
Rural							
Male Average Salary	196.65	167.65	115.77	162.94	345.14	133.69	149.32
Female Average Salary	110.41	111.19	104.96	99.86	169.61	92.83	103.28
Person Average Salary	169.93	141.53	112.84	142.4	314.88	117.36	138.67
Urban							
Male Average Salary	227.66	193.52	160.64	192.24	335.76	173.18	182.04
Female Average Salary	126.53	126.6	88.84	101.77	167.56	95.91	110.62
Person Average Salary	208.34	178.34	144.52	174.05	309.9	154.62	170.10

Source: Key Indicators of Employment and Unemployment in India, NSS 68th Round.

Table 3.13

Average Daily Wages (₹) for Casual Workers of Age 15 Years and Above Engaged in Non-public Works Across Key States, 2000

		AP	Gujarat	Karnataka	Kerala	Maharashtra	TN	AI
	Male	40.67	43.91	42.51	100.78	41.32	60.2	44.84
Rural	Female	26.48	34.43	27.14	56.65	25.28	30.78	29.01
	Person	34.14	40.73	36.23	90.59	34.01	48.14	39.64
	Male	56.75	67.13	61.01	102.35	61.7	72.27	62.26
Urban	Female	39.42	40.12	39.35	47.19	29.18	46.99	37.71
	Person	51.6	61.55	55.16	93.13	54.09	66.34	56.96

Source: Table S38, Key Indicators of Employment and Unemployment in India, NSS 55th Round.

a comparison of agricultural wage rates across Tamil Nadu districts. Firstly, the wage rates for casual labour working in rural and urban Tamil Nadu are examined comparatively (Tables 3.12 and 3.13).

Average wage/salary earnings (₹/day) received by urban male casual labourers of age 15-59 years engaged in activities other than public works was one of the highest in the country at ₹227.66 per day (Table 3.12). This wage rate can be taken to be closest to the market-determined wage rate and it was highest among major States, after Kerala. Although the difference between male and female wages continues to be high, yet the average wage for urban female workers is higher than the all-India average and ranks on the top. The high wage level is also true for rural male workers, and is again one of the highest in the country at ₹196.65. Rural female wages for casual work, even though above the all-India average, is relatively lower.

Although the wages for casual labour has been high for Tamil Nadu in relative terms even in 2000, the differences in levels *vis-à-vis* other States have not been that high. The hikes in casual wage rates may not imply better returns to labour, if the incremental increase is lower than the inflation rate. However, given the expansive social security net that the State has been known for, and the spread of universal PDS (public distribution system), it can be safely assumed that the increase in casual wage rates imply better real incomes in the State.

Table 3.14 gives the average earnings for regular workers/employees. Interestingly, unlike in the case of casual labour, the wage levels for regular waged/salaried employment in Tamil Nadu were lower than that of the all-India average (₹389 against ₹449.65 for all-India), although in comparison to casual labour wages, it is much higher. The increase in wage rates, coupled with a better spread of social security net, is likely to have implications for poverty reduction that are discussed in the next section.

Table 3.14

Average Wage/Salary Earnings (₹ per day) Received by Regular Wage/Salaried Employees—Rural + Urban—in 2011-12

	TN	*AP*	*Gujarat*	*Karnataka*	*Kerala*	*Maharashtra*	*AI*
Male Average Salary	356.65	339.55	311.39	416.69	432.23	483.37	417.08
Female Average Salary	264.53	238.41	241.5	312.17	308.28	360.68	307.72
Person Average Salary	349.75	346.87	302.38	391.45	384.81	459.32	395.82

Source: Key Indicators of Employment and Unemployment in India, NSS 68th Round.

Going by the district-wise income, there are wide disparities across districts (Table 3.15).

Table 3.15

Districts Ranked on Per Capita Income (2011-12) (Top 10 and Bottom 10 Districts)

1	Kanyakumari
2	Kancheepuram
3	Tiruppur
4	Virudhunagar
5	Thiruvallur
6	Coimbatore
7	Erode
8	Tiruchirapalli
9	Thoothukudi
10	Karur
23	Thanjavur
24	Ramanathapuram
25	Pudukottai
26	Tiruvannamalai
27	Nagapattinam
28	Theni
29	Villupuram
30	Thiruvarur
31	Perambalur
32	Ariyalur

Source: DOES,Tamil Nadu.

High income districts like Kanyakumari and Erode have more than three times the incomes of low income ones like Ariyalur and Perambalur. Other low income districts like Villupuram, Tiruvannamalai, Theni and Thiruvarur too have per capita incomes less than half of that of the highest income districts. Importantly, there have hardly been any changes in the rankings of districts, based on per capita income, in the earlier Human Development Report (HDR) with the exception of Thanjavur district. Inter-district disparities continue to persist.

Inter-district differences can also be observed in levels of urbanisation which partly overlaps with differences in PCI. Despite the fact that urbanisation levels are the highest in the country, in five districts, Villupuram, Theni, Dharmapuri, Perambalur, Cuddalore, rural population has grown at a higher rate than that of all-India. Clearly, these are also districts that rank low in terms of PCI. There are also few districts that have witnessed negative population growth in rural Tamil Nadu in the last decade; Virudhunagar, Coimbatore, Nilgiris, Thoothukudi, Kanyakumari, Karur and Tiruppur showing near zero growth. Except the Nilgiris, the other districts are home to vibrant urban growth centres driven by varying levels of manufacturing and tertiary sector growth. The Nilgiris district appears to have witnessed a phenomenon of overall out-migration as it is the only district that has seen negative urban growth as well.

The highest increments in urban population over the last decade have taken place in the following districts—Kancheepuram, Krishnagiri, Thiruvallur, Tiruppur, Kanyakumari and Karur. As mentioned earlier, Karur and Tiruppur are dynamic industrialising/urbanising regions. Kancheepuram and Thiruvallur are on the outskirts of Chennai and have witnessed rapid transformations through expansion of the Chennai metropolitan region and active efforts by the State to promote industries in sections of these districts. They have attracted in-migration considerably in the last decade with population densities growing by more than 300 and 200 persons/sq km in the last 10 years. The most slowly urbanising districts (other than Chennai which is almost 100 per cent urbanised and the Nilgiris) are Ariyalur, Thiruvarur, Nagapattinam, Theni and Thanjavur. These are also districts that have low levels of PCI. In fact, other than Thanjavur that is ranked eleventh, all the other four districts are among the 10 poorest districts in the State in terms of PCI.

We also observe that the average literacy levels tend to increase along with rising PCIs. In terms of PCI, 10 districts that fall under the lowest one-third have an average literacy of 77.33 per cent compared to that of more than 82 per cent for the top 10 districts. The causal relationship can however work both ways. While higher incomes can lead to better investments in education, it is also possible that higher literacy levels can enable better per capita incomes due to greater labour productivity. Nevertheless, in the context of specific districts, we do observe a few with high incomes but relatively lower literacy rates and vice-versa.

Trends in Poverty Reduction

This section will map changes in poverty levels (based on Tendulkar committee recommendations) using the HCR (headcount ratio) across social groups (SC, ST, OBC and minorities) and also by livelihood categories (as categorised by the NSSO) within Tamil Nadu.

Table 3.16

Changes in Incidence of Poverty (HCR) for Social Groups (Rural)

	1993-94	2004-05	2011-12
SC/ST	65.8	51.2	24.0
OBC		32.6	13.0
General*	45.6	22.2	1.0

Note: *General includes OBC population in 1993-94 as the latter was not counted separately.

Source: Kalaiyarasan (2014). Calculated using NSS CES unit record data for the respective years.

As Table 3.16 shows, the more recent phase 2004-05 to 2011-12 has witnessed sharper reductions in rural poverty compared to the previous decade across all social groups. While the poverty levels have more than halved for the SC/STs during the more recent phase, levels continue to be the highest for this group and the percentage decline has been lesser compared to other groups. It is however possible that the increase in rural casual wage rates has contributed to this decline in poverty levels.

Table 3.17 depicts changes in rural poverty levels across livelihood categories.

Table 3.17

Changes in Poverty Incidence (HCR) by Rural Livelihood Categories in Tamil Nadu

Livelihood Categories	1993-94	2004-05	2011-12
Self-employed in Non-agriculture	37.2	24.6	7.7
Wage Labour Engaged in Agriculture	69.5	54.3	25.5
Wage Labour in Non-agriculture	44.0	34.2	10.0
Self-employed in Agriculture	42.7	23.8	17.5
Others	24.2	17.1	6.4
All	51.2	37.5	15.8

Note: Others: Households which have more than one income source.

Source: Same as in previous table.

Interestingly, the levels and extent of reduction of poverty for wage labour in agriculture corresponds quite closely to those for SC/STs in the State (Table 3.16). However, while the poverty levels have declined at much faster rates for all other livelihood categories, those self-employed in agriculture have not done too well in the recent phase. In fact, as can be seen, the degree of reduction in poverty in this category has been comparatively slower in the recent phase and the associated poverty levels are closer to that of the agricultural labourers. This phenomenon does tie up with the observations made in the context of small peasant farming in the State. In fact, in 2002-03, the average income for farmer households in the State from cultivation (₹7,908) was lower than that spent on cultivation (₹8,597) (Narayanamoorthy, 2006: 471). Under such cost-price conditions, it is not surprising to find high levels of indebtedness. Seventy-five per cent of the rural households are indebted, which is next only to Andhra Pradesh in the country (Narayanamoorthy, 2006: 471). This difference in income and cost of cultivation is also higher than the all-India average. It is another aspect that warrants policy attention. Given that there has been a revival in the agricultural sector since 2005, the relatively slower reduction in poverty levels among cultivators calls for a relook at the strategies targeted at improving the incomes for farmers.

Next, the chapter turns to examine poverty incidence in the urban areas (Tables 3.18 and 3.19).

Table 3.18

Changes in Poverty Incidence (HCR) for Social-Religious Groups (Urban)

Social Groups	1993-94	2004-05	2011-12
SC/ST	54.0	40.5	9.0
OBC		17.3	6.4
General*	30.0	6.5	1.8

Note: *General includes OBC population in 1993-94 as the latter was not counted separately.

Source: Same as in previous table.

Clearly, the urban has been a site of greater reductions in poverty, particularly in the recent phase. In the case of SC/STs living in urban areas, the reduction has been sharper and in terms of levels, they along with OBCs account for bulk of poor. Breaking up urban poverty across livelihood categories (Table 3.19), we find that *the poverty levels are the highest and also substantially higher for casual labourers than other categories*. This is however again not to deny the sharp fall in the poverty levels across all groups including casual labourers in the more recent phase.

Table 3.19

Changes in Poverty Incidence (HCR) for Urban Livelihoods Categories

Livelihood Categories	1993-94	2004-05	2011-12
Self-employed	32.1	18.6	5.2
Wage/salary earners	21.2	12.2	2.8
Casual labour	59.3	49.9	14.5
Others	41.4	10.1	4.4
Total	33.8	19.7	6.6

Note: Others- Other households with multiple sources of income.

Source: Same as in previous table.

The fact, that HCR is the least for the regular wage/ salary earners, points out the importance of ensuring quality of employment. Also, more than 5 per cent of the self-employed continue to be poor.

Next, the chapter focuses on inter-district variations in poverty. In addition to NSSO estimates on MPCE for determining district-level poverty, the chapter also uses the parameters used to compute the MPI so as to analyse inter-district variations. Given the bifurcation of districts in the State between the two time periods, inferences need to be carefully drawn with regard to changes over time at the district level.

NREGA and Rural Poverty

Nationally, the NREGA is held to have considerable impacts on poverty. Given Tamil Nadu's reputation as one of the best implementing states of the Act, the impact on rural employment generation and poverty reduction is likely to be high. A study done by Princeton University (2012)[3] shows that Tamil Nadu has been ranked high in: a) ensuring women participation, b) average number of person-days worked in the programme; and c) more inclusive in terms of participation by SCs and OBCs. In 2011-12, according to the report of NSSO, 40 per cent of rural households in the State have participated in NREGA for more than 60 days. Forty-six per cent of SCs and 39 per cent of OBCs have participated for more than 60 days in Tamil Nadu.

Inter-District Patterns in Poverty Levels and Workforce Composition

To relate the poverty incidence to levels of multi-dimensional poverty across the districts, Table 3.20 provides information on MPIs for 10 districts with the highest levels of poverty incidence.

Table 3.20

Ten Districts with Highest Poverty Levels Based on Multidimensional Poverty Index

Districts	*MPI*	*Rank*
Krishnagiri	0.609	23
Nagapattinam	0.618	24
Pudukottai	0.638	25
Thanjavur	0.670	26
Vellore	0.672	27
Perambalur	0.702	28
Villupuram	0.714	29
Thirvanamalai	0.719	30
Thiruvarur	0.737	31
Ariyalur	0.747	32

Source: As calculated in Chapter 2.

There are clear overlaps between low PCI districts and those with low ranks on the MPI. Thanjavur, Vellore and Krishnagiri, despite a low rank on the MPI, do not belong to the 10 districts with the lowest

3. Cited in Kalaiyarasan (2014).

incomes, possibly due to higher inequalities in income distribution.

Considering that rural and urban poverty alleviation may require different kinds of policy interventions, the present chapter goes on to address inter-district differences in regard to rural and urban poverty. This exercise is once again based on extraction of unit-level NSSO data. Classification is done based on the absolute values obtained. Given the lower levels of urban poverty, districts with urban poverty levels greater than 10 per cent and rural poverty levels greater than 15 per cent have been identified (Tables 3.21 and 3.22).

Table 3.21

Districts with High Urban Poverty Levels in 2011-12 (>10 %)

Districts	*Percentage of Poor*
Vellore	16.3
Tiruvannamalai	20.5
Viluppuram	22.6
Salem	17.1
The Nilgiris	17.1
Ariyalur	11.4
Cuddalore	31.0
Thiruvarur	11.4
Thoothukudi	10.1
Tirunelveli	12.5
Krishnagiri	11.2
Tamil Nadu	6.6

Note: Dharmapuri and Theni have poverty levels close to 10%.

Source: Calculated using unit record data from consumption expenditure survey (CES) conducted by the NSSO, 2011-12.

Table 3.22

Districts with High Rural Poverty Levels in 2011-12 (>15%)

Districts	*Percentage of Poor*
Vellore	24.1
Tiruvannamalai	16.3
Viluppuram	58.6
The Nilgiris	28.1
Cuddalore	46.0
Sivaganga	33.1
Virudhunagar	17.7
Ramanathapuram	17.8
Thoothukudi	30.1
Tamil Nadu	15.8

Source: Calculated using unit record data from consumption expenditure survey (CES) conducted by the NSSO, 2011-12.

Though Cuddalore does not appear in the low income districts, its high urban poverty levels, along with that of Villupuram and Tiruvannamalai, are striking (Table 3.21). To understand the relationship between poverty levels and diversification of employment away from agriculture, Table 3.23 lists the districts that have high levels of agricultural labour within their working population.

Table 3.23

Districts with Highest Shares of Agricultural Labourers

Ranks	*Districts*	*Corresponding Rank for 2001*
23	Pudukkottai	19
24	Dindigul	25
25	Tiruvannamalai	24
26	Thanjavur	26
27	Cuddalore	28
28	Ariyalur	32
29	Viluppuram	26
30	Nagapattinam	29
31	Theni	25
32	Thiruvarur	31

Source: Calculated using unit record data from consumption expenditure survey (CES) conducted by the NSSO, 2011-12.

As Table 3.23 shows, there are some overlaps between the share of agricultural labourers in the district and extent of rural poverty in case of districts like Tiruvannamalai, Thiruvarur, Cuddalore, Ariyalur, Villupuram and Nagapattinam. In fact, there are a few districts where the share of agricultural labour has increased between 2001 and 2011. In Tiruvannamalai, Villupuram and the Nilgiris, there has been an increase of almost 9 per cent. Ariyalur and Pudukottai have witnessed a rise of almost 6.5 per cent, and Dindigul, Perambalur and Sivaganga districts registered a growth of 4-5 per cent. Most of the districts also rank high in terms of poverty levels. In other words, poverty levels are influenced in these districts by an inability of its residents to find more remunerative employment in the non-agricultural sector.

However other districts with high levels of rural poverty like Vellore, Nilgiris, Sivaganga, Virudhunagar, Thoothukudi and Ramanathapuram do not have significant shares of population working as agricultural labour. Given that most of these districts are dry regions, reasons for poverty may have to be sought

Table 3.24

Gini Coefficient of Distribution of Consumption: 1999-2000 to 2009-10

(MRP method for 2004-05 to 2009-10)

States	Urban			Rural		
	1999-00	2004-05	2009-10	1999-00	2004-05	2009-10
AP	0.313	0.342	0.353	0.235	0.252	0.269
Gujarat	0.286	0.295	0.309	0.234	0.251	0.252
Karnataka	0.323	0.358	0.375	0.241	0.232	0.231
Kerala	0.321	0.353	0.4	0.27	0.294	0.35
Maharashtra	0.348	0.35	0.38	0.258	0.27	0.244
TN	0.381	0.345	0.327	0.279	0.258	0.257
All India	0.342	0.348	0.371	0.26	0.266	0.276

Source: http://planningcommission.gov.in/data/datatable/data_2312/DatabookDec2014%20106.pdf

in agricultural productivity. In fact, four of these districts—Sivaganga, Virudhunagar, Thoothukudi and Ramanathapuram—are among the 10 districts with the lowest agricultural productivity levels in the State (Ramesh Chand *et al.*, 2011).

Inequality

Apart from absolute poverty, relative poverty has been identified as a major concern in fast developing economies with implications on social exclusion. The emphasis on inclusive growth emphasises not only reductions in absolute poverty, but importantly also relative poverty, i.e., the economic differences between the high and the low income earners. Income inequality can capture this dimension to an extent. Following earlier studies on inequality, this report also uses the Gini co-efficient and its changes in order to understand income inequality. Rural and urban differences noted across social and economic groups in consumption inequality will be mapped so as to understand the patterns. In this section, inequality trends across the six States during the period 1999-2000 to 2009-10 (Table 3.24).

Tamil Nadu has had the highest levels of both rural and urban inequality in 1999-2000 compared to any other State. Yet since then, incidence of inequality has declined in both rural and urban Tamil Nadu. At present, the levels are not the highest among the six States; and more importantly, it is the only State where urban inequality has declined during this period and is the lowest after Gujarat. The factors driving this process are however not clear, except for the possibility of increments in wages for casual labour and the not-so-high levels of wages/salaries for regular employees/workers that the chapter has documented earlier. Next, attention is directed towards urban and rural inequalities across districts.

Table 3.25 presents districts with above average urban inequality.

Table 3.25

Districts with Above Average Urban Income Inequality 2011-12

District	Urban	
	Mean Consumption (URP) in Rs	Inequality (Gini)
Erode	2767	0.364
The Nilgiris	1872	0.361
Coimbatore	3033	0.383
Karur	2304	0.353
Tiruchirappalli	3182	0.435
Ariyalur	1977	0.346
Tamil Nadu	2380	0.338

Source: Calculated using unit record data from consumption expenditure survey (CES) conducted by the NSSO, 2011-12.

Ariyalur not only ranks among the lowest in terms of PCI and MPI, but also exhibits high income inequality. In addition to the districts listed in Table 3.25, Chennai, Kancheepuram and Krishnagiri too have Gini co-efficients of urban inequality greater than 0.3. The rest of the districts belong either to high income or fast urbanising categories, with the exception of Niligiris. In terms of rural inequality, the following districts are found to have above average levels of Gini co-efficients (Table 3.26).

Table 3.26

Districts with Above Average Rural Income Inequality, 2011-12

	Rural	
District	*Mean Consumption (URP)*	*Inequality (Gini)*
Thiruvallur	1739	0.327
Vellore	1478	0.332
Dharmapuri	1857	0.317
Perambalur	2816	0.319
Ariyalur	1711	0.320
Pudukkottai	1979	0.367
Madurai	2107	0.418
Tamil Nadu	1505	0.301

Source: Calculated using unit record data from consumption expenditure survey (CES) conducted by the NSSO, 2011-12.

Ariyalur's presence in both the lists of districts with urban and rural inequalities needs to be noted. Perambalur, Vellore, Dharmapuri and Pudukottai are other districts that in addition to high levels of rural inequality, also have high levels of poverty as measured by the MPI.

Key Issues in Employment and the Way Forward

Based on the above analyses, the following are the key issues that need policy attention.

Poverty among Cultivators

Despite a revival in the growth of agricultural sector in the last decade, particularly in the last 7-8 years, the poverty levels among cultivators have not substantially declined. The lowering of returns from agriculture can clearly be a contributing factor. This, along with the lower incomes of agricultural labourers, either due to low labour productivity or an inability to support transition to more productive employment in some districts, are the major issues as far as rural poverty is concerned. In the case of cultivators, incomes suffer on the account of vagaries of both production and prices. In the domain of production, access to assured water has become a major problem all across the State. Depleting ground water tables, encroachment of irrigation channels, decline of community involvement in maintenance of irrigation structures, water disputes and consequent difficulties in investing in canal irrigation have collectively led to this situation, apart from erosion of soil quality due to excessive use of chemical technologies. Ensuring water, therefore, is of utmost importance, in addition to facilitating progress towards more sustainable but efficient agricultural practices.

On the prices front, there is a need to reduce the number of intermediaries in agricultural markets, while simultaneously ensuring that marketing services are rendered efficiently. Farmers' markets have worked well in some areas, but not everywhere. The reasons for non-functioning of such markets need to be explored and addressed. Importantly, as has often been noted, value addition to agricultural produce continues to be low. Interventions in this area by linking up producers to processors and to larger markets are again critical. Value additions are particularly essential, given the linkage effects generated for both labour and other inputs in the regional economy.

Issues in Manufacturing Sector Employment

Development theory has always privileged manufacturing for its much higher employment and other linkage effects. However, there is a growing realisation that manufacturing has not been able to generate as much employment in recent years as that in the past. Nevertheless, there are sectors that are more labour intensive, such as textiles and other light consumer goods, which need to be promoted. Importantly, efforts should be taken to ensure that firms in these sectors upgrade, i.e., to move into more value-adding segments, progressively with time. This will create conditions for better returns to labour. Further, there is inadequate emphasis on understanding the changing skill requirements in the ever expanding services sector on one hand, and on the segments within services sector that are more value adding and labour absorbing on the other. The extent to which the education and health sector for example can generate income, employment and other linkages and the institutional interventions required to enhance these linkages need to be identified. Steps in this direction are absolutely necessary in order to facilitate employment absorption. A sectoral approach to promotion of the segments in manufacturing and services is, therefore, suggested.

Micro-level studies also indicate a mismatch between supply and demand for skills in the labour market in the State, especially among the formally trained. The phenomenon of the 'educated unemployed' has to be studied and addressed so as to ensure that the investments made in education by households are matched by adequate returns. Part of the mismatch arises from quality issues in formal education, especially in the private sector in the case of tertiary and vocational education. There have been a series of initiatives taken by the State targeted at skill formation among the semi-literate in order to improve employability of the workforce, as the Pudhu Vaazhvu Thittam case illustrates. Sustainability and scalability of such initiatives should be given utmost attention.

Quality of Employment: Growing Casualisation

In addition to the quantum of employment, the chapter has also highlighted the growing casualisation of employment in the State over the last decade. Although casual wage rates are one of the highest in the country and poverty levels have declined among those employed in this category, this is a segment that has been expanding and one where poverty levels are relatively high compared to other segments of the workforce. Even in the organised sector, other studies have pointed to a growing reliance on contract employment and casualisation of work. The insecurity of such employment contracts clearly militates against the tenets of decent work that is seen as critical to the idea of inclusive development. Given the large-scale out-migration and in-migration of workers from and into the State, the governance of labour market arrangements becomes vital. Governance should focus not only on human capital formation, but also in protecting the rights of labour. A simultaneous focus on skill development and ensuring employment security will enable the State to take advantage of its demographic dividend.

Suggestions for a Multi-Scalar Approach to Public Intervention

The chapter, while highlighting the broad patterns and issues in employment, poverty and inequality, has sought to identify a set of issues that needs to be addressed at the State level. Simultaneously, the analyses have also revealed issues that are specific to certain districts. For instance, low agricultural productivity does not correlate completely with high levels of rural poverty, just as districts with high agricultural productivity do not necessarily have low poverty levels. Similarly, high levels of urbanisation alone do not ensure better income for labour. The chapter, therefore, makes a case for simultaneous engagement at several levels—sectoral, district and State—to tackle the problems foregrounded.

Employment Generation for Rural Youth: The Case of Pudhu Vaazhvu Thittam

Aided by the World Bank (75%) and implemented by the Ministry of Rural Development and *panchayat raj* of the State government, the Pudhu Vaazhvu Thittam has been in operation since 2006, covering 26 districts over two phases. It aims to empower the marginalised like Dalits, disabled and women by helping them design programmes for improving their livelihoods. As a part of the scheme, several youth including women have been trained and placed in the private sector. A successful example has been the case of youth being trained in repair and production of mobile phones. Members of common livelihood groups formed under the scheme through the village poverty reduction committee linked to large manufacturing firms, which then as part of its CSR (corporate social responsibility) efforts place the trainees in jobs. Similarly, there are also instances of women trainees being employed in export garment factories, and women's groups setting up tailoring units, which are then helped to market through MBA students in colleges. Another important and successful intervention has been made by way of training them for driving JCB machines used in construction. In addition, the project also helps them procure a license to help them get a job. Motorola India Private Ltd, Hyundai Motor India Ltd, India Pistons Ltd, and Rane Brakes Lining Limited are among the other firms in corporate sector that have been involved under this scheme. According to the implementing agency, close to 1,40,000 out of a total of 1,70,000 trained under this scheme have been placed in jobs with salaries ranging from ₹3,500 to ₹12,000. An advantage of this project lies in its ability to link the marginalised with the private sector for employment, allowing for a better match of skills provided and demanded. Training is done through reputed institutions in the State for various courses for youth from poor households. Importantly, the programme seeks to combine training with employment assurance. Quality assurance is done through assessment post training through National Council of Vocational Training (NCVT) approved agencies.

Annexure A-3.1

Distribution (per 10000) of Workers According to Usual Status (PS+SS) by Industry Sections of NIC-2008 for Each State/Union Territory

2011-12		*TN*	*AP*	*Gujarat*	*Karnataka*	*Kerala*	*Maharashtra*	*AI*
Section A:	Agriculture, forestry and fishing	3516	5292	4878	4994	2553	4910	4890
Section B:	Mining and quarrying	57	92	50	32	61	14	54
Section C:	Manufacturing	1995	999	1967	1231	1344	1217	1260
Section D:	Electricity, gas, steam and air conditioning supply	42	32	15	32	40	27	27
Section E:	Water supply; sewerage, waste management and remediation activities	26	4	125	10	7	19	25
Section F:	Construction	1267	807	480	606	1729	628	1060
Section G:	Wholesale and retail trade; repair of motor vehicles and motorcycles	977	871	999	913	1311	953	932
Section H:	Transportation and storage	499	511	379	426	801	486	406
Section I:	Accommodation and food service activities	286	149	189	297	295	173	164
Section J:	Information and communication	143	105	41	247	115	128	77
Section K:	Financial and insurance activities	155	86	72	99	196	174	91
Section L:	Real estate activities	39	20	8	29	34	35	20
Section M:	Professional, scientific and technical activities	43	49	54	105	83	77	55
Section N:	Administrative and support service activities	87	65	59	104	117	94	66
Section O:	Public administration and defence; compulsory social security	137	192	172	162	227	199	167
Section P:	Education	260	288	217	334	388	324	298
Section Q:	Human health and social work activities	85	91	102	95	283	112	92
Section R:	Arts, entertainment and recreation	23	18	4	45	51	27	22
Section S:	Other service activities	259	246	139	136	248	223	213
Section T:	Activities of households as employers; undifferentiated goods and services	107	83	48	103	115	181	83
Section U:	Activities of extraterritorial organisations and bodies	0	0	0	0	0	0	0
	Total	10003	10000	9998	10000	9998	10001	10002

Source: Key Indicators of Employment and Unemployment in India, NSS 68th Round.

References

Drèze, J. and A. Sen (2013). *An Uncertain Glory: India and its Contradictions*. Princeton: Princeton University Press.

Jeyaranjan, J. (2011). "Women and Pro-poor Policies in Rural Tamil Nadu: An Examination of Practices and Responses", *Economic and Political Weekly* 46(43): 64-74.

Kalaiyarasan, A. (2014). "A Comparison of Developmental Outcomes in Gujarat and Tamilnadu", *Economic and Political Weekly* 49(15): 55-63.

Narayanamoorthy, A. (2006). "State of India's Farmers", *Economic and Political Weekly* 41 (6): 471-73.

Ramesh Chand, S.S. Raju, Sanjeev Garg and Lal Mani Pandy (2011). "Instability and Regional Variation in Indian Agriculture", *Policy Paper* no 26. New Delhi: National Centre for Agricultural Economics and Policy Research.

4

Literacy and Education

Introduction

The 86th Constitutional Amendment introduced in 2002 makes access to free and compulsory education for all children in the age group of 6-14 years a Fundamental Right. The Right to Education (RTE) Act, 2009, legislated under the aforementioned Article further strengthened India's commitment towards educating her children. The Act distributed the responsibility of ensuring this right between the Centre and the States. The amendment and subsequent legislation under Article 21-A were affirmative steps towards realisation of one of the UN Millennium Development Goals (MDGs).

Education, along with food, water and hygiene, is considered a basic human right under the Universal Declaration of Human Rights. It is one of the three components used in the computation of the HDI (Human Development Index) of a country. Education among the people of a region indicates not just those who can read or write, but forms the basis for larger social, political and economic progress of the region. By the Tamil Nadu Compulsory Education Act, 1994, and the Tamil Nadu Right of Children to Free and Compulsory Education Rules, 2011, the State has laid the formal framework to attain universal primary education. Further, the State also envisages achieving universal secondary education, increasing enrolment in colleges (including vocational education) to over 50 per cent and making the State an innovation hub and a knowledge capital of India, on the strength of world class institutions in various fields and the best of human talent.

This chapter provides an overview of the progress of education in Tamil Nadu, focusing on efforts made by the State to expand literacy and provide equitable access to quality education at all levels. It maps the progress of education over the decade 2001-2011—literacy, primary and secondary education, higher education and skill development—at the State level and across districts.[1] In doing so, we also highlight the challenges that are likely to emerge.

Trends in Literacy

Although literacy is just one aspect of education, it is undeniably the most important and commonly used indicator of basic education or more simply, the ability of a population to read and write. It is computed for population aged 7 and above. According to the 2011 population census, 80.09 per cent of Tamil Nadu's population is literate, an improvement from 73.45 per cent in 2001. This is much higher than the all-India average of 74.04 per cent, positioning the State as eighth among all other States. This is remarkable, given its large size, as the only State of comparable size that ranked higher than Tamil Nadu is Maharashtra. Total literacy rate in India and Tamil Nadu has shown an increasing trend over the years. While the literacy rate of Tamil Nadu has increased from 62.66 in 1991 to 80.33 in 2011, that of India has also increased from 52.21 in 1991 to 72.99 in 2011. The difference between the national average and the State average has also decreased from slightly over 10 per cent in 1991 to over 7 per cent in 2011.

Figure 4.1

Literacy Rates in Tamil Nadu and All-India

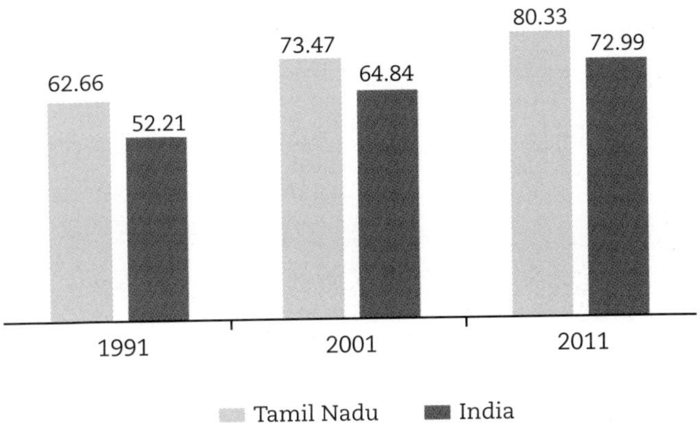

Source: Census 2001, Census 2011.

According to Census 2011, of the total rural and urban population, 24,098,521 (80.33%), 19,980,569 (73.8%) respectively are literates. Over the decade 2001-2011, the urban and rural literacy rates have increased from 82.53 to 87.24 per cent and 66.21 to 73.8 per cent respectively, with the latter exhibiting higher growth over the decade than the former. In terms of female literacy, it may be noted that while the total literacy rate for women in 2011 was 73.86 per cent, rural female literacy rate was 65.52 per cent (an increase of 10.24% from that in 2001), and urban female literacy rate was 82.67 per cent.

In order to get a sense of inter-district variations in spread of literacy, the total, rural and urban literacy rate in 2001 and 2011 are examined at the district level as shown in Table 4.1.

1. The present report is a follow-up of the Tamil Nadu Human Development Report (TNHDR) (2003), which had traced the progress of literacy and education in the state until 2001.

Table 4.1

District-wise Literacy Rates in 2001 and 2011

State/ District	Literacy Rate (2001)			Literacy Rate (2011)		
	Total	Rural	Urban	Total	Rural	Urban
Tamil Nadu	73.45	66.21	82.53	80.33	73.8	87.24
Thiruvallur	76.94	67.18	84.98	83.82	74.38	88.82
Chennai	85.33	Nil	85.33	90.33	Nil	90.33
Kancheepuram	76.85	67.28	85.12	85.29	76.6	90.25
Vellore	72.36	67.43	80.46	79.65	75.39	85.25
Dharmapuri	60.31	57.57	75.67	64.71	62.69	74.23
Krishnagiri	62.29	58.61	80.47	72.41	68.41	86.07
Tiruvannamalai	67.39	64.65	79.52	74.72	72.54	83.3
Viluppuram	63.8	60.98	80.28	72.08	69.79	85.25
Salem	65.09	57.27	74.16	73.23	66.16	79.97
Nammakkal	67.41	63.15	74.83	74.92	71.73	79.66
Erode	65.44	57.57	73.64	72.96	66	79.63
The Nilgiris	80.01	74.26	83.9	85.65	81.67	88.4
Coimbatore	78.5	65.77	83.77	84.31	72.43	88.15
Tiruppur	71.08	62.55	79.6	79.1	70.31	84.73
Dindigul	69.35	64.25	78.77	76.85	72.28	84.49
Karur	68.08	62.33	79.59	75.86	69.59	85.11
Tiruchirappalli	77.9	69.87	86.76	83.56	77.24	90
Perambalur	66.07	63.59	78.93	74.68	72.46	85.4
Ariyalur	64.08	62.32	77.74	71.99	70.79	81.49
Cuddalore	71.01	65.37	82.32	79.04	74.97	86.85
Nagapattinam	76.34	74.16	83.89	84.09	82.54	89.41
Thiruvarur	76.58	74.28	85.53	83.26	81.53	89.99
Thanjavur	75.45	70.73	84.59	82.72	79.06	89.36
Pudukkottai	71.12	68.1	85.72	77.76	74.97	89.29
Sivaganga	72.18	67.03	85.26	80.46	76.33	89.62
Madurai	77.82	67.6	85.74	81.66	70.28	88.98
Theni	71.58	66.13	76.19	77.62	72.81	81.83
Virudhunagar	73.7	68.7	79.7	80.75	76.53	84.87
Ramanathapuram	72.96	69.04	84.43	81.48	77.62	89.77
Thoothukkudi	81.34	77.54	86.65	86.52	82.57	90.46
Tirunelveli	76.15	71.76	80.79	82.92	79.49	86.4
Kanyakumari	87.55	86.17	88.29	92.14	90.95	92.4

Source: Registrar General of Census 2001, 2011.

Table 4.2

Literacy Rates by Districts, Gender and Residence, 2011

State/District	*Literacy Rate: Male (2011)*			*Literacy Rate: Female (2011)*		
	Total	*Rural*	*Urban*	*Total*	*Rural*	*Urban*
Tamil Nadu	86.81	82.08	91.82	73.86	65.52	82.67
Thiruvallur	89.18	82.45	92.7	78.39	66.33	84.85
Chennai	93.47	Nil	93.47	87.16	Nil	87.16
Kancheepuram	90.34	84.18	93.85	80.17	68.96	86.6
Vellore	86.96	84.08	90.77	72.43	66.75	79.83
Dharmapuri	69.16	67.3	78.17	60.03	57.8	70.25
Krishnagiri	79.65	76.49	90.5	64.86	59.96	81.5
Tiruvannamalai	83.73	82.29	89.46	65.71	62.77	77.23
Viluppuram	80.58	78.76	91.13	63.51	60.72	79.39
Salem	80.7	75.02	86.23	65.43	56.71	73.57
Nammakkal	83.09	80.84	86.46	66.68	62.5	72.86
Erode	80.81	74.94	86.53	65.07	56.88	72.79
The Nilgiris	92.15	89.87	93.71	79.44	73.94	83.28
Coimbatore	89.49	80.25	92.47	79.16	64.67	83.84
Tiruppur	86.07	79.36	90.33	72.07	61.29	79.05
Dindigul	84.91	81.74	90.26	68.82	62.81	78.79
Karur	84.86	80.15	91.81	67.05	59.25	78.55
Tiruchirappalli	90	86	94.08	77.24	68.64	86
Perambalur	83.39	81.88	90.73	66.11	63.19	80.18
Ariyalur	82.06	81.31	88.03	62.22	60.58	75.19
Cuddalore	86.84	84.04	92.25	71.2	65.79	81.48
Nagapattinam	90.38	89.31	94.08	78	75.96	84.94
Thiruvarur	89.65	88.53	94.1	77.02	74.69	86.05
Thanjavur	89.06	86.5	93.74	76.61	71.87	85.18
Pudukkottai	86.19	84.24	94.17	69.51	65.9	84.46
Sivaganga	88.61	86.11	94.17	72.33	66.59	85.09
Madurai	86.55	76.79	92.87	76.74	63.7	85.09
Theni	85.48	81.94	88.54	69.72	63.52	74.95
Virudhunagar	88.46	85.81	91.05	73.14	67.34	78.79
Ramanathapuram	87.89	85.23	93.52	74.93	69.89	85.87
Thoothukkudi	91.42	88.85	93.96	81.77	76.51	87.04
Tirunelveli	89.66	87.18	92.16	76.38	72.06	80.79
Kanyakumari	93.86	92.49	94.15	90.45	89.42	90.67

Source: Census 2011.

Table 4.3

Comparing Lowest/Highest Literacy Rates across Gender (2001-2011)

Sub-category		2001		2011	
		Minimum	*Maximum*	*Minimum*	*Maximum*
Total	Male	70.79	90.37	69.16	93.86
	Female	49.28	84.79	60.03	90.45
Urban	Male	81.96	92.54	78.17	94.17
	Female	64.96	85.51	70.25	90.67
Rural	Male	67.99	88.95	67.3	92.49
	Female	45.64	83.44	56.71	89.42

Source: Census 2011.

Overall, only about 50 per cent of the districts show rural and urban literacy rates above the State average in 2001 and 2011. Krishnagiri district has the highest rural literacy rate growth over the decade at 9.8 per cent and Madurai has the lowest at 2.68 per cent. In 2001, Kanyakumari had the highest rural literacy rate at 86.17, whereas Salem had the lowest at 57.27. Similarly, Kanyakumari has the highest rural literacy rate in 2011 too at 90.95 per cent (the national average is 72.99%) and Dharmapuri has the lowest at 62.69. Moving on to urban literacy rates, in 2001, Kanyakumari had the highest literacy rate at 88.29 and Erode had the lowest at 73.64. Over the decade, Kanyakumari continued to have the highest urban literacy rate at 92.4 per cent, and Dharmapuri had the lowest literacy rate at 74.23. Perambalur had the highest growth in literacy rate at a rise of 6.47 per cent over the decade 2001-2011. Dharmapuri`s literacy rate decreased by 1.44 from 74.67 in 2001[2]. Next, we present literacy rates by gender and residence across districts in Tamil Nadu for 2011 (Tables 4.2 and 4.3).

Kanyakumari district has maintained its record of attaining the highest total male and female literacy rates at 93.86 and 90.45 per cent respectively in 2011. The district with the lowest total male and female literacy rates in 2011 was again Dhamapuri with 69.16 and 60.03 per cent respectively. Kanyakumari has the highest rural male literacy rate at 92.49 per cent, whereas Pudukkottai and Sivaganga have the highest urban male literacy rate at 94.17 per cent, despite Pudukottai ranking slightly lower than the State average in overall literacy levels. Considering female literacy rates by residence, Kanyakumari has the highest rural and urban female literacy rates at 89.42 and 90.67 per cent, respectively. Dharmapuri has the lowest rural male literacy rate at 67.3 per cent, while Salem shows the lowest rural female literacy rate of 56.71 per cent. Dharmapuri also has the lowest urban male and female literacy rates at 78.17 and 70.25 per cent, respectively.

Table 4.3 presents the spread of literacy rates in 2001 and 2011 by gender and location of the residence. For males, the dispersion in total and urban literacy rates across districts is higher in 2011 than in 2001, while for females the inter-district variation has narrowed in 2011 compared to 2001.

Expansion of literacy also needs to be considered in terms of differences in the literacy rates by social groups—general population *versus* the SCs (scheduled castes) and STs (scheduled tribes) population.

According to the 2001 Census, the literacy rate in Tamil Nadu amongst the SCs was at 63.19 per cent, while that amongst the STs was at a significantly lower 41.53 per cent. Even amongst these sections, literacy rate in rural areas was lower than in the urban areas. SCs in rural areas had a literacy rate of only 59.61 per cent compared to 71.45 per cent for their urban counterparts. Similarly, STs in rural areas in 2001 had a 38.41 per cent literacy rate as opposed to 58.6 per cent in the urban areas. Men were also seen to be significantly more literate than women of the same communities in the context of both SCs and STs. The difference between men and women was approximately the same for both SCs and STs, although the former had an overall higher literacy

2. It must however be mentioned that strict inter-temporal comparisons cannot be done for all districts as new districts have been carved from old districts during this decade such as Krishnagiri from Dharmapuri, and Ariyalur from Perambalur.

Box 4.1

Library Movement in Tamil Nadu

The Tamil Nadu government has been taking various steps in promoting public libraries with an intention to nurture the reading habit among children, youth and the public at large. In pursuit of realising the goals outlined in "Vision Tamil Nadu-2023", the Department of Public Libraries has taken steps to open libraries in villages. At present, there are 4,532 libraries functioning under the directorate of Public Libraries, which was originally established in 1972.

There are 32 District Central Libraries, 1,925 branch libraries, 1,821 village libraries, 10 mobile libraries and 742 part-time libraries. There is one State Central Connemara Library and the recently opened Anna Centenary Library. In addition to this, there are few aided libraries in Tamil Nadu, like Saraswathi Mahal Library, Thanjavur, U.V Swaminatha Iyer Library, Chennai and Maraimalai Adigal Library, Chennai.

In accordance with the recommendation of the National Knowledge and Information Commission, Tamil Nadu intends to convert all libraries into Knowledge and Information Centers (KICs). All the public libraries of Tamil Nadu are being computerised. Also, a digital library is being established in Erode district. Efforts have been made by the government to create and sustain the interest of young learners in reading books.

rate. However, by 2009-10, literacy rate among the SCs in rural areas increased to 66.6 per cent, where male literacy was substantially higher than female literacy. It is also notable that in case of the ST population in rural areas, the literacy rate increased to 48.8 per cent, with males having 55.8 per cent, and females 39.2 per cent literacy (NIRD Rural Development Statistics, 2011-2012).

Figure 4.2

Gender Gap in Literacy, 1961-2011

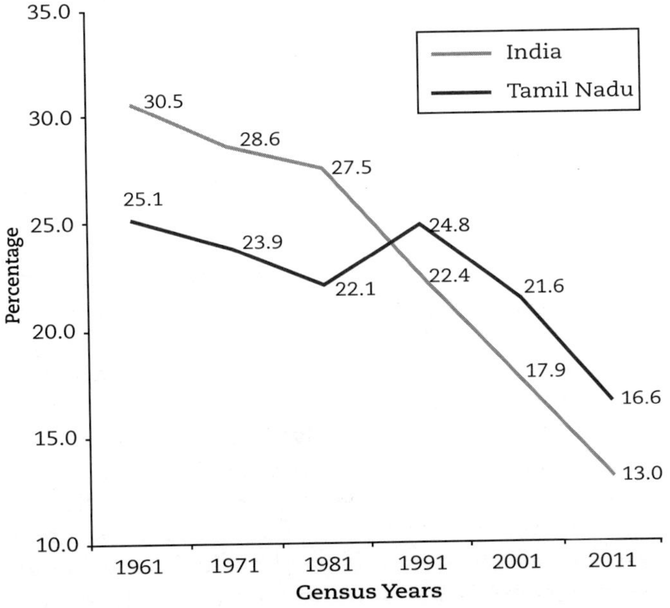

Note: For 1981-2011, literacy rate computed for population aged 7 and above; For 1961 and 1971, it is with reference to the 5+ age population.

Source: Census Tamil Nadu, Primary Census Abstract Data Highlights, p.45.

An outcome indicator that captures the spread of literacy is the reduction in gender gap in literacy. Tamil Nadu had a gender gap greater than that at the all-India level until 1981. However, since 1981, the gender gap in literacy in Tamil Nadu has recorded significant improvements. On this count, Tamil Nadu has performed better compared to improvements made at the all-India level. According to the 2011 Census, the gender gap at national level stood at 16.6, while Tamil Nadu had a gender gap of 13. This points to both the overall pace at which literacy levels have increased and also the more equitable spread of literacy in the State in terms of gender.

Having examined the levels and changes in literacy rates, we move on to other indicators of educational progress, namely the number of institutions, enrolment therein, teachers and infrastructure at various levels of education.

Primary Education

The Government of Tamil Nadu has taken the lead in launching several initiatives to improve access to and enrolment and retention in early schooling (primary and up to elementary) so as to attain the goal of UEE (universal elementary education).

One important indicator of access is number of schools, and increase over time in this indicator implies improvement in access. An analysis of the distribution of schools by management presents an idea of the providers of educational facilities in the State. The following table shows the number of government schools, private-aided schools, private-unaided schools and other management schools as a percentage of the total primary schools in the years 2002-03 and 2011-12. Interesting findings emerge from the percentage share of schools by management in the State. The State government or local bodies and government aided schools still continue to be the major providers of primary education, but the percentage of government schools offering primary education in the State has declined over last 10 years. On the other hand, the percentage of private-unaided schools has shown a large increase from 4.16 per cent in 2002-03 to 18.96 per cent in 2011-12. The ways in which this trend affects the access to primary education of children from the disadvantaged sections of society is a matter of concern. The provisions of the RTE and their effective implementation can point to possible solutions.

In Tamil Nadu, the RTE came into effect from 1 April 2010 and the Tamil Nadu Right of Children to Free and Compulsory Education Rules, 2011, were released on 8 November 2011. For implementation of the Act, 12 government orders have also been released. In a government order released in 2011, the definition for the State of Tamil Nadu was expanded to include orphans, HIV-affected children, transgender, as well as children of scavengers. This document also defined a 'child belonging to weaker section' as one whose parents or guardians earned less than Rs. 2 lakh a year. The Directorate of Teacher Education, Research and Training (DTERT) was made the nodal agency to organise and impart RTE-related training and information to the various stakeholders. An RTE cell was also set-up within the DTERT to attend to relevant queries.

Table 4.4

Distribution of Primary Schools by Management

Type of School	*Distribution by Management*		
	2002-03	2011-12	2013-14
Department of education	13.47	8.94	10.15
Tribal welfare department	3.61	3.11	3.02
Local body	63.48	52.95	51.90
Private aided	15.21	15.19	14.79
Private unaided	4.16	18.96	19.97
Other management	0.08	0.08	0.09

Source: Elementary education in India: Analytical Report, various issues.

Enrolment and Completion

The GER (Gross Enrolment Ratio) is the number of children enrolled in an educational level (primary or secondary), regardless of age, divided by population of the age group that officially corresponds to the same level. The decade from 2001 to 2011 shows a mixed trend in GER in Tamil Nadu. The GER rose in first half of the decade, peaked in 2006-07 and then showed a slight fall until 2010-11. Figure 4.3 presents year-wise GER, disaggregated by gender, for children in class I to VIII.

GER has seen an overall increase from 95.73 per cent in 2001-02 to 114.44 per cent in 2006-07 and finally, 112 per cent in 2010-11.

Figure 4.3

Gross Enrolment Ratio

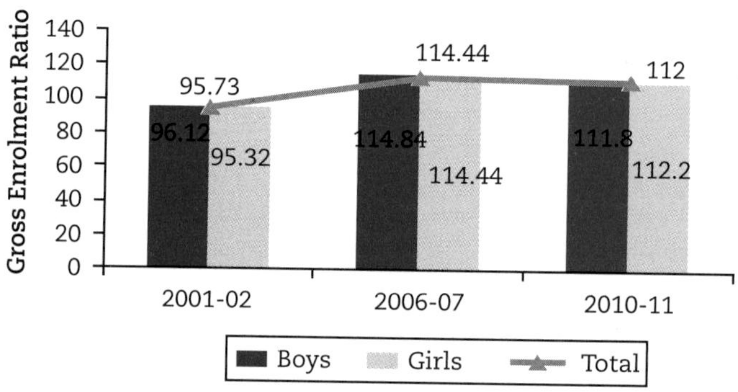

Source: Elementary education in India: Analytical Report, various issues.

A gender disaggregated analysis reveals that GER for girls has not only caught up, but has also exceeded that for boys by end of the decade. The initial years show a higher GER for boys and by 2006-07, the girls were on par with them. Data from 2010-11 shows that the GER for girls is 112.2 per cent as opposed to 111.8 per cent for boys.

The NER (Net Enrolment Ratio) shows the number of children belonging to a given age group enrolled in a particular stage of education system. The following table shows the gender-wise NER across different social categories of students, specifically SCs and STs.

This analysis of NER shows an increasing trend over the past nine years. The NER of students has substantially increased from 93 per cent in 2002-03 to 99.60 per cent in 2010-11. In 2002-03, NER of boys was 93 per cent and that of girls was 92 Per cent. This situation reversed in 2010-11; the ratio among boys (99.57%) had become lower than that among girls (99.63%), thereby showing an improvement in the gender gap. Across the different

Table 4.5

Net Enrolment Ratio

Year	*All*			*SC*			*ST*		
	Boys	*Girls*	*Total*	*Boys*	*Girls*	*Total*	*Boys*	*Girls*	*Total*
2002-2003	93.00	92.00	93.00	89.00	88.00	89.00	83.00	82.00	83.00
2003-2004	96.00	96.00	96.00	93.00	92.00	93.00	88.00	87.00	88.00
2004-2005	98.00	98.00	98.00	97.00	96.00	96.00	92.00	92.00	92.00
2005-2006	99.00	98.00	98.00	98.00	98.00	98.00	98.00	96.00	97.00
2006-2007	99.29	99.29	99.29	99.31	99.31	99.31	97.76	97.61	97.69
2007-2008	99.42	99.35	99.39	99.17	99.24	99.20	96.41	96.74	96.57
2008-2009	99.41	99.46	99.43	99.27	99.30	99.28	97.47	97.69	97.69
2009-2010	99.48	99.53	99.50	99.32	99.40	99.36	97.57	97.85	97.70
2010-2011	99.57	99.63	99.60	99.30	99.39	99.36	97.73	97.91	97.82

Source: *Elementary Education in India: Analytical Report*, various issues.

Figure 4.4

Dropout Rates in Primary Education

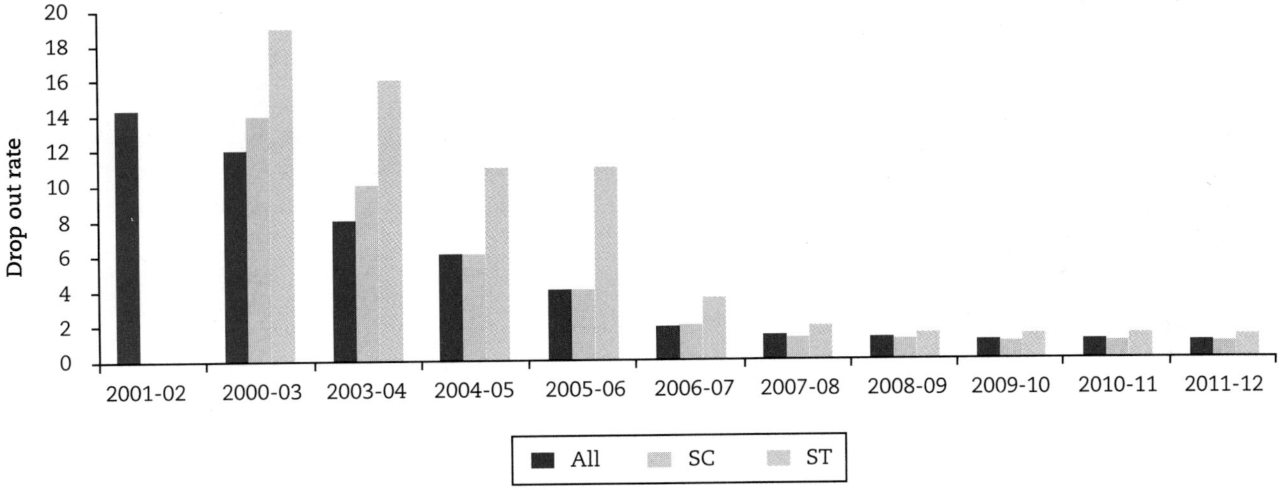

Source: *Elementary Education in India: Analytical Report*, various issues.

social strata, the NER of ST students is comparatively lower than that of SC and General Students during the given years. The greatest improvement can be observed from the year 2005-06 to 2006-07, where the NER of SC students had overtaken that of the General category students. A boost is, however, still required with regard to ST students.

One of the persistent problems in school education is early dropping out of students from schools. This leads to enormous wastage of resources. The problem is very crucial in the primary stage because this could contribute to illiteracy and even hold back achievement of the universalisation goal. Hence, it is essential to examine trends in the dropout rate in primary education.

The dropout rates in primary education among social groups have seen a downward trend over the given years, as seen in Figure 4.4. In 2011-12, the dropout rate of SC students (0.88%) is in fact lower than that of ST (1.28%) and General category (0.95%) students. These figures show a significant decrease from the levels in 2002-03 for all three categories (Figure 4.4). This steep fall in dropout rate implies higher retention rates at the primary level. This significant achievement can be attributed to the various State welfare programmes, especially in the case of SC students.

In 2002-03, completion rates of all categories of students, along with SC and ST students were 64.61 and 58 per cent respectively. By 2010-2011, these rates had seen a significant increase to 97.36, 96.84 and 92.08 per cent for the same categories respectively.

Table 4.6

Completion Rates

Year	*All*	*SC*	*ST*
2002-03	64	61	58
2003-04	69	66	61
2004-05	75	73	72
2005-06	78	74	68
2006-07	86.55	84.4	83.4
2007-08	92.46	89.88	87.1
2008-09	93.94	91.18	88.16
2009-10	97.03	96.59	91.95
2010-11	97.36	96.84	92.08

Source: Department of Education.

Yet another related problem is grade repetition. Stagnating in a class could delay completion and eventually even lead to a child dropping out of the school system. Over the last 10 years, repetition rate has shown a declining trend in Tamil Nadu. From 2002-03, the repetition rate among all categories has fallen from 24 per cent to 1.65 per cent. During the same period of time, the rate for SC students has fallen from 25 per cent to 2.25 per cent; and for ST students from 23 per cent to 6.59 per cent. From the sharp decline in dropout and repetition rates, we may infer that the State has effectively tackled the problem regarding wastage of resources allocated to primary education, thereby ensuring system efficiency.

Table 4.7

Repetition Rates

Year	*All*	*SC*	*ST*
2002-03	24	25	23
2003-04	23	24	23
2004-05	19	21	16
2005-06	19	22	21
2006-07	11.54	13.64	13.1
2007-08	6.14	8.9	11.06
2008-09	4.84	7.69	10.43
2009-10	1.95	2.47	6.69
2010-11	1.65	2.25	6.59

Source: Same as Table 4.6.

Education for All (EFA) will remain a distant goal if a sizable number of school-aged children stay out of school, and the real challenge is to enrol these out-of-school children. The district-wise analysis of out-of-school children in the school-going age for the year 2004-05 and 2010-11 have been shown in Table 4.8.

Table 4.8

Number of Students Out of School

District	*2004-05*	*2011-12*
Chennai	5502	3164
Coimbatore	5573	3403
Cuddalore	2039	895
Dharmapuri	5505	1745
Dindigul	4778	2773
Erode	2833	1087
Kancheepuram	4352	2196
Kanyakumari	1133	575
Karur	1097	545
Krishnagiri	8667	4101
Madurai	6294	1988
Nagapattinam	1691	914
Nammakkal	7405	2680
Perambalur	1989	1151
Pudukkottai	1097	593
Ramanathapuram	2324	1077
Salem	7548	2628
Sivaganga	2582	909
Thanjavur	3921	2345
Nilgiris	1095	414
Theni	2670	505
Thiruvallur	3616	1761
Thiruvarur	2053	1232
Thoothukkudi	2739	1149
Tiruchirappalli	4098	1922
Tirunelveli	4113	1730
Tiruvannamalai	4456	1981
Vellore	3489	2318
Villupuram	3868	2627
Virudhunagar	3762	2150

Source: *Elementary Education in India: Analytical Report*, various issues.

Box 4.2

Pedagogical Innovation

Activity-based Learning (ABL), grounded on the pedagogical method of learning through activity, was launched in Chennai Corporation schools in 2003 and was gradually scaled up to cover all government primary schools across Tamil Nadu by 2005. Based on pedagogical practices and materials developed at the Rishi Valley school near Madanapalle in Andhra Pradesh, the ABL initiative aimed to improve the quality of primary education in schools of Tamil Nadu: raising the achievement of students in different subjects at primary level, changing classroom practices by making them more child centred, and transforming the role of the teacher to that of a facilitator. This provides children with more freedom to express themselves, raise questions and learn through activity and peer interaction. Learning ladders allow children to track their own progress and independently 'manage' the learning process, turning to the teacher for help when required. Classrooms are child-friendly with low *chowkies* for the children to sit in groups and blackboards along the walls at child-appropriate height.

Active Learning Methodology (ALM) is a student-friendly methodology that is being implemented at the middle school level in all government schools in Tamil Nadu. An eleven day workshop by teachers from The School KFI in Chennai was organised in May 2007. The workshop explored active learning methodologies that are put to practice in the school and were adopted in the government schools of Tamil Nadu. Building upon the child-centred pedagogy of ABL at the primary level, ALM seeks to transform the middle school child into a self-directed life-long learner.

Among 30 districts in Tamil Nadu, the number of students out of their respective schools has been lowest in Nilgiris (414), Theni (505), Karur (545) and Kanyakumari (575) compared to other districts in 2011-12. The districts with the highest number of students out of school were Krishnagiri (4,101), Coimbatore (3,403) and Chennai (3,164). Salem, Krishnagiri and Madurai have recorded the most improvement, while Pudukkotai, Karur and Kanyakumari have recorded the least progress in this regard.

It is evident that the enrolment and completion rates have increased overtime even as dropout, repetition and children remaining outside the system have been largely contained. Such improvements have been made possible due to concerted efforts of the State through various interventions and incentives. The ABL methodology, a unique and major initiative of the Government of Tamil Nadu for classes I-IV, is an intervention that is worthy of mention (Box 4.2 for more details on this innovative programme). These achievements have also come about due to the increase in number of teachers as well as provision of physical infrastructure. We now turn to an examination of these.

The PTR (Pupil-Teacher Ratio) is an indicator of quality of education, and in this respect Tamil Nadu has shown a substantial improvement from 2005-06 to 2011-12. While some districts have reflected significant

Table 4.9

Pupil-Teacher Ratio

District	2005-06	2011-12
Chennai	27	25
Coimbatore	28	21
Cuddalore	33	24
Dharmapuri	31	23
Dindigul	30	25
Erode	29	21
Kancheepuram	32	21
Kanyakumari	32	23
Karur	28	21
Krishanagiri	33	26
Madurai	25	23
Nagapattinam	29	23
Nammakkal	29	22
Perambalur	34	26
Pudukkottai	36	22
Ramanathapuram	31	23
Salem	32	24
Sivaganga	27	20
Thanjavur	30	24
Nilgiris	26	17
Theni	32	27
Thiruvallur	31	19
Thiruvarur	29	21
Thoothukkudi	27	23
Tiruchirappalli	29	23
Tirunelveli	32	26
Tiruvannamalai	31	23
Vellore	29	25
Villupuram	32	27
Virudhunagar	32	27

Source: *Elementary Education in India: Analytical Report*, various issues.

improvement, betterment of the PTR has been only marginal in few other districts. The districts with the most improvement have been Pudukkottai (increase of 14%) and Thiruvallur (increase by 12%). On the other hand, districts like Madurai (2%) and Chennai (2%) have registered the least change in terms of PTR.

Figure 4.5

District-wise Distribution of Single Teacher Schools

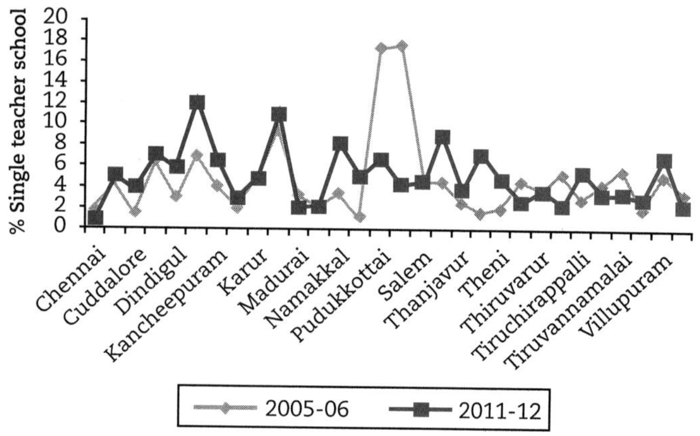

Source: Same as Table 4.9.

The percentage of primary schools with only one teacher has overall seen a decrease from 2005-06 to 2011-12. The districts that have shown the most improvement are Ramanathapuram and Pudukottai, where the rates have fallen from 17.6 per cent to 4.3 per cent and 17.3 per cent to 6.6 per cent in the given time frame respectively. This confirms the increased recruitment of teachers in these two districts. On the other hand, in the Nilgiris and Nammakkal, the percentage of schools with single teacher has shown an increase of 5.5 per cent and 4.6 per cent respectively. It is worth mentioning however, that adoption of the ABL methodology—designed for multi-grade multi-level learning—has helped mitigate problems that single teacher primary schools could face.

It is clearly evident from the Table 4.10 that the percentage of female teachers in primary schools has increased across all districts of Tamil Nadu. In 2005-2006, the participation of female teachers was highest in Chennai, followed by Madurai and Tiruchirappalli and lowest in Villupuram, Perambalur, Kancheepuram and Pudukkottai. These districts have been successful in attracting more female teachers in primary schools between 2005-06 and 2011-12 with an increase of 12.4 per cent, 11.5 per cent and 11.4 per cent, respectively.

The educational qualification of teachers is yet another indicator of the quality of teacher input. Most of the primary school teachers in 2002-03 were graduates (65.18%), followed by teachers being recruited with secondary education (15.57%) and higher secondary education (11.89%) qualifications respectively. The data available for 2011-12 shows an overall improvement in this situation with a fall in the number of teachers with 'below secondary' and 'secondary' educational qualifications, and a rise in the number of those with 'higher secondary', 'graduate' and 'postgraduate' qualifications. This is shown in Table 4.11.

Table 4.10

Percentage of Female Teachers

District	*2005-06*	*2011-12*
Chennai	95.7	96.1
Coimbatore	81.6	86.8
Cuddalore	69.1	79.8
Dharmapuri	64.6	70.9
Dindigul	75	80.5
Erode	72.2	82.3
Kancheepuram	77.5	89
Kanyakumari	85.2	91.4
Karur	73.6	81.7
Krishanagiri	66.4	71.2
Madurai	86.5	88.6
Nagapattinam	68.8	74.9
Nammakkal	70.8	79.1
Perambalur	64.9	77.3
Pudukkottai	67	78.4
Ramanathapuram	71.9	77.4
Salem	75.8	83
Sivagangai	74.2	83.4
Thanjavur	77.6	85.6
Nilgiris	74.1	82.8
Theni	76.2	81.4
Thiruvallur	76.9	86.1
Thiruvarur	71.1	80.7
Thoothukkudi	84.6	89.3
Tiruchirappalli	78.8	86.6
Tirunelveli	78.7	84.5
Tiruvannamalai	62.7	70.4
Vellore	74.3	80.4
Viluppuram	62.2	69.2
Virudhunagar	76.8	82

Source: Elementary Education in India: Analytical Report, various issues.

Table 4.11

Educational Qualification of Teachers in Primary Education Institutions

Educational Qualification	2002-03	2011-12
Below secondary	1.26	1.22
Secondary	15.57	13.17
Higher Secondary	11.89	12.01
Graduates	65.18	67.22
Postgraduate and above	5.04	6.38

Note: Values are percentages.
Source: *Elementary Education in India: Analytical Report*, various issues.

Caste-wise and gender-wise analysis of primary teachers in 2011-12 indicates that the percentage of teachers involved in primary education is the highest among the OBC (other backward classes) category females (77.45%), followed by OBC category males (75.11%). Involvement in primary education is seen to be the lowest amongst ST category females (0.92%) and ST category males (1.33%). The corresponding figures for SC females and males are 17.75 per cent and 15.03 per cent respectively; and those for the General community are 6.61 per cent amongst females and 5.81 per cent amongst males.

Infrastructure

Basic infrastructure is a crucial input in schooling as it complements the quality of education received. The factors used to measure basic infrastructure in schools are drinking water, availability of urinals for boys, separate sanitation facilities for girls and provision of electricity.

In 2002-03, the percentage of schools in Tamil Nadu with drinking water facilities, urinals for boys, separate toilets for girls and access to electricity were 80.6 per cent, 30.14 per cent, 19.02 per cent and 46.15 per cent, respectively (Table 4.12). In 2011-12, these percentage values saw a significant improvement to 100 per cent, 84.07 per cent, 65.83 per cent and 95.59 per cent respectively.

Figure 4.6

Basic Infrastructure in Primary Schools

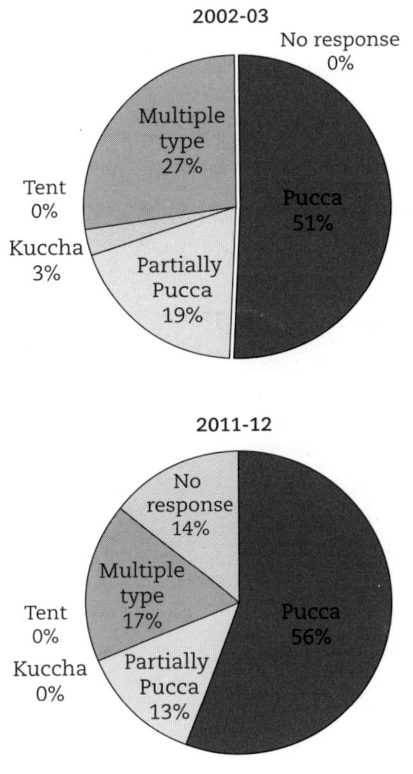

Source: DISE 2011-12, Flash Statistics.

Table 4.12

Basic Infrastructure in Primary Schools

	(2011-12)				(2002-03)			
	Percentage of schools with:				*Percentage of schools with:*			
States	*Drinking water*	*Urinal for boys*	*Separate toilet for girls*	*Electricity*	*Drinking water*	*Common Urinal*	*Separate toilet for girls*	*Electricity*
Andhra Pradesh	85.88	70.83	51.39	76.48	42.5	15.5	7.9	11.15
Karnataka	99.29	97.86	96.56	93.07	56.4	17.2	9.85	19.49
Kerala	96.89	87.83	72.14	85.66	86.8	73.26	26.49	55.21
Tamil Nadu	100	84.07	65.83	95.59	80.6	30.14	19.02	46.15
India	93.15	78.1	65.4	36.34	71.9	29.06	15.64	12.35

Source: *Elementary Education in India: Analytical Report*, various issues.

As far as physical structure of the primary school building is concerned, 50.11 per cent of the buildings were *pucca* in 2002-03. This figure increased to 55.91 per cent in 2011-12, while multiple type buildings have reduced from 26.41 to 16.6 per cent in this time period. Comparing the southern States, infrastructural development index in 2011-12 is highest in Tamil Nadu (0.748), followed by Karnataka (0.713), Kerala (0.663) and Andhra Pradesh (0.507) for primary education.

Upper Primary and Secondary Education

At the upper primary level, from 2001-02 to 2011-2012, the share of private-aided and private-unaided schools have fallen from 25.03 per cent to 16 per cent and 7.3 per cent to 0.4 per cent respectively, while the percentage of schools managed by local bodies has increased from 24.12 per cent to 79.15 per cent during this period.

Table 4.14

Gross Enrolment Ratio (Age-wise)

Year	Age group 14-16	Age group 16-18
2004-05	80.66	43.87
2005-06	82.62	45.4
2006-07	86.72	48.59
2007-08	90.79	53.74
2010-11	82.3	50.4

Source: *Elementary Education in India: Analytical Report*, various issues.

Gross enrolment ratio of students in the age group of 14-16 was 80.66 per cent in 2004-05 and increased to 90.79 per cent in 2007-08. This figure has shown a great fall in 2010-11. Same pattern can be observed among students in the age group of 16-18, where the GER of

Table 4.13

Distribution of Upper Primary and Secondary Schools by Management

Management	Distribution of schools (2002-03)				Distribution of schools (2010-11)		
	Primary with upper primary	Primary with upper primary and secondary	Upper primary only	Upper primary with sec	Senior secondary school	Upper Primary	High secondary school
Department of Education	11.43	7.27	29.41	61.61	-	-	-
Tribal welfare department	3.75	1.67	2.35	2.8	61.7	4	68
Local body	52.15	4.22	24.12	5.13	3.3	79.5	3.8
Private Aided	25.03	11.61	35.29	25.99	29.4	16	20.2
Private Un aided	7.3	73.22	7.65	4.09	5.5	0.4	8
Other Management	0.34	2.01	1.18	0.2	-	-	-

Source: *Elementary Education in India: Analytical Report*, various issues.

Table 4.15

Net Enrolment Ratio (Caste-wise)

Year	General category			SC			ST		
	Boys	Girls	Total	Boys	Girls	Total	Boys	Girls	Total
2007-08	98.64	98.6	98.62	98.78	98.82	98.8	96.27	95.78	96.04
2008-09	98.67	98.67	98.67	98.96	98.88	98.92	96.93	97.05	96.99
2009-10	98.75	98.77	98.76	99.04	98.95	99	96.9	97.16	97.03
2010-11	98.79	98.89	98.84	99.1	98.97	99.03	96.98	97.25	97.12

Source: Same as Table 4.13.

students increased from 43.87 per cent to 53.74 per cent in 2004-05 to 2007-08, followed by a fall in 2010-11.

The caste wise analysis of NER shows that the percentage of students enrolled from SC community is comparatively higher than those belonging to the General and ST categories from 2007-08 to 2010-11. This is clearly evident in Table 4.15. Gender differences in enrolment too has lessened over the years as per Table 4.16.

Table 4.16

Girls' Enrolment to Total Enrolment

Year	Upper Primary
1991-92	38.2
2001-02	43.9
2011-12	48.38

Source: Same as Table 4.13.

Table 4.17 presents the percentage of students who dropped out between 2001-02 and 2010-11.

Table 4.17

Dropout Rates

Year	(I-X)
2001-02	57.66
2005-06	42.45
2010-11	25.9

Source: Same as Table 4.13.

The time series data on dropout rates shows a mixed trend from the year 2001-02 to 2010-11. The dropout rate had significantly fallen from 57.66 per cent to 46.8 per cent from 2001-02 to 2002-03. However, this fall could not be maintained in 2003-04, where the dropout rate has steeply increased by 12.02 per cent. From the year 2003-04 to 2010-11, the dropout rates have shown a diminishing trend. In 2003-04, the dropout rate was 58.82 per cent, coming down in 2010-11 to 25.9 per cent.

A summary of the number of repeaters in Tamil Nadu for 2011-12 reveals high variation between the districts. Districts with the highest number of repeaters are (3,893 students), Cuddalore (3,304 students) and Chennai (3,057 students). Those with the lowest number of repeaters are Tiruvannamalai (27 students), Salem (74 students) and Tiruppur (143 students). When analysed along gender lines, it is seen that all districts have a larger number of boys repeating an academic year than the girls. While some districts have successfully bridged the gap to a large extent, there exists a gulf in most others. The districts with the highest gap are Nagapattinam (883 more boys), Chennai (739 more boys) and Tirunelveli (585 boys).

The PTR of all districts of Tamil Nadu is presented in Table 4.18.

Table 4.18

Pupil-Teacher Ratio

District	Primary + Secondary	
	2005-06	2011-12
Chennai	22	40
Coimbatore	28	31
Cuddalore	35	41
Dharmapuri	31	35
Dindigul	26	31
Erode	26	28
Kancheepuram	33	40
Kanyakumari	20	35
Karur	23	26
Krishnagiri	44	40
Madurai	21	23
Nagapattinam	28	34
Nammakkal	22	28
Perambalur	48	32
Pudukkottai	37	52
Ramanathapuram	39	36
Salem	26	30
Sivagangai	31	38
Thanjavur	25	33
Nilgiris	19	28
Theni	21	35
Thiruvallur	29	27
Thiruvarur	30	34
Thoothukkudi	47.3	30
Tiruchirappalli	26	30
Tirunelveli	25	36
Tiruvannamalai	31	30
Vellore	26	35
Viluppuram	29	39
Virudhunagar	24	24

Source: Same as Table 4.13.

Table 4.19

Percentage of Female Teachers

District	*Primary + Secondary*	
	2005-06	2011-12
Chennai	86.5	91.3
Coimbatore	81.6	90.4
Cuddalore	56.8	83.9
Dharmapuri	49.7	78.2
Dindigul	69.5	85.6
Erode	66.2	83.1
Kancheepuram	68.2	88.7
Kanyakumari	77.77	92.3
Karur	68.1	84.6
Krishnagiri	64.1	75.3
Madurai	80.5	88.3
Nagapattinam	59.7	56.8
Nammakkal	65.9	82.1
Perambalur	53.5	83.8
Pudukkottai	51.3	80.1
Ramanathapuram	61.2	80
Salem	64.8	70.9
Sivaganga	63	70.9
Thanjavur	65	71.3
Nilgiris	63.1	75.3
Theni	63.7	71.1
Thiruvallur	72.2	86.8
Thiruvarur	58.8	86.6
Thoothukkudi	75.7	91.9
Tiruchirappalli	72.8	85.1
Tirunelveli	65.6	77
Tiruvannamalai	52.4	78.9
Vellore	60	80.9
Villupuram	52.1	77.6
Virudhunagar	70.7	87.3

Source: Elementary Education in India: Analytical Report, various issues.

The districts with highest and lowest PTR in 2005-06 were Perambalur (48) and Nilgiris (19) respectively. In 2011-12, the highest PTR was found in Pudukottai (52) and lowest was found in Madurai (21).

In 2005-06, the percentage of female teachers in Chennai was highest at 86.5 per cent, followed by Coimbatore and Madurai at 81.6 per cent and 80.5 per cent, respectively. Percentage of female teachers was found to be lowest in Dharmapuri at 49.7 per cent. In 2011-12, Kanyakumari and Thoothukudi topped the list with highest female teacher ratio of 92.3 per cent and 91.9 per cent respectively. Percentage, in the context of Dharmapuri, has significantly increased from 49.7 per cent to 78.2 per cent during the period 2005-06 to 2011-12.

Table 4.20 shows a comparison of the educational qualifications of upper primary and secondary school teachers for the years 2002-03 and 2011-12.

In 2002-03, 43.4 per cent of the upper primary and secondary school teachers were graduates and postgraduates, while around 7 per cent of the teachers had qualifications lower than graduation. In contrast, figures for the year 2011-12 imply that the percentage of graduate and postgraduate teachers in upper primary and secondary schools has almost doubled to 80.8 per cent, while the number of teachers with qualifications lower than graduation also shows a rise of about 19.1 per cent. The data capture appears to be comprehensive for the year 2011-12, indicating a quantum improvement in information gathering and management within the school education system in Tamil Nadu.

An examination of caste-wise distribution of male and female teachers in both upper primary schools and upper primary with secondary schools for the year 2011-12 reveals that in upper primary with secondary schools, OBC males constituted 75.2 per cent of the male teachers, while OBC females make up 70.06 per cent of the female teachers. While SC and General category teachers comprise between 12 and 15 percent of the total number of teachers at this level, recruitment done among the ST population of the State is significantly low with only 1.8 per cent of female teachers. The general trend at the upper primary level is similar, with about 75 per cent of all teachers belonging to the OBC category. While there is a marginal involvement from the ST communities—1.05 per cent males and 0.97 per cent females—the recruitment from General category is significantly lower at the upper primary level. The SC males and females constitute 19.07 per

Table 4.20

Educational Qualification of Teachers

Educational Qualification	2002-03		2011-12	
	Upper Primary + Secondary	Upper Primary	Upper Primary + Secondary	Upper Primary
Below secondary	4	7	163	3
Secondary	26	166	3564	22
Higher secondary	36	99	5110	40
Graduate	615	537	19618	117
Post Graduate	443	244	15122	65
M.Phil	20	8	2619	13
Others	3	1	9	0
No response	1713	377	0	0

Source: Elementary Education in India: Analytical Report, various issues.

cent and 14.66 per cent, respectively, of the upper primary teaching staff in the State.

Infrastructure

Infrastructure in educational institutions is judged by access to drinking water and electricity as well as availability of toilets, especially for girls. In Tamil Nadu, the State average for access to drinking water and electricity is at a very high level of 94.67 per cent and 97.96 per cent respectively in 2010-11. Kanyakumari district has achieved 100 per cent access to drinking water, while Kancheepuram, Sivaganga and Kanyakumari districts have achieved 100 per cent access to electricity. Availability of separate toilets for girls is at a lower level then the State average of 68.05 per cent. The districts with the highest degree of access are Kanyakumari (93.78%), Tirunelveli (88.17%) and Coimbatore (86.59%). On the other hand, those with the least access are Tiruvannamalai (31.22%), Thanjavur (50.25%) and Thivurarur (53.33%).

Comparing the district-wise drinking water facility in the schools at secondary level, it can be seen that Perambalur has comparatively poor facility in 2010-2011. On the other hand, all the secondary schools in Kanyakumari are equipped with drinking water facility. It should be noted that as per the most recent data for 2013-14, all districts in Tamil Nadu have 100 per cent drinking water availability in secondary schools. Kanyakumari, Kanchipuram and Sivangangai are the three districts where all secondary schools have electricity facility. The rest of the districts have more than 75 per cent of the secondary schools with electricity facility. Kanyakumari has the maximum percentage of secondary schools with a separate toilet for girls, whereas districts like Tiruvannamalai and Thiruvarur needs more attention in this area.

A comparison of the infrastructure development index across the southern States reveals that Karnataka holds the first rank as far as infrastructural development index at the upper primary level is concerned, followed by Tamil Nadu, where the infrastructure development index is 0.802. Kerala and Andhra Pradesh are the States with the lowest infrastructural development index among the four southern States.

The increase observed in the number of qualified teachers and the expansion of infrastructure appear to have led to a rise in the pass percentage at both class X and class XII levels. In 2009-10, the pass percentage for class X was 82.5, which increased to 85.3 in 2010-2011. For class XII, the pass percentage in 2009-10 was 85.2, which registered a marginal increase to 85.5 in 2010-11.

Concluding the discussion on school education, it is pertinent to note that according to the EDI (Education Development Index) 2012-13 (which comprises four parameters: access, infrastructure, teachers and outcomes rankings prepared by the National University

Table 4.21

Secondary Schools- Basic Infrastructural Facility

		Drinking Water	*Electricity*	*Separate Toilet for Girls*
1	Ariyalur	91.25	93.75	53.75
2	Chennai	95.65	99.52	71.01
3	Coimbatore	92.74	97.21	86.59
4	Cuddalore	81.17	96.10	64.29
5	Dharmapuri	68.97	80.17	61.21
6	Dindigul	86.47	90.23	78.95
7	Erode	91.74	91.74	80.17
8	Kancheepuram	91.83	100.00	83.27
9	Kanyakumari	100.00	100.00	93.78
10	Karur	83.12	96.10	72.73
11	Krishanagiri	81.46	92.70	66.29
12	Madurai	86.75	95.18	63.25
13	Nagapattinam	77.61	88.81	61.94
14	Nammakkal	89.11	97.03	71.29
15	Perambalur	68.00	76.00	56
16	Pudukkottai	81.56	92.91	69.5
17	Ramanathapuram	71.11	91.11	81.11
18	Salem	81.61	93.72	69.06
19	Sivaganga	96.15	100.00	79.81
20	Thanjavur	88.94	94.97	50.25
21	The Nilgiris	94.44	95.37	76.85
22	Theni	79.49	94.87	64.1
23	Thiruvallur	79.66	94.24	61.02
24	Thiruvarur	85.56	96.67	53.33
25	Thoothukkudi	88.79	92.52	73.83
26	Tiruchirappalli	90.34	96.59	59.66
27	Tirunelveli	92.31	97.63	88.17
28	Tiruppur	79.37	78.57	70.63
29	Tiruvannamalai	69.23	85.52	31.22
30	Vellore	84.77	88.89	68.31
31	Viluppuram	88.84	95.98	56.7
32	Virudhunagar	71.94	86.33	66.91
	All Districts	85.26	93.44	68.05

Note: Data pertains to 2010-11.

Source: *Elementary Education in India: Analytical Report*, various issues.

Figure 4.7

Students Completing Class X and Class XII

Class X

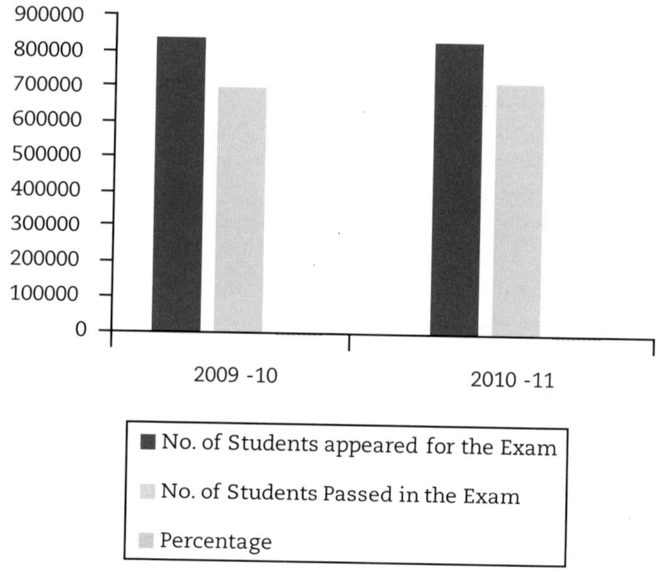

Class XII

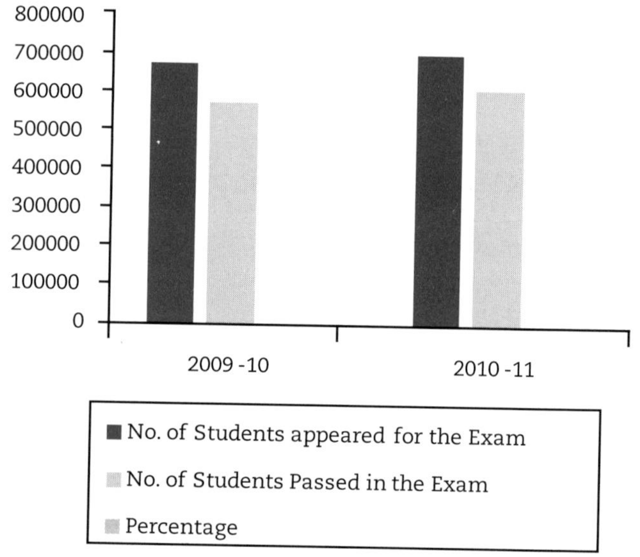

Source: Department of School Education, Govt of Tamil Nadu.

of Educational Planning and Administration [NEUPA] taking into account both the performances in primary and upper primary levels), Tamil Nadu is one of the top five States with an EDI score of 0.683, marginally behind Lakshadweep (0.712) and Puducherry (0.696).

Higher education plays a key role in giving impetus to economic development and growth. Having traced the development of school education, we now turn to the progress of higher education in Tamil Nadu.

Higher Education

One of the major challenges of the State is to tap the existing human capital potential by providing quality education to the youth. In terms of demography, Tamil Nadu is favourably placed with a population of around 77.7 lakh in the age group of 18 to 23 in 2011, where 38.8 lakh are males and 38.9 lakh are females. In terms of share in total population of the State, this age group accounts for an overall 10.8 per cent, with 10.7 per cent males and 10.8 per cent females. However, the share of graduates and above in State population is 8 per cent, with 9.7 per cent in male population and just 6.5 per cent in female population.

As per the data available for the year 2011, Tamil Nadu ranks first among all Indian States in context of the number of universities, with 59 universities, followed by Uttar Pradesh (56) and Andhra Pradesh (46). The State also ranks second in the number of State public universities (23), following Andhra Pradesh (30). Tamil Nadu has 9.5 per cent of all the universities in the country. The State also ranks first in the number of Technical Universities (14), followed by AP and Madhya Pradesh with 6 technical universities each. It can be seen from table 4.22 that the total number of universities in the State has almost doubled over the decade 2001-2011. The state has two universities set up exclusively for women and 22 dual mode universities. Notably, there is a nine-fold increase in the number of private deemed universities.

Table 4.22

Number of Universities in Tamil Nadu and India, 2001-2011

Type of University	*Tamil Nadu*	
	2001	2011
Central university	2	2
Institution of national importance	1	4
State public university	20	23
State open university	1	1
Government deemed university	0	1
Private deemed university	3	28
Grand total	31	59

Source: Annual Status of Higher Education in States and Union Territories of India, Various issues.

Table 4.23

Number of Universities in Tamil Nadu and India Based on Specialisation, 2001-2011

Specialisation	*Tamil Nadu*	
	2001	2011
General	18	29
Agriculture	1	1
Medical	1	1
Law	1	1
Technical	10	14
Veterinary	1	1
Others	0	10
Total	32	59

Source: Annual Status of Higher Education in States and Union Territories of India, Various issues.

As per AISHE 2011-12, Tamil Nadu had a total of 2302 colleges, implying a ratio of 30 colleges for a lakh population. This is higher than the all-India average (25). Further the state also a higher enrolment per college (772) compared to the all-India average of 703. Total enrolment of students in regular mode in higher education institutes in the State is around 18 lakh. Out of the total colleges in the State, 93 per cent are affiliated to universities, and the remaining is constituent/university colleges, PG/off campus or recognised direct centres of the Universities. In terms of management, Tamil Nadu colleges are dominated by the private unaided colleges, forming 88.5 per cent of all colleges in the State, followed by 5.8 per cent owned by the government and 5.6 per cent that are private aided.

Table 4.24

Enrolment in Colleges in Tamil Nadu and India, 2001-2011

Type of Management	*Tamil Nadu*	
	2001	2011
Private Unaided	98956	465980
Private Aided	231018	67877
Total Private	329974	533857
Government	90200	57245
Total	750148	591102

Source: Annual Status of Higher Education in States and Union Territories of India, Various issues.

Table 4.25

Degree-wise Distribution of Enrolment in Colleges in Tamil Nadu and India, 2001-2011

Programmes		*Tamil Nadu*	
		2001	*2011*
PhD	Male	156	4925
	Female	105	3070
	Total	261	7995
MPhil	Male	893	1847
	Female	875	2765
	Total	1768	4612
Postgraduate	Male	23614	201662
	Female	22602	187009
	Total	46216	388671
Undergraduate	Male	178758	810432
	Female	188972	764762
	Total	367730	1575194
PG Diploma	Male	715	10079
	Female	774	4842
	Total	1489	14921

Source: Department of Higher Education, Govt of Tamil Nadu.

The State-wise enrolment through regular mode at various levels was 18 lakh in 2011. The highest share of enrolment (65.4%) is at undergraduate level, followed by Diploma (16.3%) and postgraduate (16.1%), with all other levels forming only 2.1 per cent. Maximum enrolment share (78.8%) is in private unaided colleges in the State. In terms of gender, enrolment is skewed as 56.9 per cent comprising males. In terms of GER, according to the All India Higher Education Survey (AISHE) 2013-14 published by the Ministry of Human Resource Development, Government of India, the state ranks the highest among major states at 43 per cent. This is almost twice that of the all India average (23%). While the GER for SCs and STs are much lower at 31 per cent and 28.4 per cent respectively, the enrolment rates for these social groups are again much higher than the all-India average. In terms of gender, the GER is skewed towards males, with a GER of 45.6 per cent for males and 40.4 per cent for females. An examination on the basis of gender and social representation show that the share of student enrolment across backward groups is lesser than their proportionate share in population, except for Muslims. The PTR of colleges in Tamil Nadu at 7 students per teacher is considerably better than the all-India average of 15.1. Tamil Nadu has the healthiest PTR compared to other States in the country. Tamil Nadu also has nearly double number of teachers per college (82.5) compared to the all-India figure (46.4). Non-teaching staff per college (58.7) is also much higher than the corresponding all-India levels (37.3).

The expansion of technical education is another notable achievement of the State with regard to higher education. The total number of polytechnics increased from 154 in 1996-97 to 203 in 2002-2003. The numbers increased the most in self-financing colleges, which had escalated from 98 in 1996-97 to 146 in 2002-03. The total number of engineering colleges increased from 81 in 1996-97 to 222 in 2001-02. Only the self-financing colleges increased in number during this period, from 71 in 1996-97 to 212 in 2001-02. Self-financing colleges were the largest in number in all districts. We notice a massive expansion with regard to technical education over the decade 2001-2011 on examining the number of institutions and students admitted. The number of engineering colleges increased to 525 in 2011, of which 95 per cent are self-financing colleges. The number of students enrolled in these colleges has crossed 1.5 lakh in 2011. Equally impressive has been the growth of polytechnics, predominantly driven by the growth of self-financing polytechnics.

Table 4.26

Number of Engineering Colleges and Enrolled Students in Tamil Nadu (2011)

Type of Institution	*Number of Colleges*	*Number of Students Admitted*
Engineering Colleges		
Self-Financing colleges	498	149045
Anna University colleges	18	7019
Government colleges	6	2434
Government aided colleges	3	2656
Polytechnics		
Self-Financing colleges	380	98658
Government colleges	30	11035
Government aided colleges	37	11992

Source: Reports of Dept. of Technical Education, Govt. of Tamil Nadu, Various Issues.

The growth of private engineering education has been spectacular in southern States, such as Andhra Pradesh, Tamil Nadu and Karnataka along with Maharashtra, reflecting a global trend. The fast growth in the private sector is on account of the fact that during the Sixth Five Year Plan (1980-1985), when the Central and State governments were struggling to expand technical education in the country, a few State governments, especially that of Karnataka, Maharashtra, Tamil Nadu and Andhra Pradesh, took a decision to permit private registered societies and trusts to establish and run technical institutions on a self-financing basis. All these institutions were established with the permission of the respective State governments and were affiliated to universities of the region with the approval from both the State Board of Technical Education and Training (SBTET) and the All India Council for Technical Education (AICTE). Eventually, private sector acquired a dominant presence in engineering education in Tamil Nadu, occupying more than 95 per cent of the total engineering colleges. The self-financing colleges grew at an annual rate of 18.14 per cent during the period from 1993-94 to 2008-09.

A notable development in higher education in the last three years is the government's initiative to establish new State universities and colleges. Commencing in 2011-12, 12 government arts and science colleges, 24 university constituent arts and science colleges, 11 government polytechnic colleges, 4 government engineering colleges, a National Law University, 2 new government medical colleges, a Tamil Nadu Teachers' Education University (TNTEU) and 1 Indian Institute for Information Technology (IIIT) have been opened. This is indeed a historic development considering the crowding out of government institutions by private players in the State in recent past.

The inclusiveness in higher education is shown in Table 4.27. As per the table, 35 per cent of enrolments in the various engineering courses comprise girls. SCs account for nearly 15 percent of the total enrolment.

Parallel to the case of engineering education, we can identify a rapid expansion of medical education as well. A total of more than 350 medical and para-medical institutions, including Siddha, homeopathy, Unani, Ayurveda, dental, pharmacy, nursing, physiotherapy and others, function in Tamil Nadu. Both government and private unaided institutions are affiliated to the Tamil Nadu MGR Medical University. Government medical and para-medical colleges in the State occupy

Table 4.27

Admission to First Year B.E./B.Tech./Bach. Degree Course: 2013–14
Santioned Intake and Admitted Particulars

Sl. No.	Category	No. of Institutes	Sanctioned Intake	Total Admitted	OC		BC (Others)		BC (Muslim)	
					Boys	Girls	Boys	Girls	Boys	Girls
1	Government	10	3760	3156	91	65	854	650	99	41
2	Government Aided	3	2820	2685	242	128	848	554	66	23
3	Self-Financing	541	272872	170013	13122	5701	48637	29396	5308	1739
4	Anna University (Constituent Colleges)	18	7845	6401	224	184	1392	1344	162	119
	Total	572	287297	182255	13679	6078	51731	31944	5635	1922
					19757		83675		7557	

Sl. No.	Category	MBC		SC		SCA		ST		Total	
		Boys	Girls	Boys	Girls	Boys	Girls	Boys	Girls	Boys	Girls
1	Government	469	319	245	204	44	46	16	13	1818	1338
2	Government Aided	282	187	162	114	39	20	11	9	1650	1035
3	Self-Financing	26248	11727	16000	8524	1873	1020	540	178	111728	58285
4	Anna University (Constituent Colleges)	941	774	510	499	115	78	42	17	3386	3015
	Total	27940	13007	16917	9341	2071	1164	609	217	118582	63673
		40947		26258		3235		826		182255	

Source: Dept. of Technical Education Govt. of Tamil Nadu Policy Note, various issues.

Table 4.28

Medical Colleges by Management

Courses	*2006-07 in %*		*2013-14 in %*	
	Share of government institutions	*Share of private institutions*	*Share of government institutions*	*Share of private institutions*
Medical	67	33	55	45
Sidha	40	60	29	71
Homepathy	10	90	11	89
Unani	100	0	100	0
Ayurveda	0	100	16	84
Nursing	6	94	2.5	97.5

Source: Based on *www.tnmgr.univ.org*.

10 percent, while the share of medical colleges owned and run by private unaided managements is 90 per cent. Out of these institutions, more than 100 of them offer postgraduate/diploma courses. Of these postgraduate institutions, the majority (82%) are in the private sector. Almost all the para-medical courses, such as dental, pharmacy, nursing, physiotherapy, and occupational therapy, are provided by the private sector.

Expansion of higher education is also marked by attempts to improve quality. As the higher education scenario is dominated by private players, often questions on ensuring quality assume importance. National Assessment and Accreditation Council (NAAC) has been playing the role of benchmarking quality since its inception in 1994. By 2005, Tamil Nadu had the maximum number of colleges and universities accredited compared to any other States, i.e., 89 institutions consisting of 82 colleges and 7 universities. Nearly 20 per cent of the higher education institutions were accredited in Tamil Nadu, which constitutes one-third of the total accredited institutions in the country. As of 2011, NAAC has accredited 24 universities and 288 colleges in Tamil Nadu. However, compared to Karnataka, the process of accreditation in Tamil Nadu has been slow in recent years.

However, as of 2014, there are 27 universities and 529 colleges accredited in Tamil Nadu.

Tamil Nadu State Government Educational and Related Welfare Schemes

The State government, with the objective to spread education, has initiated a number of schemes so as to help the students of economically backward sections

Further, a number of performance-related incentive schemes have also been introduced such as district-level prizes for 10th/12th examination ranging between ₹500 and ₹3000 (AdiDravida and Tribal Welfare Department) and State-level prizes for 10th/12th examination of ₹10,000 and ₹25,000, respectively. Tamil-medium students are exempted from the payment of examination fees and special and/or examination fee is waived for selected economically backward students who enrol in BA (Bachelor of Arts), BSc (Bachelor of Science), BCom (Bachelor of Commerce) courses, and for girl students in postgraduate degree courses. The government also provides slates, notebooks, stationery, textbooks (1st to 12th standard) to students from BC (backward castes), MBC (most backward castes) and DNTs (denotified tribes). Other incentives include the Chief Minister's award for merit, sports, National Service Scheme and Special Prize Money Award—a one-time award to Graduates/Postgraduates and those in professional courses.

With an overarching objective of ensuring inclusion in education, the State has also launched the Integrated Education for Disabled Children (IEDC) in order to retain children with special abilities in school and integrate them with the general community. The scheme provides for books, stationery, uniforms, transport as well as cost of equipment and has been implemented across all districts with the help of NGOs (non-governmental organisations). Further, there is the Puratchi Thalaivar MGR Nutritious Meal Programme, which has been acclaimed as a pioneering effort in ensuring hunger-free school education. This

Box 4.3

Technology in Education

The centrally sponsored ICT in Schools' Scheme was launched in December 2004, and revised in 2010, to promote computer-enabled learning and usage of ICT in teaching activities of government and government aided and higher secondary schools with emphasis on educationally backward blocks and areas with concentration of SC/ST/minority/weaker sections. The scheme is implemented on a sharing basis of 75:25 ratio between Government of India and State government. In Tamil Nadu, the scheme is being implemented through BOOT Model (Build, Organise, Operate and Transfer).

There are several ICT initiatives taken by the Tamil Nadu School Education Department to promote ICT intervention in schoo ls. The department has recently launched a web portal which contains the complete database of schools, teachers, students and department officials. The portal also has information about various welfare schemes for teachers and students, events, calendar, quality initiatives of the government, recent announcements, policy notes and statistical information, etc. The link is *http://www.tnschools.gov.in*. The other ICT initiatives include SMS-based attendance, Smart Card and Education Content Server that is integrated through EMIS (Education Management Information System).

The School Education Department has also signed a memorandum of understanding (MoU) with Microsoft for the implementation of "Project Shiksha" Programme so as to provide comprehensive computer training to government school teachers. Intel® Teach Programme in association with Sarva Shiksha Abhiyan (SSA) has been launched to promote ICT integration in schools of Tamil Nadu through various programmes. As per the policy note 2012-13 of School Education Department, it has been stated that the existing computer labs would be converted into Computer Aided Language Labs by providing software and hardware materials to schools. The Government of Tamil Nadu has also recently taken efforts to provide laptop-based education for students.

is further supplemented by food grants for students of BC, MBC and minority communities who stay in government-recognised hostels. In addition, free supply of kit and sports equipment is provided by the Joint Sports Development Centre, along with supply of uniforms, mats and bed sheets (for hostels) and free bus passes for students of 1st to 8th standard. The State also introduced the distribution of free bicycles for students of BC, MBC and minority communities pursuing 11th standard in government/government-aided/partly-aided schools.

Skill Development

On recognising the major role that quality skilled manpower has played in economic development of the State and in the export of goods and services, the State has initiated a number of steps to focus attention on the production of highly skilled craftsmen. In this context, on recognising the need for upgrading Industrial Training Institutes (ITIs) in a PPP (public-private partnership) mode to achieve the goal of producing technicians of world standard, the

Box 4.4

Mid-Day-Meal Scheme

Tamil Nadu has been a pioneer of the Mid-Day-Meal (MDM) scheme, officially known as the Nutritious Meal Programme (NMP). Actually, it was started even earlier under Kamaraj in the 1960s and to a limited extent in the colonial period. Since 1984, children in the age group of 2-5 and students in classes I to X receive a hot, freshly cooked meal through the scheme, which covers more than 42,000 government, government aided and special schools. Apart from protecting children of families that live in poverty from classroom hunger, this programme also appears to have increased enrolment and attendance in schools by providing such families with an incentive to turn children away from labour and towards a school education. Going by most surveys, including official figures, we do see an increase in enrolment and a corresponding decline in school dropout rates, and it is plausible that a relatively well-implemented NMP has played a significant role in this.

Recently, Tamil Nadu government has introduced a new menu including vegetable *biriyani*, tomato rice, lemon rice, *Bisibelebhath*, egg masala, chilli fried potato, etc., to replace the routine menu of *sambar* rice and boiled egg.

government has launched a programme to upgrade ITIs over five years back A key ingredient of the government's reform agenda in this regard is to move the private sector into a lead role at all levels of decision-making—from policymaking at the central and State levels to managing individual training institutions. Other important ingredients in the government agenda of systemic reform include modernisation/ development of curricula to meet international standards, development of a qualifications framework, levelling the playing field for public and private sector providers, and designing and implementing a training fund.

As of the year 2011, there are 62 government ITIs, 627 ITCs (industrial training centres), and 987 industrial schools in Tamil Nadu. On an average, these institutions turn out 0.83 lakh students, along with 1.16 lakh diploma holders. The State Skill Development Mission (TNSDM) acts as a single agency to conduct training programmes for qualifications upto 12th standard. TNSDM also accredits training institutions.

A recent initiative has been undertaken to set up a world-class vocational training institute so as to train youth in high technology areas, like aviation, shipping, etc., with a willing industry partner under PPP mode. Further, a faculty development institute in order to provide adequate exposure of industry and technology trends to the trainers in ITIs/ITCs has also been established. It is planned that successful students of National Trade Certificate (NTC) will be issued Smart Cards that will contain information about the individual, which is expected to benefit around 25,000 successful NTC holders and 50,000 persons under the Modular Employable Skills (MES) programme.

The Skill Development Mission conducts skill training for college students with a target of around 25,000 government arts and science college students. There is also a collaboration with the British Council for imparting English languages skills. The State has implemented a project on vocational training improvement with the assistance of World Bank. The objective of the project is to achieve the government's goal of improving the employment outcomes for graduates from the vocational training system by making the design and delivery of training more demand responsive. The project aims to produce high quality craftsmen from publicly-funded ITIs,to enhance knowledge and skills of ITI instructors and trainers,to promote innovations andtobring about systemic reforms.The idea is to establish Centres of Excellence (CoEs) and upgrade the training of conventional trades in ITI.

ICT Academy of Tamil Nadu (ICTACT) has been implementing various skill development initiatives for up-skilling the teachers in the ICT domain, thereby benefitting the students to become employable in the State of Tamil Nadu. ICTACT has launched SKILLEDGE, a skill development initiative dedicated to create and enhance employability skills among the graduating students in both engineering as well as arts and science colleges. SKILLEDGE trains teachers on the Industry-relevant content and assists in delivering classes to students in colleges. Students who have cleared all the courses of SKILLEDGE will get an opportunity to participate in placement drives organised by ICTACT.

Community colleges have emerged as an important institution in recent years in terms of imparting skill enhancement. Community college refers to an alternative system of education, which aims to empower disadvantaged and underprivileged groups through appropriate skills development, leading to gainful employment, in collaboration with local industry and local community. The community colleges promote job-oriented, work-related, skill-based and life-coping education. They provide education for earning a livelihood, responding to the challenges of exclusion and elimination from the formal system, mismatch between education and employment capability, poverty and problems of unemployment, under-employment, unemployability and school dropouts.

Tamil Nadu Open University has recognised 185 community colleges in Tamil Nadu as per Government Order No. 163. More than 22 academic programmes are being conducted by community colleges from 2005, including life coping skills and communication skills. Profile of Tamil Nadu Open University community college students is provided in Table 4.29.

Table 4.29

Profile of Tamil Nadu Open University Community College Students (upto 2010-11)

Particulars	*Students*
Type	
Male	11417
Female	30832
Total	42249
Marital Status	
Unmarried	36369
Married	5475
Widows	294

Divorced	111
Total	42249
Age-wise	
18 – 22	31676
23 – 26	6342
26 – 30	2371
31 - Above	1860
Total	42249
Education	
Below 10th	7722
10th Passed	11596
12th Passed	20883
Degree	2048
Total	42249
Caste-wise	
SC	14868
ST	626
MBC	9145
BC	15949
OC	1661
Total	42249
Religion-wise	
Hindus	26926
Christians	12678
Muslims	2613
Others	32
Total	42249
Monthly Income-wise	
Below-1,000	13353
1,001-2,000	15278
2,001-3,000	8667
3,001-above	4951
Total	42249
Category-wise	
Physically Challenged	469
Others	41780
Total	42249
Employment Status	
Employed	40763
Higher Education	1486
Total	42249

Source (for entire grid): Tamil Nadu Open University, Report 2012.

Using innovative technology, both print media and multimedia approach, job-oriented vocational education programmes, such as that of House-Electrician, Refrigeration and Air-Conditioning Technician, Four Wheeler Mechanic, Health Assistant, Early Childhood Care and Education, Garment Making, Apparel and Fashion Design, Beautician, DTP-Operator, Plumbing Technician, Multimedia, Animation, Hardware Serving, Catering Assistant, etc., are offered to learners for immediate employment.

Box 4.5

Success Story of a Community College Student

I am Sumathi. I have completed my secondary and high secondary studies and was married soon after. After the sudden death of my husband, I thought that everything had come to an end. But when Madam Selvin came to my house and talked to me, I began to forget my sorrows. Madam asked me to join Udhayam Rural Community College. I never thought that I would pursue my studies after twelfth standard. But I joined Diploma in Early Childhood Care Education (DECE) trade in the community college approved by Tamil Nadu Open University, Chennai and did well. Now I am working and taking care of myself with sufficient income. Life skills taught in the community college have changed my perception and outlook towards life. I have gained enough confidence to withstand any amount of hardships in my life. I am grateful to my community college.

Financing of Education

The social sector comprising sub-sectors of education, health and medical care, housing and water supply, is very essential for the economic development of any State. Social development paves the way for sustained and sustainable economic development. Most of the social sector subjects fall within the purview of the States, for which funding is provided through CSS (centrally sponsored schemes). Here too, Tamil Nadu sets a model for other States in India, with the State government playing a very significant role in development of the social sector.

The share of revenue expenditure in the social sector expenditure of Tamil Nadu was 83.48 per cent in the year 1990-91 and it was 77.79 per cent in the year 2009-2010. This points to a reduction in revenue expenditure of the social sector in recent years. At the same time, the share of capital expenditure was 16.52 per cent in the year 1990-91 and 22.21 per cent in 2009-10. These figures imply that in the recent past, importance has been given to physical infrastructure development in the social sector.

Table 4.30

Composition of Social Sector Expenditure in Tamil Nadu

	Percentage to total social sector expenditure				
Year	*Education*	*Health*	*Water supply*	*Housing*	*Others*
2000-01	45.85	10.38	7.01	0.66	35.44
2001-02	46.79	10.9	7.41	0.75	33.4
2002-03	43.04	10.51	6.75	1.04	37.62
2003-04	36.72	9.19	6	1.32	45.46
2004-05	34.49	8.51	11.25	3.02	39.71
2005-06	36.88	9.46	3.16	1.19	48.11
2006-07	36.88	8.34	3.29	3.23	45.04
2007-08	35.35	7.58	3.29	2.42	48.94
2008-09	34.52	7.83	2.88	5.04	44.68
2009-10	38.98	10.22	4.32	3.16	40.16

Source: RBI, *Handbook of Statistics on State Government Finances*, various issues.

Table 4.30 shows the composition of social sector expenditure in Tamil Nadu for the period 2001-01 to 2009-10. It can be inferred that even though the education sector has accounted for a larger share in the social sector expenditure, its share is declining since the year 2000. This assumes importance as Tamil Nadu, having achieved high levels of enrolment at the school level now is faced with the challenge of enhancing the quality of education at the school level and expansion of higher education. The share of health sector is less compared to that of education. The "Others" category includes urban development and other social welfare measures, which have increased their share over the years. It can be concluded that the decade since 2000 was a decisive period for the State, in terms of altering the compositional share of the sub-sectors of social sector.

Viewed from a different angle, the period since 2011 shows an increasing share for education in total social services expenditure. Currently, education accounts for 45 percent of the social service expenditure, which is the same share it had in 2000. Equally important is the fact that education has been accorded top priority in the State's expenditure, with nearly 17 per cent of the total expenditure devoted to it. Nearly one-third of the total development expenditure is allocated to education since 2011, which points to a return of the emphasis on education and human capital formation as a priority of the State's development plan.

Figure 4.8

Allocation of Education Expenditure

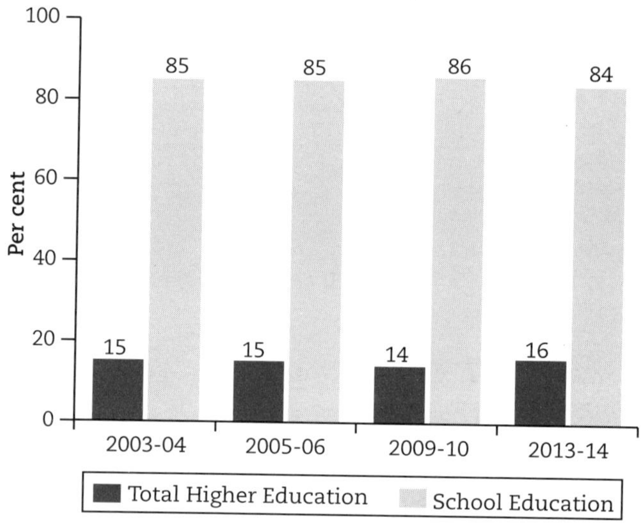

Source: Govt. of Tamil Nadu, *Budget Document*, various years.

An examination of allocation within education reveals that school education accounts for more than 80 per cent of the total expenditure on education.

Table 4.31

Social Sector Expenditure: Recent Trends

	2011-12	2012-13	2013-14
Share of Education, Sports, Art and Culture in Social services expenditure	45.90	43.46	45.97
Share of Education, Sports, Art and Culture in Development expenditure	32.20	29.92	29.74
Share of Education, Sports, Art and Culture in Total expenditure	18.21	17.26	16.94

Note: All values are percentages.

Source: RBI, *Handbook of Statistics on State Government Finances*, various issues.

Regardless of a marginal increase in the share of higher education, the expenditure pattern seems to be highly skewed. This pattern needs to be re-examined with the demographic changes that are taking place in the State.

Figure 4.9

Break-up of Expenditure

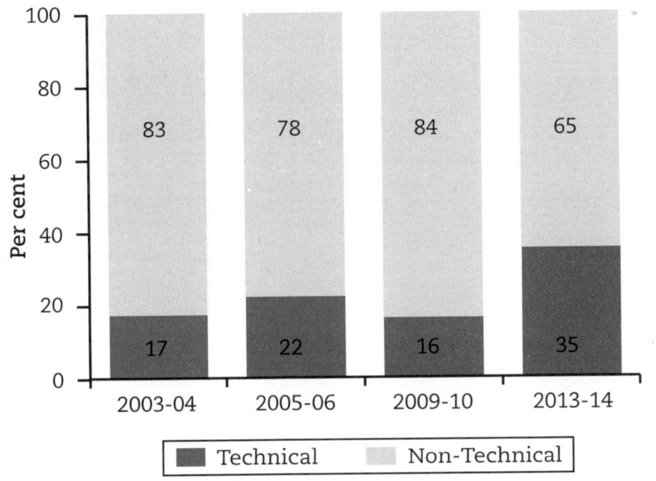

Source: Same as Figure 4.8.

There seems to be a quantum jump in the share of technical education within higher education. The share has more than doubled since 2009-10. This is an indication of emphasis of the State on nurturing human capital. Apart from additional teaching faculty being recruited, the thrust on technical education quality improvement programme (TEQIP), phase II, has resulted in the purchase of equipment, machinery, books and journals to modernise laboratories and libraries.

Future Challenges for Tamil Nadu

The school education sector in Tamil Nadu is overwhelmingly public, and much of the future expenditure both in terms of enrolment and in improving quality has to be incurred by the State government. However, there are several areas where the private sector can contribute in a significant way by means of innovative institutional mechanisms within the ambit of Sarva Shiksha Abhiyaan (SSA) and beyond. For example, residential schools for never-enrolled and dropout girl students from poor communities can be set up. This scheme can be scaled up to reach out-of-school girl students, and extended to the secondary level so as to reduce chances of dropout after the elementary stage.

Community participation is a cornerstone of the SSA design and implementation. Given sufficient training and capacity improvement, the community can help in mobilising out-of-school children, supervision of maintenance works, enforcing accountability of teachers and contributing extra resources. While SSA's commitment is to provide opportunities for elementary education until the age of 14, there also has to be a long-term strategy to absorb the extra students into higher education. The ratio of enrolment in secondary to elementary education needs to be improved.

The share of education in total budgetary expenditure should at least be stabilised, if not increased, to focus on improving quality of education. There is also a wide variation in the number of dropout children and incompletion rates in elementary education across districts. Some degree of decentralisation in the school education scene should be considered, with local bodies being more involved in the process to ensure accountability. There exists huge potential for enhancing involvement of the private sector, especially in upgrading the quality of education in government institutions. The government can play the role of a co-financier and a facilitator in the process.

Regarding higher education, in a system dominated by private players, university/college administration may have to play a greater role to ensure the effectiveness of other actors and institutions in this sector. Recent experiences reveal that the enabling environment has been created by autonomous—both government and private—institutions of higher education. Academic freedom and compliance with duties and responsibilities require autonomy of institutions. Autonomy is that degree of self-governance necessary for effective decision-making by institutions regarding curriculum development and related activities consistent with systems of public accountability. Financial constraints pose barriers in recruiting staff required for proper functioning. It is important to establish such terms and conditions of employment that will be most conducive for effective teaching, research, scholarship and extension work. To achieve this, the State government has to facilitate greater interaction with the department of education, universities, University Grants Commission (UGC) and the central Ministry of Human Resource Development (MHRD). Preparing a perspective plan of development for a span of time and making the financial allocations and adjustments for prioritised activities will enable institutions to move in the desired direction.

References

Clarke, Prema (1997). "School Curriculum in the Periphery: The Case of South India",(in H. Dean Nielson and William Cummings (eds.), *Quality Education For All: Community-Oriented Approaches*. New York: Garland Publishing.

DPEP State Project Directorate (2001). *Progress Performance and Achievements of DPEP*. Chennai.

Duraiswamy, P., E. James, J. Lane and J. Tan (1997). "Is there a Quantity-Quality Tradeoff as Enrollments Increase?: Evidence from Tamil Nadu, India", *Policy Research Working Papers*. The World Bank.

Haq, Mahbub and Khadija Haq (1998). *Human Development in South Asia 1998: The Education Challenge*. Dhaka: Oxford University Press.

Mukhopadhyay, M. and M. Parhar (1999). *Indian Education: Developments Since Independence*. New Delhi: Vikas Publishing House Pvt. Ltd.

Ministry of Human Resources Development (2001). *Sarva Shiksha Abhiyan: A Framework for Implementation*. Ministry of Human Resources Development, India.

Shukla S., V.P. Garg, V.K. Jain, S. Rajput, and O.P. Arora (1994). *Attainment of Primary School Children in Various States*. New Delhi: NCERT.

Tilak, Jandhyala B.G. (1999). "Education and Poverty in South Asia", *Prospects* 29(4): 517-33. December.

Varghese, N.V. (1996). "Quality of Education: What Do We Learn From Research", *Indian Journal of Education and Social Change*. World Bank.

Data Sources

DISE Statistics

Government of India, Census 2001 and 2011

Government of Tamil Nadu, Department of Education, various publications

Reserve Bank of India, *Handbook of Statistics on State Government Finances*, various issues

Appendix A-4.1

A. Elementary Education in India: Where do we Stand?
State Elementary Education Report Card 2013-14

Total Districts	30	Districts Covered	30	State Code	33		TAMIL NADU		
Primary Cycle	1-5	Upper Primary Cycle	6-8	Ratio of P. to U.P. School/Section			2.26		
Data Reported	Blocks/Taluks		413	Clusters	4,088	Villages	19,295	Schools	56,785
Basic Data: 2011	Total Population in ('000's)		72139.0	%Urban Population			38.1	% 0-6 Population	9.6
Decadal Growth Rate	15.6	Sex Ratio	995	% SC Population			20.0	% ST Population	1.1
Overall Literacy Rate	80.3	Female Literacy Rate		73.9				Male Literacy Rate	86.8

Key Data	*Primary only*	*Pry. with U. Pry*	*Pry with UP & Sec+H Sec*	*U. Pry. only*	*UP with Sec+H Sec*	*Pry. with UP & Sec*	*UP with Sec*	*No Res & Other Cat.*	*Total*
Total Schools (2013-14)	35,177	9,22	4,035	128	7,823	0	0	0	56,785
Total Schools (2012-13)	35,185	9,656	3,832	144	7,718	0	0	0	56,535
Government Schools	23,928	7,250	91	13	5,718	0	0	0	37,000
Private Schools	11,234	2,343	3,942	114	2,102	0	0	0	19,735
Madrasas & Unreco. sch.	15	29	2	1	3	0	0	0	50
Government Schools: Rural	21,401	6,182	47	12	4,623	0	0	0	32,265
Private SChools: Rural	6,674,	1,372	1,757	97	985	0	0	0	10,885
Total Enrolment (2013-14)	2,960,356	1,997,695	2,554,072	10,887	1,873,431	0	0	0	9,396,441
Total Enrolment (2012-13)	3,146,144	2,043,342	2,610,589	14,487	1,863,914	0	0	0	9,678,476
Enrdment in Govt. Schools	1,487,031	1,249,624	45,606	1,137	1,074,774	0	0	0	3,858,172
Enrdment in Pvt. Schools	1,472,549	741,668	2,507,715	9,740	798,491	0	0	0	5,530,163
Enr. in Madrasas & Unreco.	776	6,403	751	10	166	0	0	0	8,106
Enr. in Govt. Schools: Rural	1,258,356	1,020,397	21,676	1,071	801,485	0	0	0	3,102,958
Enr. in Pvt. Schools: Rural	715,602	347,829	1,001,254	7,520	290,295	0	0	0	2,362,500
Total Teachers (2012-13)	137,811	77,413	115,523	951	142,513	0	0	0	474,211
Government Teachers	64,864	50,479	2,406	71	100,485	0	0	0	218,305
Private Teachers	78,229	27,034	134,185	706	49,706	0	0	0	289,860
Tch. in Madrasas & Unreco.	95	450	45	3	30	0	0	0	623

Perfomance indicators (in percentage)	*Primary only*		*P + UP*		*P + UP + Sec + HS*		*UP only*		*UP + Sec + HS*		*P + UP + Sec*		*U.P. + Sec*		*All Schools*	
	12-13	13-14	12-13	13-14	12-13	13-14	12-13	13-14	12-13	13-14	12-13	13-14	12-13	13-14	12-13	13-14
Single–Classroom Schools	1.2		0.0	0.0	0.1	0.0	0.7	0.0	2.1	0.0					1.0	0.0
Single–Teacher Schools	6.9	3.7	0.4	0.3	0.0	0.0	2.1	0.0	0.2	0.2					4.4	2.3
Sch Aproachable by All Road	97.2	97.7	97.3	97.8	99.2	99.1	97.2	98.4	98.1	98.4					97.5	98.0
Schools with Playground	73.0	73.9	73.2	74.1	97.3	98.0	86.1	88.3	76.0	76.2					75.1	76.0
Schools with Boundary Wall	73.3	74.4	80.2	81.6	97.3	97.2	80.6	83.6	80.5	83.0					77.1	78.4
Schools with Girls Toilet	94.0	86.3	99.1	97.4	100.0	100.0	97.1	94.3	97.0	96.5					95.6	90.5
Schools with Boys Toilet	52.7	99.6	75.7	99.9	95.6	100.0	79.8	97.0	76.4	99.1					62.6	99.6
Schools with Drinking Water	99.4	100.0	99.6	100.0	99.7	100.0	97.2	100.0	97.8	100.0					99.2	100.0
School Provided MDM#	98.8	99.1	99.2	99.5	49.1	50.0	68.0	98.0	98.5	98.6					98.5	98.8
Schools with Electricity	96.0	96.5	98.4	98.7	99.5	99.7	95.8	96.1	95.0	95.9					96.5	97.0
Schools with Computer	34.9	35.5	81.6	82.6	98.1	99.0	75.0	78.1	77.9	79.2					53.1	54.1
Sch. with Ramp, if required		83.6		89.1		82.1		77.1		86.3						85.2
Sch. Established since 2001	13.0	13.3	6.7	7.3	21.4	25.3	50.0	54.7	20.6	20.1					13.6	14.2
Schools with Kitchen–shed	89.8	95.3	94.1	96.7	46.8	94.4	59.2	97.9	80.1	89.3					88.8	94.7
Sch. with Enrdment<=50	49.9	51.6	3.3	3.7	1.1	1.4	38.9	35.9	4.4	5.0					32.4	33.5
Schools with SMC#	95.7	95.0	94.9	94.3	52.5	52.8	47.2	79.6	93.6	92.7					94.8	94.3
Pupil–Teacher Ratio	23	21	26	26	23	19	15	14	13	12					20	18
Studen–Classroom Ratio	20	19	27	26	37	34	23	20	44	43					28	27
average Tch. per School	3.9	4.1	8.0	8.0	30.1	33.9	6.6	6.1	18.5	19.2					8.4	9.0
Female Teachers	82.6	82.8	71.0	82.6	82.6	83.0	82.4	57.1	57.9						73.1	73.7
Enr. in Single–Tch Schools	2.7	1.5	0.2	0.2	0.0	0.0	0.1	0.0	0.1	0.0					0.9	0.5
Enr. in Govt. Schools	48.0	50.2	62.3	62.6	1.7	1.8	43.0	10.4	58.0	57.4					40.4	41.1
Girls Enrolment	49.6	49.7	49.6	49.6	45.9	45.7	65.3	65.4	50.3	50.1					48.8	48.7

% Sch. with Pre–pry.	*pry. level*	21.1	*Total Grossness*	*Primary*	*Upper Primary*	*Transition Rate (Pry. to Upper Pry.)*	95.4
% Enr. in Pre–pry.		20.2		15.5	22.0	*ratio of Grade V to Grade I*	

Incentives (previous year)	Text books			Uniform			*% Sch with SCR >*		*% SCR with PTR >*	
Number of Beneficiaries	*All*	*SC*	*ST*	*All*	*SC*	*ST*	*30 at Pr. Level*	*35 at U.P. Level*	*30 at Pr. Level*	*35 at U.P. Level*
Primary Level	2,881,097	937,990	81,625	1,722,257	602,459	44,397				
Upper Primary Level	2,351,033	701,951	43,371	1,188,174	396,807	23,571	18.3	37.0	13.0	16.5

= Govt + Aided

NR=Not Required

Some totals may not match due to no response in classificatory data items

B. Secondary Educatio: State Report Cards

State Secondary Education Report Card: 2013–14

Number of Districts Covered			30	State Code	33	TAMIL NADU			
Ratio of U.P. to Sec.Schools/Sections			1.82	Ratio of Sec. to Hr Sec. schools/Sections				1.00	
Date reported from	Blocks	413	Clusters	3746	Villaes	6685	Schools	11901	
Basic data: 2011	Total population in (000's)		72139	% Urban population		48.45	Sex ratio	995	
Decadal growth rate	15.60	% SC population		20.00		% ST population		1.10	
Overall literacy rate	80.33	Male literacy rate		86.81		Female literacy rate		73.86	130058

Key Data	*Prim. with U.P. & Sec. & HSec.*	*U.P. Sec. & HSec*	*Prim. with U.P. & Sec.*	*U.P. with Sec.*	*Sec. only*	*Sec. with H.Sec.*	*H. Sec. only*	*Other Categories*	*Total*
Total Schools	4035	7823	0	0	8	24	11	-	11901
Schools: Rural	1805	5610	0	0	7	11	3	-	7436
Schools: Urban	2230	2213	0	0	1	13	8	-	4465
Total Enrolment	894643	3060403	0	0	692	8607	4354	0	3968699
Enr. in Rural Areas	314734	1643983	0	0	604	3779	1027	0	1964127
Enr. in Urban Areas	579909	1416420	0	0	88	4828	3327	0	2004572
Total Teachers	49689	105406	0	0	43	337	215	0	155689
Tch. in Rural Areas	20249	62564	0	0	36	158	50	0	83057
Tch. in urban areas	29440	42841	0	0	7	179	165	0	72632

Performance Indicators	*Prim. with U.p. & Sec. & HSec.*	*U.P. with Sec. & HSec.*	*prim with U.p. & Sec.*	*U.p. with Sec.*	*Sec. Only*	*Sec. with H. Sec.*	*H.Sec. Only*	*All Schools*
% Single–Classroom schools	2.65	1.07			0.00	0.00	0.00	1.60
% Single–Teacher schools	0.02	0.15			0.00	4.17	0.00	0.12
% Schools with Building	99.53	99.22			100.00	100.00	99.33	
% Schools with Girls' Toilet	99.95	98.41			100.00	100.00	100.00	98.96
% Schools with boys' Toilet	99.67	93.75			85.71	100.00	100.00	96.89
% Schools with Toilet for CWSN	19.55	11.75			12.50	16.67	18.18	14.41
% Sch. with Drinking Water	100.00	100.00			100.00	100.00	100.00	100.00
% Schools with Electricity	99.73	97.03			100.00	100.00	100.00	97.96
% Schools with Ramp. if needed	82.09	86.29			100.00	100.00	50.00	85.69
% Schools with Library	99.85	97.09			100.00	95.83	90.91	98.02
% Schools with Full time Librarian	55.44	8.45			0.00	25.00	63.64	24.46
% Schools with Boundary Wall	97.25	82.97			87.50	87.50	100.00	87.84
% Schools Exclusively for CWSN	1.76	0.37			0.00	0.00	0.00	0.84
% Schools with Lab. Assistant	42.50	24.04			0.00	25.00	81.82	30.34
% Schools with Head Master Room	97.84	66.09			62.50	75.00	90.91	76.89
% Schools with Hostel for Boys	10.14	8.39			0.00	8.33	9.09	8.97
% Schools with Hostel for Girls	9.84	6.31			0.00	29.17	9.09	7.55
% Schools with Computer & Internet	92.81	69.93			25.00	79.17	81.82	77.69
% Schools with ICT Laboratory	38.49	10.19			12.50	20.83	27.27	19.82
% Schools with Playground	98.02	76.25			75.00	83.33	72.73	83.64
% Sch. Conducted medical Check–up	82.03	95.49			100.00	79.17	81.82	90.88
% Schools having SMDC	5.77	76.89			25.00	37.50	9.09	52.60
% Sch. with School Bld. Committee	8.72	44.24			12.50	8.33	9.09	32.07
% Schools having PTA	37.47	89.39			50.00	62.50	36.36	71.66
% Schools Established Since 2006	12.96	14.47			12.50	4.17	9.09	13.93
Pupil–Teacher Ratio	18	29			16	26	20	25
Student–Classroom Ratio	31	42			28	32	34	39
Avg. no. of Teachers per School	12	13			5	14	20	13
% Female Teachers	73.59	55.34			72.09	51.04	70.70	61.18
% Girls eneolment	47.31	51.47			46.24	42.23	41.20	50.50
PTA Parent Teacher Association	SMDC–School management & Development Committee				CWS–Children with Special Need			

C. Elementary Education: State Report Cards

Ratio of Girls to Boys Enr: Grades I to V				0.95	Retention Rates (Pry.)			96.29				
Enrolment 2013–14					Total Repeaters	Repetition rate	Drop out rate	SC/ST/OBC Enrolment			Enrolment ratio	
Grade	Total	Girls enrolment	CWSN						Primary	U.Pry.	GER Primary	102.6
			Boys	Girls				% SC enr.	24.2	24.3	GER U. Pry.	98.3
I	1,169,855	569,502	7,031	5,072	1,244	0.10	5.94	% SC enr.	48.9	49.0	NER Primary	86.7
II	1,131,279	550,861	8,896	6,157	1,104	0.09	3.43	% ST enr.	1.9	1.4	NER U. Pry	76.7
III	1,133,013	51,291	9,003	6,820	1,031	0.09	3.48	% ST girls	47.8	48.4	Non-Tec Assignment	
IV	1,160,886	564,714	8,507	6,812	993	0.08	2.90	% OBC enr.	70.0	70.0	% Teachers involved	1.9
V	1,174,652	570,626	8,374	6,683	1,034	0.08	4.53	% OBC girls	48.6	48.6		
VI	1,177,180	574,670	11,475	8,699	885	0.07					Number of days involved	10
VII	1,205,708	586,966	11,915	9,301	952	0.08		% Muslim enr.	6.2	5.9	Average Instructional Days	
VIII	1,243,868	604,365	11,310	9,678	874	0.07						
Pry (I–V)	5,769,685	2,806,994	41,811	31,544	5,406	0.09	4.06	% Muslim girls	48.8	49.3	Pr. level	U. Pr. level
U. Pry.	3,626,756	1,766,001	34,700	27,678	2,711	0.07	1.24				216	213

Classooms/Others Rooms

School category	*Average Cls.*	*Total Classrooms*	*% Good cond.*	*% Minor repair*	*% Major repair*	*Other rooms*
Pry. only	4.4	155,782	88.71	8.27	3.02	30,791
Pry. + U. pry.	8.1	77,639	87.24	9.35	3.41	14,257
P + UP + Sec +HS	18.7	75,621	99.70	0.29	0.01	28,664
U. pry. only	4.3	553	98.01	1.81	0.18	257
U.P. + Sec. + HS	5.6	43,554	90.11	7.37	2.52	32,689
P + U.P. +Sec						
U.P. + Sec						

Teachers by Edu. Qualification (Other than contract teacher)

School category	Below Sec.	Sec.	Hr. Sec.	Grad.	Post Grad.	M Phil/ PhD	Post Doc.	No Res.
Pry. nly	1,758	14,651	45,421	52,224	23,897	2,135	31	61
Pry + U. Pry	522	4,621	16,387	29,911	22,994	2,842	14	7
P + UP + Sec + HS	1,923	3,975	9,816	59,675	49,911	7,263	76	108
U. Pry. only	12	44	64	381	193	20	0	0
U.P. + Sec + HS	514	5,091	7,612	40,921	70,031	25,094	97	17
P + U.P. + Sec								
U.P. + Sec								
Contract	121	447	1,359	4,279	1,986	270	9	3

Enrolment by nature of Disability

Nature of Disability	I	II	III	IV	V	VI	VII	VIII
Blind	523	344	345	287	243	516	314	331
Low-sion	769	1108	1297	1471	1378	3045	4142	4241
Hearing	1136	1469	1993	1379	1550	2019	2112	2512
Speech	685	923	917	1032	892	890	840	1013
Loco–motor	1385	1803	2020	2028	1953	2560	2637	2653
Mentally ratarded	5348	6551	6466	6539	6788	862	7736	7441
Learning	74	117	155	149	129	156	224	164
Carebral palsy	645	1101	806	941	798	1005	1384	664
Autism	226	287	356	215	194	268	347	378
Multiple	1312	1350	1468	1278	1132	1653	1480	1591

% Professionally Trained Teachers

Gender	Government		
	Regular	Contract	Private
Male	99.4	97.1	97.5
Female	99.6	94.1	94.6
All Teachers	99.5	95.4	95.2

Teachers by Gender & Caste		*Regular Teachers*			*Contractual teachers*			*SC Teachers*		*ST Teachers*	
School category	*Total*	*Male*	*Female*	*No res*	*Male*	*Females*	*No res*	*Male*	*Female*	*Male*	*Female*
Primary only	143,188	24,438	115,740	0	141	2,869	0	4,415	18,468	390	1,238
Primary + U. pry	77,963	21,727	55,571	0	144	521	0	4,387	7,942	305	522
P + UP + Sec + HS	136,636	23,229	109,518	0	611	3,278	0	4,050	11,472	208	808
Upper Pry. only	780	130	584	0	7	59	0	11	140	1	27
U.P. + Sec + HS	150,21	62,991	86,386	0	325	519	0	11,750	11,749	478	535
P + U.P. + Sec											
U.P.+ Sec											

Enrolment by Medium of Instructions						*% Sch*	
School category	*Tamil*	*English*	*Others*		*Urdu*	*TLM*	*SD Grant*
Primary only	2090223	821380	775		15954	18.7	81.9
Primary with Upper Primary	1728836	231103	48		9173	21.6	90.6
Primary with UP. Pri & Sec & HS	66987	241776	237		64	0.9	2.8
Upper primary only	10459	318	438		0	5.5	35.9
Upper Primary with Sec & HS	1530237	244657	41671		4946	18.3	91.1
Primary with up & Sec							
Upper Primary with Sec							

% Teachers Received In–Service Training (Previous year)								*% Teachers by Age (In year)@*			*% Grants Utilized*	
	P. only	P+ UP	P+ UP+ Sec+ HS	UP only	UP+ Sec+ HS	P+ UP+ SEC	UP+Sec	55–56	57–58	59–60	TLM	SD Grant
Male	81.2	81.2	1.2	48.9	20.8			3.43	2.79	0.44	99.7	99.8
Female	51.9	71.6	1.3	48.4	25.8			1.86	1.52	0.35		
All Tch.	56.9	74.3	1.3	48.5	23.7			2.27	1.85	0.37		

Source: National University of Educational Planning and Administration.

5

Health and Nutrition

Good health and access to healthcare, as shown in Figure 5.1, are facilitated by factors from within and outside health sector, from private and public sector, and are shaped by intra-national and global institutions.

In India, although several major national programmes financed by the Government of India (GoI) (such as national blindness control programme, national malaria control programme, national HIV/AIDS control programme), have played and continue to play a significant role in building healthcare systems across States, State governments have a greater role and responsibility in building a sustainable delivery system in the long run. Over the years, Tamil Nadu has acquired the distinction of having implemented various national and State-level health programmes more effectively than most other States (Muraleedharan *et al.*, 2011). The people of Tamil Nadu also enjoy a far better health status than those in most parts of India. Yet, there are several challenges that persist. This chapter will highlight both the achievements and challenges, and indicate the steps that the government can take to build an affordable and effective healthcare system and to improve health status of the people of Tamil Nadu.

This chapter is organised as follows:

Section II presents major policy and programmatic initiatives in the State in the last decade, since early 2000s. Section III provides available evidence on access to health services and cost of care, and progress in overall health status of the State over the past decade. Section IV addresses attainments and gaps in nutrition and sanitation facilities in the State that are critical for improving health status. Comparison with other States and inter-district comparisons are provided wherever possible. The present chapter concludes by highlighting some of the major prevailing challenges, and suggests ways forward to strengthen the healthcare system, including the State's private health sector.

Programmatic Initiatives

Tamil Nadu's performance in health sector has improved significantly over the past decade. The State has witnessed dramatic improvements in primary care and secondary care facilities through the establishment of several professional medical teaching institutions and significant improvements made in the higher secondary and tertiary care facilities. The effective implementation of National Rural Health

Figure 5.1

Conceptual Framework: Good Health at Low Cost

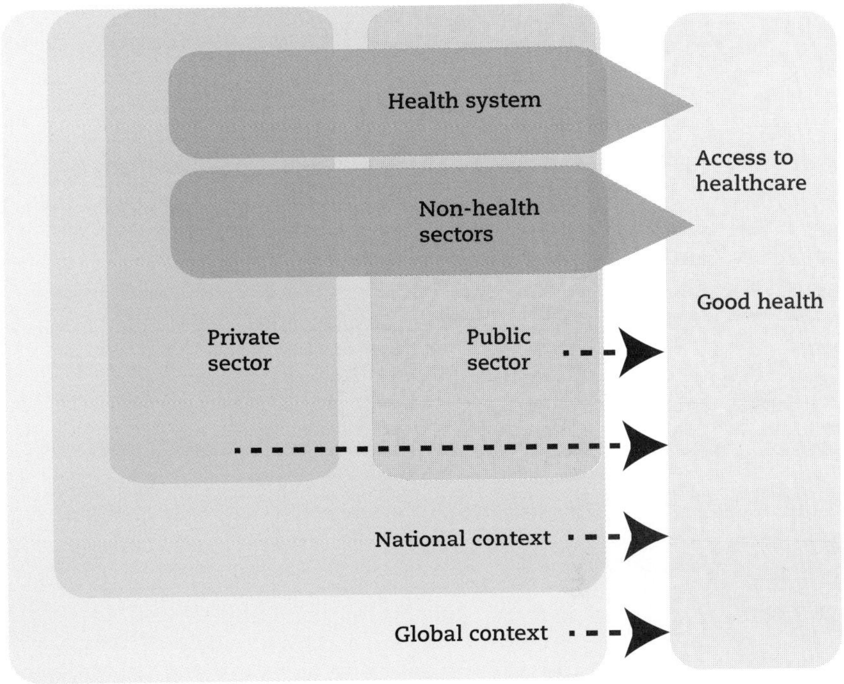

Source: Balabanova *et al.*, 2011.

Mission (NRHM), a national level flagship programme of the GoI, and the State Health System Project (SHSP) with the support of World Bank and State government, since 2005, have contributed significantly in improving the quality and quantum of services delivered through public healthcare facilities in the State. The major developments since early 2000 are highlighted here.

Public Financing

The budgetary provisions for public healthcare delivery system has steadily increased over the decades. It has grown from ₹410 crore in 1991-92 to about ₹8,245.41 crore in 2015-16 (Health and Family Welfare (HFW), Policy Note, 2015). This is partly due to "The conditions[1] for receiving funds under NRHM" and partly for launching newer schemes, such as the State insurance scheme for tertiary care, and huge increase in maternity benefits scheme. Another interesting feature of the State budget for health is the fact that nearly 40 per cent of this budget is spent on primary healthcare, which is observed to be higher than the amount spent by most Indian States. The share of tertiary care in the budget has fallen from 33 per cent in 1990 to 25 per cent in 2012 with the secondary sector's share rising correspondingly, possibly due to the increased flow of funds from SHSP (Muraleedharan *et al.*, 2011: 169). The consistent commitment of resources to the health sector by successive governments has made it possible for the State to make the best use of Central schemes, which often require matching resources and funding for staff from the State government. The State also has the distinction of having spent a larger share of the budget on drugs and other non-staff items compared to that of other States (Kumar *et al.*, 2011). The State budget during 2005-2012 had been on a rise on an average at 19 per cent per annum, while the contribution of NRHM had been growing at about 16 per cent per annum during the same period. It is important to note here that the State's capacity to absorb and utilise central funding has remained on average above 95 per cent over the past decade, reflecting overall systematic efforts being made to strengthen the public delivery system. In the year 2013-14, the State has received about ₹1,300 crore under NRHM budget, which is one of the highest amount received and utilised among all States.

While such positive features reflect State's commitment to strengthen public health delivery system, we should also flag the fact that the government's spending for health sector is about 1 per cent of the State GDP (Gross Domestic Product). Estimates show that government spending on healthcare per capita was about ₹223, while the total health spending (including private spending) per capita was about ₹1,256 (which works out to 3.99% of SGDP) (MoHFW, National Health Accounts, 2004-05; 2009). Although NRHM has brought considerable additional resources, the overall public spending has not been able to keep pace with the increased private spending. Over the years, government spending on health accounts for about 4.2 per cent of the total State budget.

Service Delivery

Strengthening PHCs/HSCs: Since mid-1980s and through 1990s, the State witnessed a massive expansion in the primary healthcare delivery system. A fairly robust network of Primary Health Centres (PHCs) and Health Sub Centres (SHCs or sub-health centres) across the State (as per population norms) along with a huge deployment of field functionaries and sustained bureaucratic and political commitment, helped effective implementation of NRHM in the following decade. But for the existence of a fairly effective primary healthcare delivery system, already in place by early 2000, the benefits of NRHM may not have been appropriately realised. During 2005-2015, about 200 new PHCs were built using NRHM funds; but one must note here that a significant portion of NRHM funds was systematically utilised to upgrade a large number of PHCs (close to 300, with additional buildings, beds, staff and equipment) during this same period (Interview with a former Secretary, HFW, GoTN, 10 July 2014).

It should be noted here that (as of 2015) out of 1,750 PHCs, 1,564 are functioning in government buildings (HFW, Policy Note, 2015), compared to 1,360 in 2004-05, and a mere 660 in 1999-2000.

As of 2015,748 PHCs have been awarded ISO certification. There has been a concerted effort to upgrade at least 2 PHCs from each district to ISO 9000 standards over next few years.

The State has been upgrading 1 PHC in each block with 30 beds and providing them with additional facilities (such as operation theatre, x-ray machine, an ambulance) and manpower (5 additional doctors in each upgraded PHC). As of 2013, 398 upgraded PHCs have been functioning in 365 blocks.

Mobile Medical Units: In addition, Tamil Nadu has also been at the forefront in deploying Mobile Medical Units

1. A main condition imposed by the Central Government being that the state health budget should increase annually by 15 per cent to receive NRHM funds.

(MMUs) at block level, to improve access in remote and underserved areas. Each MMU consists of a dedicated team, including a doctor, a nurse and an attendant, provides family welfare services and treatment for minor ailments. At present, there are about 396 MMUs; one in each block in the State, funded by NRHM. On an average, each MMU conducts 40 camps per month, and covers about 50-80 patients per camp.

Mobile Units in Tribal Areas: Twenty mobile units (in 13 districts) have been deployed exclusively in tribal areas. Women tribal counsellors have been appointed in about 42 PHCs/hospitals in tribal regions, with additional funding to augment bed availability in some regions. Special efforts have been made in tribal regions to survey the prevalence of sickle cell Anaemia, and for treatment and counselling. Birth waiting rooms (for 2 weeks prior to delivery date) in PHCs in tribal areas, initiated with NRHM funds, are increasingly being utilised.

Anecdotal impression is that MMUs have improved access to primary care in remote areas, but their impact on access to care and outcomes are yet to be systematically assessed. 396 MMUs are being deployed across the State, utilising considerable amount of resources from NRHM. It is therefore important to rationalise their use in order to maximise their reach and utility among the target population.

Hospitals and Comprehensive Emergency and Obstetric and Neonatal Care (CEmONC) Centres

The State has 30 district-level hospitals (providing up to higher secondary care), besides 160 Taluk and 80 non-Taluk hospitals providing a link between primary care and secondary care services.

The facilities at higher levels of care have also been substantially augmented. Under SHS project, about 700 buildings were newly built/renovated. Several of these are located at taluk headquarters. Tamil Nadu was the first State to establish 24-hour functioning CEmONC by early 2000. At present, there are 125 CEmONC centres with additional permanent staff. These along with several other initiatives, as a result, have substantially reduced maternal deaths over the past decade. The number of complicated deliveries made in CEmONC centres has increased from about 1.07 lakh in 2007-08 to about 1.85 lakh in 2013-14. Their capacity to handle complicated neonatal admissions has also been doubled over the last six years.

Neonatal Intensive Care Units (NICUs): There are 42 Neonatal Intensive Care Units (NICUs) attached to CEmONC centres, all with additional staff nurses and physicians. All staff members in NICUs receive special 14-day training in NICU management. The overall quality of these NICUs is so high that private providers see them as competitors, and as a result, many private providers have substantially reduced the charges for neonatal services to attract and retain their patients (interviews with private physicians in Thoothukudi and Ramnad Districts, July 2014)

108-Ambulance Service: As of February 2014, 638 vans have been deployed to provide 108-emergency management services (EMRI scheme). Each van does 3 to 4 trips per day, travelling on average 50 to 60 km per trip. Recent estimates shows that on average it takes about 16 minutes to reach the patient from the time of call, about 11 minutes at the "incident location" and about an hour to reach a hospital from the time of call.

Non-Communicable Diseases: The State has also been a forerunner in providing primary care services to those suffering from NCDs (non-communicable diseases). NCD clinics have been established in all district, taluk and non-taluk hospitals, and upgraded PHCs in the State. PHCs in the State have a staff nurse (funded by SHSP) exclusively for screening patients for NCDs. All PHCs provide free drugs to patients with diabetes and blood pressure, which is important given that a study conducted in Tamil Nadu (ICMR–INDIAB study), reported that the prevalence of diabetes was 10.4 per cent (Anjana *et al.*, 2011). All government hospitals regularly carry out screening for breast and cervical cancer for women above 30 years of age. Besides that, the Department of Education, Labour and Education are also involved in addressing NCDs at schools and work-related sites. Funds from centrally-funded National Programme for Prevention and Control of Cancer, Diabetes, Cardiovascular Diseases and Stroke (NPCDCS), and District Mental Health Programme (DMHP) have substantially strengthened efforts to address NCDs in the recent past. The DMHP assumes importance in the context of relatively high suicide rates in Tamil Nadu. National Crime Records Bureau's report on accidental deaths and suicides in India (National Crime Records Bureau, 2014) indicate that the States with the highest suicide rates (number of suicides per one lakh population) in 2013 were Sikkim (29.3), Tripura (25.9), Kerala (24.6) and Tamil Nadu (24.3).

Quality of Care: As part of efforts to improve quality of care and services provided in public hospitals, SHS project has developed a set of 14 quality of care indicators, and 12 parameters to be fulfilled for International Association for Business and Health

(IABH) accreditation. So far, 3 government hospitals and 25 private hospitals have been accredited. Besides, the State (with in-house expertise) has brought out a Standard Treatment Guidelines (in 2010). Several other States have adopted this manual.

Also, steps are underway to accredit 12 secondary hospitals under the National Accreditation Board for Hospitals and Health Care (NABH) under the Tamil Nadu Health Systems Project (TNHSP). What is needed at this point seems to be a major policy thrust to incorporate the principles of quality management into the functioning of the entire public health system.

Under National Health Mission (NHM), the State has made a special effort to improve healthcare in urban areas. All towns/cities with a population of more than 50,000 will have their existing urban health post upgraded and new centres added.

Besides that, special initiatives have been launched (though at pilot stage) with regard to Palliative care, Early Intervention Centres, Poison Management Centres, and Upgraded Dental Care Scheme across the State.

State-Sponsored Insurance for Tertiary Care: In an effort to further reduce financial burden arising from catastrophic expenses in tertiary care, a State-sponsored insurance scheme was introduced in 2009.

This scheme, which was further improved with more comprehensive features and increased coverage of up to ₹1 lakh per year per household in 2011, covers nearly 1.36 crore families, i.e., nearly 40 per cent of the population having an income of less than ₹72,000 per annum (HFW, Policy Note 2012: 104). The government pays the entire premium for the scheme and the scheme is implemented through public and private providers at a cost of more than ₹700 crore. The revised scheme has been successful in involving the public sector hospitals, which receive nearly 30 per cent of the claim amount, since certain basic surgical procedures have been reserved for these hospitals. However, the scheme is yet to be evaluated for its effect on out-of-pocket expenses. The scheme does not receive any funding from NRHM and the State has also opted out of participating in the Rashtriya Swasthya Bima Yojna (RSBY). About 2.2 lakh and 3.3 lakh claims have been made in 2010-11 and 2012-13 respectively (Interviews with offices, CMCHIS, October 2014).

Dr Muthulakshmi Reddy Maternity Benefit Scheme: In the year 2006-07, the government launched a maternity benefit scheme in the name of Dr Muthulakshmi Reddy Maternity Benefit Scheme (MRMBS). Until 2011, all poor pregnant women were given a financial assistance of ₹6,000 so as to protect them adequately from wage losses during the pregnancy period, and from experiencing lack of nutrition, in turn reducing the incidence of low birth deliveries. Within a year since its launch, the proportion of women using government institutions for deliveries increased substantially, from 6.22 lakh in 2006-07 to 6.83 lakh beneficiaries in 2007-08. Thereafter, every year, nearly 6 lakh women/mothers benefit from this scheme. Since 2011, this amount has been increased to ₹12,000 per delivery, provided it is made in public facilities. It is important to note that this scheme also covers pregnant women of Sri Lankan Refugees. There are certain salient features of this scheme, unique across the entire country. The amount is distributed in three equal instalments: the first is given during the 7th month of pregnancy to those who have availed prescribed health services (antenatal care services); the second instalment is given to those who deliver in government institutions; and the third instalment is given to mothers on completion of 3rd dose of DPT and other post-delivery services to the child. All disbursements are now made electronically from the treasury to beneficiary bank accounts. A sum of ₹652 crore was disbursed (for 6.63 lakh beneficiaries in 2013-14), compared to ₹100 crore for 2.41 lakh beneficiaries in 2006-07.

National Disease Control Programmes: All national programmes are being implemented in Tamil Nadu. The following specific programmatic efforts deserve a special mention. Vector borne diseases (VBDs), particularly Malaria, Dengue, Chikungunya, Filarias, are common in several districts in the State, with Filaria being regionally more widespread (Table 5.1). Tamil Nadu is one of the States in India to have reported Japanese Encephalitis, and it is being reported from newer regions in the State. VBDs continue to remain as a major public health problem in the State.

The State has established 1 Apple Laboratory, besides 30 sentinel surveillance hospitals, and has more than 70 entomologists in place. The number of confirmed cases has steadily gone up, reflecting the system's capacity to detect follow-up action. The trend during 2009-2011 is given in Table 5.1 (SHS, PIP, 2012-13).

Leprosy programme was integrated with the general healthcare system (as part of primary healthcare) in mid-1990s and has made remarkable progress in containing the incidence of leprosy in the State. The number of new cases detected has come down from 8.1 (in 2006-07) to 6.7 (in 2015-16) per 1 lakh population.

Table 5.1

Cases and Deaths Due to Vector Borne Diseases in Tamil Nadu, 2012-2015

Year	*Malaria Cases*	*Malaria Deaths*	*Dengue Cases*	*Dengue Deaths*	*Chikungunya Cases*	*AES Cases*	*AES Deaths*	*JE Cases*	*JE Deaths*	*Microfilaria Rate*
2012	18869	0	13204	66	514	954	72	33	5	0.14
2013	15081	0	6122	0	859	77	8	33	0	0.07
2014	8729	0	2804	3	543	346	4	36	3	0.07
2015	5653	0	4535	12	329	847	0	53	0	—

Source: State Health Society SHS, PIP, 2012-13.

The State's remarkable achievement over the years in controlling HIV/AIDS is well recognised. The overall control strategy of Tamil Nadu State Aids Control Society (TNSACS) and NGOs (non-governmental organisations) in particular has played a significant role in this regard (Muraleedharan *et al.*, 2011).

HIV-TB intensified package is being implemented in the State. Close to 80 per cent of TB (tuberculosis) patients were tested for HIV in 2012. Both cure rate and success rate under the Revised National Tuberculosis Control Program (RNTCP) have been around 84 per cent since early 2000.

Indian System of Medicine (ISM): Historically, Tamil Nadu is known for promoting ISM. About 1000 PHCs, 30 district hospitals and nearly 230 government hospitals (taluk and non-taluk) have incorporated ISM. Nearly 450 ISM facilities were established with additional funding from NRHM. One must note here that drugs prescribed under ISM are produced by Tamil Nadu Medicinal Plant Farms and Herbal Medicines Corportion Ltd (TAMPCOL), established by the Tamil Nadu government, since 1983.

Human Resources

Here we focus on both the efforts being made to establish a large number of educational institutions leading to creation of medical and paramedical professionals, and to create employment opportunities for these professionals.

Medical Education: A notable development has been the decision to institute a large number of publicly-financed medical colleges across the State. As of 2013, there are 18 government medical colleges, with total intake of about 2,400 seats for undergraduate programme in medicine. This has been a substantial growth over the last 20 years: by mid-1990s, there were 9 government medical colleges with capacity of about 1,100 seats for undergraduate programme. Of these, 3 were and are in Chennai. The additional 9 government colleges over the past 20 years have been established systematically in other regions/districts of the State, resulting in substantial improvement in hospitals attached to these medical colleges. As a result, public hospitals are now in a position to exert pressure on the large private facilities to reduce costs of care for comparable services. Besides these medical colleges, there are 23 government nursing schools (offering Diploma in Nursing), and 4 government nursing colleges (offering BSc/MSc courses in nursing). Also, there has been a proliferation of private educational institutions offering training in basic medical and super speciality services and in allied paramedical subjects. There are 11 private medical colleges and 166 private nursing colleges. Nearly 10 private medical colleges have been established since mid-1990s. As a result, over the past two decades, 19 new medical colleges have been established, thereby increasing the total number of medical colleges in the State to 29, and the overall capacity of producing health professionals.

Besides these schools, there are a large number of private institutions offering two year training in Auxiliary Nursing and Midwifery (ANM) courses and a large number of health-based NGOs who employ female field workers to implement their own out-reach services. How much of these professionally trained manpower get absorbed in the State health system, how much is absorbed by the private health system, and of which how many remain as stand-alone practitioners? We have little knowledge of the career paths of those not entering the government system.

The Department of Health and Family Welfare has about one lakh employees, of which nearly 42 per cent is employed under the Directorate of Public Health and Preventive Medicine. About 33 per cent comes under the Medical Education Department and about 25 per cent comes under Directorate of Medical and Rural Services (*Source*: DPH office). Evidently, primary care services, both in terms of total manpower deployed and its overall share in the State health budget, have received much attention.

With the creation of Medical Recruitment Board (MRB), direct recruitment of physicians and paramedical professionals (including nurses and radiographers) on contract basis has become possible. MRB has already made a large number of direct recruitment and has filled vacancies on a fast track mode. Over the past three years, more than 2000 doctors have been recruited directly into services through MRB.

Over last 8 years, since 2007-08, about 10,000 assistant surgeons have been recruited through Tamil Nadu Public Service Commission. About 1,000 male (health inspectors) and about 200 village health nurses (VHNs) were appointed over the same period. Evidently, while there has been a significant increase in the employment of physicians; contrarily, the rise in the number of paramedical staff has been too low.

However, every wave of recruitment faces legal hurdles that delay the process of deployment of human resources, thereby limiting access to effective care. In higher level facilities, particularly at taluk and district level public hospitals, there has mostly been an acute shortage of nurses and other paramedical staff, in particular.

Drugs Supply and Diagnostic Services

The role of Tamil Nadu Medical Services Corporation (TNMSC) deserves special attention. Over the years, since its creation in mid-1990s, TNMSC has strengthened substantially the public drug delivery system in the State and its contributions are widely recognised, nationally and internationally. Its role has expanded from procurement and distribution of essential drugs to public facilities, to include investing substantially on diagnostic equipment in these facilities. Across the State, TNMSC now provides the following diagnostic services on payment basis: 61 CT scan centres (with at least one in each district), 15 MRI scan centres, 2 Lithotripsy centre, and a sales counter (at Chennai Kilpauk Hospital) where life-saving drugs are sold to the public at a rate much less than market prices. The essential drug list is updated once every two years, based on drug utilisation and inclusion of new drugs for maternal and child health and safe abortion (SHS, PIP, TN 2012-13).

The overall budgetary provisions have gone up from about ₹175 crore in 2008-09 to about ₹350 crore in 2013-14. The Corporation with about 650 employees has managed most effectively the drugs supply system in the State. All warehouses (located in district headquarters) maintain five months' physical stocks to prevent any shortage of drugs.

Health Management Information System

Health Information Management System: Health Management Information System (HIMS) in the State has been bolstered with support from SHSP. Tata Consultancy Services (TCS) and ELCOT have been involved in building the HIMS. At present, each hospital maintains patient records but they are not fully networked and integrated. But to an extent, these hospitals that are involved in CM's Insurance Scheme, are also integrated. The State, with the help of Indian Council of Medical Research (ICMR), has recently set up a State Health Data Resource Centre (SHDRC). It is yet to get stabilised, but its mandate is clear and has the potential to contribute to effective monitoring and policy formulation in the future.

Integrated Disease Surveillance Project (IDSP): IDSP in Tamil Nadu was launched in 2005 in order to establish a decentralised system of surveillance of the communicable and non-communicable diseases with a view to provide timely and effective public health interventions. More specifically, IDSP will address a few specific diseases and risk factors, integrate surveillance activities at district and State level, improve laboratories for disease surveillance, deploy human resources development for surveillance and establish a system of data collection, reporting, analysis and feedback using IT (information technology) (SHS, PIP, TN 2012-13).

Owing to strengthening of District Surveillance Units (DSUs)—there are 32 DSUs—a drastic improvement in the laboratory confirmation of outbreaks has been noticed over the years. It went up from 2008—19 per cent, 2009—31 per cent, 2010—29 per cent, 2011—82 per cent, 2012—93 per cent, 2013—93 per cent, 2014—84 per cent, 2015—89 per cent. Also over the years, there has been a significant improvement in the reporting of outbreaks of communicable diseases: 2008—81, 2015—153. Yet, it should be noted that several Health Unit Districts (HUDs) do not have DSUs in place and in that case, these regions are yet to benefit from IDSP.

Outcomes

How do we assess the combined and cumulative effects of several of these initiatives? Intuitively, one could expect positive impact of these initiatives in terms of: (a) increased utilisation of services provided in public facilities; (b) reduction in the out-of-pocket expenditure by patients, in particular among the poor; and (c) improvements in the overall health status of people. This section provides an overview of changes that the State has witnessed over the past decade or so, in these contexts.

Quite evidently, we cannot directly relate the impact of these measures on overall improvements in the health status of populations, for the simple fact that health status (survival chances and quality of life after treatment) is significantly determined by factors, such as nutrition, housing, overall economic status, pollution and lifestyle.

Utilisation of Public Healthcare Services

Data from the National Sample Survey Organization (NSSO, 2006) 60th Round study on Morbidity and Health Care, shows that self-reported ailments in Tamil Nadu are comparable to that of rest of the country, whereas the rate of hospitalisation is distinctly higher. The percentage of those not seeking care is relatively low at 13 per cent, the major reasons given being unavailability of healthcare and its high cost. Further, considering the all-India figures, it is seen that 75 per cent of outpatient care and 60 per cent of inpatient care in the State are availed in the private sector. The share of the private sector in both these cases are higher in urban than in rural areas. Another interesting fact is that as on 1 January 2002, it was estimated that 78 per cent of hospital beds in Tamil Nadu are in the public sector (CBHI, 2003). Although the public healthcare infrastructure in the State is comparatively better than rest of the country, it does not seem to have resulted in an increased proportion of utilisation of public inpatient or outpatient care, except in the case of child birth. This indicates a preference of the population for availing healthcare from the private sector, raising questions about the quality of services provided by the public health facilities. With a largely unregulated private sector and rising healthcare costs, there is an urgent need to improve utilisation of the public healthcare system so as to avoid wastage of precious government resources and to ensure that the poor and underprivileged are not denied access to healthcare for economic reasons.

The data presented here on utilisation of healthcare is based on the NSSO study done in 2004 and it can merely serve as a base line for studying the impact of NRHM on this parameter, which is a good proxy for access to healthcare. State health department data show that the average figures for outpatient attendance in the PHCs has increased from 123 per day in 2005-06 to above 142 in 2011-12. This indicates a possible shift towards better utilisation of the public sector in the State for outpatient care. As stated above, utilisation of public health services is very closely aligned with the public perception of quality of services rendered by the public health facilities.

Equity in Utilisation of Healthcare

Equity is an important dimension of provision of health services to the population. Equity studies help to reveal whether or not the public funds invested in healthcare services have reached the poorest, the target population. Studies by Mahal *et al.* (2000) done on the utilisation of public healthcare services in the State, using the 52nd Round of NSSO on Morbidity and Treatment of Ailments, have clearly shown that public immunisation and maternity services were pro-poor in the State; that is, the poorest quintile used more than its proportionate share of these services, even in 1995-96. At this time, the rural inpatient services and urban outpatient services were pro-rich. Further research using the 60th Round of NSSO reveals that over this period, utilisation of all forms of public healthcare services, which include inpatient, outpatient, maternity and immunisation, has become more equitable in the State, with all the services becoming pro-poor (Acharya *et al.*, 2011: 19-29). Figure 5.2 illustrates the-poor utilisation of public facilities for maternal deliveries. The figure also shows that over a period (1995-96 to 2004), greater proportions of those utilising public facilities belonged to bottom-most quintiles. Further studies on how equity and utilisation of public healthcare in the State have fared owing to NRHM, can only be carried out after results of the 71st Round of NSSO on Morbidity and Health Care become available.

Figure 5.2

Distribution of Maternal Deliveries in Public Facilities in Tamil Nadu, 1995-96, and 2004, by Socio-economic Groups

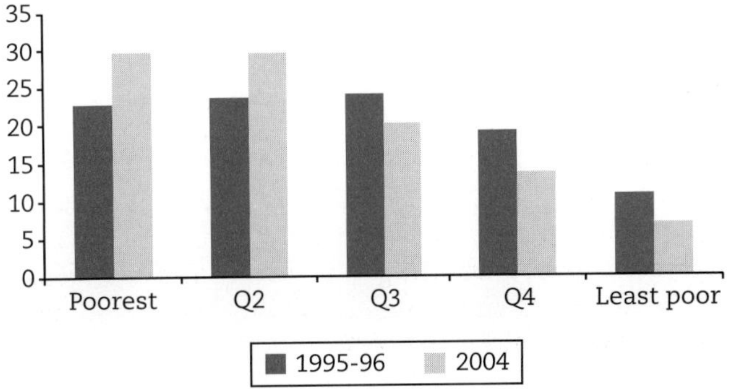

Source: Acharya *et al.* (2011).

Maternal and Child Health: Coverage and Outcome Indicators

Many inputs provided under the Reproductive and Child Health (RCH) component of NRHM, including provision of 24x7 delivery services, ensuring availability of emergency obstetric care and setting up of NICUs, have been designed to improve Maternal and Child Health (MCH). The coverage and outcome parameters of MCH services are relatively easy to measure and can be used as a proxy to study performance of the overall health system in terms of access and effectiveness.

MCH coverage indicators show that Tamil Nadu had met most of the benchmarks set by NRHM by 2005 itself. The proportion of institutional deliveries in the State, which was only 64 per cent in 1992-93, had gone up to nearly 98 per cent by 2005 (Muraleedharan *et al.*, 2011: 178-80). In fact, data from the District Level Household and Facility Survey in 2007-08 (DLHS 3) shows that institutional delivery was near universal in both rural and urban areas of Tamil Nadu (Table 5.2). The one significant change noted since 2005 is the increase in proportion of deliveries conducted in the PHCs, their share of total deliveries going up from 7.9 per cent to more than 25 per cent between 2005-06 and 2009-10. This has been accompanied by a corresponding fall in the share of deliveries conducted by the private institutions over the same period. The shift in utilisation from private to the public sector can be taken as a positive indicator of improved health service delivery for maternity care, resulting from the additional inputs provided under NRHM. However, the payment of ₹6,000 (and later ₹12,000) as a maternity benefit for all poor women under the State-funded Muthulakshmi Reddy Maternity Benefit Scheme (HFW, Policy Note, 2013: 42) also had some role to play in the improved utilisation of PHCs for maternal deliveries. Similarly, the proportion of women who received at least three antenatal visits increased dramatically from about 20 per cent in the early 1990s to 95 per cent by 2005 (HFW, Policy Note, 2013: 178-80). Information from Table 5.2 shows that the proportion of mothers who received three or more antenatal visit was the highest in Tamil Nadu (95.6%) and those with full antenatal coverage was much higher than the national average in Tamil Nadu (51.8%), except Kerala and Karnataka. However, there were rural-urban disparities, with full ANC (antenatal care) coverage being relatively higher in urban than rural Tamil Nadu. Latest information from the United Nations Children's Fund's (UNICEF) Coverage Evaluation Survey (CES) 2009[2] shows a decline in full antenatal coverage in Tamil Nadu to 44.1 per cent (UNICEF, 2010). During the same period, full antenatal care coverage improved in the country as a whole and also in Andhra Pradesh (united), Kerala, Maharashtra and Gujarat, while declining in Karnataka and Maharashtra. Tamil Nadu has a higher proportion of mothers who received postnatal care within two weeks of delivery (89.2%) than the other States under comparison, except Kerala. Moreover, the proportion was higher in rural than urban areas in Tamil Nadu. Information from UNICEF's CES 2009 reveals that 98.4 per cent of the deliveries took place in institutions in Tamil Nadu, which reflects an increase since 2007-08.

Another example of Tamil Nadu's nearly universal coverage of services for women and children is its successful immunisation programme. Tamil Nadu has always been a pioneer in immunisation services and had ranked first among all the States in India in terms of coverage by the early 1990s. By the late 1990s, 99 per cent of rural and 100 per cent of urban children in the State had received at least one dose of immunisation, while more than 80 per cent children received full vaccination—a level of performance that has been maintained over the past 15 years (DPH Office 2014). Data from DLHS 3 for 2007-08, however, show a fall in the full vaccination coverage (to about 81.8%) compared to 91.4 per cent in DLHS 2 in 2002-2004[3] (International Institute for Population Sciences (IIPS), 2010). This declining trend in full immunisation coverage in Tamil Nadu is also corroborated by UNICEF's CES 2009, which indicate that 77.3 per cent of the children aged 12-23 months were fully immunised in Tamil Nadu (UNICEF, 2010a). There was a higher utilisation of private health facilities for immunisation in Kerala (21%) and Tamil Nadu (20%), which affected full immunisation of children (UNICEF, 2010a). In Tamil Nadu, according to CES 2009 (UNICEF, 2010b), full immunisation shows variation across caste, where children belonging to STs (Scheduled Tribes) (54.3%), SCs (Scheduled Castes) (74.5%) and OBCs (Other Backward Classes) (77.7%) have lower levels of immunisation than those from other castes (90.3%). While immunisation improves among children belonging to higher wealth quintiles, there

2. UNICEF's CES used questionnaires similar to National Family Health Survey (NFHS) and DLHS. The data on antenatal care pertains to women who delivered 12 months preceding the survey.

3. It is important to note that DLHS 2 administered the questionnaire only to currently married women, whereas DLHS 3 administered the questionnaire to every married woman.

Table 5.2

Maternal (Married Women Aged 15-49 Years) and Child Health Coverage in Tamil Nadu, Andhra Pradesh (United), Karnataka, Kerala and Maharashtra 2007-08 (as %)

S. No.	State	Place of residence	Mothers who had 3 or more antenatal check-up	Mothers who had full antenatal check-up	Institutional delivery	Mothers who received post-natal care within two weeks of delivery	Children age 12-23 months fully immunised
		Rural	94.8	47.7	91.8	86.9	82.9
1	Tamil Nadu	Urban	97.0	58.3	97.5	92.7	80.0
		Total	95.6	51.8	94.0	89.2	81.8
		Rural	87.2	37.6	65.7	76.4	65.0
2	Andhra Pradesh (united)	Urban	96.3	49.7	90.9	89.0	73.2
		Total	89.4	40.5	71.8	79.4	67.1
		Rural	78.5	48.7	59.7	64.8	76.5
4	Karnataka	Urban	88.6	57.3	79.8	81.5	77.3
		Total	81.2	51.0	65.1	69.3	76.7
		Rural	95.2	72.4	99.2	99.3	80.3
5	Kerala	Urban	95.5	71.4	99.9	99.9	77.0
		Total	95.2	72.2	99.4	99.4	79.6
		Rural	70.5	32.6	54.1	76.0	67.6
6	Maharashtra	Urban	84.3	37.1	87.2	89.1	72.6
		Total	74.4	33.9	63.5	79.7	69.0
		Rural	48.0	16.0	48.0	52.8	51.3
7	Gujarat	Urban	77.3	32.7	83.7	81.1	66.8
		Total	54.8	19.9	56.4	59.4	54.8
		Rural	42.8	14.7	37.8	41.7	50.0
	All India	Urban	67.5	29.5	70.4	69.7	62.5
		Total	49.7	18.8	46.9	49.5	53.5

Source: District Level Household and Facility Survey 3, 2007-08.

is surprisingly a decline among children belonging to the highest wealth quintile. They may have most likely used private health facilities. CES 2009 points out that Goa, Sikkim and Punjab have the highest proportion of children aged 12-23 fully immunised in India. As Pentavalent vaccines have been introduced in select States, beginning with Tamil Nadu and Kerala in 2011, results from NFHS 4 will provide an idea of coverage under the new Universal Immunisation Programme (UIP).

Considering the aggregate outcome indicators on maternal and child health, Tamil Nadu has already achieved the NRHM goal of Maternal Mortality Rate (MMR) below 100, reaching a value of 97 per one lakh live births, based on the Sample Registration Survey (SRS) data of 2007-09 (RGI, 2011). The MMR figures for the year 2010-11 based on State programme data (maternal death line listing) show a value of 79, which has reflected a further fall to 71 in the year 2011-12 (SHS, 2012: 10). However, the SRS figures for MMR in 2010-12 show that it has declined to only 90 (Table 5.3). This discrepancy needs to be reconciled and the early momentum in reduction of MMR has to be regained.

On the child health front, the Infant Mortality Rate (IMR) has fallen to 21 in 2013, well below the NRHM target of 30 per thousand live births (RGI, 2013a). The rate of fall of the IMR has also been faster in the years following NRHM than those preceding it. In the period between 2005 and 2013, the State recorded one of the largest falls in IMR in the country (Table 5.4).

Table 5.3

MMR for Tamil Nadu and Other Southern States (2011-12, 2007-2009, and 2004-2006)

India and Southern States	*Sample Female Population*	*Live Births*	*MMR 2010-2012*	*MMR 2007-2009*	*MMR 2004-2006*
India	6169091	430170	178	212	254
Andhra Pradesh	357699	22427	110	134	154
Karnataka	390941	21909	144	178	213
Kerala	305268	15351	66	81	95
Tamil Nadu	410769	22622	90	97	111
Subtotal	1464677	82309	105	127	149

Source: Registrar General of India (RGI, 2013b).

However, the State has witnessed a certain degree of deceleration in the improvement of IMR over the last two years—the causes for which need to be examined in detail and addressed. Figure 5.3 shows changes in IMR for rural and urban TN from early 1970s and Figure 5.4 shows IMR in major states of India, as of 2012. Table 5.4 shows that the State fares better across all health indicators compared to the all-India averages in many respects. TN CDR has however remained stagnant over the period 2005-2012 at 7.4, while all-India average has fallen to 7 by 2012.

Table 5.4

Tamil Nadu's Health Status in Comparison with All-India Status: Key Indicators

Health Indicators	2005		2012	
	TN	*All India*	*TN*	*All India*
CBR	16.5	23.8	15.6	21.4
CDR	7.4	7.5	7.3	7.0
TFR	1.7	2.9	1.7	2.3
IMR	37	58	21.0	40.0
MMR	111	254	79	167
U5M	36	69 (2008)	23	49
LE at Birth	66.7 (1997)	63.8 (m) 66.1 ((f) 2001-2005	68.6 (m) 71.8 (f)	67.3 (m) 69.6 (f)

Note: Crude Birth Rate (CBR), Crude Death Rate (CDR), Total Fertility Rate (TFR), Infant Mortality Rate (IMR), Maternal Mortality Ratio (MMR), Under 5 mortality (U5M) and Life Expectancy at Birth (LE).

Source: SRS 2011-2013 (RGI).

Figure 5.3

IMR for Tamil Nadu by Place of Residence

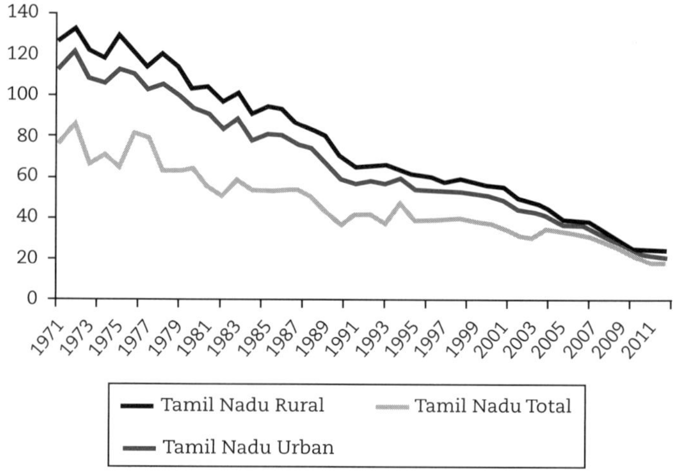

Source: RGI, 2013a.

While the State can be justifiably proud of these achievements, it is well documented that there are inequities in health outcomes across districts as measured by the departmental MMR figures. Similar variation is seen in the IMR figures as measured by the Vital Events Survey in 2008 (SHS, 2011). Studies based on the NFHS-3 also show inequities in mortality and morbidity indicators across income and caste (Krishnamurthy, 2008). The State cannot afford to ignore these differences, even though the reasons for their existence may not lie within the health system alone.

The State has always been a star performer in family welfare, with the Total Fertility Rate (TFR) falling to 2 by 1997, reaching the national goal of 2.1 well before

Figure 5.4

IMR in Tamil Nadu and Other Major States of India

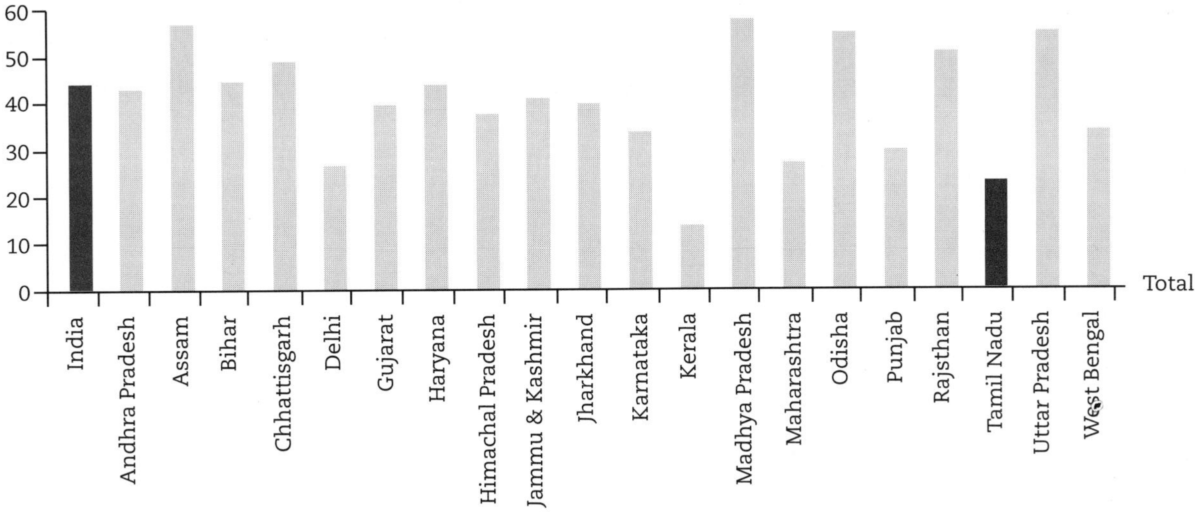

Source: RGI, 2013a.

Figure 5.5

Total Fertility Rate, Tamil Nadu and Other Major States of India, 2011

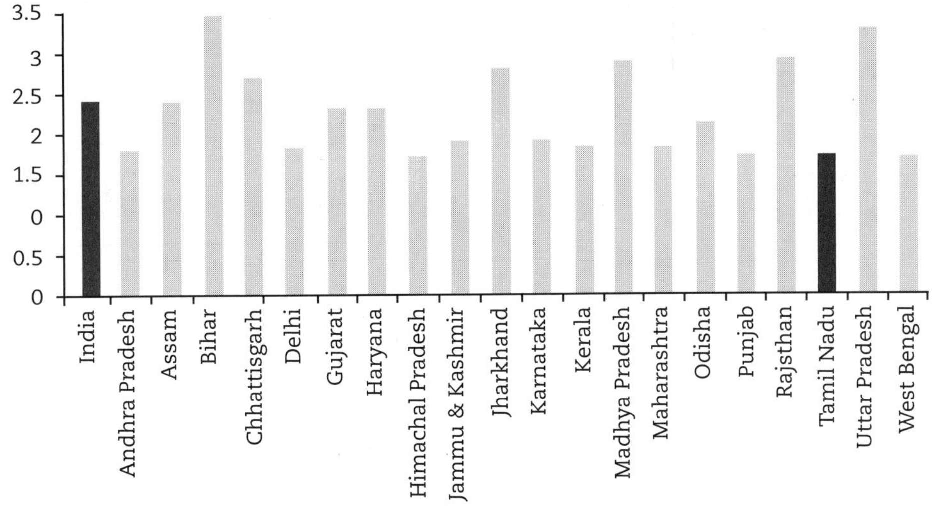

Source: SRS Statistical Report 2012.

the introduction of NRHM. As of 2013, Tamil Nadu's TFR stands at 1.7 (see Figure 5.5).

However, there is excessive dependence on female sterilisation, with 53.8 per cent of women reporting it as a method of family planning in comparison with 0.2 per cent of men (International Institute of Population Sciences, 2010). DLHS 3 had revealed that nearly three-fourth (73.6%) of the terminal methods of family planning were practiced in a government health facility, whereas only 24 per cent accessed a spacing method from government health facilities in Tamil Nadu. Further, in 2013-14, 25 per cent (81,554) of all the sterilisations were conducted in PHCs and 41 per cent in government hospitals (Government of Tamil Nadu, 2014). There is very low priority given to provision of accessible, safe abortion services in the public sector.

Cost of Care: Out-of-pocket Expenditure on Healthcare

Unlike most other States, Tamil Nadu has the distinction of having the lowest out-of-pocket

Table 5.5

Availability of Drinking Water, Toilet Facilities and Prevalence of Open Defecation Tamil Nadu, Andhra Pradesh (United), Karnataka, Kerala, Maharashtra, Gujarat and All-India, 2011 (as %)

S. No.	State	Place of residence	Drinking water –Tap water from treated source	Location of drinking water source within premises	Households having latrine facility within premises	Households having bathroom within premises	Open defecation
1	Tamil Nadu	Rural	46.1	17.0	23.2	26.1	73.3
		Urban	66.3	54.0	75.1	75.5	16.2
		Total	55.8	34.9	48.3	49.9	45.7
2	Andhra Pradesh (united)	Rural	36.4	31.5	32.2	33.9	65.1
		Urban	75.5	67.9	86.1	85.6	11.9
		Total	49.0	43.2	49.6	50.6	48
3	Karnataka	Rural	22.9	26.6	28.4	63.4	68.1
		Urban	68.4	70.9	84.9	91.7	10.7
		Total	41.2	44.5	51.2	74.8	45.0
4	Kerala	Rural	17.2	72.9	93.2	74.5	5.6
		Urban	30.4	83.3	97.4	88.8	1.7
		Total	23.4	77.7	95.2	81.2	3.8
5	Maharashtra	Rural	32.0	42.9	38.0	46.2	55.8
		Urban	85.7	79.3	71.3	86.0	7.7
		Total	56.3	59.4	53.1	64.3	34.0
6	Gujarat	Rural	16.7	48.3	33	33.6	65.8
		Urban	68.8	83.7	87.7	85.0	8.7
		Total	39.8	64.0	57.3	56.5	40.4
	All-India	Rural	17.9	35.0	30.7	25.4	67.3
		Urban	62.0	71.2	81.4	77.5	12.6
		Total	32.0	46.6	46.9	42.0	49.8

Source: Census of India (2011).

expenditure amongst those utilising public facilities. The out-of-pocket expenditure for hospitalisation in rural Tamil Nadu was only ₹637 as against ₹3,238 in the rest of India (NSSO, 2006: 29-35). However, the corresponding out-of-pocket expenditure in a private facility summed up to ₹8,360, and was higher than the all-India average value of ₹7,408 (NSSO, 2006: 42). The out-of-pocket cost for hospitalisation in public facilities for the poorest quintile was only ₹152, which was around 6 per cent of the all-India figure of ₹2,469, thereby proving that even before the advent of NRHM, the poorest were able to get inpatient care at very low cost in the State. In this context, it is significant to note that Tamil Nadu was the only State where the Patient Welfare Societies (PWS) were not authorised to collect user fees as a method of raising resources, regardless of being part of the NRHM mandate.

Water, Sanitation and Nutrition

No discussion on health is complete without a reference to access to water, sanitation and nutrition status of a population. Proportion of households having access to improved water[4] has increased from 94.7 per cent in 2007-08 to 97.4 per cent in 2012-13 (IIPS, 2014). Similarly, those with access to improved toilet facility increased from 38.8 per cent to 52.5 per cent during the same period. However, when compared to other southern States, Census of India (2011) shows that although a larger proportion of households in Tamil Nadu used tap water from treated source as drinking water, a lower proportion of households did have a proper drinking water source,

4. Improved source of water includes pipe water into dwelling, piped to yard/plot, public tap/standpipe/hand pump/tube well/bore well/well covered/protected spring, tanker/truck, cart with small tank/drum and packaged/bottled water

Table 5.6

Availability of Drinking Water, Toilet Facilities and Prevalence of Open Defecation in Districts of Tamil Nadu, 2011 (as %)

S. No.	Name of the district	Drinking water– Tap water from treated source	Location of drinking water source within premises	Households having latrine facility within the premises	Households having bathroom within the premises	Open defecation
1	Ariyalur	44.1	16.6	18.1	14.7	80.1
2	Chennai	79.0	76.3	95.6	95.6	0.6
3	Coimbatore	87.6	59.2	66.7	73.6	22.2
4	Cuddalore	49.5	33.4	36.1	32.6	61.8
5	Dharmapuri	27.6	9.9	19	24.2	79.0
6	Dindigul	50.9	25.0	33.3	43.7	58.7
7	Erode	63.8	35.6	49	52.5	41.9
8	Kancheepuram	56.7	43.8	65.5	67.6	32.5
9	Kanyakumari	45.5	38.8	87.5	51.7	7.1
10	Karur	58.5	36.9	41.2	43.4	53.2
11	Krishnagiri	47.3	18.9	33.0	44.2	64.3
12	Madurai	65.5	37.4	59.2	60.8	35.5
13	Nagapattinam	40.9	25.3	39.5	29.1	57.8
14	Namakkal	57.9	29.4	40.7	48.5	43.8
15	The Nilgiris	60.1	21.4	51.9	63.7	36.7
16	Perambalur	27.9	19.2	22.2	26.6	73.5
17	Pudukkottai	44.6	14.6	28.0	22.5	69.7
18	Ramanathapuram	29.1	10.5	36.6	30.7	60.0
19	Salem	62.1	24.7	35.0	43.2	53.9
20	Sivagangai	40.1	24.7	40.7	36.3	55.6
21	Thanjavur	30.2	34.7	45.1	35.6	50.9
22	Theni	76.0	39.3	39.3	62.7	40.1
23	Tiruchirappalli	66.6	41.0	48.5	48.3	43.1
24	Thiruvallur	46.0	36.6	67.9	69.6	29.9
25	Thiruvarur	23.0	25.0	39.7	27.3	56.8
26	Tirunelveli	72.5	36.2	47.6	45.3	43.1
27	Tiruppur	75.4	46.5	57.2	62.6	35.4
28	Tiruvannamalai	44.0	26.6	22.8	26.8	75.8
29	Thoothukudi	63.0	30.4	50.0	49.8	46.1
30	Vellore	49.9	35.0	41.1	48.8	56.5
31	Villupuram	41.5	16.7	21.1	22.6	77.2
32	Virudhunagar	45.0	21.5	30.9	46.9	52.4
	Tamil Nadu	55.8	34.9	48.3	49.9	45.7

Source: Census of India (2011).

latrine and bathroom within their homes (Table 5.6). Further, a larger proportion of households in Tamil Nadu defecate in the open than in Kerala, Karnataka, Maharashtra and Gujarat. Although Kerala has a lower proportion of households that use treated tap water for drinking, the State performs better than the States under comparison in terms of having drinking water source, bathroom and latrine within premises and very low proportion of households that report open defecation.

The district-wise pattern on sanitation show that Chennai and Coimbatore perform better than all the other districts (Table 5.6). While Chennai and Coimbatore have the highest proportion of households using tap water from a treated source for drinking, Chennai, Coimbatore, Kanyakumari and Thiruvallur have the lowest proportion of households defecating in the open.

Malnutrition (both under and over nutrition) among children and adults has the potential to depress human capability, increase vulnerability and reduce resilience of a population; or in other words, it has potential to reverse human development. If left unaddressed, undernutrition causes poor health among children, leaving them susceptible to illness and mortality. It also causes cognitive impairments leading to sub-optimal educational completion, which by reducing opportunities reinforces poverty and multiple deprivations. The consequences of obesity are no less, as it is a risk factor for NCDs. Access to food and dietary composition is no doubt a critical determinant of child undernutrition, but not the only one; the others being women's autonomy, maternal education, maternal nutritional status, utilisation of maternal healthcare services, caste, early marriage and early child bearing, birth order, child care and feeding practices, sanitation and hygiene, income group, traditional beliefs/taboos about food and living arrangements. It has been argued that the main factor that explains high level of stunting among Indian children is the practice of open defecation (Coffey *et al.*, 2013). India's shocking record in under-five child undernutrition up to 2005-06 has received considerable attention prompting the Supreme Court to order that the Integrated Child Development Scheme (ICDS) and Midday Meal Scheme (MDMS) be universalised, which is the world's largest child feeding programme. Information gathered from the NFHS (population-based survey) conducted in 2005-06 revealed that in India, 42.5 per cent of children under the age of five were underweight, 48 per cent were stunted and 19.8 per cent were wasted. Child underweight (weight for age minus 2 standard deviation [SD]) is a comprehensive indicator of nutritional status, as it reflects chronic and acute malnutrition; stunting (height for age minus 2 SD) reflects linear growth retardation and indicates chronic undernutrition; and wasting (weight for height minus 2 SD) is an indicator of acute malnutrition as a result of recent illness. When compared to the national average, in 2005-06, the situation in Tamil Nadu was better with lower percentage of underweight children (29.8%) and stunted children (30.9%), although the State had a higher percentage of children who were wasted (22.2%). It is evident that Tamil Nadu's long history in implementing social security schemes (described in the chapter on social security) for nutrition, education and health, particularly the public distribution system, MDMS, ICDS and those focussing on girl's education, has played a role in enabling such a situation. In fact, the State performs comparatively well in maintaining lower rates of chronic malnutrition (stunting) among children, exhibiting the third lowest rate after Kerala (24.5%) and Goa (25.6%), although the prevalence of malnutrition was fairly high even among these better performing States. The earlier discussion on sanitation has highlighted that Tamil Nadu had relatively higher proportion of households defecating in the open, which could be one of the reasons for 30 per cent of the under-five children to be stunted in 2005-06.

Figure 5.6

Nutrition Status of Children Below Three Years in Tamil Nadu, Between 1998-99 and 2005-06

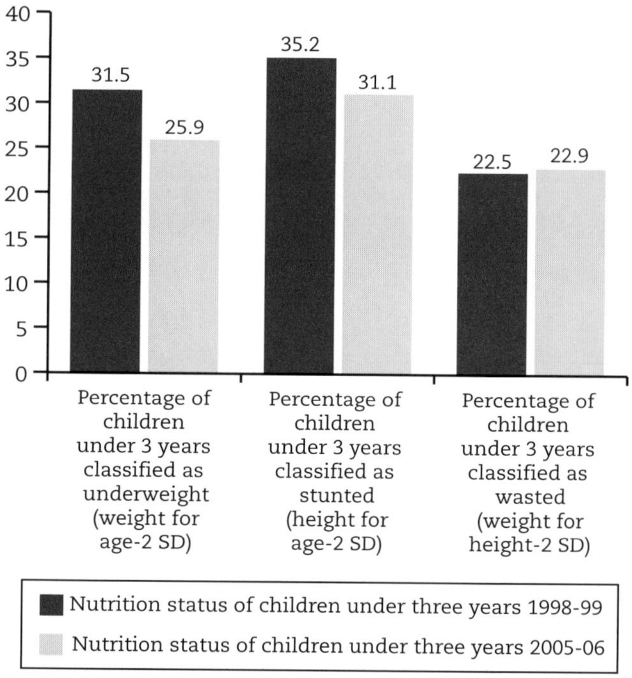

Source: International Institute of Population Sciences (IIPS) and Macro International (2008).

On the nutrition front, both positive and negative trends are observed over time in Tamil Nadu, when data on undernutrition for children under three years is compared between NFHS 2 and NFHS 3[5] (Figure 5.6): Firstly, the proportion of underweight children (below age 3) has decreased from 31.5 per cent in

5. As NFHS 2 collected information on children under three years, for comparison, NFHS 3 data on the same has been used. All indicators of malnutrition are expressed in SD units from the median of the 2006 WHO International Reference Population.

Table 5.7

Nutritional Status of Children Below Five Years and Pregnant Women in Tamil Nadu, Andhra Pradesh, Karnataka, Kerala, Maharashtra and Gujarat, 2005-06 (as %)

S No	State	Place of residence	Percentage of children under 5 years classified as underweight (weight for age-2 SD)	Percentage of children under 5 years classified as stunted (height for age-2 SD)	Percentage of children under 5 years classified as wasted (weight for height-2 SD)	Percentage of children (6-59 months) with anaemia	Percentage of adult women (age 15-49 years) with anaemia
1	Tamil Nadu	Rural	32.1	31.3	22.6	63.4	54.2
		Urban	27.1	30.5	21.6	65.1	52.0
		Total	29.8	30.9	22.2	64.2	53.2
2	Andhra Pradesh	Rural	34.8	45.8	13.0	72.7	64.6
		Urban	28.0	36.7	10.7	66.8	59.7
		Total	32.5	42.7	12.2	70.8	62.9
3	Karnataka	Rural	41.1	47.7	18.2	72.0	53.5
		Urban	30.7	36.0	16.5	67.1	48.3
		Total	37.6	43.7	17.6	70.4	51.5
4	Kerala	Rural	26.4	25.6	18.2	44.6	32.2
		Urban	15.4	22.2	10.9	44.4	34.1
		Total	22.9	24.5	15.9	44.5	32.8
5	Maharashtra	Rural	41.6	49.1	18.2	66.8	50.6
		Urban	30.7	42.3	14.1	58.7	46.0
		Total	37.0	46.3	16.5	63.4	48.4
6	Gujarat	Rural	47.9	54.8	19.9	74.6	58.7
		Urban	39.2	46.6	16.7	61.9	50.9
		Total	44.6	51.7	18.7	69.7	55.3
	All India	Rural	45.6	50.7	20.7	71.5	57.4
		Urban	32.7	39.6	16.9	63.0	50.9
		Total	42.5	48.0	19.8	69.5	55.3

Source: National Family Health Survey 3, 2005-06.

1998-99 to 25.9 per cent in 2005-06; secondly, stunting among under-3 children has declined from 35.2 per cent to 31.1 per cent over the same period; but lastly, wasting (weight for height) among under-3 children has worsened from 22.5 per cent in 1998-99 to 22.9 per cent by 2005-06.

Anaemia among children under five years was high at 69 per cent in 2005-06. Furthermore, anaemia among children under three years increased from 69 per cent in 1998-99 to 72.7 per cent in 2005-06. Under-five anaemia was higher among male children, children of mothers without education, those with anaemic mothers, Hindus, SCs, and children living with both parents instead of one and in urban areas (IIPS, 2008). This observation has to be read with the fact that 53.2 per cent of adult women in Tamil Nadu had anaemia.

Among the States under comparison, Kerala had the lowest proportion of children under five years who were underweight and stunted, Andhra Pradesh had the lowest prevalence of wasting and Gujarat had the highest proportion of children who were underweight and stunted.

A higher percentage of children who were small at birth (38.8%) were underweight than those who were normal or average size at birth (24.9%) in Tamil Nadu (IIPS, 2008). In 2005-06, Tamil Nadu has a lower proportion of infants (less than 6 months) being exclusively breastfed (34.1%) than Kerala (56.2%). A larger proportion of boys than girls were underweight, stunted and wasted (Table 5.7). The need to focus attention on birth spacing is brought out by the fact that under five, underweight and stunting rates decline

Table 5.8

Nutritional Status of Children Below Five Years in Tamil Nadu by Background Characteristics, 2005-06 (as %)

Background characteristics		*Percentage of children under 5 years classified as underweight (weight for age -2 SD)*	*Percentage of children under 5 years classified as stunted (height for age -2 SD)*	*Percentage of children under 5 years classified as wasted (weight for height -2 SD)*
Gender	Male	31.5	32.7	31.5
	Female	28.0	29.0	28.0
Birth interval in months	First birth	28.3	27.0	21.4
	<24	34.7	42.7	19.9
	24-47	32.4	34.8	24.9
	48+	23.8	25.4	16.7
Birth order	1	28.2	26.9	21.5
	2-3	29.6	33.2	19.5
	4-5	40.6	45.6	33.9
Mother's education	No education	41.6	44.4	27.4
	<5 years complete	35.4	37.0	20.9
	5-9 years complete	33.5	34.0	25.6
	10 or more years complete	17.7	19.1	14.1
Religion	Hindu	31.8	32.7	22.9
	Muslim	15.0	13.6	26.8
	Christian	13.4	19.1	7.9
Caste/tribe	SC	40.2	39.7	26.7
	ST	NA	NA	NA
	OBC	26.3	28.2	20.8
	Others	15.9	10.6	15.4
Mother's nutritional status	Underweight (BMI<18.5)	37.7	37.6	26.7
	Normal (BMI 18.5-24.9)	29.7	30.9	21.8
	Overweight (BMI>25.0)	18.8	22.4	14.8
Child's living arrangements	Living with both parents	31.0	31.8	22.0
	Living with one or neither parent	24.4	26.6	22.8
Wealth index	Lowest	43.1	40.1	27.7
	Second	38.0	37.7	31.4
	Middle	34.1	35.4	22.0
	Fourth	26.7	28.3	20.4
	Highest	9.2	13.2	13.4

Source: IIPS, National Family Health Survey 3, 2005-06.

with increase in birth interval. Wasting is lowest when the birth interval is more than four years. Similarly, underweight and stunting prevalence increases with birth order. Maternal education has an important role in child development. In Tamil Nadu, underweight and stunting was higher among children whose mothers had no education (41.6% and 44.4% respectively) than those whose mothers had 10 or more years of education (33.5% and 34% respectively), thereby indicating the important role that education plays in improving capabilities (Table 5.8). The proportion of underweight and stunted children was highest among Hindus and least among Muslims, whereas wasting was highest among Muslims and least among Christians. The SC children exhibited a higher prevalence of underweight, stunting and wasting. The proportion of children who were underweight, stunted and wasted was greater among those whose mothers were underweight, underscoring the important role that maternal health plays in determining child undernutrition. Under-five stunting and underweight were lower among children who lived with single parents or no parent than those living with both parents, which could be because single parents are more independent in taking decisions about their child's health. Economic background of the household also plays a role in influencing children's undernutrition, with prevalence of underweight and stunting declining with increasing wealth quintile.

Information from NFHS 3 on child care practices will offer some insights about determinants of undernutrition. Incorrect feeding practices among children were higher in Tamil Nadu than in Kerala, with 20.6 per cent of the children being given a pre-lacteal feeding when compared to 10.8 per cent in Kerala (IIPS, 2007). In addition, in Tamil Nadu, only 34.1 per cent of infants less than 6 months were exclusively breastfed (24-hour recall period). Further, 28.9 per cent of all children (6-23 months) were fed with recommended Infant and Young Child Feeding (IYCF) practices in Tamil Nadu, whereas it was 61 per cent of the children (6-23 months)in Kerala. In addition, only 12 per cent of the children (age 6-59 months) in Tamil Nadu were given deworming medication six months preceding the survey, compared to 44.7 per cent in Kerala (IIPS, 2007). The relatively higher proportion of under-five wasting in Tamil Nadu can be associated with poor knowledge and practice about management of diarrhoea, apart from poor sanitation and management of other illnesses. Information from NFHS 3 had shown that in Tamil Nadu, only 9.6 per cent of the children suffering from diarrhoea were given more fluids as per UNICEF guidelines, compared to 44.1 per cent in Kerala (IIPS, 2007). Besides management of diarrhoea, another factor that can cut down wasting is safe disposal of children's excrement, which prevents spreading of infections. Only 22.1 per cent of children's excrement was disposed safely in Tamil Nadu, in comparison with 73.7 per cent in Kerala and 73.5 per cent in Sikkim (IIPS, 2007).

As discussed earlier, maternal undernutrition (low BMI or body mass index) is a risk factor for child undernutrition. A BMI of less than 18.5 indicates Chronic Energy Deficiency (CED). Information from NFHS 3 highlights that a relatively low percentage of adult men and women in Tamil Nadu and Kerala had CED compared to the other southern States, Maharashtra and Gujarat (Table 5.9). CED was higher among women than men in all the States under comparison, except Kerala. Tamil Nadu and Kerala also had the highest proportion of adult men and women who were obese and obesity was considerably higher among adult women than men, implying that these two States face a higher risk of NCDs among women

Table 5.9

Chronic Energy Deficiency and Obesity according to BMI Grades among Adults (18 Years and Above) in Tamil Nadu, Andhra Pradesh, Karnataka, Kerala, Maharashtra and Gujarat, 2005-06 (as %)

S. No.	*State*	*Chronic energy deficiency (<18.5)*		*Obesity (>30)*	
		Male	*Female*	*Male*	*Female*
1	Tamil Nadu	27.1	28.4	2.0	5.1
2	Andhra Pradesh	30.8	33.5	1.9	4.1
3	Karnataka	33.9	35.5	1.7	3.7
4	Kerala	21.5	18.0	2.1	5.0
5	Maharashtra	33.5	36.2	1.6	3.6
6	Gujarat	36.1	36.3	2.0	4.6
	All India	34.2	35.6	1.3	2.8

Source: IIPS, National Family Health Survey 3, 2005-06.

Way Forward

Several challenges persist even in the present day. But it is important to address a few key issues in the immediate future as they are likely to have long-term implications.

1. There are considerable variations within and across district in IMR, MMR, and neonatal deaths. Most districts have blocks that are suffering from the lack of access to primary and secondary care services; this is so, even in most developed districts such as Coimbatore, where children continue to suffer from highly preventable conditions such as dysentery and diarrhoea. While efforts are being made to reduce such inequities in health status, significant improvements in the overall health status can be addressed, only if such inequities are reduced systematically as the primary objective of public health policy of the State.

2. While it is obvious that government spending in absolute amount has gone up significantly over the past five years, its share in the overall State budget has remained the same around four per cent; in terms of State domestic product, it is just about 1 per cent. The share

of health and family welfare in the total State budget should be much more than it is now.

3. Despite the recent spurt in recruitment of medical and paramedical persons both in primary and secondary delivery system, there is a huge shortage of manpower at various levels in the delivery system. Not only specialists, but even field functionaries at primary care level are in short supply. Every round of recruitment faces unexpected legal and other barriers, but it is important to address this bottleneck and strengthen the manpower required to improve access to effective care. Several secondary level facilities, particularly district hospitals, require careful and immediate attention to strengthen paramedical staff specifically. There is a clear case for strengthening human resources at the sub-centre level across the State. There is an urgent need to (re)open training institutions for VHNs and other functionaries and also continue training for enhancing quality of services delivered by them. The State is now in the process of re-establishing training institutions and in augmenting the strength of VHNs at HSC level. This needs immediate attention.

4. Tamil Nadu's primary healthcare delivery system has received considerable attention over the years and is being viewed as a model system for rest of the country. Yet, it is true that HSCs (Health Sub Centres) over the years have not received as much attention as PHCs. Both building infrastructure and additional staff (VHNs) at HSC level require immediate attention. This will have visible and immediate positive impact on overall functioning of the public primary healthcare system and the extent to which this can reduce the financial burden of people.

5. Private health sector has grown passively over the year. The presence of private providers in the tertiary sector is noteworthy. Yet, a concern is noticed from various quarters with regard to the overall quality and cost of care obtained through private providers. The State must implement the Private Clinical Establishment Act, which was introduced more than 15 years ago, but is yet to be implemented. This will go a long way in facilitating improved governance of private health sector and ensure accountability.

6. The State should formulate and implement specific policy measures, with a view to achieve Universal Health Coverage (UHC) before the end of the current decade.

7. Despite improvements in overall health parameters, the state needs to address the issue of malnutrition among pregnant women and children. Importantly, the state's relatively poor performance in terms of provisioning sanitation facilities despite good economic development emerges as a policy issue that requires urgent attention.

References

Acharya, D., G. Vaidyanathan, V.R. Muraleedharan, S.D. Vaishnavi and U. Dash (2011). *Do the Poor Benefit from Public Spending on Healthcare in India? Results from Benefit (Utilisation) Incidence Analysis in Tamil Nadu and Orissa.* The Consortium for Research on Equitable Health Systems (CREHS) London: London School of Hygiene and Tropical Medicine. pp.19-29.

Anjana R.M., R. Pradeepa, M. Deepa, M. Datta, V. Sudha, R. Unnikrishnan, A. Bhansali, S.R. Joshi, P.P. Joshi, C.S. Yajnik, V.K. Dhandhania, L.M. Nath, A.K. Das, P.V. Rao, S.V. Madhu, D.K. Shukla, T. Kaur, M. Priya, E. Nirmal, S.J. Parvathi, S. Subhashini, R. Subashini, M.K. Ali, V. Mohan (2011). "Prevalence of Diabetes and Pre-Diabetes (Impaired Fasting Glucose and/or Impaired Glucose Tolerance) in Urban and Rural India: Phase I Results of the ICMR-INDIAB Study", *Diabetologia 54: 3022-27.*

Balabanova, D., M. Mckee and A. Mills (eds.). *Good Health at Low Cost: 25 Years on—What Makes a Successful Health System.*London: London School of Hygiene and Tropical Medicine. pp.159-92.

Central Bureau of Health Intelligence (CBHI) (2003). *Medical Care Statistics.* New Delhi: Ministry of Health and Family Welfare.

Health and Family Welfare Department (HFW) (2011). *Policy Note 2011-12.* Chennai: Government of Tamil Nadu.

———. (2012). *Policy Note 2012-13.* Chennai: Government of Tamil Nadu.

———. (2013). *Policy Note 2013-14.* Chennai: Government of Tamil Nadu.

———. (2014) *Policy Note 2014-15.* Chennai: Government of Tamil Nadu.

International Institute for Population Sciences (IIPS) (2010). *District Level Household and Facility Survey (DLHS-3), 2007-08: India. Tamil Nadu*: Mumbai: IIPS.

———. (2014). *District Level Household and Facility Survey (DLHS-4), 2012-13: State Fact Sheet Tamil Nadu*: Mumbai: IIPS.

International Institute for Population Sciences (IIPS) and Macro International. (2007). *National Family Health Survey (NFHS-3), 2005–06: India: Volume I.* Mumbai: IIPS.

———. (2008). *National Family Health Survey (NFHS 3) India 2005-06 Tamil Nadu.* Mumbai: International Institute of Population Sciences. p.53.

Krishnamurthy, S. (2008). *Inequalities in Health Status and in Access and Utilisation of Healthcare Services in Tamil Nadu: Evidences from the National Family Health Surveys*. Chengalpattu, Tamil Nadu: Rural Women's Social Education Centre (RUWSEC).

Kumar A.K.S., L.C. Chen, M. Choudhury, S. Ganju, V. Mahajan and A. Sinha (2011). "Financing Health Care For All: Challenges and Opportunities", *The Lancet* 377(9766): 668-79.

Mahal A, J. Singh, F. Afridi, V. Lamba, A. Gumber and V. Selvaraju (2000). *Who Benefits from Public Health Spending in India*. New Delhi: National Council for Applied Economic Research.

Ministry of Health and Family Welfare (MoHFW) (2009). *National Health Accounts 2004-05*. New Delhi: Government of India. pp. 5-8.

Muraleedharan, V.R., U. Dash and L. Gilson (2011). "Tamil Nadu 1980–2005: A Success Story in India", in D. Balabanova, M. Mckee and A. Mills (eds.), *Good Health at Low Cost: 25 Years On—What Makes a Successful Health System*. London: London School of Hygiene and Tropical Medicine. pp. 159-92.

National Crime Records Bureau (2014). *Accidental Deaths and Suicides in India 2013*. New Delhi: Ministry of Home Affairs

National Sample Survey Organization (NSSO) (2006). *Morbidity Health Care and the Condition of the Aged*. New Delhi: Ministry of Statistics and Programme Implementation. pp.18-42.

Registrar General, India (RGI) (2011). *Sample Registration System: Special Bulletin on Maternal Mortality in India 2007-09*. New Delhi: Government of India.

———. (2012). *SRS Based Abridged Life Tables 2003-07 To 2006-10*. New Delhi: Government of India. pp.1-28.

———. (2013a). *Sample Registration System: SRS Bulletin 2012*. New Delhi: Government of India.

———. (2013b). *Sample Registration System: Special Bulletin on Maternal Mortality in India 2010-12*. New Delhi: Government of India.

State Health Society (SHS) (2011). *Vital Events Survey 2008*. Chennai: State Health Society and Directorate of Public Health and Preventive Medicine.

State Health Society (SHS) (2012). *Project Implementation Plan (PIP) 2012-13*. Chennai: Government of Tamil Nadu.

Tamil Nadu State Planning Commission (TNSPC) (2003). *Tamil Nadu Human Development Report*. Chennai: Government of Tamil Nadu and New Delhi: Social Sciences Press. pp.13-14.

UNICEF (2010a), Coverage Evaluation Survey: All India Report, New Delhi: UNICEF

———. (2010b).*Coverage Evaluation Survey: Tamil Nadu Fact Sheet*. New Delhi: UNICEF.

6

Gender in Human Development

The promotion of gender equality and empowerment of women is one of the eight Millennium Development Goals (MDGs) to which India is a signatory. Including women's empowerment and gender equality in one MDG goal implicitly recognises that gender equality and women's empowerment are both equally relevant and importantly inter-linked. The concepts are multidimensional, resulting in a large number of potential indicators. Indicators of empowerment/disempowerment and gender equality/inequality are typically designed to compare the status of women and men on particular characteristics of interest and are not relative figures. In common parlance, the terms gender and sex are often used interchangeably; however, they are distinct concepts. Then again, sex of individuals is largely determined by biology while their gender is socially constructed and comprises of the roles, of rights, and obligations attached to them on the basis of their sex. Kishor (2006) identifies three important aspects of gender, namely:

a) Gender is not value neutral. The roles, rights, and obligations assigned to each sex are not just different, but also unequal, with male roles and rights generally being valued more highly than that of females.

b) Gender involves differences in power, both 'power to' and 'power over'. The concept of power encompasses legal and informal rights, access to resources, and pursuit of knowledge and personal goals. This cuts across most domains of human functioning, including familial, cultural and institutional domains. 'Power over' refers to control over societal and household resources, and decisions, cultural and religious ideology, and one's own and others' bodies. Importantly, men tend to have greater power than women, and, in some domains, even have power over women.

c) Gender is neither static nor immutable. Being socially constructed, gender roles, rights, and expectations can change over time and across geographical space as societal needs, opportunities, and customs change.

The characteristics stated as (a) and (b) reflect inequalities based on gender, as also the disempowerment of females, which is pervasive in most patriarchal societies. Gender-based differences in power and resource access have consequences for quality of life of the population. The inequalities find expression in many ways—explicit and implicit. The explicit measures can be tracked and are revealed in statistics depicting differences in sex ratio, child infanticide, literacy rates, health and nutrition indicators, wage differentials and ownership of land and property. Implicit measures are not visible and are embedded in power and culture. These intra-household inequalities result in unequal distribution of power, unequal control over resources and decision-making; and unfair, unequal distribution of work, drudgery and even food. Gender disaggregated data and indices are a tools that helps to identify genders inequalities, determine issues to be addressed, take steps to redress the inequalities, provide feedback on effectiveness of the actions and re-prioritise allocation of resources.

The development of any nation or area does not necessarily follow a uniform path. Also, the direction, pace or intensity of growth do not exhibit unique patterns (Kelley, 1991; Krishnaji, 1997; Rustagi, 2000). That is to say, any impetus or stimulant introduced into the existing state of affairs does not always lead to a predetermined outcome and even the path adopted to attain or reach the goal set out often varies from one case to another. This is because the trajectory of growth is a dynamic process. The presence and operation of these multiple factors, each of which can assume a different form with the slightest change occurring in any dimension, makes the process dynamic. The objective of gender development indicators is to be able to generate specific sets of information that can be usefully utilised for identification and intervention for improvement in the status of women.

The chapter seeks to address the following issues in separate sections.

- Comparisons based on Gender Inequality Index (GII).
- Status of women:
  - Sex ratio—adult and child—comparison and analysis *vis-à-vis* India and State.
  - Changes in ratio—favourable/adverse status of women.
- Socio-Economic Empowerment of Women:
  - Female literacy rate and gender gap.
  - Girls in higher education.
  - Female wages and WFPR (workforce participation rate).
  - Crimes and violence against women.
  - Political participation.
- Female-headed households:
  - Family size.

- Access to facilities—toilets, water, assets and credit.
- Gender-specific concerns and interventions at policy and programmatic levels, including legal provisions.

Gender Inequality Index

The GII is designed to reveal the extent to which achievements in these aspects of human development are eroded by gender inequality, and to provide empirical foundations for policy analysis and advocacy efforts. Table 6.1 ranks the districts into better faring and poorly districts.

Table 6.1

GII Index: District-wise

	GII Index	
District	*Index*	*Rank*
Top 5 Districts		
The Nilgiris	0.036	1
Virudhunagar	0.048	2
Vellore	0.051	3
Nammakkal	0.054	4
Perambalur	0.057	5
Middle Districts		
Erode	0.065	11
Kanyakumari	0.066	12
Karur	0.070	13
Tirupur	0.070	14
Dharmapuri	0.074	15
Bottom 5 Districts		
Chennai	0.111	28
Madurai	0.112	29
Villupuram	0.113	30
Sivagangai	0.114	31
Ariyalur	0.118	32

The GII of the State is best in the Nilgiris district where gender inequality is closest to zero (0.036), whereas inequality is highest in Ariyalur district whose index is 0.118. In Ariyalur district, most of the gender related indicators—female literacy rates, female agricultural wage rates, etc.—are low. A lower score in terms of indicators relating to capabilities, livelihood and empowerment has widened gender inequality in the district. Kanyakumari's health indicators appears favourable in terms of low MMR (Maternal Mortality Ratio) and high institutional deliveries, but due to other factors, its position has moved to the middle level at rank 12 despite a high HDI (human development index). Kanyakumari's inequality is more due to the high differential in the livelihood indicator as one finds that female wage rates are half of the male's wage and their workforce participation rate is also considerably lower. Madurai is one of the districts which had high MMR and so the district has moved to the bottom five districts in GII. Virudhunagar had the highest female political representation, while Nilgiris had the lowest. Female agricultural wage as stated in the earlier section was the highest in Salem and lowest in Villupuram.

One of the key indicators that reflect the position of women in the society is sex ratio (SR), which is being dealt in the first section.

Sex Ratio

A strong correlation exists between poor human development indicators and gender disparity. However, there are other forms of gender discrimination which are worse in places, where traditional human development indicators are good. It is more apparent in aversion towards daughters, also manifesting as 'son preference'. The intensity of this form of gender discrimination is evident from the worsening sex ratios, but is often not correlated with poor human development indicators.

Sex Ratio Differences in the Census Period

Figure 6.1 Indicates that the northern parts of India have reported far lower rates of sex ratio when compared to southern India. But even among the southern states there are marked differentials in the sex ratio.

The sex ratio of Tamil Nadu declined every census period until 1971 since 1901; but post-1991, there has been an increase (Figure 6.2). The State has in the 2011 census crossed the sex ratio that was recorded in 1961. Though the State's overall sex ratio has improved, there are inter-district disparities. Nilgiris district in the State has the highest sex ratio with 1041 and Dharmapuri with 946 has the lowest sex ratio (Table 6.2). Thoothukudi, which held the first rank in terms of sex ratio in the previous census, has now moved down to the fourth rank. Ramanathapuram, which was at the fourth rank in the previous census, is now among the bottom five districts with adverse sex ratio. In Tamil Nadu, a few districts with adverse sex ratio were identified and specific interventions were undertaken.

The changes in sex ratio in the last two censuses

Figure 6.1

India: Sex Ratio Map, 2011

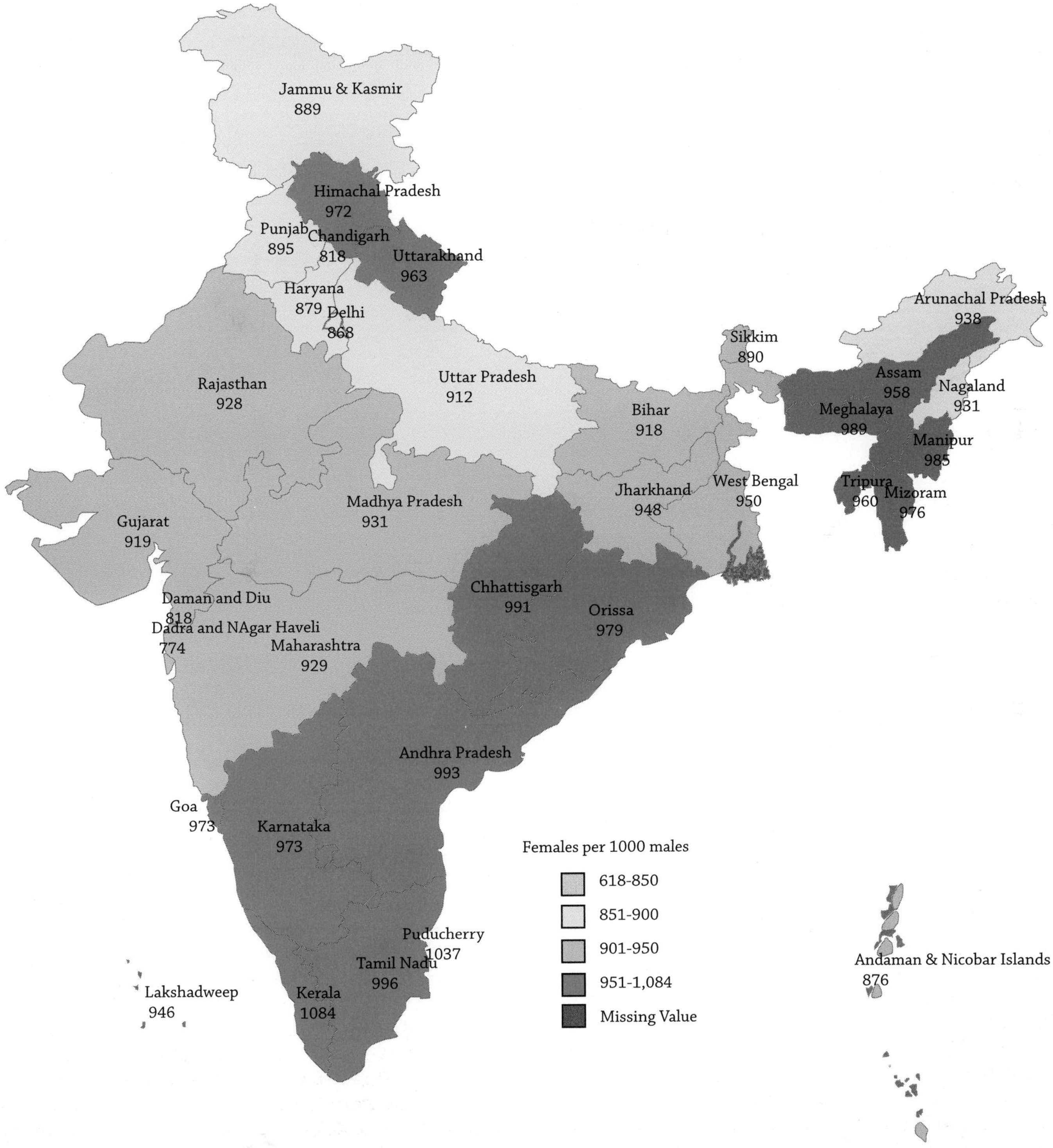

Note: The sex ratio map of India indicates sex ratio as per the 2011 Census. There are disparities in the sex ratio across States. Kerala has the highest sex ratio and Haryana has the lowest with 877. The Union Territories of Daman and Diu and Dadra and Nagar Haveli, Chandigarh and New Delhi fare worse than many States.

Source: Maps of India, 2011.

Figure 6.2

Tamil Nadu Sex Ratio, 1901-2011

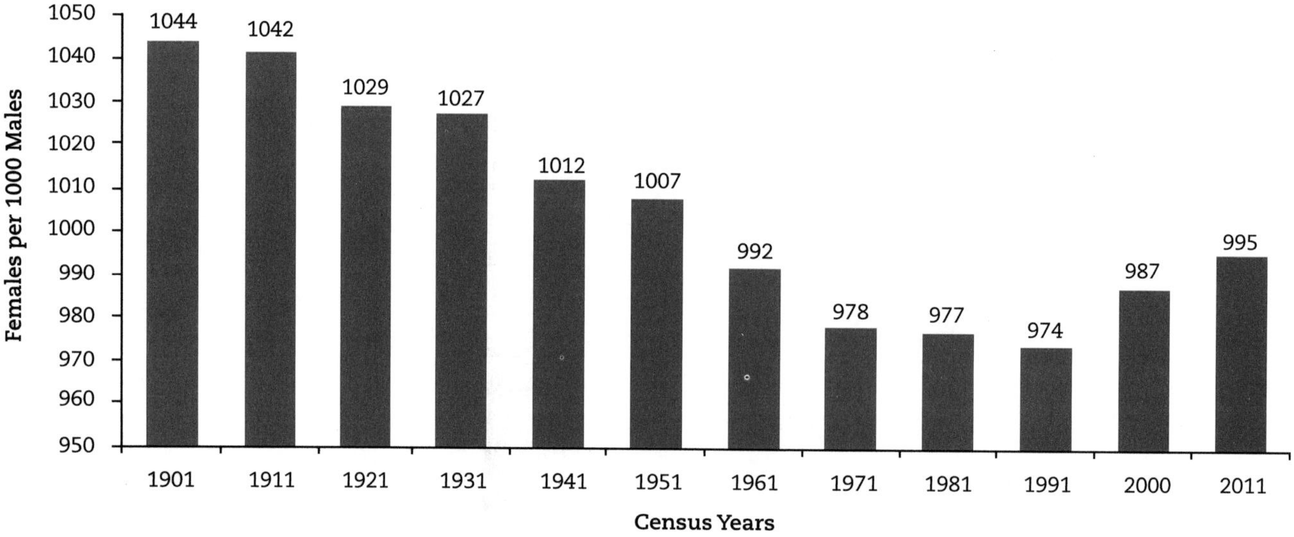

Source: Census of India, 2011.

have been presented in Figure 6.3(a) for a clear understanding of the districts, in which there have been extreme changes. There has been a decline in 10 districts when compared to the previous census. The maximum differentials are mostly seen in the districts of Theni, Ramnathapuram, Sivaganga, Thoothukudi and Tirunelveli.

According to available data, the practice of female infanticide was prevalent in the districts of Dharmapuri, Salem, Namakkal, Theni, Madurai, Karur, Dindugul, Erode and Vellore, with occasional occurrence in others (Gender Profile of Tamil Nadu, NCW, 2004).

Table 6.2

Changes in Sex Ratio in the Inter-Census Period (2001-2011)

State/District	*2001*	*2011*	*Change in SR 2011-2001*
Tamil Nadu	987	995	8
Thiruvalur	971	983	12
Chennai	957	986	29
Kancheepuram	975	985	10
Vellore	997	1004	7
Dharmapuri	932	946	14
Krishanagiri	944	956	12
Tiruvannamalai	995	993	-2
Vilupuram	984	985	1
Salem	929	954	25
Namakkal	966	986	20
Erode	968	992	24
The Nilgris	1014	1041	27
Coimbatore	968	1001	33
Tiruppur	**963**	**988**	**25**
Dindigul	986	998	12
Karur	1010	1015	5
Tiruchirappalli	1001	1013	12
Perambalur	1006	1006	0
Ariyalur	1006	1016	10
Cuddalore	986	984	-2
Nagappattinam	1014	1025	11
Thiruvarur	1014	1020	6
Thanjavur	1021	1013	-8
Pudukkottai	1015	1015	0
Sivaganga	1038	1000	-38
Madurai	978	990	12
Theni	978	900	-78
Virudhunagar	1012	1009	-3
Ramanathapuram	1036	997	-39
Thoothukkudi	1050	1024	-26
Tirunelveli	1042	1024	-18
Kanyakumari	1014	1010	-4

Source: Census of India, 2011.

Figure 6.3

Tamil Nadu Sex Ratio 2011

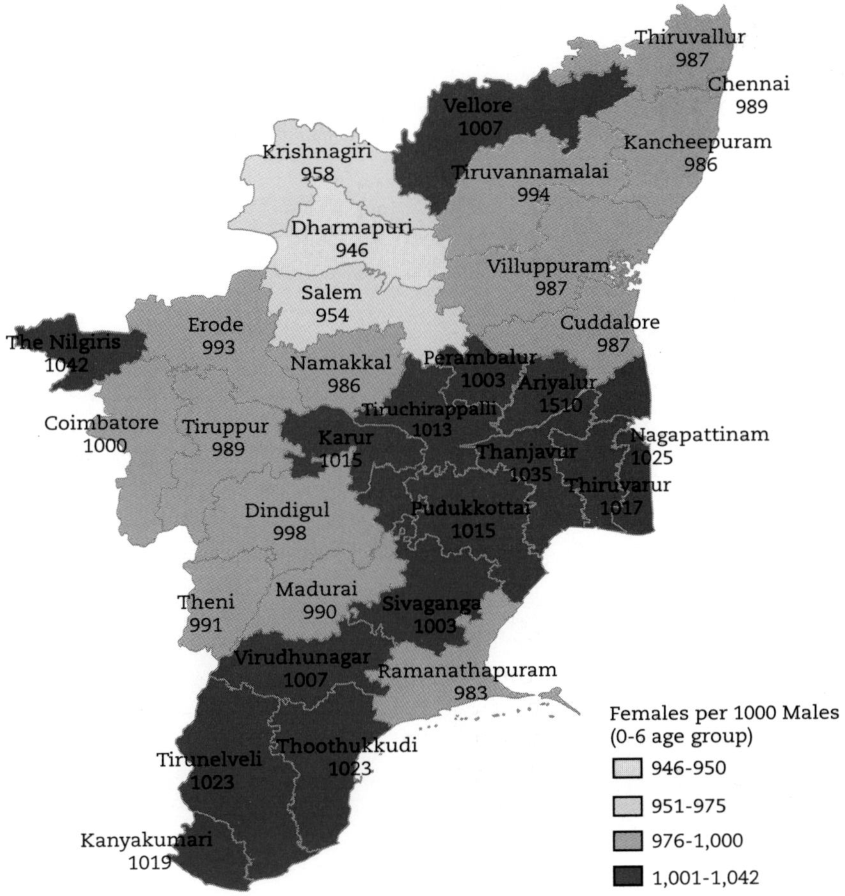

Source: Census of India, 2011.

Figure 6.3(a)

Tamil Nadu: Change in Sex Ratio, 2001-2011

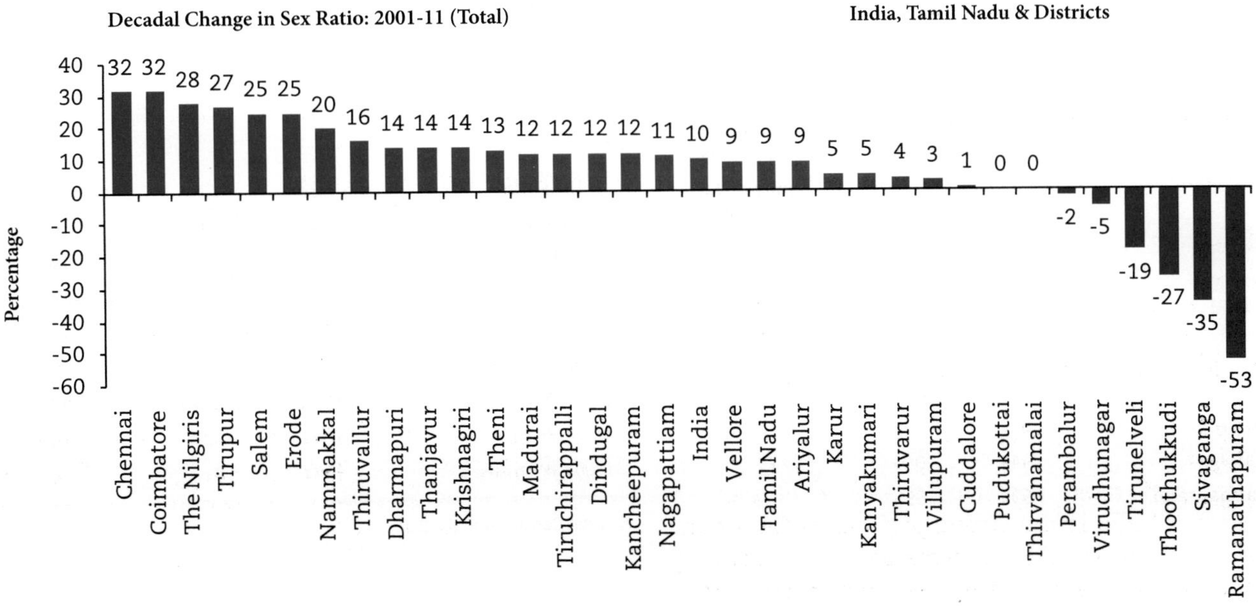

Note: Chennai district has been excluded as it is entirely urban.

Figure 6.4 presents the results of interventions and the corresponding rise in SR in the districts. The districts of Dharmapuri, Salem, Theni and Namakkal have shown improvement in the past two censuses. An increase by 85 points in Dharmapuri district was noted, where there was a campaign mode intervention through Kalajathas in order to address this adverse SR. Campaign against female infanticide has been successful with involvement of the government, community and leaders of the local bodies where it was launched with intensity, as in the case of Dharmapuri (Athreya and Chunkath, 2000).

Figure 6.4

Improvements in Districts with History of Low Chid Sex Ratio

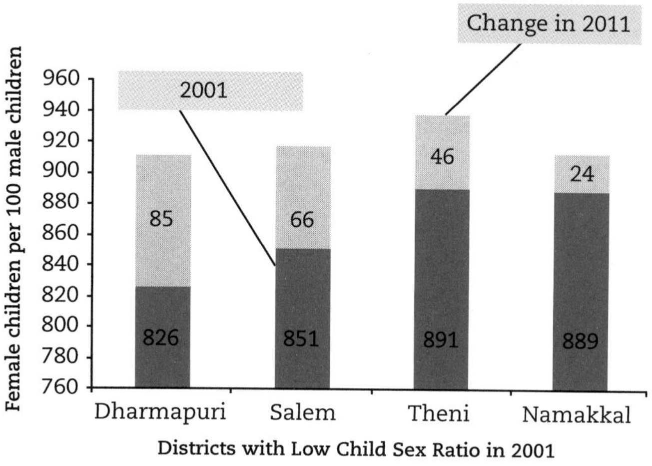

Source: Department of Social Welfare.

The Twelfth Five Year Plan (FYP) of Tamil Nadu highlights this issue and discusses how reception centres were being opened in the above districts to address the same. The role of the State attains significance in preventing harm and protecting girls and women on one hand, and promoting women empowerment, gender equality and male transformation on the other.

The next section discusses child sex ratio in detail. Among the States/Union Territories, the highest child sex ratio (0-6 years) is reported by Mizoram (971), followed by Meghalaya (970), Andaman & Nicobar Islands (966), Puducherry (965) and Chhattisgarh (964).

Child Sex Ratio

A critical and most powerful indicator of gender inequality in India is the strong preference for a son, which manifests itself as adverse sex ratio, limiting the birth and survival of girls. The decline over time in the child sex ratio could be attributed to one or more of the three possible main causes: a decrease in the sex ratio at birth by using technologies that enable sex selection; an increase in the mortality of girl children when compared to that of boy children, suggesting intensification of the already documented discrimination against the former; or a systematic undercount of female children, compared with male children under the age of seven (Miller, 1981; Das Gupta, 1987; Kishor, 1993).

The population SR is inclusive of migration and hence it needs to be looked at along with the child sex ratio and particularly sex ratio at birth. The child sex ratio of the State as a whole has improved marginally from 942 in 2001 to 946 in 2011, while it declined from 927 to 919 in the same period for the nation as a whole. In 18 of the 29 States in India, the sex ratio at birth is below normal. Notably, all four of the southern States, including Kerala, have lower than normal sex ratios at birth. On the contrary, States and Union Territories which have reported lowest child sex ratio (0-6 years) are: Haryana (830), followed by Punjab (846), Jammu & Kashmir (859), NCT of Delhi (866) and Chandigarh (867).

Sex Ratio Differences in the Census Period

In 27 States and Union Territories, including Delhi, the child SR has declined. "The rate of decline ranges from normal to alarming" as per Census of India reports. It can be estimated that2 million women in the country go "missing" every year; 12 per cent disappear at birth due to sex selective infanticide or abortion and 25 per cent die in childhood, predominantly due to lack of access to the same level of healthcare and nutrition available to their male counterparts. The rural sex ratio of 947 in 2011 has witnessed a decline of 32 points from 1901 to 2011, with the maximum figure of 979 being recorded in 1901. The urban sex ratio of 926 females per thousand males has shown an upward trend by recording an increase of 16 points from 1901 to 2011, where the highest figure of 926 has been recorded in 2011. The changes in the child sex ratio over the last two censuses, 2001 and 2011, in Tamil Nadu has been represented in Figure 6.5. Figure 6.5(a) indicates that at least in 2 districts, Ariyalur and Cuddalore, there has been a sharp decline of 25 points and more, and the child sex ratio was below 925. The adverse changes in child SR indicate a strong case of son preference in the State.

Figure 6.5

Tamil Nadu Child Sex Ratio 2011

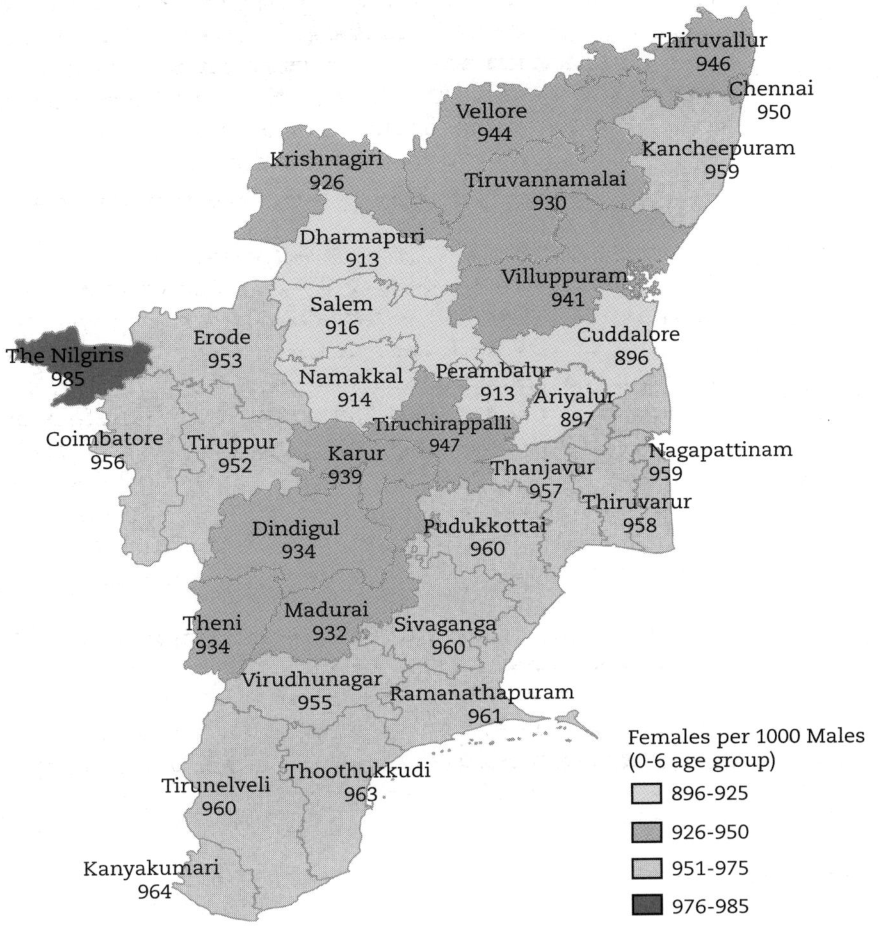

Source: Census of India, Maps.

Figure 6.5a

Tamil Nadu: District-wise Changes in Child Sex Ratio 2011

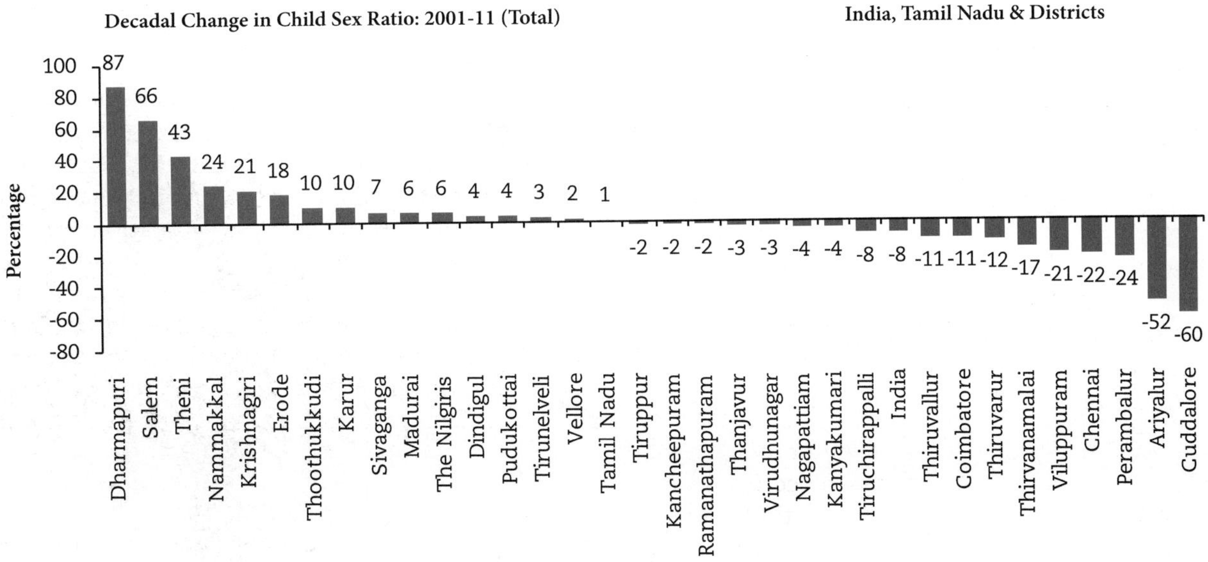

Note: Chennai district has been excluded as it is entirely urban.

Looking at Figure 6.6, one can see that six districts have sex ratios lower than the all-India average: Ariyalur, Cuddalore, Dharmapuri, Namakkal Salem and Perambalur. Cuddalore, Ariyalur, Perambalur, Villupuram and Tiruvanamalai show sharp decline in child sex ratio in the recent census. This is indicative of the fact that the process of sex selection is not confined to the traditional female infanticide areas, but has moved to other backward districts as well. These districts require immediate attention.

There are eight districts between the State average and the all-India average. On the whole, nearly 14 districts indicate adverse sex ratios that are lower than the State average. Although overall child sex ratios are falling for the country, recent analysis of the 2011 census by Diamond-Smith and Bishai (2014) suggests that the States and districts that have historically had the lowest child sex ratios are beginning to show signs of improvement (the corresponding ratios are becoming less skewed, or slowing down in their rate of decline).

It is necessary to reiterate that any efforts to address adverse sex ratio needs to be adopted across the State. There are newer districts showing adverse sex ratio and more urban and literate areas seem to exhibit declining sex ratios, thereby indicating that patriarchal system in combination with small family norms may have contributed to this phenomenon.

Son preference and devaluation of girls cannot be attributed to one single factor in Tamil Nadu. An economic cost-benefit analysis of having sons versus daughters may play an important role among impoverished families, but should not affect affluent families who can afford to equally invest in their sons' and daughters' education and well-being. Additionally, there has been a decline in dowry payments among educated, affluent families (Mitra, 2014). Yet, there is a persistence of son preference among both the rich and the poor, educated and illiterate families. Deep-rooted culture and traditions, coupled with patriarchal kinship patterns and lower status of women in different parts of the State are still contributing to this trend. The sex ratio is particularly low among couples whose first born is a daughter, compared to those who have a boy as their first born (Jha *et al.*, 2011).

The Cradle Baby scheme launched by the state government had played an important role in addressing adverse sex ratios. Under the scheme, cradles were placed in important places, such as hospitals, primary health centres, and children homes, in order to rescue the female children abandoned by their biological parents due to various social circumstances. As Figure 6.7 shows, this scheme has had a substantial number of beneficiaries over the years.

More importantly, as Table 6.3 shows, the sex ratio has improved in all the districts where the scheme was implemented.

Figure 6.6

India, Tamil Nadu and Districts: Child Sex Ratio 2011

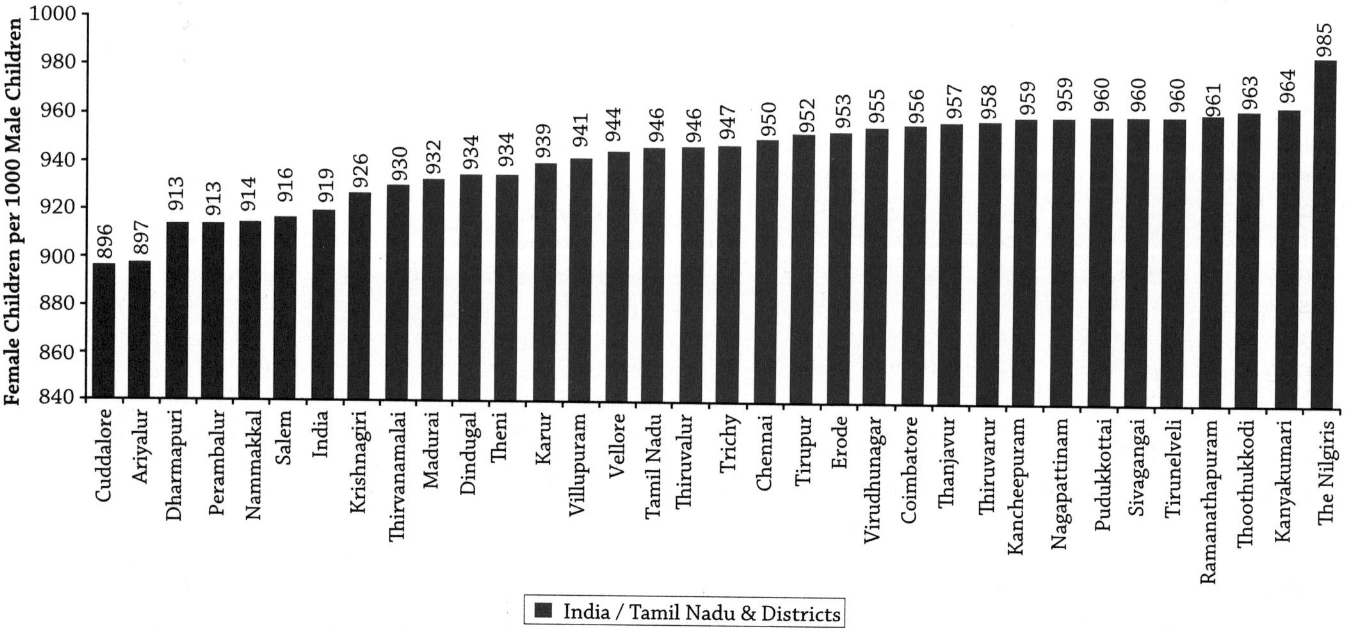

Source: Census of India, 2011.

Figure 6.7

Cradle Baby Scheme: Allotment and Beneficiaries

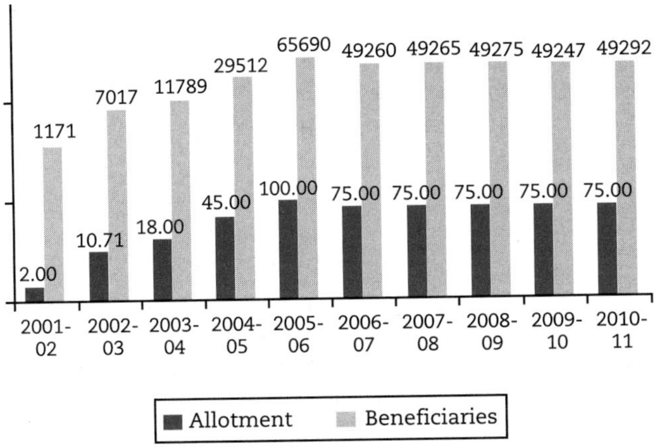

Source: Department of Social Welfare, Chennai.

Table 6.3

Cradle Baby Scheme: Improvement in Sex Ratio, District-wise

Name of the Districts	*2001 Census Child Sex Ratio (per 1000 males)*	*2011 Census Child Sex Ratio (per 1000 males)*
Salem	851	917
Madurai	926	939
Theni	891	937
Dindigul	930	942
Dharmapuri	826	911

Source: Department of Social Welfare, Chennai.

Women and Literacy

Eliminating gender differences in access to education and educational attainment are key elements on the path to attaining gender equality and restraining the disempowerment of women. At the national level, pace of increase in female literacy rate was perceptibly higher in rural areas. It has increased from 46.13 per cent in 2001 to 58.75 per cent in 2011. Gender gap in literacy rate narrowed down considerably over the censuses, but continues to be high (19.81). This gap is largest in Rajasthan (31.2 points). The gender gap in literacy as per the 2011 census is presented in the map with different colour shades.

The literacy rate for Tamil Nadu in 2011 has increased to 80.33 per cent from 73.45 per cent in the 2001 census. Among the males, 86.81 per cent were literates, whereas among the females, the rate is 73.86 per cent. The corresponding rates in 2001 were 82.42 per cent for males and 64.43 per cent for females. It may be observed that more than three-fourth of the population is literate among males in all the districts (except Dharmapuri), while more than two-third of the population is literate among females in all districts, except eight; namely Dharmapuri (60.03), Krishnagiri (64.86), Tiruvannamalai (65.71), Villupuram (63.51), Salem (65.43), Erode (65.07), Perambalur (66.11) and Ariyalur (62.22). Among the districts, Kanyakumari district has reported the highest literacy rate of 92.14 per cent, while Dharmapuri district accounts for the lowest rate of 64.71 per cent.

The female literacy map for the two census periods in Figure 6.8 indicate that although the number of districts in the highest quintile have remained more or less the same, the number in the second lowest quintile has moved to the second highest quintile.

Figure 6.9 is the graphical representation of female literacy rates in the districts. Six districts of the State—Salem, Erode, Krishnagiri, Villupuram, Ariyalur and Dharmapuri—had literacy rates lower than the national average. Twelve districts have female literacy rates lower than the State average, but above national average. Only 14 districts have female literacy rates above the State average (73.86%). Differential between Kanyakumari with the highest female literacy rate and Dharmapuri with the lowest literacy rate is quite high (nearly 30 percentage points).

Although there are stark inter-district variations across districts, the gender gap in literacy is narrowing down and is evident from Figure 6.10.

Five districts have a gender gap less than 10. Fourteen districts have a gender gap in literacy between 10 and 15 percentage points. The remaining districts have greater than 15 percentage points.

In terms of school enrolment and access to schools across gender, there was near equal access in the primary and upper primary levels. However, as girls move above middle school, a sizeable proportion drop out, thus increasing the gender gap in higher education. Graphical representation of the district-wise enrolment in high schools is presented in Figure 6.11. It shows that overall in the State, nearly 50 per cent of the girls are in schools. Ensuring that girls continue their education for a longer time has the twin benefits, in terms of knowledge attainment and also delaying the age of marriage.

Moving onto gender differences in enrolment at the high school level, the highest percentage of girls enrolled in high school is in Thoothukudi (67.2) and

Figure 6.8

Tamil Nadu: Female Literacy Rate (Rural), 2011

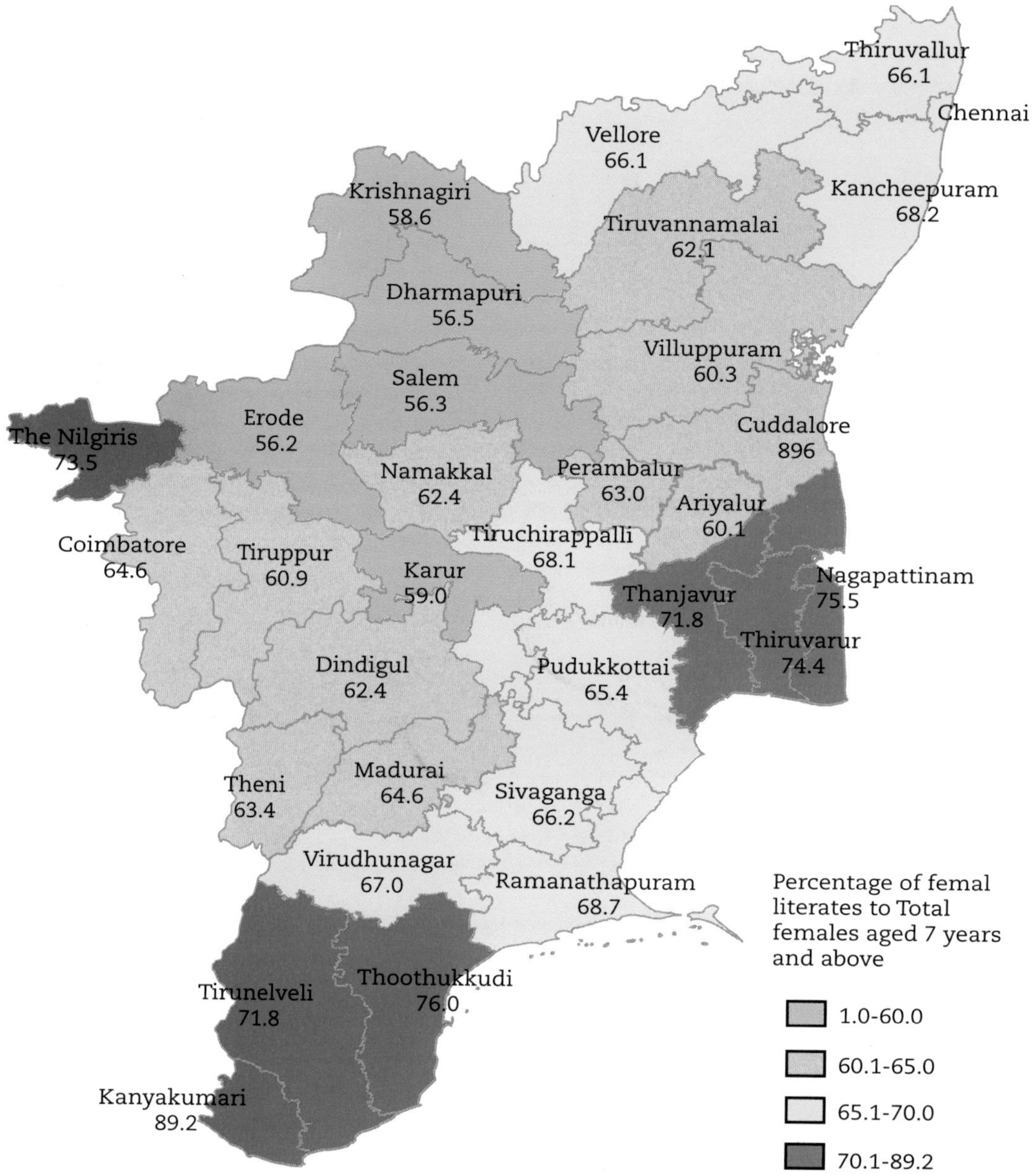

Source: Census of India, 2011.

Figure 6.9

Ranking of Districts by Female Literacy Rate, 2011

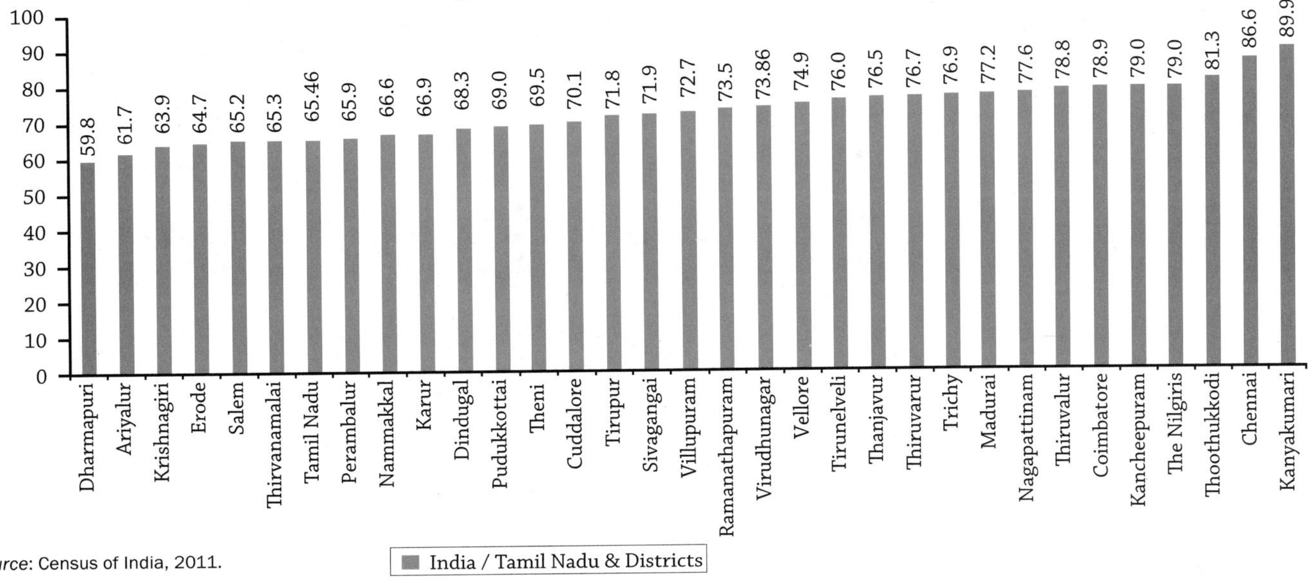

Source: Census of India, 2011.

Figure 6.10

Tamil Nadu: Gender Gap in Literacy, 2011

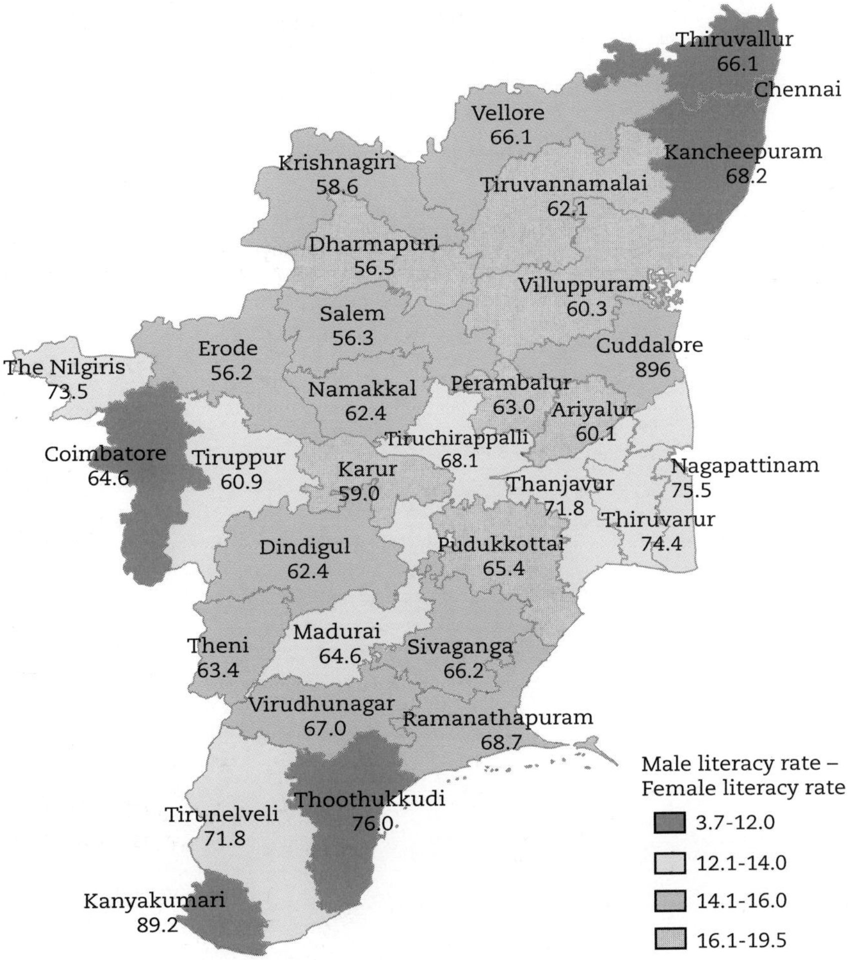

Source: Census of India, 2011.

the lowest is in Madurai district (45.9). The high school enrolment gap between the highest and the lowest is therefore nearly 18 percentage points and is an issue that needs to be addressed in earnest.

It would also be interesting to look at the higher education pattern of women and their educational choices. A CII–Deloitte study conducted on higher education highlights that the number of women who enrol for M.Phil is higher than that of the males (Figure 6.12). It was also evident that in professional PG diploma, male enrolment was higher. Enrolment of women was the highest for certificate courses.

The difference in the enrolment and completion rates at the higher education levels is quite evident. This is also an indicator of the fact that the percentage of women qualified for higher paid professional jobs is comparatively lower. In addition, the number of professionally qualified women who are able to manage both family and career become rather limited. This is evident from data available on women taking

Figure 6.11

Percentage of Female Students in High School

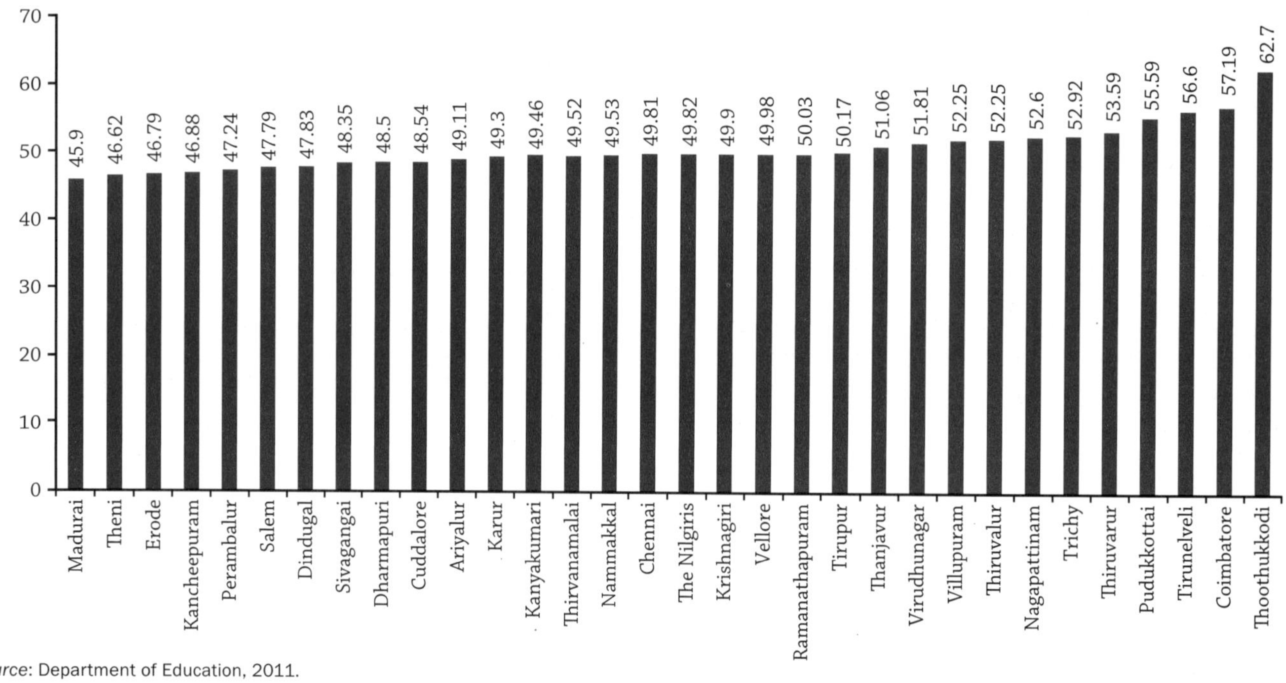

Source: Department of Education, 2011.

Figure 6.12

State-wise Enrolment through Regular Mode of Various Levels: Tamil Nadu

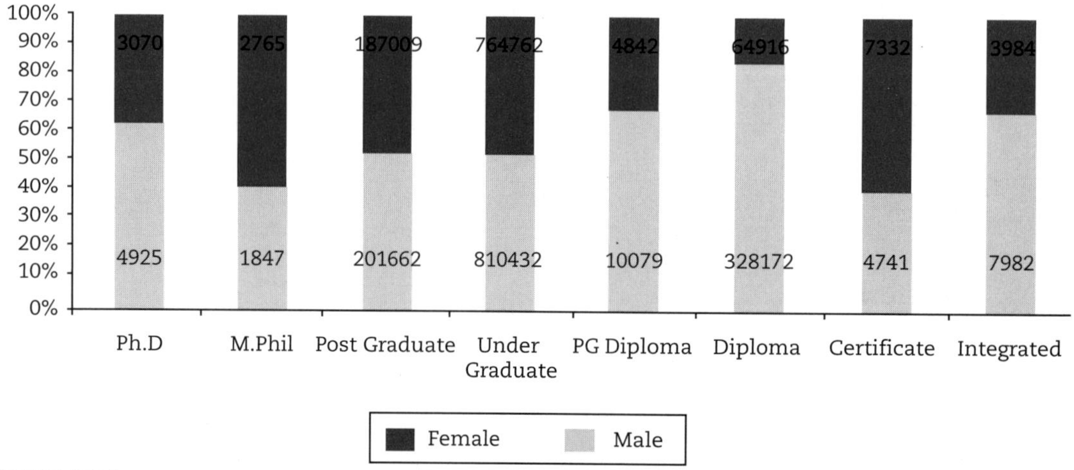

Source: CII-Deolitte study report.

up lower paid jobs and also very few being posted at high paid professional jobs.

Access to education is the most powerful instrument to improve women's position in society. Education also brings about reduction in inequalities and also acts as a means to improve their status within the family. In order to encourage education of women at all levels and to dilute gender bias in the provision of education; schools, colleges and even universities were established exclusively for women in the State. To bring in more girl children, especially from marginalised BPL (below poverty line) families into mainstream education, the government provides a package of concessions in the form of free supply of books, uniform, boarding and lodging, clothing, mid-day meals, scholarships, free bicycles and so on. Scholarships, laptops and bicycles are all given free of cost in order to encourage girl children to pursue their education.

Female Workforce Participation Rate

Along with education, women's employment is a critical factor in their progression towards economic independence and is also considered as an indicator of their overall status in society (Mammen and Paxson, 2008). Women's contribution to the economy remains significantly invisible in national accounts. Although a certain degree of statistical invisibility of women in the economy is a global phenomenon, it is particularly predominant in India and other South Asian nations due to the orthodox socio-cultural milieu.

While the female workforce participation rate declined marginally at the all-India level between the 2001 and 2011 censuses (from 25.6 to 25.5), Tamil Nadu has witnessed a slight increase, from 31.5 to 31.8 during this period. Figure 6.13 on female workforce participation rate across the districts in the state reveals that Perambalur had the highest percentage in the labour market, while both Kancheepuram and Kanyakumari had low workforce participation rate. The WFPR may not be reflective of the lower status of women. Many studies indicate that when family income goes up to a certain extent, women prefer leisure to work and withdraw from the labour market. A U-shaped relationship has been noticed in several studies on economic development and women's economic activity. (Goldin, 1994; Tansel, 2002; Fatima and Sultana, 2009; Kottis, 1990). Female labour force participation is noticed to decline initially with economic development, and then form a plateau before rising again, giving it the U-shape. This has been argued as being reflective of structural shifts in the economy, changing influence of income and substitution effects, and a increasing education levels of women in the population (Goldin, 1994).

Analysing National Sample Survey (NSS) data for 1993-94, Das and Desai (2003) find that educated women in India are less likely to be employed, which is attributed to a lack of employment opportunities rather than social norms restricting their movement. Klasen and Pieters (2012) argue that women with low-levels of education are forced to work in order to contribute towards household income; whereas women with very high levels of education are attracted towards the labour market due to high wages. Based on ILO's research, explanations include increasing educational enrolment, improvement in earnings of male workers that discourages women's economic participation, and the lack of employment opportunities at certain level of skills and qualifications discouraging women to seek work. (ILO, 2014)

Figure 6.13

Female WPR

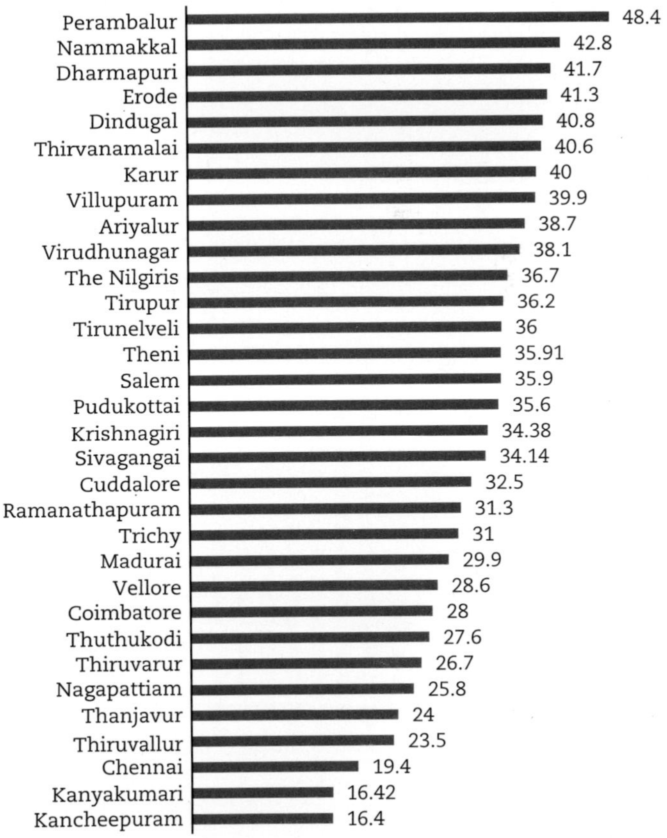

Source: Census of India, 2011.

Occupational structure of female work participation indicates that a greater share of women workers are still engaged in primary sector in India. Indian women workers are heavily concentrated in this low productive work. Globalisation had and continues to have different impacts on men and women (Basu, 1995). The following section deals with the gender differences in wages taking agricultural wages as a proxy.

Average Female Agricultural Wages

Most women in India work and contribute to the economy in one form or another, but a significant portion of their work has not been documented or accounted for in official statistics. Since there are strong gender barriers in India for women to access jobs in the formal sector, the informal sector is particularly important for them as a means of employment. There are estimates that over 90 per cent of the working women are involved in the informal sector. Bulk of the women are employed in the agricultural sector, which has in fact witnessed a growing feminisation of employment in India. Other informal jobs include self-employment of various kinds, particularly vending, domestic help, small traders or artisanal work. Clearly, most of these jobs are unskilled and low paying, and do not provide social security benefits to the worker. Tamil Nadu, however, has instituted a range of schemes addressed at marginalised women as highlighted in the chapter on social security.

Apart from gender-based segmentation across sectors, segmentation has been observed even within sectors and within same jobs. Considering levels and male-female differences in agricultural wage rates in the State, Salem and Kanyakumari have the highest average female agricultural wage of ₹258.11 and ₹215.7 respectively. The higher wage rate in these two districts can be attributed to the availability of non-farm employment, which offers a decent alternative. Villupuram has the lowest average agricultural wage rate of ₹74.88. This has been presented in Figure 6.14.

Proponents of the Mahatma Gandhi National Rural Employment Guarantee Act (MGNREGA) scheme believe that the wages provided ensures an alternative source of income, raising the reservation wage (the fall-back position if a bargain is not struck) of all workers and implicitly offering them better bargaining power. This must be seen as a positive development, as the Indian labour market, due to inequitable social and power dynamics, has suppressed wages far below the competitive wages for the rural labour force.

It will also be worthwhile to study the inter-district wage differentials between male and female agricultural wages as presented in Table 6.4. It was found that in almost all districts, there were variations

Figure 6.14

Agri-Wage Rate (2011-12)

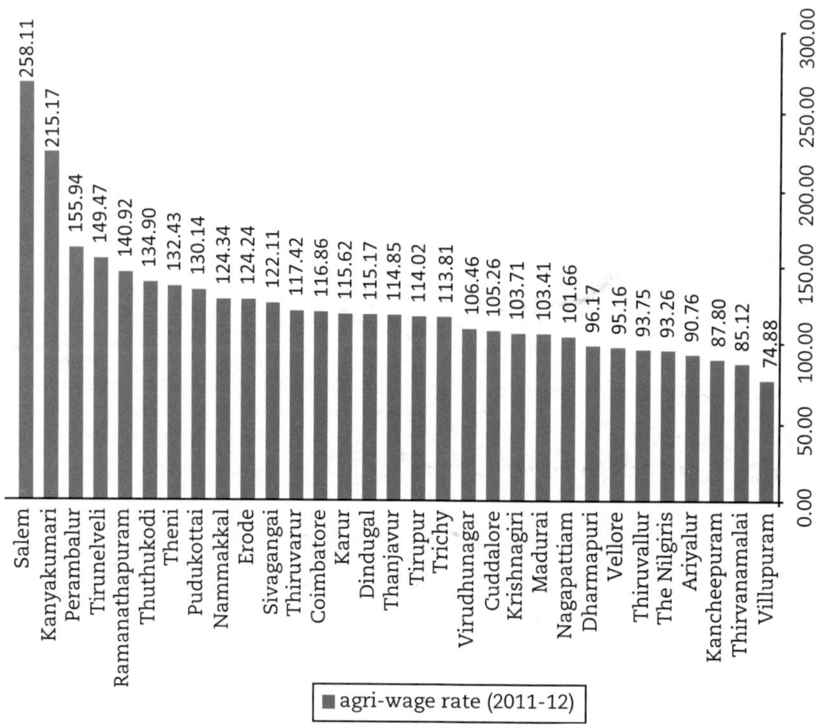

Source: Season and crop report, 2011-12.

in wage rates, with the male agricultural wage being higher. The maximum wage differentials were noted in Kanyakumari district with ₹347.79. Minimum wage differentials were noted in Salem, which incidentally has the highest female agricultural wage rate.

Table 6.4

Male and Female Agricultural Wage Rates

Districts	*Male Agricultural Wage rate*	*Female Agricultural Wage rate*	*Differential in wages (male wages- female wages)*
Salem	305.05	258.11	46.95
Ramanathapuram	198.71	140.92	57.79
Karur	199.94	115.62	84.32
Dindugal	204.97	115.17	89.80
Vellore	187.90	95.16	92.74
Thiruvallur	189.13	93.75	95.38
Kancheepuram	188.54	87.80	100.74
The Nilgiris	197.75	93.26	104.48
Perambalur	263.49	155.94	107.55
Thuthukodi	248.36	134.90	113.46
Nammakkal	245.18	124.34	120.84
Trichy	247.36	113.81	133.55
Cuddalore	238.93	105.26	133.67
Tirupur	248.36	114.02	134.34
Thanjavur	251.79	114.85	136.94
Virudhunagar	244.23	106.46	137.77
Thiruvarur	260.94	117.42	143.52
Madurai	247.33	103.41	143.92
Dharmapuri	244.58	96.17	148.40
Villupuram	230.07	74.88	155.19
Erode	283.65	124.24	159.41
Nagapattiam	262.08	101.66	160.42
Theni	307.44	132.43	175.01
Krishnagiri	280.61	103.71	176.90
Thirvanamalai	267.85	85.12	182.73
Pudukottai	315.57	130.14	185.43
Tirunelveli	340.06	149.47	190.59
Coimbatore	324.24	116.86	207.38
Ariyalur	328.68	90.76	237.92
Sivagangai	464.86	122.11	342.75
Kanyakumari	562.96	215.17	347.79

Source: Season and crop report of agriculture department, 2011-12.

Only six districts have less than ₹100 wage differential between the male and female agricultural wage rate, indicating that wage parity in the agricultural sector is yet to be achieved. In addition to farm employment, non-farm employment opportunities are also available, including self-employment that is encouraged by the Women Development Corporation, Pudhu Vazhu Project etc., through the SHG (self-help group) concept.

Women and Political Participation

Political equality regardless of birth, sex, colour, etc., is one of the basic premise of democracy. Political equality includes not only equal right to franchise, but also more importantly, the right to access institutionalised centres of power. Thus, political participation of women means not only using the right to vote, but also power sharing, co-decision-making and co-policymaking at all levels. The active participation of women in political sphere is integral to their empowerment. Women's political empowerment has three fundamental and non-negotiable principles: (a) the equality between women and men; (b) women's right to complete development of their potential; and (c) women's right to self-representation and self-determination.

Political empowerment on a standard basis is assessed by the number of female elected representatives. Although there are reservations for women as per the 33 per cent seats under reserved category in the State, only in some *panchayats*, women exert considerable influence and are able to exercise their powers. The mere presence of women can initiate change, but cannot ensure that priorities set by patriarchal frameworks are transformed. Redefining of the democratic space of the *panchayats* also requires policy changes by way of defining a focus and creating operational guidelines to prioritise and support this outcome. Social indicators of gender equality are matters of concern today, and engagement of Panchayat Raj Institutions (PRIs) on strategic gender issues cannot be left to chance. Any development that is bereft of equality and justice loses its meaning. The district-wise female elected representatives in the *panchayats* is presented in Figure 6.15. The lowest count is in Nilgiris and the highest number of elected representatives is in Virudhunagar district.

Women are moving into leadership positions in both reserved and unreserved seats and many perceive positive outcomes due to being in the position of a *panchayat* member, including increased self-confidence and improved status in the family and community. But women often face number of barriers, such as low education attainment, poor preparatory training, high household work burden and negative attitude faced by them while holding public office, that constrain their

Figure 6.15

District-Level Female Elected Representatives

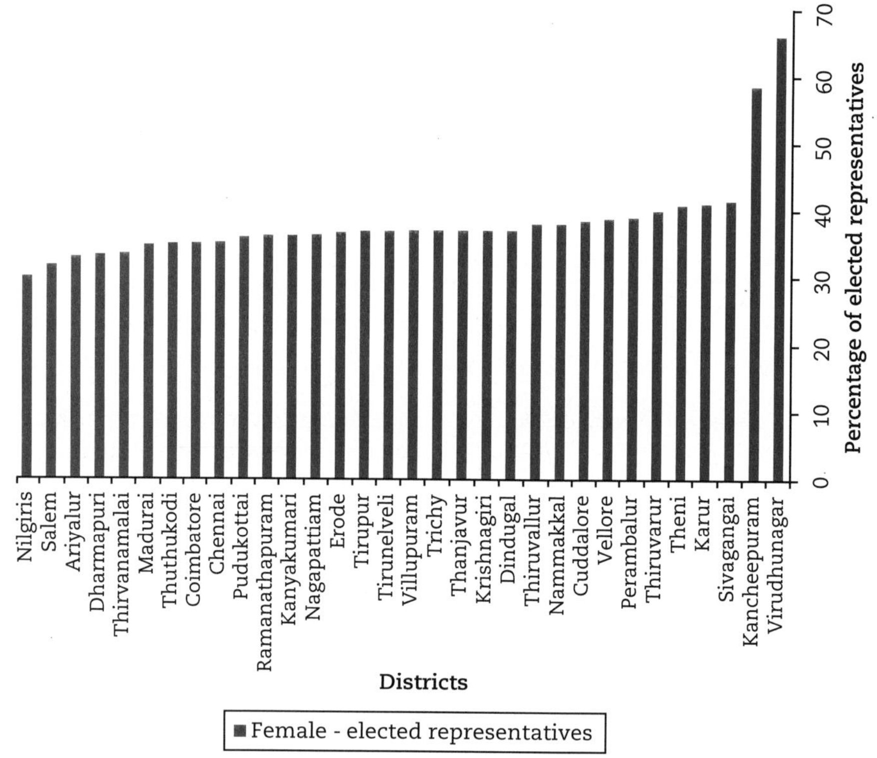

Source: Data provided by State Planning Commission.

Figure 6.16

Rate of Crimes Against Women, 2011

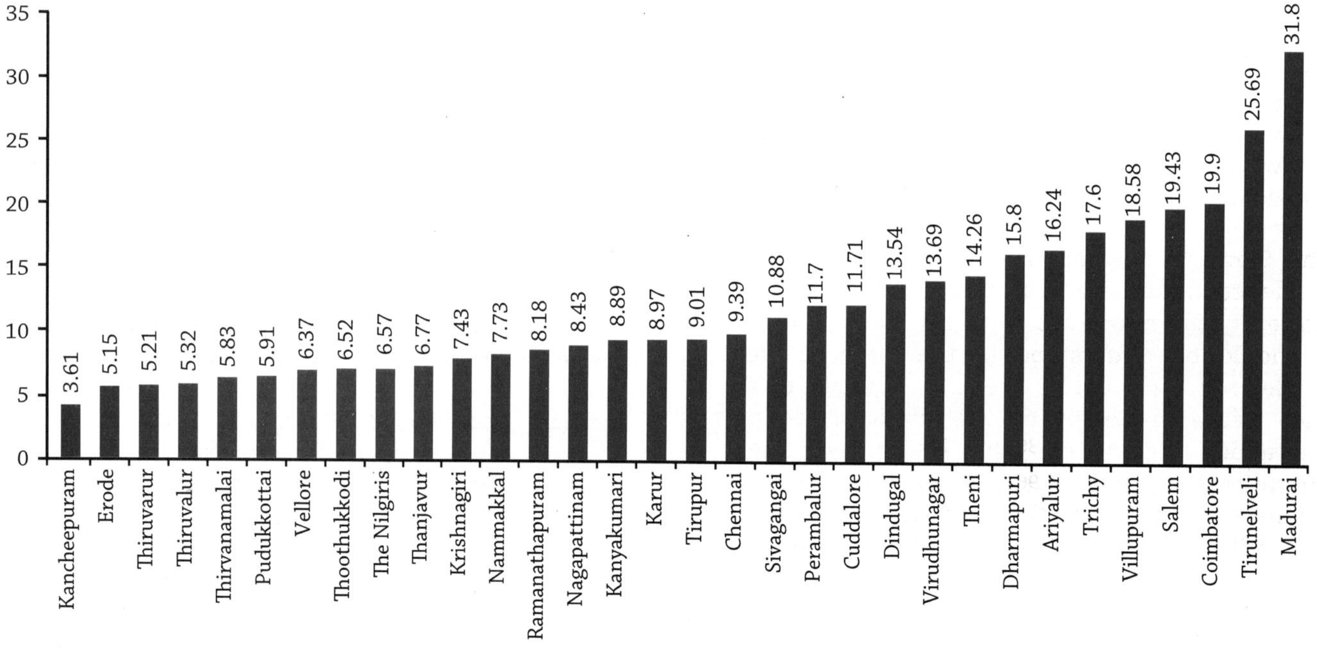

Source: Crime Records Bureau, 2011.

ability to function effectively or which makes them unlikely to re-contest. However, *Panchayats'* mandate on development concerns like water, sanitation, transportation and eligibility for social schemes is all important for meeting a number of women's practical needs.

In the previous section, we were able to assess the economic and political aspects in the empowerment of women. However, empowerment is constrained by the safety and security in work and public places too. It is essential to take into account the conditions of women's safety and security.

Safety and Security of Women

Tamil Nadu is the first Indian State to set up "all women police stations" to deal with crimes against women. After the infamous rape and death incident in Delhi in 2012, the Tamil Nadu government unveiled a 13-point action plan in 2013, which includes installation of closed-circuit television (CCTV) in all public buildings and booking offenders under the Goondas Act of 1982 that gives non-bailable detention up to one year. The Acts under which cases are filed for protection of women include Indecent Representation of Women Act, Child Marriage Restraint Act, Tamil Nadu Prohibition of Harassment of Women (Amended) Act 2002, Tamil Nadu Prohibition of Sexual Harassment of Women Act 2000, and Dowry Prohibition Act. However, there are variations across districts in the crimes reported against women.

Analysis of district-wise crimes against women data maintained by the police department reveals that the highest incidence of crimes committed against women occurred in Chennai City (not marked separately) (Figure 6.16). Most cases reported in the city were against sexual harassment. Kidnapping and molestation was found to be highest in Villupuram.

The State as a whole has recorded highest crime incidence under cruelty by husband and his relatives. However, when one looks at the data of reporting, it should be understood in the larger context of gender relations, which socialises women to accept such treatment meted out by relatives, particularly husbands, in silence. In other words, reporting does not quite correspond to the actual extent of violence against women and may be indicative of the awareness and ability of women to seek judicial action against the same. The following discussion on domestic violence substantiates the argument to a large extent.

Domestic violence is not just a violation of the human rights of women, but has significant economic costs. These include the loss of women's labour hours, as well as an increased need for healthcare investments at both the household and societal levels. Further, a growing body of research points to both short- and long-term detrimental effects of domestic violence on the health and welfare of women and their children (Garcia-Moreno *et al.*, 2006; Hindin, Kishor, and Ansara, 2007; Kishor and Johnson 2006; 2004). In addition to other costs, experiencing and living with the constant threat of domestic violence is a source of disempowerment for women.

Surprisingly, as Figure 6.17 reveals, women who experienced domestic violence have been socialised to believe that their acts or lack of appropriate responses have warranted the act of violence. Population Council's recent report on "Violence within marriage among young people in Tamil Nadu" reinforces the observations made by other studies in the past. The majority believe that wife beating is justified; and 34 per cent of men admitted to have beaten their wives.

As a part of a nation-wide survey, a sub-national study in Tamil Nadu, was put together with responses from 7,996 young men and women, including 1,322 married men and 2,007 married women. The National Family Health Survey (NFHS)-III done in 2005-06 reported that 35 per cent of women in the country had experienced physical or sexual violence. It also pegged Tamil Nadu in the top slot with States that have 40 per cent or higher prevalence of spousal physical/sexual violence, along with Tripura, Manipur, Uttar Pradesh (UP), West Bengal, and Assam.

As shown in Figure 6.18, a substantial share of women respondents felt justified in being at the receiving end of violence. The extent of physical and sexual violence was quite high and more so in the rural areas. It can also be observed that education levels of women did not have much impact on the incidence of domestic violence and in fact, in the case of educated women, sexual violence dominated. The State has enacted laws for seeking redressal in case of domestic violence and provides more rights to women to curb the issue. Further, it was found that many of the victims of domestic violence have either refused to name the perpetrator of the assault or attributed the injuries to other reasons (Daga *et al.*, 1999).

As it is a phenomenon deep rooted in widely accepted socio-cultural practices with both the perpetrators as well as victims taking it as 'normal', there is a strong

Figure 6.17

Domestic Violence in Tamil Nadu

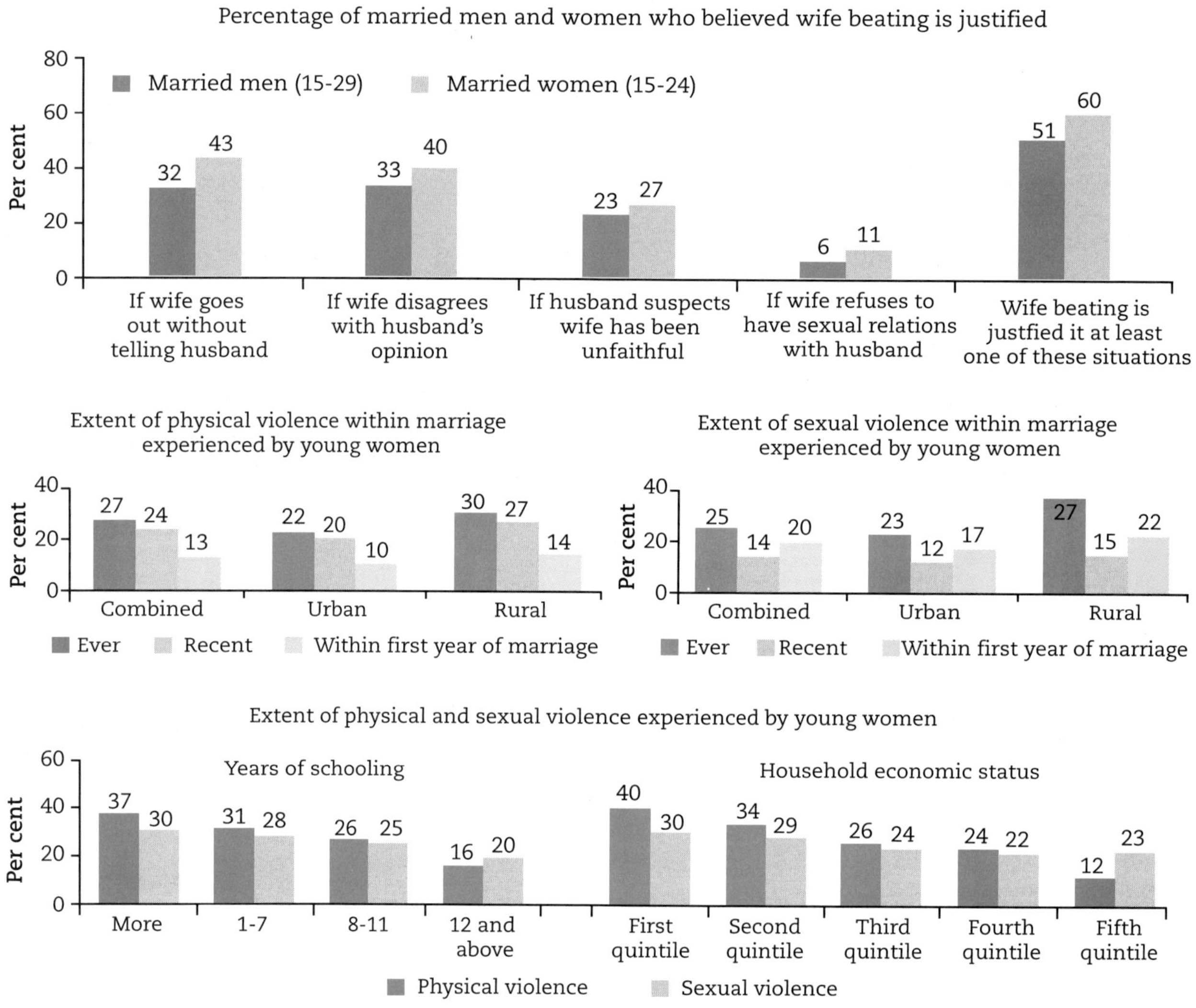

Source: Population Council of India.

need for major public and civil society interventions to alter such perceptions. In order to address the problem, social norms and values towards gender roles should be transformed to facilitate the implementation of appropriate and meaningful responses to domestic violence and ultimately to prevent the occurrence altogether (Strategic Management Group analysed multiple government sources and surveys to generate the Well Being Index and Female Security Index for India 2013). It was found that two clusters—Punjab, Haryana, Delhi and Himachal Pradesh; and Kerala, Tamil Nadu and Andhra Pradesh topped the Well Being Index. On the Female Security Index (FSI), Hyderabad and Delhi were the lowest-ranked amongst the urban agglomerations (UAs) while Chennai and Bengaluru were at the top. Southern States, Gujarat and most north-eastern States emerged as the most secure for women while Haryana, Madhya Pradesh, Punjab, Delhi and Rajasthan had the lowest FSI ranking. Social parameters consisting of gender ratio in the 0-6 year age group, dowry deaths, rape and other crimes against women were used to create the FSI ranking of all the districts. Tata Strategic used FSI to measure the safety of women in Indian society. Tamil Nadu has been listed among the better States with greater security for women.

Figure 6.18

Women Headed Households

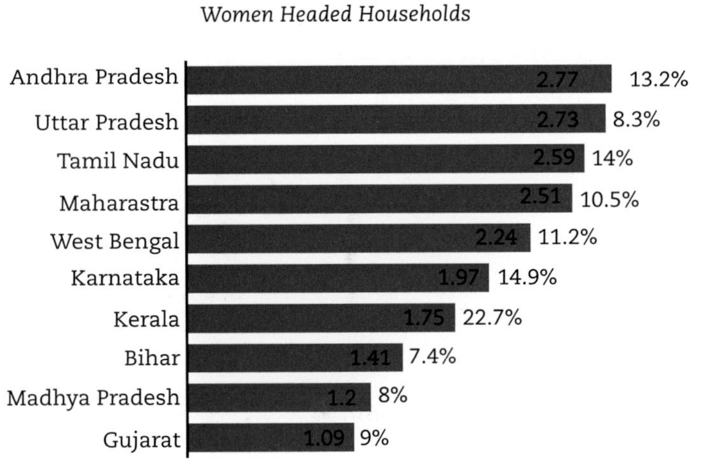

Note: Figures in million; Percentage figures=As % of all households.
Source: Census 2011.

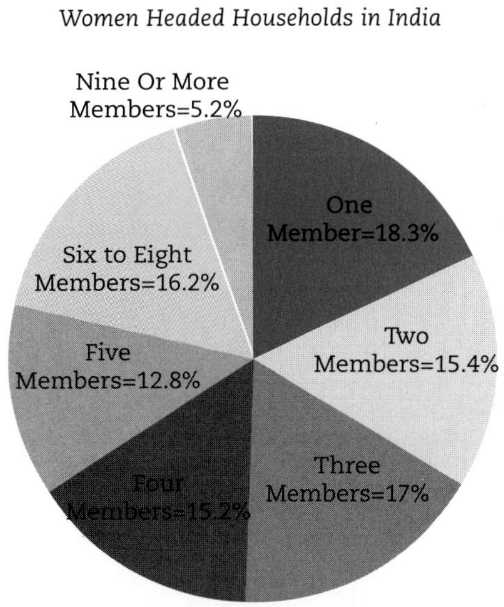

Source: Census 2011.

Female-Headed Households

It is for the first time in the history of Census that a separate category, Female-headed Households has been included and data has been collected accordingly. She is generally the person who bears the chief responsibility for maintenance of the household and takes decisions on behalf of the households as per Census of India Guidelines, 2011.

a. The broad range of domestic situations typically characterized by the absence of a resident male head, *viz.*, widowhood, divorce, separation and desertion.

b. Migration of male members for long periods.

c. Loss of economic function by resident males due to severe unemployment, disability, illness and male reluctance to accept jobs seen as status reducing, etc.

d. Households with no mature sons.

e. Sons residing in independent nuclear units.

The female-headed households distributed across the States are presented in Figure 6.19

Figure 6.18 indicates that 14 per cent of the total households are female headed in Tamil Nadu. It is also evident from the graph that in absolute numbers, the State nearly has 2.59 million female-headed households, the third largest in the country. In terms of percentage to total households also, Tamil Nadu has 14 per cent households and stands third, next to Kerala and Karnataka. A study of the family size in a woman-headed household indicates that nearly 18.3 per cent of these are single-member households. This has a larger social policy implication since the State has to ensure a safety net for social services of these single women.

The female-headed households' distribution across the country is presented as per 2011 census in Figure 6.19. The percentage of women-headed households is more in the southern districts of India. Central and northern parts of the State have lower percentage of female-headed households. There are about 27 million female-headed households in the country. They constitute 10.9 per cent of the total households present. In seven major States, the proportion of single-member female-headed HH (households) is more than 20 per cent. Chhattisgarh (29.9%), Madhya Pradesh (24.9%), and Tamil Nadu (26.1%), Andhra Pradesh (27.1%), Maharashtra (22.2%), Odisha (22.1%) and Gujarat (20.4%)

Figure 6.19

India: Female Headed Households (Total), 2011

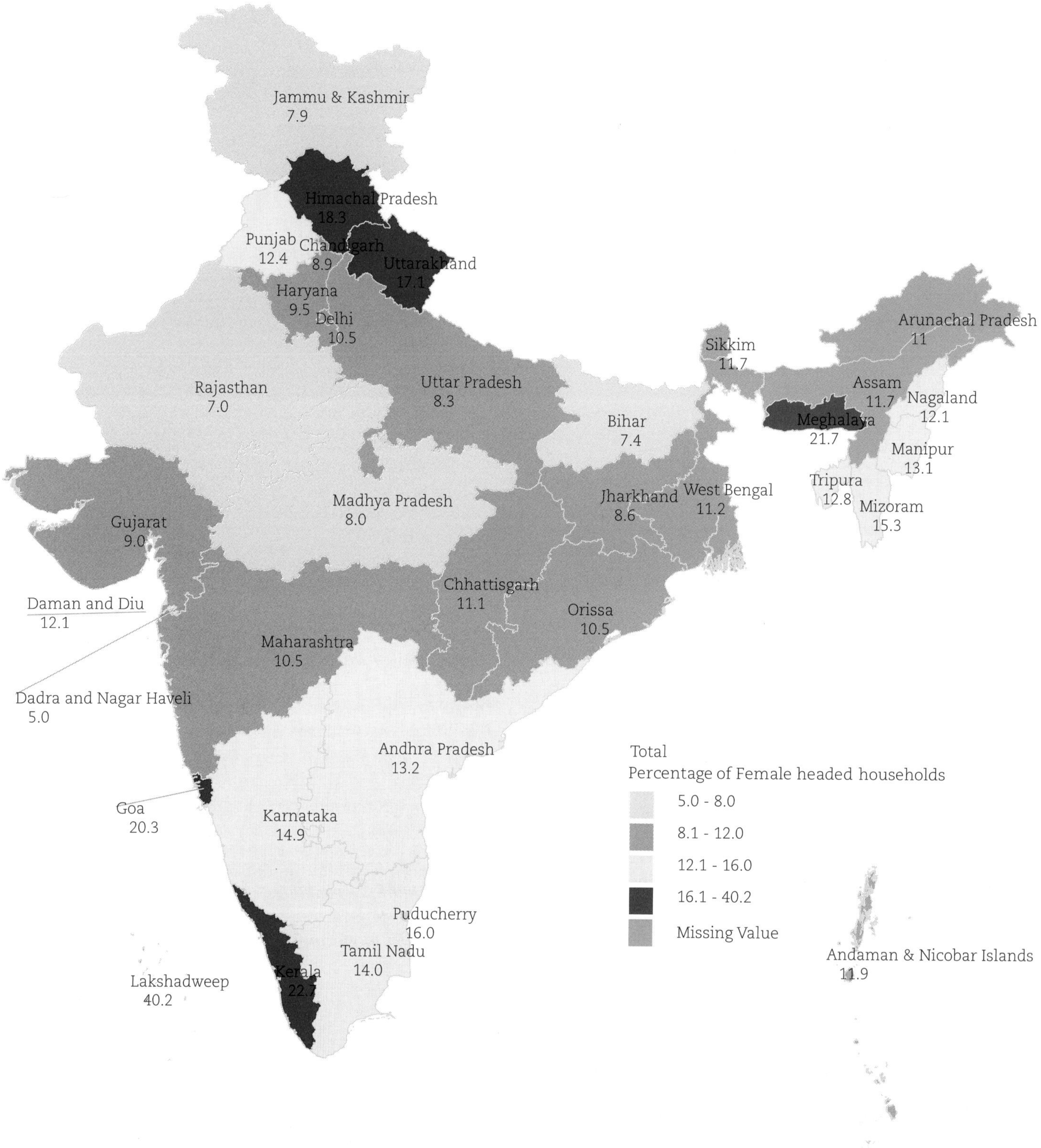

Source: Census of India.

A larger proportion of female-headed households live in 'no exclusive room' and in 'one room' dwelling units compared to male-headed households. The size of houses in case of female-headed households tend to be smaller than the male-headed ones. The proportion of households possessing different assets are lower in case of female-headed HHs in relation to the male-headed HHs.

The analysis of asset position of the female-headed households across the country suggests that there were large number of female-headed households with no assets. A matter of particular concern is vulnerability of the SC (Scheduled Caste) and ST (Scheduled Tribe) population that are female headed and are without any particular assets to support them during economic crisis. Such multiple deprivations need to be considered for appropriate policy interventions.

Wealth inequality is an integral aspect of economic inequality at a given point in time, evident across generations. Disparities in wealth can also translate into the same in economic security. For a substantial portion of the Indian population that is dependent on agriculture, land is the major source of livelihood. Inequalities in quantity and fertility of the land owned are a significant determinant of economic inequality among households.

Figure 6.20 indicates that ST female-headed households that have no assets are more in number in the central and western parts of India. In States like Tamil Nadu, the number of female-headed households without any assets is lower. Even among the SC and ST population, States like Tamil Nadu show a better status of women.

The all-India average of women-headed households that availed banking services was 58.4 per cent. Figure 6.21 indicates that the Tamil Nadu average was considerably lower than the all-India average. The average access percentage was 40.74 and it was the 6th State from the bottom, thus giving scope for improvement. It is essential for the State to ensure that the households' access to credit for this group and bank linkages are enhanced through the SHG movement and other welfare schemes.

The discussion so far has centred on the differential access of women in the State. It would now be worthwhile to look at some of the policies and programmes implemented by the State.

Livelihood Interventions: MahalirThittam and PudhuVazhvuThittam

Tamil Nadu Corporation for Development of Women (TNCDW) implements Mahalir Thittam, a scheme for empowerment of women. TNCDW became the focal point for women empowerment activities in the State due to its key role in spearheading the SHG movement therein. Mahalir Thittam is implemented in partnership with NGOs (non-governmental organisations) and community-based organisations, such as Panchayat Level Federations (PLFs), which are affiliated to TNCDW and who extend support in the formation of SHGs, capacity-building activities and in guiding and monitoring. As on February 2012, there were 5.35 lakh SHGs functioning with 82.85 lakh members. The total savings was ₹3,225 crore. The number of SHGs that were credit linked was 476,854 and total credit worked out to ₹15,015 crore.

The Pudhu Vazhvu Thittam has been implemented in 16 districts with a total outlay of ₹717 crore, benefitting 5.8 lakh households for a period up to September 2014. With additional financing, the project expanded its operations to 10 more districts for a period of 3 years until September 2014 with an outlay of ₹950 crore benefitting 3.8 lakh target poor households. The project design is based on a CDD (community-driven development) approach to empower poorest of the poor through promotion of strong CBOs (community-based organisations), thereby providing a voice for rural poor, especially women in community decision-making and in shaping developmental endeavours. Both the above programmes contribute to improved livelihood security and access to credit for women.

Marriage Assistance Schemes and Girl Child Protection Schemes

The scheme of giving 4 grams of 22 carat gold coin (1/2 sovereign) for making Thirumangalyam, in addition to the financial assistance, through existing marriage assistance schemes to mitigate the hardships faced by these below poverty line parents to get their educated daughters married. This has been implemented since 2011-12 and has been discussed in detail in the chapter on social security. The financial assistance has been increased to ₹50,000 for graduates/diploma holders.

Girl Child Protection Scheme

Tamil Nadu has enhanced the monetary incentive under the Girl Child Protection Scheme from ₹22,200 to ₹50,000, in the case of the parents undergoing

Figure 6.20

Possession of Assets

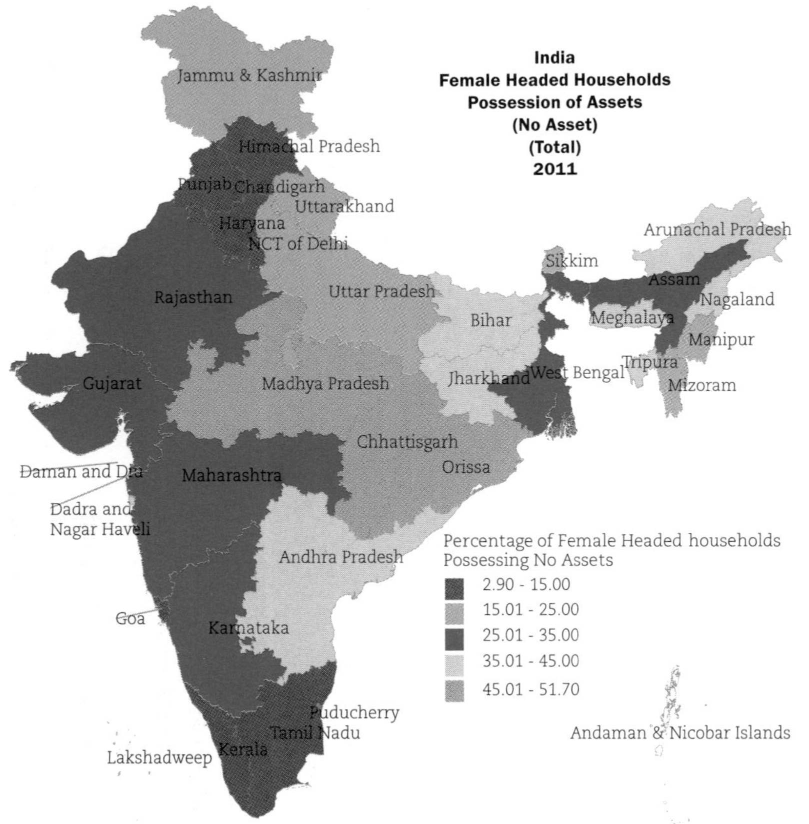

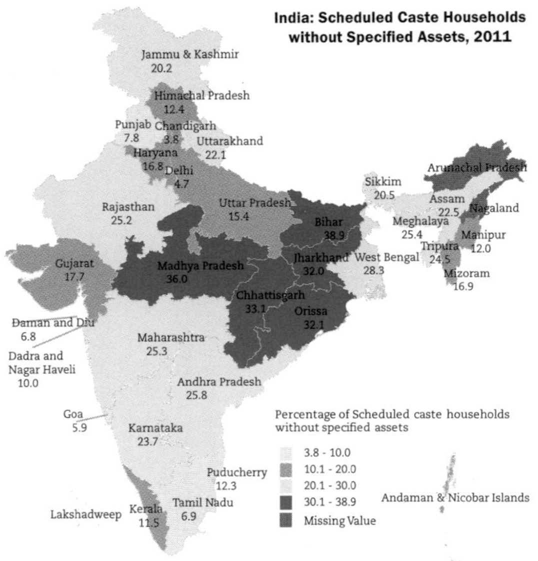

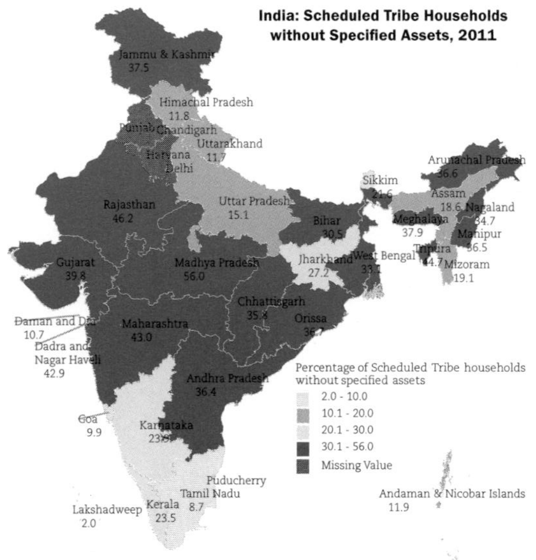

Source: Census of India.

Figure 6.21

Availing Banking Services in India (Female-headed HH in %)

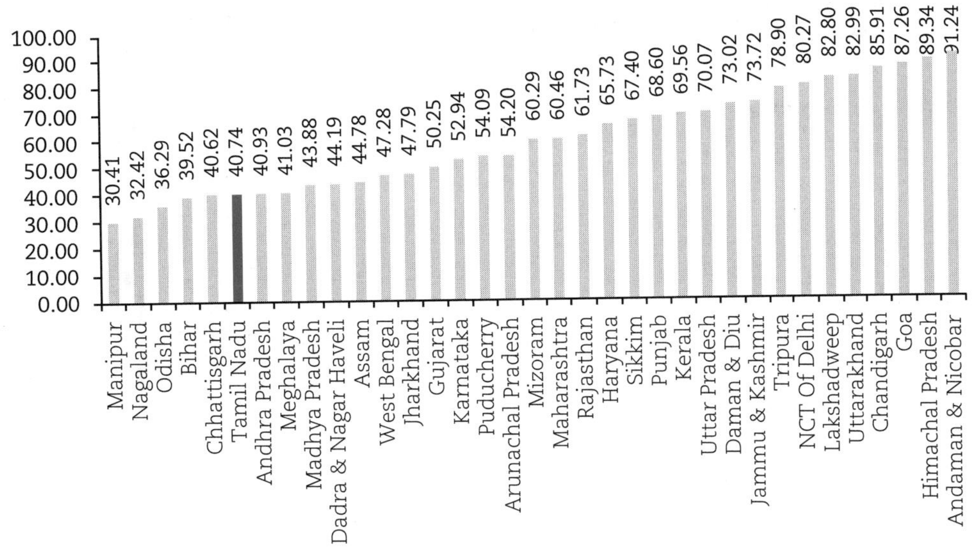

Source: Census of India.

family planning surgery after the first girl child; and from ₹15,200 to ₹25,000 for each child in the event of the parents undergoing family planning surgery after the second girl child.

Legislative Provisions for Social Security

The legislative provisions for social security have been enacted to provide sufficient security for the vulnerable sections of women and children. Some of the best practices adopted by the State are:

- Stakeholders training.
- Training of Medical Officers (MOs).
- Good linkage with the judiciary.
- Counseling under Section 14 ordered by the courts.
- Issue of interim orders.
- Issue of handbooks published by Lawyers Collective to all the Protection Officers (POs), Deputy Superintendents of Police (DSPs) and 100 Magistrates.
- Provision of bare act in local language to all the POs.
- Ensure stock of Printed DIR Application-12, Form III Affidavit in green sheet and supplied to all the POs.

Protection of Women from Domestic Violence Act, 2005

This Act formally recognises a woman's right to live in a violence-free home. The issues are low awareness, indifferent attitude of police personnel and ineffective free legal aid. This may be addressed through application of the act in simplified manner, training the stakeholders and providing free legal aid with competent and experienced gender-sensitive judges.

Dowry Prohibition Act, 1961

This law is framed to combat the evils of dowry. The issues are misinformation about the act, lack of gender perspective and low level of legal literacy. Village level women's committees are to be set up exclusively for dealing with these cases. Members of the committees are to be trained by experts and linked up with police stations and protection officers within the district. The committees are to provide support to the women in terms of mobility and child care, receive complaints, and assist them while filing the complaints.

Pre-conception (PC) and Pre-natal Diagnostic Technique (Prohibition of Sex Selection Act) Act, 1994 (PC and PNDT Act)

Even though the Act has been implemented effectively, it has to be thoroughly reviewed in order to evaluate its progress and monitoring mechanism. Frequent inspections without prior notice are to be conducted in the districts with the worst child sex ratio.

Immoral Traffic Prevention Act, 1956

Rehabilitation homes are have been established with enabling environments, coupled with facilities for alternative livelihood training.

Sexual Harassment of Women at Work Place

This Act has not been enacted, but the bill has been tabled in the Parliament. Action has been taken based on the Supreme Court Guidelines.

Tamil Nadu Women Harassment Act, 2000

The target population is not adequately aware of the act and its provisions. Provisions of the act should be disseminated through various communication strategies to all schools and colleges, orphanages, shelter homes, work places, and among all stakeholders.

Tamil Nadu is one of the States that have enacted various statutory provisions for the protection of women. Various capacity-building initiatives and State-level sensitisation workshops for stakeholders such as women, police officials, lawyers, judges, etc., have been held. In the Twelfth Plan, the Department of Social Work proposes to create awareness about legal rights and remedies. Formation of village level women's committees to deal with legal issues, training of PLFs and preparation of manual for training of federation members is being proposed in coordination with TNCDW. Many of the central Acts (the first six) have a State-based implementation unit and the POs and Social Welfare department closely monitor the fallout.

Tamil Nadu Hostels and Homes for Women and Children (Regulation) Act, 2014

The Act mandates compulsory registration and licensing of all hostels and homes with the District Collector and also follow certain basic guidelines prescribed by the Government of Tamil Nadu.

Way Forward and Areas for Policy Intervention

- Declining child sex ratios necessitates that the specialised girl child protection schemes be extended across all districts and throughout the State. Various programmes to check foeticide and female infanticide were devised with focus on ante-natal care including special surveillance to check foeticide which won a national award for excellence in public administration. Such interventions can be replicated and scaled up across the State to increase Sex ratio.

- Female literacy requires some attention as gender gap in literacy needs to be reduced. Literacy circles in MGNREGA sites, etc., could be a good option

- Domestic violence figures indicate scope for improvement and need to use SHGs and apply peer pressure for local community-based interventions. There is a need for improving the projection of the status of women in media and for adopting a rights-based approach to safety and security.

- Social security net needs to be improved for female-headed households who are responsible for children as well as geriatric population as they are the most vulnerable.

The process of gender budgeting that has been under planning process is yet to take off in the State. The classification of all programmes for women under the gamut of TNCDW reduces the reach of different sectoral schemes. There are several departments that do not have specific programmes to address the specific development requirements of women. There is a need for specialised gender cells that can conduct research, document and draw the attention of policy planners to the emerging needs and issues of women.

Working towards development that also encompasses women, it is necessary to focus on women in the context of policies and various developmental programmes. This is a paradigm shift from the welfare approach that relegates women to become mere recipients of various beneficiary projects, often under the assumption that some of the benefits would eventually trickle down to them. The patriarchal structures aid the prevalence and perpetuation of gender inequalities, despite the constitutional provision of equality. Equality refers to equal opportunities in terms of access to sources of livelihood, health, and education, as well as to social, economic and political participation without discrimination. It is expected that the State would continue and gear up its policies to tackle the issues of women and promote an engendered development.

References

Athreya, Venkatesh B. and Sheela Rani Chunkath (2000). "Tackling Female Infanticide: Social Mobilisation in Dharmapuri, 1997-99", *Economic and Political Weekly* 35(49): 4345-48.

Basu, S. (1995). *She Comes to Take Her Rights: Indian Women, Property, and Propriety*. State University of New York Press.

Chaudhary, Ruchika and Sher Verick (2014). "Female Labour Force Participation in India and Beyond", *ILO Asia-Pacific Working Paper Series*.

Daga, A.S., S. Jejeebhoy and S. Rajgopal (1999). "Domestic Violence against Women: An Investigation of Hospital Causality Records, Mumbai", *Journal of Family Welfare* 45(1): 1-11.

Das, M. and Sonalde Desai (2003). "Why Are Educated Women Less Likely to Be Employed in India?: Testing Competing Hypotheses", Social Protection Discussion Paper Series. *http://www.sonaldedesai.org/das_and_desai_2003_on_women.pdf*

Dasgupta, M. and P.N.M. Bhat (1995). "Intensified Gender Bias in India: A Consequence of Fertility Decline", *Working paper* No. 2. Centre for Population and Development Studies, Harvard University.

Dheeraja, C. and H. Rao (2010). *Changing Gender Relations: A Study of MGNREGS across Different States*. Hyderabad: National Institute of Rural Development (NIRD).

Diamond-Smith, N. and D. Bishai (2014). "Evidence of Self-correction of Child Sex Ratios in India: A District Level Aanalysis of Child Sex Ratios in India from 1981-2011", *Demography* (in Press).

Fatima, Ambreen and Humera Sultana (2009). "Tracing Out the U-shape Relationship between Female Labor Force Participation Rate and Economic Development for Pakistan", *International Journal of Social Economics* 36(1/2): 182-98. doi: 10.1108/03068290910921253. *http://www.emeraldinsight.com/ 10.1108/03068290910921253*

Garcia-Moreno, C., H.A. Jansen, M. Ellsberg, L. Heise and C.H. Watts (2006). "Prevalence of Intimate Partner Violence: Findings from the WHO Multi-Country Study on Women's Health and Domestic Violence", *Lancet* 368(9543): 1260-69.

Ghosh, J. (2009)."Equity and Inclusion through Public Expenditure: The potential of the NREGS", *Paper for International Conference on NREGA*, New Delhi. 21–22 January.

Goldin, C. (1994). "The U-shaped Female Labour Force Functions in Economic Development and Economic History", *NBER Working Paper* No. 470. Cambridge: National Bureau of Economic Research.

Hindin, M.J., S. Kishor and D.L. Ansara (2008). "Intimate Partner Violence among Couples in 10 DHS Countries: Predictors and Health Outcomes", *DHS Analytical Studies* No. 18 Calverton, Maryland, USA: Macro International Inc.

ICRW (2012). *Opportunities and Challenges of Women's Political Participation in India: A Synthesis of Research Findings from Select Districts in India*.

Jejeebhoy, S. (1998). "Wife Beating in Rural India: A Husband's Right? Evidence from Survey Data", *Economic and Political Weekly* 33(15): 855-62.

Jha, P., M. Keslar and R. Kumar (2011). "Trends in Selective Abortions of Girls in India: Analysis of Nationally Representative Birth Histories from 1990 to 2005 and census data from 1991 to 2011", *Lancet* 377(9781): 1921-28.

Kelley, A.C. (1991). "The Human Development Index: Handle with Care", *Population and Development Review* 17(2): 315-24.

Kishor, S. (1993). "May God Give Sons to All: Gender and Child Mortality in India", *American Sociological Review* 58(2).

Kishor, S. (2006)."Population and Gender", in G. Ritzer (ed.), *Blackwell Encyclopaedia of Sociology*. Oxford UK: Blackwell Publishing.

Kottis, A.P. (1990). "Shifts over Time and Regional Variation in Women's Labor Force Participation Rates in a Developing Economy: The Case of Greece", *Journal of Development Economics* 33: 117–32. *http:// www.sciencedirect.com/science/article/pii/030438789090009Z*

Klasen, S. and J. Pieters (2012). *"Push or Pull? Drivers of Female Labor Force Participation During India's Economic Boom", IZA Discussion Paper Series, Working Paper* No. 6395. Bonn: Institute for the Study of Labor.

Kottis, A.P. (1990). "Shifts Over Time and Regional Variation in Women's Labour Force Participation Rates in a Developing Economy: The Case of Greece", *Journal of Development Economics* 33(1): 117-32.

Krishnaji, N. (1997). "Human Development Index; A Critique", *Economic and Political Weekly* 32(35): 2202-05.

Mammen, Kristin and Christina Paxson (2008). "Women's Work and Economic Development", *The Journal of Economic Perspectives* 14(4): 141–64.

Mitra, Aparna (2014). "Son Preference in India: Implications for Gender Development", *Journal of Economic Issues* 48(4): 1021-37, December.

Miller, B.D. (1981). *The Endangered Sex*. Ithaca, New York: Cornell University Press.

———. (1989). Changing Patterns of Juvenile Sex Ratios in Rural India: 1961 to 1971, *Economic and Political Weekly* 24(22): 1229-35.

Rustagi, Preet (2000). "Identifying Gender Backward Districts Using Selected Indicators", *Economic and Political Weekly* 35(48): 4276-86.

Tansel, Aysit (2002). "Economic Development and Female Labor Force Participation in Turkey: Time-series Evidence and Cross-section Estimates", METU/ERC Working Paper. *http://papers.ssrn.com/sol3/papers.cfm?abstract_id=301946*

Sahoo, Harihar and Manas Ranjan Pradhan (2013). "Domestic Violence in India: An Empirical Analysis", in *Well Being and Female Security Indices*. Tata Strategic Management Group. March 5.

7

Social Security

Introduction

Social security is a set of means that influences human development by addressing deprivations, and improving living standards and access to entitlements. According to Dreze and Sen (1995: 99), "Social security is an essential requirement of social justice". Social security assumes a crucial role in dealing with chronic deprivations and uncertainties that characterise the developing countries. "Short-term, often acute downward fluctuations in living standards are superimposed upon long-term persistent deprivation associated with generally low standards of living"(Burgess and Stern, 1991: 41). The contrast with developed countries is striking—while deprivations do prevail in developed countries, the magnitude and consequences are less severe. Burgess and Stern (1991) attribute this difference partly to government social security programmes in most developed countries. Guhan (1994) has advocated adoption of a combination of promotional, preventive and protective social security measures in developing countries, which are characterised by high occupational diversity and employment instability associated with the unorganised sector.

Tamil Nadu Vision 2023 emphasises state provision of social security net to the disadvantaged, vulnerable and destitute groups so that economic growth is inclusive. "To those sections of society who are too old, helpless and destitute, the state will provide though its social security net, the necessary helping hand in terms of income support, food, shelter and healthcare so that there is no fundamental deprivation at any level in the state. Tamil Nadu Vision 2023 resolves that by 2023 nobody in Tamil Nadu will be left behind" (Government of Tamil Nadu, 2012). According to Dreze and Sen (2013), achievements of Tamil Nadu, Kerala and Himachal Pradesh (HP) are examples of those attained through state intervention in health, education, nutrition and related social sector schemes. Tamil Nadu has witnessed reduction in poverty and improvement in health, education and nutrition with a social security programme comprising in-kind transfers and cash transfers for vulnerable groups like women, children, workers in organised and unorganised sector, elderly, sexual minorities (transgender), widows, SCs (Scheduled Castes), STs (Scheduled Tribes), minorities and PWD (persons with disability). The state is known for successful implementation of the universal programmes like PDS (public distribution system), Puratchi Thalaivar MGR Nutritious Meal Programme PT MGR (NMP) and Integrated Child Development Scheme (ICDS); and is in fact the first state to initiate a school noon meal programme. Tamil Nadu has a number of innovative social security programmes to its credit, besides the PT MGR NMP—social security pensions for vulnerable population, public provisioning of health and education, Labour Welfare Board, Transgender Welfare Board, Amma Unavagams (canteens) and disability component in Mahatma Gandhi National Rural Employment Guarantee Scheme (MGNREGS). The state has judiciously used some conditional transfers, such as ICDS, Chief Ministers Girl Child Protection Scheme (CMGCPS) and Dr Muthulakshmi Reddy Maternity Benefit Scheme (MRMBS), supply of free notebook, textbook and bicycles scheme to attain educational and health goals like growth monitoring of children, pre-school education, improvement in nutrition, enrolment of girl children in schools, increased educational attainment of girl children, increased age of marriage, institutional birth, immunisation of children, etc. Tamil Nadu provides unconditional transfers (both cash and in kind), like social security pensions for vulnerable groups, PDS, etc., in order to protect the population from destitution and improve their standard of living. Marginalised groups like homeless population, SCs, STs, religious minorities, children in conflict with law and sexual minorities, are included in the state's social security schemes. The CCTs (conditional cash transfers) have made a considerable impact on some indicators, primarily because Tamil Nadu has not substituted CCTs for service delivery. Earlier chapters have dealt with education and health in detail. Social security in Tamil Nadu has enabled people's access to education, healthcare, food and nutrition and played an important role in breaking inter-generational transmission of poverty and in enhancing resilience. Although social security is not just a government activity, this chapter examines some of the important social security schemes of the Government of Tamil Nadu (GoTN), classifying those according to the approach discussed by Dreze and Sen (2013). The classification is provided in Annexure Table A-7.1.

Social Sector Expenditure in Tamil Nadu

Information gathered on the composition of expenditure made on the four social welfare schemes in Tamil Nadu between 2000 and 2010 shows that, by 2009-10, expenditure on social security and welfare was the highest at 12.9 per cent, followed by nutrition at 8 per cent (Table 7.1). Expenditure on the welfare of SCs, STs and OBCs (Other Backward Classes), and labour welfare as a proportion to expenditure on social services declined between 2000 and 2010.

Table 7.1

Composition of Expenditure on Social Welfare Schemes to Total Expenditure on Social Services in Tamil Nadu from 2000-2009 (as %)

S. No.	Year	*Proportion of Welfare Schemes to Social Services*			
		Welfare of Scheduled Castes, Scheduled Tribes and Other Backward Classes	*Labour and Labour Welfare*	*Social Security and Welfare*	*Nutrition*
1	2000-01	6.4	1.4	8.5	7.0
2	2001-02	6.2	1.4	9.0	6.0
3	2002-03	6.3	1.4	7.9	6.6
4	2003-04	6.4	1.7	9.7	7.9
5	2004-05	6.3	1.1	9.6	7.1
6	2005-06	6.8	1.1	10.6	6.9
7	2006-07	6.7	1.1	12.2	6.7
8	2007-08	6.1	0.9	15.1	7.2
9	2008-09	5.3	1.0	12.4	6.7
10	2009-10	5.6	1.1	12.9	8.0

Note: Includes plan and non-plan expenditure.

Source: *http://www.rbi.org.in/, Handbook of Statistics on State Government Finances*, 2010.

Nutrition Security Schemes

In India, PDS increased the per capita calorie intake of the population by nearly 6 per cent in 2009-10 (Himanshu and Sen, 2013). Further, in the context of calorie intake of the population being below the RDA (recommended dietary allowance), the absence of PDS would have resulted in heightening out-of-pocket consumption expenditure by 15 per cent than the actual so as to maintain even the low level of calorie intake (Himanshu and Sen, 2013). The decline in household intake of food (recommended dietary intake) was discernible in the National Nutrition Monitoring Bureau (NNMB) States between 1975-1979 and 2011-12, in the case of nutrients like protein, energy, calcium and iron (National Nutrition Monitoring Bureau, 2012). Tamil Nadu government's commitment to food and nutrition security by provision of universal in-kind transfers, like PDS, MDM and ICDS, has ensured that majority of the households have access to food. Data from the National Sample Survey Organisation (NSSO), which will be presented in the following discussion, clearly demonstrates the universal nature of PDS in Tamil Nadu, with nearly all households belonging to the consumption poor groups utilising the PDS, thus minimising exclusion errors. Although the ICDS is a Central government scheme which has a specific programme design, it is in implementation that Tamil Nadu differs from other states. A study on ICDS indicated that the level of political commitment, accountability and women's agency distinguished Tamil Nadu from other states. (Citizens' Initiative for Rights of Children Under Six, 2006). Although, access to food is ensured in Tamil Nadu, child undernutrition data, from a population-based survey, which has been discussed in detail in the Health chapter, shows that population level estimates of child undernutrition remain an area of concern, regardless of the improvements made between National Family Health Survey (NFHS)-2 and NFHS-3. The following discussion will highlight improved nutritional outcomes among children who utilise ICDS centres, attesting to the crucial role that the government plays in achieving public health goals.

Puratchi Thalaivar MGR Nutritious Meal Programme

Tamil Nadu has to its credit one of the most innovative in-kind, universal, conditional transfers to combat malnutrition and hunger and to improve human capability—Puratchi Thalaivar MGR Nutritious Meal Programme (PT MGR NMP) launched in 1982, which has been replicated by the central government across the country. School children, irrespective of caste, religion, income and gender, from classes 1-10 can take part in the programme on all school working days, provided they are enrolled in a school (government schools, government-aided schools, National Child Labour Project (NCLP) Special schools, madrasas), attend class and are willing to participate. The meal is cooked fresh in the school and provides employment to women belonging to disadvantaged sections of the population. It is important to note that mere provision of noon meals alone will not ensure increased enrolment rate in schools. This scheme works effectively in States that have well functioning schools run by the government and private schools which are aided by the government. The chapter on Education had highlighted improvements in PTR (pupil-teacher ratio) in all districts between 2005-06 and 2011-12, a large proportion of qualified teachers and high rank on infrastructural development index for schools in Tamil Nadu.

Prior to the introduction of this scheme, Madras Municipal Corporation (MMC) had a Midday Meal Programme for disadvantaged children in 1925. In 1956, the erstwhile Madras State ran a Mid-day Meal (MDM) programme in elementary schools with contributions from the government and community. Owing to the work burden on school teachers who were expected to cook the noon meal, this scheme was modified in 1967 with a centralised kitchen, which turned out to be more expensive than the meals cooked there (Rajivan,2001). PT MGR NMP, which was introduced in 1982, initially covered children in the age group 2-5 years in pre-school noon meal centres and primary school children in rural areas. Within a few months, the scheme was extended to urban areas, and by 1984, it also covered children in the age group 10-15 years in their schools. In 1983, the scheme included the Old Age Pension (OAP) beneficiaries and by 1990s, pregnant and lactating women as well. The pre-school NMP centres were merged with the ICDS.

On all school days, school children are provided with hot meals comprising rice, lentils curry (sambar), vegetables and eggs (banana in lieu of eggs for children who do not eat eggs). Since 2013, the State government has introduced variety in the meals programme with a different menu on each day, keeping in mind nutritional requirements as well as taste on a pilot basis in one block in each district. The government has also introduced a millet pilot in two districts (Box 7.1).

In the government and government aided schools, 75.5 per cent of children benefitted from PT MGR NMP (data provided by Tamil Nadu State Planning Commission). Tamil Nadu provides higher calories and proteins to beneficiary children under PT MGR NMP than recommended by the Government of India (GoI). For instance, while the GoI norms for MDM is 450 kcl of calories for primary and 700 kcl for upper primary children, Tamil Nadu provides 533.3 kcl for primary and 733.86 kcl for upper primary school children. Similarly, while the GoI norm for proteins is 12 gm for primary and 20 gm for upper primary school children, Tamil Nadu provides 18.12 gm for primary and 21.64 gm for upper primary school children. Importantly, Tamil Nadu puts in more than the required fund contribution from the State, although the MDM norms have fixed the Centre-State fund sharing ratio as 75:25. Although the Centre-State ratio for per day MDM cost norm is ₹3.34, where the Centre contributes ₹2.51 and the State contribution is supposed to be ₹0.83 for primary school children, Tamil Nadu puts in an additional contribution of ₹3.26, taking the per child per day expenditure to ₹6.60. In the case of upper primary school children, while the MDM norm is ₹5, with the Centre's share as ₹3.75 and the State's share as ₹1.25, Tamil Nadu makes an additional contribution of ₹2.43, making the per child per day expenditure to be ₹7.43 (data provided by the State Planning Commission). Tamil Nadu contributes the entire expenditure on PT MGR NMP for school children in the 9th and 10th standards. In addition to increased financial outlays, the State organises regular training programmes for the staff involved on hygiene, waste disposal and cooking methods. To monitor the programme, government officials regularly inspect the centres. The government has also installed a Management Information System (MIS) on a pilot basis in 208 blocks in which basic information is entered into a database.

The chapter on Education had discussed a marginal decline in the percentage of government schools offering primary education in the State and a

Box 7.1

Improving Micronutrient Intake: Ariyalur and Perambalur Pilot

In 2013, Tamil Nadu has introduced a pilot programme in Ariyalur and Perambalur districts to improve nutrient intake with provision of cookies, *laddoos* and *chikkies* made of millets as a special initiative. As millets are rich in mineral and fibre content and have comparable levels of protein and energy content similar to rice and wheat, the government decided to include this nutrition powerhouse in PT MGR NMP. The state government has allocated ₹500 crore for the pilot programme benefitting 63,426 children. Data from the schools have shown that intake of millets has resulted in weight gain among children.

Table 7.2

Number of Beneficiaries and Expenditure under Social Welfare Schemes for Nutrition in Tamil Nadu, 2009-10 to 2013-14

S. No.	Name of Scheme	Achievement	2010-11	2011-12	2012-13	2013-14
1	PT MGR Nutritious Meal Programme (schools)	Number of centres	42824	42886	43787	42490
		Number of beneficiaries	5774673	5480340	5014245	5352111
		Expenditure (₹ in crore)	1060.81	1267.74	1229.55	1473.54
2	PT MGR Nutritious Meal Programme (anganwadi centres)	Number of beneficiaries	1138831	1130238	1156017	1104148
		Expenditure (₹ in lakh)	7425.82	7865.06	7986.50	6210.23
3	Integrated Child Development Service Scheme (number of supplementary nutrition beneficiaries)	Number of centres	54439	54439	54439	54439
		Number of children in age group 6-12 months	267552	346784	364067	358460
		Number of children in age group 13-24 months	533473	612332	668030	694208
		Number of children in age group 25 to 36 months children	507165	619114	656870	689059
		Number of children in age group 37 to 60 months children	631666	511138	751863	699610
		Number of antenatal/postnatal women	523889	619845	670266	688683
		Number of senior citizen pensioners	22384	18414	5915	2307
		Number of adolescent Girls	-	382050	383777	404378

Note: The scheme for adolescent girls was taken over by Rajiv Gandhi Scheme for Empowerment of Adolescent Girls in 2010-11.

Source: Government of Tamil Nadu, Social Welfare and Nutritious Meal Programme Department, Performance Budget 2014-15.

considerable increase in the percentage of private-unaided schools between 2002-03 and 2011-12. Increased participation of the unaided private sector in education, which is out of the scope of the MDM scheme, could well have an impact on enrolment for PT MGR NMP, thereby rendering those sections of population vulnerable in the event of food inflation or adverse events. Table 7.2 shows a decline in the number of noon meal centres as well as beneficiaries in the last four years. The number of centres and beneficiaries has come down from 42,824 and 57,74,673 in 2010-11 to 42,490 and 53,52,111 in 2013-14, respectively.

Table 7.3 is based on information gathered from the NSSO in 2007-08, 64th Round (2010) on Education in India, which covers students in the age group 5-29 years. NSSO data indicate the extent to which government schools and MDM retain importance even at the population level. It reflects the extent to which the child population is protected against random shocks, like food inflation, unemployment of parents, etc., which could result in children being withdrawn from schools.

Tamil Nadu (62%) had the largest proportion of currently enrolled students receiving MDM from the government, followed by Karnataka (58.6%). Further, in rural Tamil Nadu, nearly three-fourth of the students benefitted from the government MDM. Even in urban areas of Tamil Nadu, nearly half the students has gained from the scheme.

Integrated Child Development Service Scheme (ICDS)

ICDS was initiated by the central government in 1975 with an aim to improve the nutritional and health status of children in the age group 0-6 years and it offers a package of services such as supplementary nutrition, immunisation, health check-up, referral services, pre-school non-formal education and nutrition and health education. Besides children under six years, the scheme also covers adolescents and pregnant and lactating women. Tamil Nadu has included elderly (OAP beneficiaries) and destitute pensioners (widows, deserted wives, differently-abled individuals and unmarried women) in the scheme, whereby they can participate in the noon meal.

Table 7.2 indicates an increase in the number of children in the age group 6-36 months receiving food from the Anganwadi Centres (AWCs) and in that of

Table 7.3

Proportion of the Students of Age 5-29 Years Pursuing General Education and Receiving Mid-Day Meals (MDM) from the Government in Tamil Nadu, Andhra Pradesh (United), Karnataka, Kerala, Maharashtra, Gujarat and All-India, 2007-08 (as %)

S. No.	State	Place of residence	Proportion of students receiving mid-day meals (MDM)
1	Tamil Nadu	Rural	72.9
		Urban	47.2
		Total	62.0
2	Andhra Pradesh (United)	Rural	41.7
		Urban	16.6
		Total	34.5
3	Karnataka	Rural	72.1
		Urban	30.0
		Total	58.6
4	Kerala	Rural	46.2
		Urban	30.9
		Total	42.6
5	Maharashtra	Rural	44.3
		Urban	22.7
		Total	35.4
6	Gujarat	Rural	65.8
		Urban	23.1
		Total	50.1
	All-India	Rural	48.7
		Urban	21.1
		Total	41.7

Source: National Sample Survey Organisation, 2010; Education in India: Participation and Expenditure 2007-08, 64th Round.

antenatal and postnatal women receiving food by more than 30 percentage points between 2009-10 and 2012-13. However, the number of elderly and destitute pension beneficiaries receiving food from the AWCs has declined considerably, probably because OAP in the State was increased to ₹1,000. The Performance Budget 2014-15 of Social Welfare and Nutritious Meal Programme Department, GoTN, shows that in AWCs, there was a 12.2 percentage points increase in the proportion of children in the age group 0-60 months with normal weight; and 11.6 percentage points decline in moderate underweight children in the same age group, demonstrating effective programme outcomes (Figure 7.1).[1] Under the Special Weight Taking Campaign conducted at AWCs, monthly progress reports show further improvements, with a decline in the proportion of underweight children to 14 per cent in 2014-15.

Table 7.4 presents information collected from NFHS-3 on utilisation of ICDS services. Tamil Nadu has a higher proportion of children under the age six who has received any service from an AWC over the past one year, as opposed to the other southern States, although it is lower than that of Maharashtra and Gujarat.

Nearly one-third of the children under six years received food supplements from an AWC in Tamil Nadu. The State has the largest proportion of mothers who received counselling from an AWC after their child was weighed (75.7%). Tamil Nadu does better than the other States under comparison, considering the percentage of pregnant women and lactating mothers who received supplementary food from AWCs.

Public Distribution System (PDS)

The PDS is an unconditional in-kind transfer. Tamil Nadu is one of the few States in India, besides Chhattisgarh, to have a nearly universal PDS, although the GoI introduced Targeted Public Distribution System (TPDS) from 1997. Universal PDS has played a crucial role in protecting the poor from food price inflation. Calculations based on the Tendulkar national poverty line, made by Dreze and Khera (2013), revealed that PDS had reduced the headcount ratio (HCR) of the poor by 44.4 per cent and the poverty gap index by 61.3 per cent in rural Tamil Nadu (Table 7.5). Poverty reduction was sharper on using the consumer price index for agricultural labourers (CPI-AL), which shows that the PDS had reduced HCR of the poor by 80.3 per cent and poverty gap index by 83.4 per cent in rural Tamil Nadu.

Tamil Nadu has the highest implicit per capita monthly subsidy on PDS at ₹107.3 in rural areas and ₹86.0 in urban areas among all States (Dreze and Khera, 2013).The GoTN provides 20 kg of rice free of cost per month per card throughout the State and has a special scheme for Nilgiris district, where the limit ranges from 16-24 kg. Rice entitlement for Antyodaya card holders stands at 35 kg per month, which is free of cost. There are 33,948 fair price shops in Tamil Nadu, which undertake the distribution of commodities at subsidised price. As on March 2014, there were 1,98,02,532 cards in circulation in Tamil Nadu.

Rice is 19.7 times cheaper in the PDS than from other sources in rural Tamil Nadu and 25.6 times cheaper than other sources in urban Tamil Nadu (National Sample Survey Organisation, 2013). Table 7.6, which

1. This data pertains only to children who utilise AWCs in Tamil Nadu and is not a population-based estimate.

Figure 7.1

Nutritional Status of Children Enrolled in Anganwadi Centre

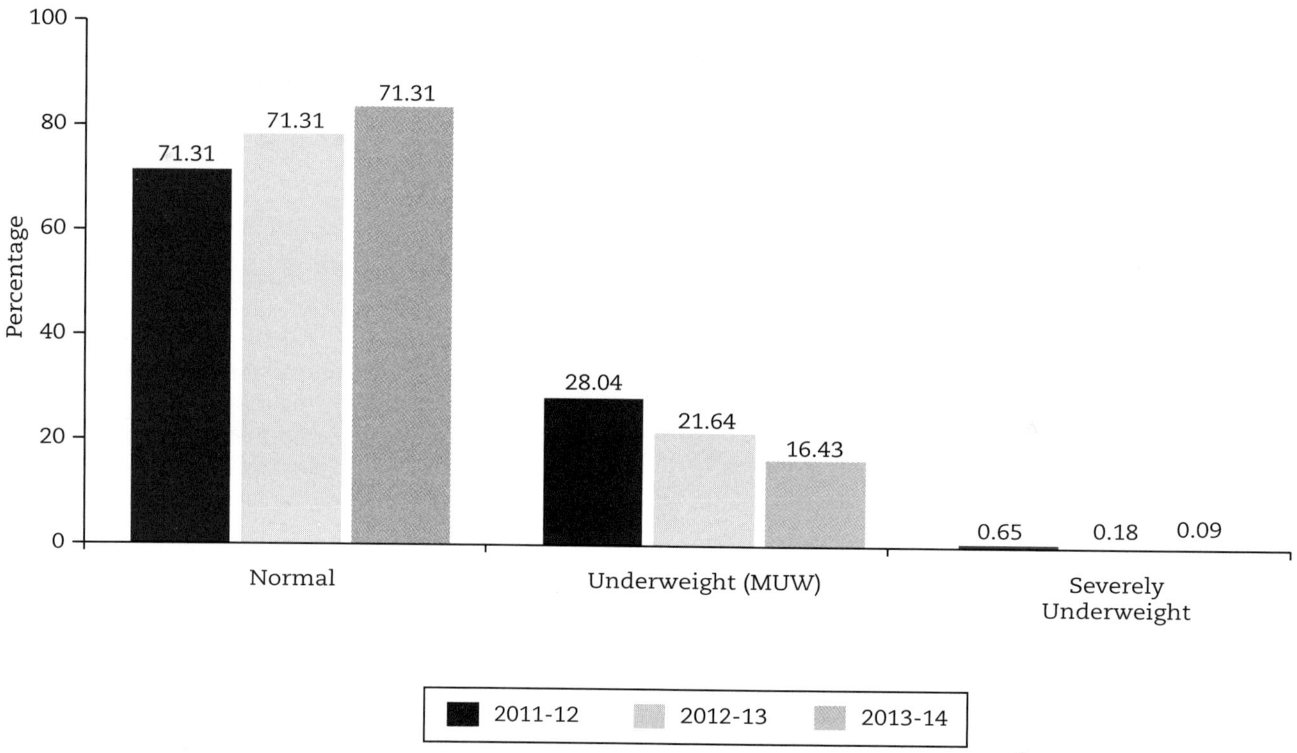

Source: Government of Tamil Nadu, 2014; Social Welfare and Nutritious Meal Programme Department, Performance Budget 2014-15.

presents information on PDS consumption shows that almost 91 per cent of the households in rural areas and 61 per cent of the households in urban areas of Tamil Nadu received rice from the System in 2009-10. This is much higher than the all-India average and that of all the States under comparison, thereby attesting to the universal nature of PDS in Tamil Nadu. The table also shows a marked increase in consumption of rice and wheat in all the States under comparison, except for Gujarat, between 2004-05 and 2009-10. It is important to note that the year 2009-10 witnessed very high food inflation.

We can see that coverage of the universal PDS is much higher among lower MPCE (monthly per capita expenditure) decile groups than targeted PDS. The data (Table A 7.2) demonstrates the importance of PDS for all MPCE decile groups, though a lesser proportion of households in the top two deciles in rural Tamil Nadu and top 4 deciles in urban Tamil Nadu consume rice from the PDS. Nearly all the households in rural (99.3%) and urban (95.3%) Tamil Nadu, belonging to the bottom decile, consume rice obtained from PDS. Further, in rural Tamil Nadu, 67.1 per cent of the households belonging to the top MPCE decile consume rice from the PDS, as opposed to 39.2 per cent in rural India. The State government has introduced subsidised food canteens in order to provide nutritious food to the urban poor (Box 7.2).

Social Security Schemes for Women

Livelihood Schemes

Since 1979, Tamil Nadu has a scheme that promotes income earning opportunities for women by supplying sewing machines free-of-cost to vulnerable groups, such as widows, deserted wives, destitute women, differently-abled men and women in the age group 20-40 years and Sri Lankan refugees. The objective of the scheme is to promote self-employment among poor women. The government also has a Special Programme for Women since 1978-79, which aims to improve the economic status of poor women by providing employment opportunities in training centres, like palm leaf training centre, tailoring training centre, mat training centre and cloth doll making training centre, where 498 women were trained at an expense of ₹213.8 lakh in 2013-14 (Government of Tamil Nadu, 2014). The government also has industrial cooperatives societies in which poor women above the age of 18 years can become members. There are 98 such societies including

Table 7.4

Utilisation of ICDS Services in Tamil Nadu, Andhra Pradesh (United), Karnataka, Kerala, Maharashtra, Gujarat and All-India During 12 Months Preceding the Survey, 2005-06

S. No.	State	Percentage of children age 0-71 months who received any services from AWC	Percentage of children under age six years who received food supplements from AWC	Percentage whose mothers received counselling from an AWC after child was weighed	Percentage of women who received supplementary food during pregnancy	Percentage of lactating mothers who received supplementary food
1	Tamil Nadu	42.5	32.2	75.7	50.4	42.5
2	Andhra Pradesh (United)	30.5	28.0	56.5	22.9	17.4
3	Karnataka	35.5	28.0	52.5	30.3	18.4
4	Kerala	30.8	24.7	56.1	15.8	10.5
5	Maharashtra	49.5	42.4	40.2	25.8	17.5
6	Gujarat	43.9	31.7	45.1	19.1	12.1
	All-India	32.9	26.3	48.9	20.5	16.5

Note: Supplementary food includes food cooked and served at the AWC on a daily basis or given in the form of take-home rations; AWC stands for Anganwadi Centre; Information relates to children under age six years in areas covered by an AWC.

Source: International Institute for Population Sciences (IIPS) and Macro International, 2007.

Table 7.5

Reduction of Rural Poverty Due to PDS in Tamil Nadu, Andhra Pradesh (United), Karnataka, Kerala, Maharashtra, Gujarat and All-India, 2009-10 (as %)

S. No.	States	Tendulkar national poverty line		Consumer price index for agricultural labourers (CPI-AL) based poverty line	
		Headcount ratio	Poverty gap index	Headcount ratio	Poverty gap index
1	Tamil Nadu	44.4	61.3	80.3	83.4
2	Andhra Pradesh (United)	32.8	40.6	56.1	57.2
3	Karnataka	22.2	33.1	34.6	45.5
4	Kerala	33.0	36.7	39.6	38.2
5	Maharashtra	18.9	30.0	35.5	30.1
6	Gujarat	11.8	15.3	18.7	18.7
	All-India	10.6	17.6	16.4	22.4

Source: Reproduced from Dreze and Khera (2013).

tailoring societies, chalk, crayon, stationery and coir-making societies with a membership of 72,891 in 2013-2014. Tailoring societies stitch and supply uniforms for children studying in the government schools.

Social Security Schemes for Children

Educational Schemes for School Children

Government of Tamil Nadu provides in-kind and cash transfers to encourage completion of schooling among children who attend government/government-aided schools. This is an important measure to develop human capability, which enhances choices of children so that they can live a long and healthy life and enjoy a decent standard of living. In-kind transfers like free textbooks, notebooks, laptops, bicycles, noon meals and residential accommodation, as well as cash transfers, are provided to children who are enrolled in schools. All of these schemes have contributed to improvements made in the GER (gross enrolment ratio), particularly among girls and decline in overall dropout rate as shown in the Chapter on Education. As per a survey commissioned by the Ministry of Human Resources Development (MHRD) in 2014, 0.66 per cent of children aged 6-13 years were out-of-school in Tamil Nadu (Social and Rural Research Institute and EdCIL, 2014). In addition, a slightly smaller proportion of girls (0.62%) than boys (0.7%) aged 6-13 years were out-of-school, which is different from the all-India pattern, indicating the role played by various social security schemes dedicated towards girl children in Tamil Nadu. It is interesting to note that Goa is the only state where no children were out-of-school. In Tamil Nadu, a lesser proportion of Muslim children aged 6-13 (0.54%) than that of Hindus (0.65%) and Christians (1.24%) were out-of-school. However, a larger proportion of SC children aged 6-13 (0.85%) compared to the STs (0.73%), OBCs (0.41%) and others (0.41%) were out-of-school in Tamil Nadu. Social security schemes and the education system will have to focus attention on Children with Special Needs (CWSN), as 26.97 per cent of them aged 6-13 years were out-of-school in the State. Andhra Pradesh (united) does better than all the south Indian states with only 11.65 per cent of CWSN aged 6-13 years being out-of-school. Further, although Tamil Nadu has a relatively lower

Table 7.6

Percentage of Households Reporting Consumption from Public Distribution System During 30 Days in Tamil Nadu, Andhra Pradesh (United), Karnataka, Kerala, Maharashtra, Gujarat and All-India, 2004-05 and 2009-10

State	*Commodity*	*Percentage of households reporting consumption from PDS during past 30 days*			
		2004-05		2009-10	
		Rural	*Urban*	*Rural*	*Urban*
Tamil Nadu	Rice	78.9	47.7	91.0	67.0
	Wheat	8.9	10.7	57.3	50.8
	Sugar	64.8	64.1	86.4	77.7
	Kerosene	79.0	39.0	81.2	40.5
Andhra Pradesh (United)	Rice	62.2	31.1	83.9	42.7
	Wheat	0.6	0.7	1.7	2.8
	Sugar	35.8	15.0	57.0	31.8
	Kerosene	63.0	26.0	79.1	27.7
Karnataka	Rice	58.5	21.0	74.6	24.8
	Wheat	45.6	14.6	69.2	23.3
	Sugar	15.2	4.8	47.0	13.2
	Kerosene	74.0	31.0	84.5	30.5
Kerala	Rice	34.6	23.3	54.3	42.5
	Wheat	12.2	12.1	32.8	28.5
	Sugar	7.2	5.2	21.7	16.1
	Kerosene	73.0	57.0	79.3	59.0
Maharashtra	Rice	27.5	6.0	46.8	10.0
	Wheat	25.8	6.9	44.2	10.7
	Sugar	3.4	0.9	20.3	7.8
	Kerosene	56.0	23.0	79.6	19.8
Gujarat	Rice	31.5	7.2	33.8	8.3
	Wheat	28.7	6.8	34.5	10.5
	Sugar	25.3	6.7	28.3	6.2
	Kerosene	78.0	25.0	74.5	18.3
All India	Rice	24.4	13.1	39.2	20.6
	Wheat	11.0	5.8	27.6	17.6
	Sugar	15.9	11.5	27.8	18.7
	Kerosene	73.0	33.0	81.8	33.0

Note: Both the PDS survey rounds used a 30-day reference period to collect information on households reporting consumption from the PDS.

Source: National Sample Survey Organisation, 2007;National Sample Survey Organisation, 2013.

Box 7.2

***Amma Unavagam* (Urban Cafeterias)**

Tamil Nadu is one of the highly urbanised states according to the Census of India 2011, with nearly 48.4 per cent of the population residing in urban areas. The GoTN has launched an innovative programme financed by municipal corporations—*Amma Unavagams* (canteens)—in 2013 to address urban food insecurity. This initiative aims to provide subsidised and hygienic cooked food in the urban areas in municipal corporations to protect health and economic conditions of the poor and downtrodden. It was intended to benefit workers in the unorganised sector, labourers, migrant workers and the urban poor. The Chapter on Income, Poverty and Employment shows that a larger proportion of casual labourers, compared to other categories of workers, were poor. *Amma Unavagam* will offer a buffer against fluctuating food prices for such vulnerable groups. There are 298 *Amma Unavagams*, of which 207 are in Chennai Corporation, 11 in Madurai Corporation, and 10 each in Coimbatore, Tiruchirappalli, Salem, Tirunelveli, Tiruppur, Erode, Vellore and Thoothukudi Corporations. The canteens are managed by women belonging to self-help groups (SHGs). It has been reported that nearly 2.5 lakh people eat at these canteens every day in Chennai. This initiative has drawn the attention of other States, like Rajasthan, Andhra Pradesh and Gujarat, which are considering replication of the programme.

proportion of children out-of-school, 284,232 children were in the workforce; or in other words, child labour comprised 2.4 per cent of all children in the age group 5-14 years (Census of India, 2011), indicating the need to strengthen coverage of free educational services and continue emphasis on social security schemes in order to prevent parents/caregivers from making their children work. It is important to note that children without parents living with elderly caregivers/others from socio-economically disadvantaged backgrounds would be particularly vulnerable to be engaged in work, even though the government has care homes, albeit a limited number, and hostels for those without caregivers.

Tamil Nadu government provides free textbooks and four sets of free uniform to all students from classes 1 to 12 and free notebooks to all those studying in classes 1 to 10. The free laptop scheme was introduced in 2011-12, and the free notebook and educational kits scheme in 2012-13. The educational kit comprised school bag, geometry box, crayons/colour pencils and an atlas. The government has introduced a special cash incentive scheme from 2011-2012 to reduce the dropouts at secondary level and to encourage the children to continue their secondary education. An amount of ₹1,500 for students studying in 10th and 11th standards and ₹2,000 for those in 12th standard in government/government-aided schools is deposited in the Tamil Nadu Power Finance Corporation, which is later handed over to the students on completion of their higher secondary education. In the case of those studying in the government/government-aided schools (classes 1-12), whose income earning parent has passed away or has become permanently incapacitated in an accident, the government provides financial assistance of ₹50,000 deposited in the name of the student in a public sector undertaking so that children do not drop out of school. As Sarva Shiksha Abhiyan (SSA) promotes inclusive education, the State government has allocated ₹2.37 crore for 1,49214 CWSN in 2013-14 (Government of Tamil Nadu, 2014).

In order to enhance enrolment of SC/ST girls and to reduce dropouts, the government has been providing cash transfer since 1994-95. This scheme aims to incentivise the completion of primary schooling among SC/ST girls and is currently implemented in all districts. The monthly cash incentive for SC/ST girls studying in classes 3-5 works out to ₹50 per child for 10 months in a year and the same for classes 6-8 is ₹100. The scheme has benefitted 4,83473 girl students from classes 3-8 in 2013-14 (Government of Tamil Nadu, 2014).

The government has an important initiative to reduce dropouts among SC, ST, BC, MBC (most backward classes) and Minority school children—hostel facilities. In 2013-14, there were 2,604 hostels for school children (comprising AdiDravida Welfare Hostels, Tribal Hostels, Government Tribal Residential Schools, hostels for Backward Classes, Most Backward Classes, Denotified Communities and Minority school children) with 1,81,750 students utilising the facilities (Table 7.7). The government subsidises expenditure on food and toiletries at the hostels and provides library facilities, incinerators, water purifiers, colour television and bedding for resident students. Although provision of accommodation for children belonging to SC, ST, BC, MBC, Denotified Communities (DNCs) and Minorities have enabled a large number of poor children to complete schooling, there is concern about the safety of these children, particularly girls, who reside in the hostels and the maintenance of hostels. In order to address these concerns, the government has ensured that all hostels for women and children in the state are regulated under the Tamil Nadu Hostels and Homes for Women and Children (Regulations) Act 2014.

Table 7.7

Number of Residential Hostels for SC, ST, BC, MBC, DNC and Minority School Children in Tamil Nadu, 2013

Sl. No.	*Classification of hostels*	*Number of hostels*	*Number of students*
1	Adi Dravidar Welfare Hostels	1143	82130
2	Tribal hostels	42	2782
3	Government Tribal Residential Schools	301	31594
4	Hostels for Backward Classes	611	34325
5	Hostels for Most Backward Classes	360	19485
6	Hostels for Denotified Communities	136	10534
7	Hostels for Minorities	11	900
	Total	2604	181750

Source: Government of Tamil Nadu, 2014, Department of Adi Dravidar and Tribal Welfare, Performance budget 2014-15; Government of Tamil Nadu, 2014, Department of Backward Classes, Most Backward Classes, Denotified Communities and Minority Welfare, Performance budget 2014-15.

The government could allocate additional resources to maintain the existing hostels.

Schemes for Children in Need of Care and Protection and Children in Conflict with Law

The Department of Social Defence administers schemes to protect the interest of children in need of care and those in conflict with law under the Juvenile Justice Act. The Rajya Sabha has passed a new Juvenile Justice (Care and Protection of Children) Bill in 2015. Tamil Nadu was the first State in India to notify the Tamil Nadu Juvenile Justice (Care and Protection) Rules, 2001. Presently these schemes are governed under the Juvenile Justice (Care and Protection of Children) Act 2015. There are 11 government children homes with 84 children and 24 children homes run by Non Government Organisations (NGOs) with 1,391 children in Tamil Nadu (Government of Tamil Nadu 2014). In 2013-14, the government spent ₹1,505.41 lakh on the government children homes and ₹515.63 lakh on children homes run by NGOs. The government also runs 27 government orphanages and 9 service homes, which cater to 4,036 children. In addition, there are 167 children homes run by NGOs, which benefit 8,521 children and the government expenditure on these homes amount to ₹1,924.75 lakh (data provided by State Planning Commission. Children admitted to these homes are provided with education and vocational training. These homes serve as a safe shelter and have the potential to play an important role in preventing child labour.

The Department of Social Defence has observation homes, special homes for boys and girls and government aftercare organisations for children in conflict with law. In 2013-14, the government has spent ₹13.02 lakh on observation homes, ₹134.54 lakh on special homes and ₹129.34 lakh on government aftercare homes. Observation homes admit children in conflict with law who are facing enquiry before Juvenile Justice Boards. In Tamil Nadu, there are six government observation homes with 127 children and two NGO-run observation homes with 45 children. Children who are found guilty by the Juvenile Justice Board are admitted to the special homes for rehabilitation. There are two special homes in Tamil Nadu with 27 children (Government of Tamil Nadu, 2014). The homes are supposed to provide education, vocational training and counselling as part of rehabilitating the children. After the children admitted in children homes and special homes complete their 18 years, they are discharged and admitted in aftercare organisations and provided with vocational training. There are three government aftercare organisations with 57 children in Tamil Nadu.

Labour Welfare Boards

The labour welfare board schemes primarily provide protection for workers in the case of employment related injury, unemployment, disability, maternity and death of breadwinner of the family.

Labour Welfare Board for Organised Sector Workers

In 1975, Tamil Nadu constituted the Tamil Nadu Labour Welfare Board under the Tamil Nadu Labour Welfare Fund Act, 1972, for organised sector workers. The schemes are contributory with employers and employees working in factories, plantations, motor transport undertakings, shop and catering establishment. Employers contribute ₹14 per worker per year, employees contribute ₹7 per year and the government contributes ₹7. During the period 1 April 2013 to 31 March 2014, 18,942 persons benefitted from various schemes under the board and ₹10,448,185 was spent (Government of Tamil Nadu, 2014). Table 7.8 presents information on various welfare schemes under this board.

Table 7.8

Schemes of Tamil Nadu Labour Welfare Board

S. No.	*Type of scheme*	*Nature of assistance*
1	Labour welfare centres	Tailoring section, pre-school and reading room.
2	Scholarships for various courses	Postgraduate course ₹6000 Graduates course ₹4000 Diploma course ₹2500 Higher secondary course ₹2000 ITI course ₹2000
3	Educational incentive	For first 10 rank holders in each educational district 10th standard - ₹2000 12th standard - ₹3000
4	Book allowance	Postgraduate course ₹3000 Graduate course ₹2000 Diploma course ₹1500 Higher secondary course ₹1000 (For private school students only)
5	Assistance for basic computer training	₹1000 for five employees/dependants in each district.
6	Marriage assistance	₹5000 for female and ₹3000 for male workers and their wards.
7	Spectacles assistance	Upto ₹500 for workers
8	Typewriting /Shorthand assistance	Typewriting higher ₹600 Typewriting lower ₹1000 Shorthand inter/high speed ₹750 Shorthand lower/higher ₹1500
9	Death assistance and funeral expenses	Death assistance of ₹25,000 and funeral expenses of ₹2000 to the legal heir of the worker.
10	Accident death assistance and funeral expenses	Accident death assistance of ₹100000 and funeral expenses of ₹2000 to the legal heir of the worker.
11	Hearing aid, artificial limbs and three Wheelers	Upto ₹1000 for Hearing aid, government prescribed price for artificial limbs and free supply of three wheelers.
12	TB Wards in various sanatoria	Tambaram Sanatorium (Chennai), Tiruppur, Asaripallam (Kanniyakumari), Austinpatti (Madurai) and Kizhpennathur (Tiruvannamalai)
13	Holiday homes for workers	Mamallapuram, Courtallam and Valparai.
14	JeevaIllam	A rest house for trade union representatives.
15	Magazine for workers	Monthly magazine,UzhaippavarUlagam, which consists of court judgments, labour acts, question and answers, as well as consumer price index.

Source: Government of Tamil Nadu, 2014c, Labour and Employment Department, Policy Note 2014-15.

Welfare Boards for Unorganised Sector Workers

As the reports produced by the National Commission for Enterprises in the Unorganised Sector (NCEUS) have pointed out, close to 90 per cent of India's workforce are employed in the informal sector with no security of employment or income. Even segments of workers in the formal sector, the NCEUS points out, are increasingly being employed as contract or as casual workers in recent years. The experience of Tamil Nadu is not very different as the chapter on Income, Poverty and Employment points out.

Over time, there has been a visible casualisation of employment in the State (NSS 55th and 68th Rounds). While 36.9 per cent of the total workforce in the State was casually employed in 2000-01, the share has increased to 42.8 per cent in 2011-12. While this increase has partly been the result of a decline in the number of self-employed, from 34.5 per cent to 31.7 per cent during this time period, additions made to the casual labour force has also been due to reductions in the share of the regularly employed—from 28.6 to 25.5 per cent. Importantly, as per the NCEUS report, in

Table 7.9

Conditions of Work Among Employees (Principal Status and Subsidiary Status) in AGEGC and Non-Agriculture Sectors for Different Statuses in Employment in Tamil Nadu, 2011-12 (as %)

S. No.	Conditions of employment	Category of Employees	Rural			Urban		
			Male	Female	Person	Male	Female	Person
1	Employees without a written job contract	Regular wage/salaried employees	73.8	78.7	75.1	82.9	82.9	82.9
		Casual labour	97.9	91.3	94. 6	99.3	99.8	99.4
		All workers	86.9	88. 5	87. 5	88.1	86.7	87.8
2	Employees not eligible for paid leave	Regular wage/salaried employees	50. 6	54.0	51. 5	48.7	46.3	48.1
		Casual labour	99.2	98.4	98.8	99.8	100	99.8
		All workers	76.9	88.4	81.7	64.9	58.4	63. 5
3	Employees not eligible for any social security benefit	Regular wage/salaried employees	63.2	59. 6	62.3	54.2	59.7	55. 6
		Casual labour	96.8	95.9	96.3	97. 6	97.3	97. 5
		All workers	81.4	87.7	84.1	68.0	68.2	68.0

Note: Social security benefits considered in the survey were PF/ pension, gratuity, healthcare and maternity benefit.

Source: National Sample Survey Organisation, 2014, Informal Sector and Conditions of Employment in India, 2011-12.

India, condition of the self-employed are rarely better than that of casual labour and are more often distress-induced due to inability to enter the labour market as wage labour. Information from the NSSO show poor conditions of employment among employees in the AGEGC (agriculture-related activities excluding crop production) and non-agriculture sectors workers in India, with 84.6 per cent in rural areas and 72.5 per cent in urban areas not having a written job contract; 80.5 per cent in rural areas and 60.7 per cent in urban areas not eligible for paid leave; and 80 per cent in rural areas and 63.5 per cent in urban areas not eligible for any social security benefit like provident fund (PF)/ pension, gratuity, healthcare and maternity benefit (National Sample Survey Organisation, 2014). The situation was worse among employees in the AGEGC and non-agriculture sectors in Tamil Nadu, with 87.5 per cent in rural areas and 87.8 per cent in urban areas without a written job contract; 81.7 per cent in rural areas and 63. 5 per cent in urban areas not eligible for paid leave; and 84.1 per cent in rural areas and 68.0 per cent in urban areas not eligible for any social security benefit (Table 7.9).

It is in this context that ensuring a degree of social security for different segments of the workforce becomes important. Tamil Nadu has 17 welfare boards for unorganised sector workers, which cover various occupations such as manual workers, construction workers, tailors, artists, handloom workers, power loom workers, handicraft workers, potters, palm tree workers, etc. (Table 7.10). In the period between 1 April 2013 and 31 March 2014, 3,71,303 unorganised workers have benefitted from various welfare schemes under the board, which has spent ₹9,3055,7703.

Tamil Nadu and Kerala were among the earliest states to start a welfare fund for construction workers. This is particularly important given that a major rise in employment over the last decade or so has happened in the construction sector. Subsequent to the passing of Tamil Nadu Manual Workers (Regulation of Employment and Conditions of Work) Act, 1982, the State government constituted the Tamil Nadu Construction Workers Welfare Board in 1994 in order to maintain and administer the Manual Workers General Welfare Fund of the Board and to provide welfare measures for 38 categories of workers in the construction sector. The funds are built up solely through contribution by the employers. Employers are supposed to pay 0.3 per cent of the total estimated cost of the proposed construction work. Workers who are registered with the board are eligible for the following benefits.

(1) Crèches.

(2) Personal accident relief.

(3) Pension scheme.

(4) Assistance for the funeral expenses.

(5) Assistance for education of the son or daughter of registered workers.

(6) Assistance for marriage of self and the son/daughter of a worker.

(7) Assistance for the delivery of a child or for the miscarriage during pregnancy or for the termination of pregnancy.

(8) Assistance for natural death.

(9) Spectacles.

Table 7.10

Welfare Boards for Unorganised Sector Workers in Tamil Nadu

S. No.	*Name of Welfare Board*	*Year of Inception*	*Number of Beneficiaries in 2013-14*
1	Tamil Nadu Construction Workers Welfare Board	1994	114101
2	Tamil Nadu Manual Workers Welfare Board	1999	41272
3	Tamil Nadu Unorganised Drivers Welfare Board	2006	11853
4	Tamil Nadu Tailoring Workers Welfare Board	2006	70077
5	Tamil Nadu Hair Dressers Welfare Board	2006	2219
6	Tamil Nadu Washermen Welfare Board	2006	3129
7	Tamil Nadu Palm Tree Workers Welfare Board	2006	2461
8	Tamil Nadu Handicraft Workers Welfare Board	2008	10560
9	Tamil Nadu Handloom and Handloom Silk Weaving Workers Welfare Board	2006	27238
10	Tamil Nadu Folk Artists'	2006	1110
11	Tamil Nadu Artists Welfare Board	2006	331
12	Tamil Nadu Goldsmiths Welfare Board	2006	3373
13	Tamil Nadu Pottery Workers Welfare Board	2006	1948
14	Tamil Nadu Domestic Workers Welfare Board	2007	9367
15	Tamil Nadu Powerloom Weaving Workers Welfare Board.	2009	16623
16	Tamil Nadu Street Vending and Shops and Establishments Workers Welfare Board	2010	55641
17	Tamil Nadu Cooking Food Workers Welfare Board	2011	-

Source: Government of Tamil Nadu, 2014, Labour and Employment Department, Performance Budget, 2014-15 and data provided by Tamil Nadu State Planning Commission.

Registration with the board renders the workers eligible for a pension of ₹1,000 per month, once they have attained 60 years or earlier in case they are unable to work due to illness or injury. As on 30 September 2013, 23,22,743 workers have been registered with the board (data provided by the State Planning Commission). However, of the total, only 7,41,416 workers have claimed benefits under this scheme, out of which 13,176 workers have availed the pension scheme. Given that the fund has a balance of nearly ₹500 crore after current disbursals, there is a clear need to put in more efforts to enrol workers in the welfare board and also to disseminate information among the members on benefits of being a registered member. The enactment and implementation of the welfare board was driven to a considerable extent by strong public action by workers' organizations since the late 1970s and early 1980s. While this public action led to greater awareness among the workers during that period, recent labour in the state's construction sector is increasingly drawn from inter-state migrants who are less aware of these schemes. This once again reiterates the case for active State and civil society action to create better awareness about the welfare board among new entrants into the construction sector's labour market.

In addition to the welfare board for labour in the construction sector, the State has constituted 16 other such boards for workers engaged in different segments of the unorganised sector. Funds for these boards are mobilised through cess, taxes and government grants. The government constituted the Tamil Nadu Manual Workers Welfare Board on 17 September 1999 and formulated the Tamil Nadu Manual Workers Social Security and Welfare Scheme in 2001. Later on, the scheme was substituted by the Tamil Nadu Manual Workers Social Security and Welfare Scheme, 2006. In the year 2012-13, 1,62,842 workers have registered in Tamil Nadu Manual Workers Welfare Board and other 14 boards. Another 11,525 workers have registered under the Unorganised Drivers Welfare Board. The welfare schemes are similar to the ones offered by the construction workers welfare board. The data provided by the social welfare department reveals that between 1 April 2013 and 31 December 2013, 1,86,749 workers had become beneficiaries of the welfare schemes provisioned by various welfare boards (apart from the construction sector). However, the welfare benefits per person works out to a State average of ₹2,142 for this period, which is not substantial. In fact, only 1,346 members have availed of the pension scheme so far. Clearly, in terms of the numbers registered and the quantum of benefits availed per registered member, there is a need for structured expansion.

Given the growing casualisation of employment, efforts should be made to considerably increase the registration count. Resource mobilisation should also be stepped up to ensure adequate resources available for a comprehensive social security net for those in temporary or casual work.

Despite the decline in shares of self-employment, the State continues to be home to a large number of self-employed artisanal workers, such as those involved in weaving, handicrafts and fishing. In addition to schemes for manual workers in general, there are separate schemes for handloom and fish workers. The following table provides a list of the various schemes and the number of beneficiaries under each scheme in the year 2013-14 for handloom weavers (Table 7.11). In the year 2013-14, the State government had a financial commitment of ₹300.16 crore directed at the set of schemes listed below.

Table 7.11

Welfare Schemes for Cooperative Handloom Weavers in Tamil Nadu

S. No.	*Name of Welfare Schemes*	*Amount*	*Number of Beneficiaries*
1	Cooperative Handloom Weavers' Family Pension Scheme	₹1000 per month	1299
2	Cooperative Handloom Weavers' Old Age Pension Scheme	₹1000 per month	17238
3	Cooperative Handloom Weavers' Savings and Security Scheme	Not applicable	71741
4	Health Insurance Scheme for Handloom Weavers	Upto ₹15000 per month	270046
5	Mahatma Gandhi Bunkar BimaYojana (Life and Accident Insurance)	Upto ₹150000	234608
6	Free Electricity to Handloom Weavers	Upto 100 units bimonthly	140005
7	Free Electricity to Handloom Weavers	Upto 500 units bimonthly	103653

Note: Scheme (4) is supported considerably by the central government. Scheme (5) is supported by the central government and Life Insurance Corporation of India

Source: Data provided by the Director of Handlooms and Textiles, Tamil Nadu.

Fish-workers too are provided with a number of welfare schemes. In addition to a separate set of economic support and schemes for those involved in inland fisheries, the State has 11 social security schemes, besides a range of subsidies for mechanisation and fuel. It includes fishermen and fisherwomen savings and relief schemes, assistance to fish-workers' families during fishing ban and fishing lean periods, and personal and group accident insurance schemes. During the ban period, the government provides ₹2,000 per family; whereas ₹4,000 is given to each family in order to offset loss of income during the lean seasons.

Welfare Schemes for Vulnerable Social Groups

Census of India 2011 shows that there were 1,44,38,445 SCs and 7,94,697 STs in Tamil Nadu. Inequalities among social groups on various indicators persist—while 80.1 per cent of the general population was literate, only 73 per cent of SCs and 54.3 per cent of STs were literate. The chapter on employment had shown that while the proportion of SCs/STs below the poverty line had decreased during the period 1993-94 to 2011-12, from 65.8 per cent to 24 per cent in rural Tamil Nadu, a much larger proportion of SCs/STs were poor when compared to the general population and OBCs. Tamil Nadu government has initiated welfare boards similar to that of the Tamil Nadu Labour Welfare Board for social security provision to the most vulnerable among SCs/STs and Muslims. The welfare boards for vulnerable social groups are Tamil Nadu Scavengers Welfare Board, Tamil Nadu Puthirai Vannar Welfare Board under the Adi Dravidar and Tribal Welfare Department and Denotified Communities Welfare Board, Tamil Nadu Narikoravar Welfare Board and Ulemas and Other Personnel Welfare Board under the Backward Classes, Most Backward Classes and Minorities Welfare Department (Table 7.12).

Scheduled Castes and Scheduled Tribes

Tamil Nadu Adi Dravidar Housing and Development Corporation Limited (TAHDCO)

Tamil Nadu Adi Dravidar Housing and Development Corporation (TAHDCO), which was established in 1974 under the Companies Act, 1956, with the aim of achieving socio-economic improvement of Adi Dravidar (SC) population was initially conceived as a construction company to build houses for SCs. However, by 1980-81, its scope was extended to betterment of SC/ST population through need-based formulation and implementation of economic activities. The economic development programmes implemented through TAHDCO are micro-enterprise development for poor families, vocational job-oriented skill training programmes and individual entrepreneur schemes supported by appropriate training and subsidy programmes. The following are schemes implemented for SCs through TAHDCO:

- Land Purchase Scheme exclusively for women
- Land Development Scheme
- Entrepreneur Development Programme (EDP)
- Special Scheme under EDP: Assistance for Petrol/Diesel/Gas retail outlets
- Self Employment Programme for Youth (SEPY)
- Self Employment Programme for setting up of Clinic—(SEPY Special)
- Economic Assistance to Self-Help Groups.
- Revolving Fund to Self-Help Groups.
- Collectors' Discretionary Fund.
- Managing Director's Discretionary Fund
- Financial Assistance to Civil Service Aspirants (UPSC)
- Financial Assistance to State Civil Service Aspirants (Tamil Nadu Public Health Service [TNPSC] Group-I)
- Financial Assistance to Law Graduates to set up their profession
- Financial Assistance to Chartered Accountant/ Cost Accountant to set up their profession.

During 2012-13, ₹13.45 crore had been allocated by the government to impart Skill Development Training programme to 13,130 youth belonging to the Adi Dravidar and SC/ST who had converted to Christianity (Government of Tamil Nadu, 2013). To improve the chances of absorption of SCs and STs into the labour market, TAHDCO offers the following skill development training programmes:

- AC mechanic.
- Apparel manufacturing training.
- Beautician.
- CAD/CAM.
- CAT/XAT.
- Diesel mechanic.
- Electrician.
- Fitter.
- Food production, food and beverages.
- Footwear and leather product manufacturing.
- JCB, Fork Lift Operation.
- Motor mechanic.
- Plastic product manufacturing.
- Tally.
- Tailoring.

Table 7.12

Welfare Boards for Vulnerable Social Groups in Tamil Nadu

S. No.	*Name of Welfare Board*	*Year of Inception*
1	Tamil Nadu Scavengers Welfare Board	2007
2	Tamil Nadu Puthirai Vannar Welfare Board	2010
3	Tamil Nadu Narikoravar Welfare Board	2008
4	Tamil Nadu Ulemas Welfare Board	2009
5	Tamil Nadu Denotified Communities Welfare Board	2007
6	Tamil Nadu Fisheries Welfare Board	2009
7	Tamil Nadu Tribal Welfare Board	2007
8	Tamil Nadu Traders' Welfare Board	1989
9	Tamil Nadu Grama Koil Poosarigal Welfare Board	2007
10	Tamil Nadu Folk and Artists' Welfare Board	2007
11	Tamil Nadu Agricultural Workers' Welfare Board	2006
12	Tamil Nadu Cable TV Operators' Welfare Board	2008
13	Tamil Nadu Film Artists' Welfare Board	2009
14	Tamil Nadu Transgenders' Welfare Board	2008
15	Tamil Nadu Khadi Spinners and Weavers Welfare Board	2010
16	Tamil Nadu Welfare Board for Differently-abled Persons	2007
17	Tamil Nadu Coconut Farmers' Welfare Board	2010

Source: Data provided by Tamil Nadu State Planning Commission

Provision of House Sites for Adi Dravidars

The Department of Adi Dravidar and Tribal Welfare provides free house-site *pattas* to the poor houseless SC and ST families, whose annual income is less than ₹40,000 in rural areas and ₹60,000 in urban areas. The extent of each house-site is one cent in corporations, one and a half cent in Municipalities and three cents in rural areas. During 2013-14, a sum of ₹252.51 lakh was spent and ₹512.93 lakh had been provided for 2014-15 (Government of Tamil Nadu, 2014).

Backward Classes, Most Backward Classes, Denotified Communities and Minorities

Distribution of Sewing Machines for Backward Classes, Most Backward Classes and Denotified Communities

In order to promote livelihood opportunities among BCs, MBCs and DNCs, the government implemented a sewing machine distribution scheme from the year 2001-02. The eligibility criteria for the scheme was that beneficiaries should belong to BCs, MBCs and DNCs in the age group 20-45 years, should have knowledge in tailoring and whose annual income limit is within ₹40,000 in rural areas and ₹60,000 in urban areas. In 2013-14, 2,418 sewing machines were distributed among the beneficiaries at a cost of ₹82.6 lakh. The government has allocated ₹82.8 lakh under this scheme for the year 2014-15. Distribution of sewing machines were focused on eight districts that were ranked low on the HDI (human development index), namely, Perambalur, Sivagangai, Tiruvannamalai, Villupuram, Dharmapuri, Dindigul, Krishnagiri and Cuddalore.

Skill development training scheme for Backward Classes, Most Backward Classes and Denotified Communities

The government has skill development training programmes, which are imparted through State/Central government training institutions so as to help BCs, MBCs and DNCs to acquire specific skills, to enhance employability and to take up self-employment which will contribute to their socio-economic improvement. The entire course fee is borne by the government. The eligibility criteria states that the candidate's parents' annual income should not exceed ₹1 lakh. Since 2012-13, the trainees have been sanctioned with a sum of ₹400 per month as stipend. The year 2012-13 onwards, skill development training programmes conducted by various departments of the State were implemented through the Tamil Nadu Skill Development Mission (TNSDM). By 2013-14, 36 types of training programmes have been conducted and 2,711 youths were trained at a total cost of ₹382.15 lakh (Government of Tamil Nadu, 2014).

Distribution of house site *pattas* for Backward Classes, Most Backward Classes and Denotified Communities

To provide access to land for construction of houses, the government distributes house-site *pattas* free of cost to the houseless persons belonging to BCs, MBCs and DNCs, whose annual income do not exceed ₹40,000 in rural areas and ₹60,000 in urban areas. Under this scheme, 2,20,296 house-site *pattas* have been distributed among the BCs, MBCs and DCs so far. In 2013-14, ₹262.47 lakh was spent on 1,407 beneficiaries. A sum of ₹200.01 lakh for Backward Classes Welfare Department and ₹100 lakh for Most Backward Classes and Denotified Communities Welfare Department, adding up to ₹300.01 lakh, have been provided under this scheme for the year 2014-15 (Government of Tamil Nadu, 2014).

Tamil Nadu Minorities Economic Development Corporation (TAMCO): Skill Development Training to Minority Youth

Tamil Nadu Minorities Economic Development Corporation (TAMCO) implements various welfare schemes to promote socio-economic development of religious minorities viz., Muslims, Christians, Buddhist, Sikhs, Parsis and Jains, whose annual income is within ₹40,000 in rural areas and ₹55,000 in urban areas. To improve employability of minority community, skill development training is provided free of cost in apparel manufacturing technology, leather goods designing and production technology, manufacturing technology, digital still photography, video camera, beautician skills, advanced automobile technology, air conditioning and refrigeration, certificate in foot wear manufacturing, food production, craftsmanship, light and heavy motor vehicle driving and various computer hardware/software. Training has been provided to 41,316 minorities at a cost of ₹12.0 crore between 2007-2008 and 2011-12 (Government of Tamil Nadu, 2013). It has been planned to implement these programmes through TNSDM.

Tamil Nadu Transgender Welfare Board

Data from the Census of India, 2011, reveal that there were 22,364 transgender persons in Tamil Nadu (Table 7.13). Andhra Pradesh (united) and Maharashtra have a larger number of third gender persons. Literacy rate among this particular group in Tamil Nadu (57.8%) was lower than that in Kerala (84.6%), Maharashtra (67.6%), Gujarat (62.8%) and Karnataka (58.8%). Then again, work participation rate among third gender persons in Tamil Nadu (43.7%) was higher than the all-India average (34%) and other states under comparison.

Tamil Nadu is the first state in the country to establish a welfare board for transgender individuals in 2008-2009, recognising the need to rehabilitate and integrate them in mainstream society, as they have been marginalised from access to social, cultural and economic opportunities since they do not conform to gender norms. As a result of these exclusions, transgender individuals face difficulty in accessing housing, healthcare, education and work participation. The Transgender Welfare Board (TGWB) comes under the Social Welfare and Nutritious Meal Programme department, and all transgender individuals who are natives of Tamil Nadu and possess an identity card issued by the TGWB are eligible to become members of the board. The State government conducted a survey across all districts in the State to identify transgender individuals. District-level screening committees constituting the district collector, deputy director of medical and rural health services, district social welfare officer, clinical psychologist/psychiatrist and a representative of the transgender community certify transgender individuals. These individual sare registered as members with TGWB and issued an identity card. The following types of assistance are provided by the TGWB:

- Identity card.
- Ration card.
- Voter identity card.
- House patta.
- Free housing.
- Medical facilities.
- Educational loan.
- Skill training.
- Assistance for self-improvement.
- Short stay homes.
- 25 per cent subsidy for Transgender SHGs for economic activities.

The Steering Committee had identified 3,471 transgender individuals in Tamil Nadu. In 2011-2012, 1,502 transgender individuals were given ration cards, 963 were given house *pattas*, 108 were given sewing machines, 589 were given health insurance cards and 442 were given 25 per cent subsidy from Transgender SHGs for economic activities. In 2012-13, the government spent ₹35 lakh on TGWB.

Since 2012-13, Tamil Nadu government has started a monthly pension scheme of ₹1,000 for destitute transgender individuals in order to assist those aged 40 years and above and are unable to earn a proper livelihood. Transgender individuals aged 40 years and above who possess a TGWB identity card and is unable to work are eligible for the monthly pension. In 2013-2014, 743 transgender individuals received the pension and the government spent ₹89.16 lakh on the scheme (Government of Tamil Nadu, 2014).

Tamil Nadu Welfare Board for Differently-abled Persons

According to Census of India, 2011, there were 1,17,9963 persons with disability (PWD hereafter) in Tamil Nadu, comprising 1.6 per cent of the total population (Table 7.14). The proportion of PWD in Tamil Nadu was lower than the national average. The work participation rate among PWD in Tamil Nadu (31.4%) was higher than the all-India average (28.2%). Literacy among PWD (64.1%) in Tamil Nadu was lower than that of the general population.

Figure 7.2 shows that among PWD, movement (24%) and hearing (19%) disability comprised a relatively large share. The NSSO's (2003) survey of disabled persons in India demonstrate the extreme vulnerability of PWD, as only 45.3 per cent were literate and 23.8 per cent were in the workforce.

Table 7.15 shows that 37.2 per cent of PWD were working before the onset of disability and among them, 55.3 per cent lost their job due to the same. Loss of job due to disability was highest among those with mental illness and blindness.

In order to address multiple deprivations of PWD, Tamil Nadu government instituted the Tamil Nadu Welfare Board for Differently-abled Persons under the Department for the Welfare of Differently-Abled Persons. This department has 67 schemes for the welfare of PWDs, which are grouped under the following thematic areas:

- Issue of identity card (1 scheme).
- Early intervention (3 schemes).
- Special education (14 schemes).
- Training and employment (13 schemes).
- Reservation (4 schemes).
- Assistive devices (12 schemes).
- Maintenance allowance (4 schemes).
- Other schemes (9 schemes).
- Social security schemes (7 schemes).

The board administers social security schemes similar to that of labour welfare boards, comprising cash transfers and in-kind transfers like personal accident relief, financial assistance to meet funeral expenses, financial assistance on natural death of PWD, scholarship to son and daughter of PWD, marriage assistance, maternity assistance and assistance for the purchase of spectacles. The achievements of major welfare schemes under the Department for the Welfare of Differently-abled Persons are highlighted in

Table 7.13

Socio-demographic Characteristics of Third Gender Population in Tamil Nadu, Andhra Pradesh (United), Karnataka, Kerala, Maharashtra, Gujarat and All-India, 2011 (as %)

S. No.	State	PoR	Absolute number	Literacy rate (7+ years)	WPR
1	Tamil Nadu	R	10909	45.3	51.2
		U	11455	69.9	36.6
		T	22364	57.8	43.7
2	Andhra Pradesh (United)	R	24838	43.1	46.9
		U	18931	67.2	30.1
		T	43769	53.3	39.7
3	Karnataka	R	11536	48.4	43.7
		U	8730	72.7	34.7
		T	20266	58.8	39.8
4	Kerala	R	2013	83.2	24.2
		U	1889	86.1	21.0
		T	3902	84.6	22.7
5	Maharashtra	R	21036	61.2	45.0
		U	19855	74.4	30.4
		T	40891	67.6	37.9
6	Gujarat	R	5318	51.0	39.3
		U	6226	72.6	33.2
		T	11544	62.8	36.0
	All-India	R	323120	48.8	35.7
		U	164683	69.9	30.7
		T	487803	56.1	34.0

Note: WPR stands for Worker Population Ratio.
Source: Census of India, 2011.

Table 7.16. In 2013-14, 92,680 persons with intellectual disabilities, 14,163 severely affected persons, 1,743 persons with muscular dystrophy and 4,970 persons affected with leprosy received maintenance allowance of ₹1,000 per month (Government of Tamil Nadu, 2014).

Night Shelters for Homeless Population

The Census of India has published information on the homeless (referred to as houseless by the Census) population in India. Persons who are not living in 'census houses' are considered to be homeless by the Census. Census houses refers to a structure with roof, hence the enumerators are instructed by Census officials to take note of the possible places where the houseless population is likely to live, such as on the roadside, pavements, drainage pipes, under staircases, or in the open, places of religious worship, platforms and the like. Homeless population are extremely vulnerable, as they are denied one of the basic human rights—shelter. A survey commissioned by the Planning Commission had shown that 73.8 per cent of homeless population in Chennai attributed their homelessness to poverty (Mander, 2008). In 2001, there were 86,472 homeless persons in Tamil Nadu, which declined to 50,929 in 2011. While the number of homeless population can be an underestimate in both time points, the temporal decline in the figures can be due to decline in poverty and effective implementation of social security schemes in Tamil Nadu. Table 7.17 points out that there are 17,73,040 homeless persons in India, with a larger concentration in the urban areas. The proportion of SCs among houseless population was relatively higher in Tamil Nadu and Karnataka, and that of STs was higher in Gujarat, Maharashtra and Andhra Pradesh. Men outnumber women among the homeless population in all the states under comparison. Literacy rate among the houseless population was highest in Kerala (58.4%), Maharashtra (50.2%) and Tamil Nadu (50.1%).

As a response to the issue of homelessness, Tamil Nadu has started 37 night shelters in urban areas across the State. There are 28 night shelters in Chennai, 2 in Tiruchirappalli, 1 each in Tiruppur, Vellore, Erode, Salem, Tirunelveli and Coimbatore. There are night shelters for women and children, men, families, PWD, persons with mental health issues, elderly and transgender individuals. Apart from accommodation and food, the night shelters also provide free legal aid, assistance in accessing government social security schemes and identity cards, admission to anganwadis and schools, admission to hospitals and referral to livelihood schemes of the government.

Social Security Pension

Tamil Nadu has experienced a rapid demographic transition and a concomitant increase in the proportion of elderly (age 60 years and above) population. In 2011, elderly constituted 10.4 per cent of the population in Tamil Nadu, which was higher than the all-India average of 8.6 per cent but lower than that of Kerala's 12.6 per cent (Table 7.18). The index of ageing, which is a ratio of the elderly to child population, is higher than the national average in south Indian States, particularly in Kerala and Tamil Nadu. The age dependency ratio was much higher than the national average in Kerala. In all the States under consideration, elderly women outnumbered elderly men, indicating that problems of ageing are dominantly faced by elderly women. The worker population ratio (WPR) among the elderly in Tamil Nadu was higher than the all-India average and that of the other states under comparison. In the

Table 7.14

Socio-demographic Characteristics of Persons with Disability (PWD) in Tamil Nadu, Andhra Pradesh (United), Karnataka, Kerala, Maharashtra, Gujarat and All-India, 2011 (as %)

S. No.	State	PoR	Absolute number	Proportion	Sex ratio (number of females per 1000 males)	Literacy rate (7+ years)	WPR
1	Tamil Nadu	R	621745	1.7	993	56.5	31.7
		U	558218	1.6	1000	72.4	31.1
		T	1179963	1.6	996	64.1	31.4
2	Andhra Pradesh (United)	R	1512961	2.7	996	42.5	33.2
		U	753646	2.7	987	69.2	29.1
		T	2266607	2.7	993	51.2	31.8
3	Karnataka	R	792694	2.1	979	55.4	31.5
		U	531511	2.2	963	76.9	32.8
		T	1324205	2.2	973	63.9	32.0
4	Kerala	R	414875	2.4	1078	71.8	19.0
		U	346968	2.2	1091	75.1	18.5
		T	761843	2.3	1084	73.3	18.8
5	Maharashtra	R	1666135	2.7	952	66.9	39.9
		U	1297257	2.6	903	80.8	34.3
		T	2963392	2.6	929	73.0	37.4
6	Gujarat	R	570479	1.6	949	59.3	29.5
		U	521823	2.0	880	77.0	29.6
		T	1092302	1.8	919	67.7	29.6
	All-India	R	18636358	2.2	949	53.0	28.0
		U	8178636	2.2	929	72.6	28.7
		T	26814994	2.2	943	59.0	28.2

Note: WPR stands for Worker Population Ratio.PoR stand for Place of Residence, R stands for Rural, U for Urban and T for Total

Source: Census of India, 2011.

Figure 7.2

Distribution of Persons with Disability by Type of Disability in Tamil Nadu, 2011 (as %)

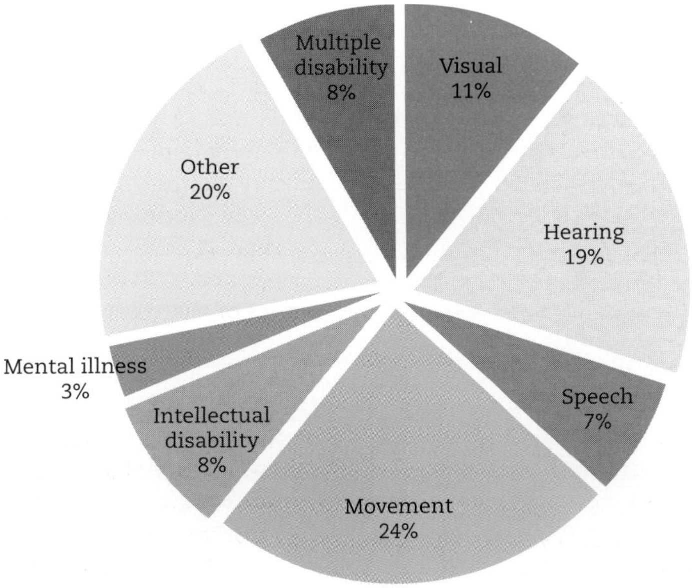

Source: Census of India, 2011.

Table 7.15

Proportion of Persons with Disability Working Before Onset of Disability and Change in Work Status Due to Disability, All India, 2002 (as %)

S No	Type of disability	Working before onset of disability	Change in work status due to disability			
			Loss of work	Change of work	No change	Not recorded
1	Intellectual disability	3.9	61.7	9.7	28.4	0.2
2	Mental illness	50.5	76.9	7.6	15.5	0
3	Blindness	54.0	77.6	7.1	15.3	0
4	Low vision	60.3	60.1	12.6	27.3	0
5	Hearing disability	50.9	23.9	8.4	67.5	0.1
6	Speech	9.2	23.7	8.3	68.0	0
7	Locomotor	35.7	56.5	17.1	26.4	0.0
	Any disability	37.2	55.3	13.2	31.4	0

Note: Intellectual disability refers to the diagnostic categories F70-F79, classified as mental retardation under the International Classification of Diseases 10 (ICD 10) of the World Health Organisation.

Source: National Sample Survey Organisation, 2003, Disabled persons in India.

absence of occupational pensions for a vast majority of the elderly, a significant proportion of them continue to work. The earlier discussion on the poor conditions of labour had shown that majority of the workers did not have any social security benefits. Hence, the elderly have to continue working until their health does not permit. Information from the NSSO (1998) show that among the elderly who had stopped working, the proportion without any retirement benefits was higher in rural areas (68.2%) than the urban areas (32.8%) in Tamil Nadu. Table 7.19 shows that the proportion of elderly persons has increased from 5.6 per cent in 1961 to 10.4 per cent in 2011 in Tamil Nadu. The age dependency ratio has also increased between 1961 and 2011. The index of ageing has increased sharply from 14.9 per cent to 44.2 per cent between 1991 and 2011. In Tamil Nadu, women constitute a larger share of the elderly. Since 2001, the gender composition of elderly has changed with a predominance of elderly women. The degree of urbanisation of the elderly has also escalated from 22.7 in 1961 to 46.4 per cent in 2011

A significant proportion of the elderly who are economically independent do support dependant family members. NSSO's (1998) report on elderly population highlights low incidence of ownership of property and financial assets among elderly women when compared to elderly men in Tamil Nadu. Further, 68.8 per cent of elderly women were completely dependent on others for day-to-day economic sustenance, whereas it is 31.8 per cent for elderly men (Table 7.20). Furthermore, a higher proportion of elderly women than men lived alone. While most elderly men lived with their spouse, most elderly women lived with their adult children. Nearly 30 per cent of elderly individuals reported suffering from some illness. The data on suicides in 2013 indicate that 15.5 per cent (179 out of 11,449) of all elderly persons who committed suicide in India were from Tamil Nadu and 14.8 per cent (198 out of 11,449) were from Kerala (National Crime Records Bureau, 2014), suggesting the high level of socio-economic stress associated with ageing.

In the earlier sections on welfare boards, we had discussed some of the deprivations faced by PWD, SC/ ST and transgender individuals. Table 7.21 presents information on the proportion of elderly population, PWD, SC, ST and number of transgender individuals across districts of Tamil Nadu. Erode had the highest proportion of elderly (12.9%), followed by Namakkal (12.4%), Karur (12.4%), Kanniyakumari (12.2%) and Ariyalur (11.6%).

The table also indicates that a larger proportion of SCs are found in Thiruvarur (34.1%), followed by Nilgiris (32.1%), Nagapattinam (31.5%), Perambalur (31%) and Villupuram (29.4%); and a larger proportion of STs are seen in Nilgiris (4.5%), followed by Dharmapuri (4.2%), Tiruvannamalai (3.7%), Salem (3.4%) and Namakkal (3.3%). Ramanathapuram (2.1%), Nilgiris (2%), Ariyalur (2%), Chennai (1.9%) and Tiruchirappalli (1.9%) have a relatively greater proportion of PWD. The State

Table 7.16

Number of Beneficiaries and Expenditure on Select Social Security Schemes of Government of Tamil Nadu for PWD, 2013-14

S. No.	Social security schemes		Number of beneficiaries	Expenditure (₹ in lakh)
1	Maintenance allowance	Severely affected	14163	1699
		Intellectual disabilities	92680	11121
		Muscular dystrophy	1743	204.12
		Leprosy	4970	596.4
2	Assistive devices	Tricycles	356	19.04
		Wheelchairs	412	20.18
		Braille watches	533	3.99
		Solar rechargeable batteries	1394	4.01
		Goggles and folding sticks	859	0.81
		Callipers	170	5.98
		Crutches	895	2.46
		Reflecting folding sticks	185	0.39
3	Employment	Motorised sewing machines	1879	71.97
		Self-employment scheme	785	78.34
		Unemployment allowance	25247	968.39
4	Special education	Cash incentive to prevent dropout	1279	19.77

Source: Data provided by Tamil Nadu State Planning Commission.

government transgender identification process claims that the number of transgender individuals was highest in Chennai (638), Coimbatore (332), Madurai (237), Salem (189) and Villupuram (149).

A survey known as the Public Evaluation of Entitlements Programme conducted in 2013 across 10 States of India, namely Bihar, Chhattisgarh, Himachal Pradesh, Jharkhand, Maharashtra, Madhya Pradesh, Odisha, Rajasthan, Tamil Nadu and Uttar Pradesh, highlighted the critical role that social assistance pensions play in the lives of elderly people (Chopra and Pudussery, 2014). The survey found that food, healthcare and subsistence needs accounted for abulk of spending done from the pensions for 80 per cent of the elderly.

Tamil Nadu had introduced several social security pension schemes much before the GoI started the same. The State has a long history of providing non-contributory social security pension to vulnerable groups like elderly, widows, deserted wives, unmarried destitute women, differently-abled persons, and agricultural labourers. These schemes cater to the below poverty line (BPL) population. Further, the government also organises grievance redressal/public hearings, where the public can report difficulties faced in accessing social security pension. The GoTN had introduced an Old Age Pension in 1962. This scheme is currently administered under the GoI scheme known as Indira Gandhi National Old Age Pension Scheme (IGNOAPS) since 2010. The State government also started Destitute Widow's Pension (DWP) in 1975, Destitute Agricultural Labourers Pension scheme (DALP) in 1981, Destitute Differently-abled Pension scheme (DDAP) in 1974, Destitute or Deserted Wives Pension Scheme (DDWP) in 1986 and Unmarried Women's Pension (UWP) in 2008. The DALP, which was started in 1981, is administered as Chief Minister's Uzhavar Padhukappu Thittam since 2013-14. The State government was the first to introduce a social security pension for transgender individuals in 2012-13. Sri Lankan Tamil refugees are eligible for State government social security pension schemes like Old Age Pension to Sri Lankan Tamils, Widows Pension to Sri Lankan Tamils, and Differently-abled Pension to Sri Lankan Tamils and Deserted Wives Pension to Sri Lankan Tamils. The State also provides maintenance allowance without an income ceiling through the Department for Welfare of Differently-abled Persons to those with intellectual disabilities, severely affected persons, ones with muscular dystrophy and leprosy-cured persons (discussed under Welfare Boards). The

Table 7.17

Socio-demographic Characteristics of Homeless Population in Tamil Nadu, Andhra Pradesh, Karnataka, Kerala, Maharashtra, Gujarat and All-India, 2011, (as %)

S. No.	State		Absolute number of houseless population	Proportion of houseless population	Proportion of SC	Proportion of ST	Proportion of children under six years	Sex ratio (number of females per 1000 males)	Literacy rate (7+ years)	WPR
1	Tamil Nadu	R	13812	0.04	19.4	11.4	14.3	873	43.9	49.1
		U	37117	0.11	31.2	3.3	10.8	789	52.3	44.7
		T	50929	0.07	28.0	5.5	11.7	811	50.1	45.9
2	Andhra Pradesh (United)	R	69354	0.12	16.5	20.1	15.8	978	37.5	53.9
		U	75857	0.27	10.4	7.8	12.9	867	55.0	42.3
		T	145211	0.17	13.3	13.7	14.3	919	46.8	47.9
3	Karnataka	R	41262	0.11	36.4	9.3	17.1	852	41.8	60.7
		U	35473	0.15	25.6	6.2	14.0	723	50.4	53.3
		T	76735	0.13	31.4	7.9	15.6	790	45.8	57.3
4	Kerala	R	4092	0.02	9.0	6.1	9.4	589	62.6	44.3
		U	7761	0.05	5.6	0.9	6.4	500	56.2	46.6
		T	11853	0.04	6.8	2.7	7.4	529	58.4	45.8
5	Maharashtra	R	99535	0.16	9.3	30.9	18.5	876	45.8	58.6
		U	111373	0.22	7.0	9.5	10.6	490	53.9	58.0
		T	210908	0.19	8.1	19.6	14.3	650	50.2	58.3
6	Gujarat	R	59484	0.17	2.5	31.8	20.1	882	32.4	55.1
		U	84822	0.33	3.6	25.9	15.3	620	36.5	58.8
		T	144306	0.24	3.1	28.3	17.3	719	34.9	57.3
	All-India	R	834692	0.10	21.2	17.4	18.9	878	37.2	50.9
		U	938348	0.25	13.8	8.4	12.0	558	40.8	52.8
		T	1773040	0.15	17.3	12.6	15.3	694	39.2	51.9

Note: WPR stands for worker population ratio. Census refers to homeless population as 'houseless population'.

Source: Census of India, 2011.

Table 7.18

Socio-demographic Characteristics of Elderly Population (60 years and above) in Tamil Nadu, Andhra Pradesh (United), Karnataka, Kerala, Maharashtra, Gujarat and All-India, 2011, (as %)

S. No.	State		*Proportion of elderly*	*Absolute number of elderly*	*Index of ageing (ratio of 60+ to 0-14 years)*	*Aged dependency ratio (ratio of 60+ to 15-59 years)*	*Sex ratio (number of females per 1000 males)*	*Proportion of literate elderly*	*WPR of elderly*
1	Tamil Nadu	R	10.8	4029097	44.4	16.7	1041	36.4	53.7
		U	10.0	3480661	43.9	14.8	1063	65.4	32.1
		T	10.4	7509758	44.2	15.8	1051	49.8	43.7
2	Andhra Pradesh (United)	R	10.8	6108091	41.4	17.4	1126	23.8	47.1
		U	7.7	2170150	30.8	11.6	1100	55.6	30.7
		T	9.8	8278241	38.0	15.4	1119	32.1	42.8
3	Karnataka	R	10.4	3897069	38.4	16.7	1127	33.0	46.7
		U	8.0	1893963	32.2	12.0	1070	65.4	28.6
		T	9.5	5791032	36.1	14.8	1108	43.6	40.8
4	Kerala	R	12. 6	2197552	53.2	19.8	1219	76.5	27.6
		U	12. 5	1995841	54.0	19.5	1234	82.2	20.9
		T	12.6	4193393	53.5	19.6	1226	79.2	24.4
5	Maharashtra	R	11.3	6969540	40.2	18.8	1152	42.4	52.1
		U	8.1	4137395	32.9	12.2	1054	71.9	24.8
		T	9.9	11106935	37.1	15.7	1114	53.4	41.9
6	Gujarat	R	8.3	2884326	26.7	13.8	1173	37.2	42.3
		U	7.4	1902233	28.6	11.1	1071	69.5	25.2
		T	7.9	4786559	27.4	12.6	1132	50.0	35.5
	All-India	R	8.8	73293822	26.8	15.1	1036	34.2	47.1
		U	8.1	30555218	30.9	12.4	1027	66.0	28.5
		T	8.6	103849040	27.9	14.2	1033	43.5	41.6

Note: WPR stands for worker population ratio. PoR stands for Place of Residence, R stands for Rural, U for Urban and T for Total

Source: Census of India, 2011.

Table 7.19

Demographic Characteristics of Elderly Population (60 years and above) in Tamil Nadu, 1961-2011 (as %)

Demographic characteristics of the elderly		*1961*	*1971*	*1981*	*1991*	*2001*	*2011*
1 Proportion		5.6	5.7	6.4	7.5	8.8	10.4
2 Decadal growth rate	-	25.4	31.3	34.1	32.3	36.4	
3 Age	Proportion of youngold (60-69 years)	3.9	4.0	4.3	4.8	5.5	6.4
	Proportion of oldold (70 years and above)	1.8	1.8	2.1	2.6	3.3	4.0
4 Dependency ratio	Age dependency ratio	9.9	10.2	11.0	12.1	13.9	15.8
	Child dependency ratio	66.2	66.9	59.8	50.2	42.0	35.8
5 Index of ageing		14.9	15.2	18.3	24.2	33.0	44.2
6 Gender composition	Male	50.2	50.9	51.4	52.0	49.7	48.8
	Female	49.8	49.1	48.6	48.0	50.3	51.2
	Person	100.0	100.0	100.0	100.0	100.0	100.0
7 Rural urban composition	Rural	77.3	72.9	70.2	68.7	58.5	53.6
	Urban	22.7	27.1	29.8	31.3	41.5	46.4
	Total	100.0	100.0	100.0	100.0	100.0	100.0
8 Proportion of literate elderly	Male	40.4	NA	47.9	49.9	60.6	65.8
	Female	5.7	NA	10.9	16.1	25.9	34.6
9 WPR among elderly	Male	73.4	70.2	61.8	57.1	60.3	60.2
	Female	24.8	13.3	19.4	21.3	26.1	28.0

Note: WPR stands for worker population ratio.

Source: Census of India various years.

pension amounts disbursed are the same at ₹1,000 per month. When the OAP was first introduced in 1962, the pension amount was ₹20 and by 2011 it was ₹1,000 (Figure 7.3). In the initial years, OAP had stringent eligibility criteria with only destitute elderly above the age of 65 years without male children being eligible, and there were ceilings on the number of beneficiaries. In fact, Tamil Nadu Human Development Report (TNHDR) 2003 had recommended revision of the two eligibility criteria for OAP, namely that the pensioner should have no family support and no means of subsistence. The government has removed these eligibility criteria reflecting a high degree of policy sensitivity.

Since 1991-92, the government has been providing grants to NGOs to run old age homes and from 2011-12 integrated complexes of special homes for senior citizens and destitute children. In 2013-14 the government spent ₹31.91 lakhs on 28 old age homes with 611 elderly residents and ₹499.30 lakh on 64 integrated complexes with 1821 beneficiaries (Government of Tamil Nadu, 2014).

Figure 7.3

Change in Social Security Pension Amount in Tamil Nadu, 1962-2011

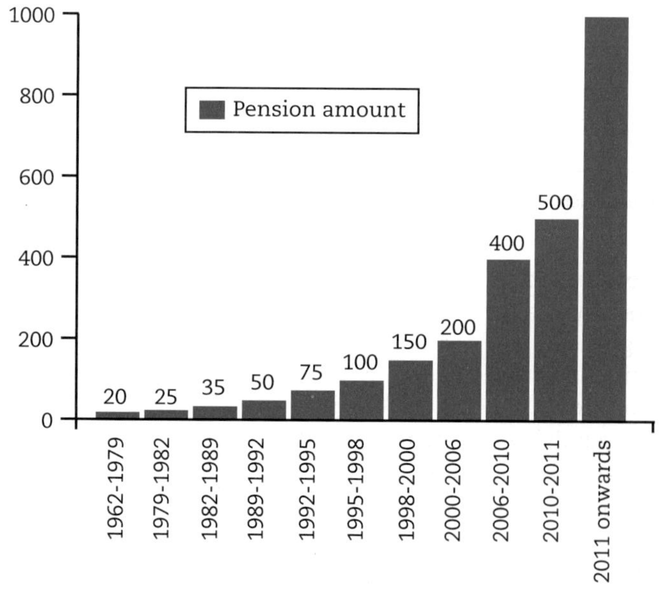

Source: GoTN (2014). *Performance Budget 2014-15*. Social Welfare and Nutritious Meal Programme Department.

Table 7.20

Socio-economic Characteristics and Morbidity of the Elderly in Tamil Nadu, 2004 (as %)

Social characteristics		*Rural*			*Urban*		
		Male	*Female*	*Person*	*Male*	*Female*	*Person*
Level of economic dependence	Not dependent on others	48.7	19.3	33.9	54.3	19.3	35.7
	Partially dependent	15.9	16.5	16.2	13.9	11.9	12.8
	Fully dependent	35.5	64.2	49.9	31.8	68.8	51.4
Number of dependants among elderly who are economically independent	0	7.2	46.0	18.3	13.7	54.7	25.4
	1	42.0	28.5	38.2	37.4	12.7	30.3
	2	24.5	21.2	23.6	26.9	26.1	26.7
	3	12.5	2.1	9.5	10.8	4.6	9.1
	4	5.4	0	3.8	4.6	0.6	3.4
	5	4.6	1.9	3.8	3.8	1.4	3.1
	6-8	3.5	0.3	2.6	2.4	0	1.7
	9 and above	0.4	0	0.3	0.4	0	0.3
Category of persons supporting elderly	Spouse	9.9	10.9	10.5	5.1	15.2	11.8
	Own children	86.7	78.8	81.9	85.6	73.8	77.7
	Grandchildren	1.2	3.0	2.3	2.5	3.1	2.9
	Others	2.2	7.2	5.3	6.8	7.9	7.5
Living arrangement	As inmate of old age home	0	0	0	0.8	0	0.4
	Alone	5.2	19.4	12.3	2.7	12.0	7.7
	With spouse only	30.2	11.0	205	22.1	9.9	15.7
	With spouse and other members	51.6	20.4	35.9	58.7	19.9	38.1
	With children	10.4	39.1	24.8	12.1	48.0	31.2
	With relations	2.7	8.9	5.8	3.3	9.7	6.7
	With other non relations	0	1.1	6	0.3	0.3	0.3
Proportion of elderly reporting ailment (15-day recall)		28.7	29.6	29.2	30.3	34.6	32.6

Source: National Sample Survey Organisation, 2006, Morbidity, healthcare and the condition of the aged, 2004.

However, due to targeted nature of these pensions, documentation requirements are found to be quite high, leaving scope for corruption. Moreover, there is evidence from the India Human Development Survey conducted in 2004-05, which reveals that targeting does not result in more benefits for the poor and that universal programmes, like MDM, have higher utilisation among the poor, SC and ST households (Desai *et al.*, 2010). For instance, 55 per cent of the children belonging to the bottom quintile were covered by MDM, whereas only 15 per cent of elderly and widows from the same quintile were covered by the old age/widow pension. Besides, the government does not identify beneficiaries (except in the case of transgender individuals); rather the poor and disabled are expected to apply for benefits and submit documentation to support their claims. Available estimates of the coverage of elderly and widows by government social security pensions such as old age pension, widow pension, disability pension, etc from the 2011–12 round of the India Human Development Survey (IHDS) shows an increase in the proportion of elderly households in India receiving pensions from17 per cent in 2004–05 to 42 per cent in 2011–12 (Barik *et al.*, 2015).

Table 7.21

District-wise Proportion of Elderly, Persons with Disability (PWD), Scheduled Castes (SCs), Scheduled Tribes (STs) and Number of Transgender Individuals, 2011 (as %)

S. No.	District	Proportion of elderly (%)	Proportion of PWD (%)	Proportion of Scheduled Castes (%)	Proportion of Scheduled Tribes (%)	Number of transgender individuals identified
1	Ariyalur	11.6	2.0	23.3	1.4	24
2	Chennai	9.8	1.9	16.8	0.2	638
3	Coimbatore	11.3	1.7	15.5	0.8	332
4	Cuddalore	9.3	1.6	29.3	0.6	131
5	Dharmapuri	9.3	1.5	16.3	4.2	87
6	Dindigul	10.9	1.7	20.9	0.4	148
7	Erode	12.9	1.3	16.4	1.0	141
8	Kancheepuram	9.1	1.5	23.7	1.0	85
9	Kanniyakumari	12.2	1.6	4.0	0.4	41
10	Karur	12.4	1.4	20.8	0.1	44
11	Krishnagiri	8.6	1.5	14.2	1.2	26
12	Madurai	10.0	1.3	13.5	0.4	237
13	Nagapattinam	10.5	1.5	31.5	0.2	36
14	Namakkal	12.5	1.8	20.0	3.3	123
15	Nilgiris	9.7	2.0	32.1	4.5	1
16	Perambalur	11.0	1.6	31.0	0.5	19
17	Pudukkottai	10.2	1.7	17.6	0.1	14
18	Ramanathapuram	9.8	2.1	18.4	0.1	51
19	Salem	10.9	1.5	16.7	3.4	189
20	Sivagangai	11.3	1.5	17.0	0.1	32
21	Thanjavur	10.8	1.8	18.9	0.1	40
22	Theni	10.7	1.5	20.7	0.1	125
23	Thiruvallur	8.4	1.7	22.0	1.3	105
24	Tiruvannamalai	10.5	1.5	22.9	3.7	86
25	Thiruvarur	10.5	1.7	34.1	0.2	14
26	Tirunelveli	11.3	1.8	18.5	0.3	62
27	Tiruppur	10.7	1.7	16.0	0.2	45
28	Tiruchirappalli	11.1	1.9	17.1	0.7	127
29	Thoothukudi	11.4	1.7	19.9	0.3	62
30	Vellore	9.6	1.5	21.9	1.9	143
31	Villupuram	9.6	1.5	29.4	2.2	149
32	Virudhunagar	10.3	1.4	20.6	0.1	114
	Tamil Nadu	10.4	1.6	20.0	1.1	3471

Note: The data on transgender individuals are for the period 2008-09.

Source: Census of India 2011; *Transgender Survey of Government of Tamil Nadu, 2008-09.*

Table 7.22 shows that 35.6 lakh people in Tamil Nadu have benefitted from social security pensions. Of the total social security beneficiaries, the largest number is that of elderly and widowed pensioners. Coverage under the pension schemes could not be calculated due to lack of updated data on BPL population. All these schemes are targeted towards BPL population.

Employment Security

Mahatma Gandhi Rural Employment Guarantee Scheme

The Mahatma Gandhi Rural Employment Guarantee Scheme (MGNREGS) is a landmark social protection scheme, which was notified as an Act in 2005 to ensure social protection for the most vulnerable people living in rural areas, particularly women, SCs and STs by providing employment opportunities while creating durable assets, facilitating improved water security, soil conservation and higher land productivity, along with decentralised planning (Ministry of Rural Development, 2012). MGNREGS, a combination of an unconditional in-kind transfer (employment) and conditional cash transfer of wage, is conferred as a legal right to any adult member of a rural household who is willing to undertake unskilled manual work. Due to nature of the work, only those who are willing to do manual work self-select into the scheme, regardless of it being universal. The State-wise wage rate, as notified by the GoI, is paid to beneficiaries. Table 7.23 shows that Tamil Nadu had the largest number of households participating in MGNREGS, as well as the highest number of person-days generated among the States under comparison. Tamil Nadu had provided employment to 62.6 lakh households in 2013-2014.

Nearly 84 per cent of MGNREGS workers were women and 29.6 per cent were SCs, indicating that the scheme has reached vulnerable sections of the population. The table also shows that Tamil Nadu and Andhra Pradesh had the highest proportion of rural households with a MGNREGS job card. Further, 75 per cent of persons aged 18 years and above who had registered for MGNREGS job card were able to get work in Tamil Nadu, which is considerably higher than the all-India average and of all other States under comparison, thereby indicating higher efficiency in governing the scheme. However, Tamil Nadu and Gujarat had the lowest daily wage rate among all the states under comparison.

Tamil Nadu is the first State in India to initiate a pilot for inclusion of PWD in MGNREGS. PWD were paid full days' wages for four hours of work (Box 7.3). In 2013-14, 79,645 PWD worked in MGNREGS and generated 4,037,694 person-days. The largest number of households participating in MGNREGS is in Villupuram, Cuddalore, Tiruvannamalai and Vellore (Table 7.24).

Health Insurance

According to estimates presented in the National Health Accounts 2004-05, India has one of the highest out-of-pocket expenditures on health, where private health expenditure constitutes 79.9 per cent of the total amount (Ministry of Health and Family Welfare, 2009). Public expenditure on health comprises a meagre 0.84 per cent of GDP (gross domestic product), while private health expenditure accounts to 3.32 per cent. A State-wise analysis reveals that the situation was no different in Tamil Nadu, with public health expenditure comprising 0.71 per cent of GSDP (gross state domestic product). The GoI has introduced a health insurance called the Rashtriya Swasthya Bima Yojana (RSBY) in 2008 to protect poor households from catastrophic out-of-pocket expenditure. Findings from a study on out-of-pocket expenditure on health, comparing RSBY intervention districts with non-intervention districts, showed that there was an increase in expenditure in the former (Selvaraj and Karan, 2012).

Information from the NSSO (2006) shows that 71 per cent of outpatient treatment in rural areas and 78 per cent in urban areas of Tamil Nadu took place in private hospitals. However, in the case of hospitalisation, 40.8 per cent in rural and 37.2 per cent in urban areas availed treatment from government hospitals, thus demonstrating the important role of public provisioning of healthcare. Medical expenditure per person on outpatient treatment in rural Tamil Nadu was nil in government hospitals and much lower than private hospitals in urban areas (Figure 7.4).

The difference was comparatively sharper in the case of hospitalisation in both rural and urban Tamil Nadu, with the expenditure being considerably higher in the private health sector (Figure 7.5).

The GoTN launched a public non-contributory health insurance scheme called Chief Minister New Insurance Scheme in 2009, targeted at members of 26 welfare boards in Tamil Nadu as well as those with an annual income of less than ₹72,000. Nearly 1.33 crore families were enrolled in the scheme. In 2011, a new non-contributory public health insurance scheme, called Chief Minister's Comprehensive Health Insurance Scheme (CMCHIS), was launched with the objective of improving access to poor families to quality medical care, where surgical and medical treatment were provided with cashless reimbursement. Families

Table 7.22

Number of Beneficiaries of Social Security Pension Schemes in Tamil Nadu as on 31-03-2014

District	Number of beneficiaries under social pension schemes (as on 31-03-2014)								
	IGNOAPS	IGNDPS	IGNWPS	DDAP	DWP	DDWP	UWP	CMUPT	Total
Ariyalur	33524	667	5378	4791	8889	687	181	11874	65991
Chennai	97076	2551	67686	8953	61620	9376	1285	0	248547
Coimbatore	57084	1381	14409	8522	1464	2634	754	1034	87282
Cuddalore	59399	4619	27637	6166	1448	10347	396	14701	124713
Dharmapuri	26490	1263	12185	2773	4510	2918	428	24222	74789
Dindigul	35090	422	10746	4688	322	10214	1062	21716	84260
Erode	57331	4274	19283	7016	6774	2594	305	7110	104687
Kancheepuram	61344	3029	31577	10129	14829	5344	626	4674	131552
Kanniyakumari	32386	1978	9589	7227	10399	2949	1857	4065	70450
Karur	20349	496	4154	2597	4776	1992	247	1084	35695
Krishnagiri	37666	1795	12589	10496	13387	5972	485	52280	134670
Madurai	45958	2318	46069	7063	9889	15353	1573	24687	152910
Nagapattinam	35078	2006	15978	4340	17448	1742	541	27142	104275
Namakkal	40242	231	12984	16062	13178	5155	262	26989	115103
Nilgiris	8697	309	4628	962	799	1225	1842	5060	23522
Perambalur	21543	549	9846	3458	8332	1137	228	16457	61550
Pudukottai	33359	1106	3839	4558	4275	1227	451	7467	56282
Ramanathapuram	28118	1287	14190	3007	2855	7541	353	36409	93760
Salem	56803	3883	61808	3573	13082	18046	528	60855	218578
Sivagangai	26824	866	6639	9989	10126	1549	312	22870	79175
Thanjavur	20902	2913	20821	2771	1135	6660	474	11478	67154
Theni	14037	553	17936	5845	4091	11882	496	42780	97620
Tiruvallur	92287	1517	27859	8465	29689	4160	642	1862	166481
Tiruvannamalai	42829	539	16826	9109	54482	12533	520	46046	182884
Tiruvarur	22136	1238	11354	2075	7316	1370	234	4461	50184
Tirunelveli	52560	2493	14268	5645	3195	14111	975	27716	120963
Tiruppur	34856	825	5556	3792	4234	6471	455	743	56932
Tiruchirapalli	35580	1272	34913	6101	16272	2164	1370	21379	119051
Thoothukudi	25628	1426	10253	2184	7248	2159	311	1275	50484
Vellore	191420	9745	53256	19478	20801	35179	2063	1855	333797
Villupuram	52346	5472	25549	12859	31036	2528	351	57994	188135
Virudhunagar	37502	2868	14889	1858	1702	1786	524	1515	62644
TOTAL	1436444	65891	644694	206552	389603	209005	22131	589800	3564120

Note: IGNOAPS stands for Indira Gandhi National Old Age Pension Scheme; IGNDPS stands for Indira Gandhi National Disability Pension Scheme; IGNWPS stands for Indira Gandhi National Widow Pension Scheme; DDAP stands for Destitute Differently-abled Pension scheme; DWP stands for Destitute Widow's Pension; DDWP stands for Destitute or Deserted Wives Pension Scheme; UWP stands for Unmarried Women's Pension; CMUPT stands for Chief Minister's UzhavarPadhukappuThittam.

Source: Data provided by Tamil Nadu State Planning Commission

Table 7.23

Total Households Worked, Total Person-days in MGNREGS, Proportion of Adults with MGNREG Job Card in Tamil Nadu, Andhra Pradesh (United), Karnataka, Kerala, Maharashtra, Gujarat and All-India, 2013-14

S. No.	State	Total households worked	Total person-days	Proportion of households having MGNREG job card	Proportion of persons of age 18 years and above registered for MGNREG job card	Proportion of persons of age 18 years and above registered for MGNREG job card and got work	MNREG per day wage rate in 2014
1	Tamil Nadu	6267704	367722584	48.3	28.2	75.0	167.0
2	Andhra Pradesh (United)	5975167	296514322	49.5	41.6	58.6	169.0
3	Karnataka	1450457	71886018	20.2	12.4	43.4	191.0
4	Kerala	1523812	86593980	29.1	12.5	58.7	212.0
5	Maharashtra	1142662	51714111	16.7	12.5	24.0	168.0
6	Gujarat	578676	23029659	23.8	17.2	31.4	167.00
	All India	49976775	2294384530	38.4	23.7	50.5	NA

Note: NSSO data are for the period 2011-12.

Source: http://www.nrega.nic.in; National Sample Survey Organisation 2014, 68th Round, Employment and Unemployment Situation in India.

Box 7.3

Inclusion of Persons with Disability in MGNREGS

Tamil Nadu's unique initiative to include PWD, including individuals with mental illness, in MGNREGS began with a time and motion study conducted in four districts of Tamil Nadu, namely Kancheepuram, Madurai, Tirunelveli and Coimbatore, by four organisations in each of the four districts; they are Banyan Academy of Leadership in Mental Health and The Banyan, MS Chellamuthu Trust, Amar Seva Sangam and Sri Ramakrishna Mission respectively. Persons with different types of disabilities, like locomotor disability, hearing impairment, visual impairment, intellectual disability and mental illness, were included in the pilot. The objective of the time and motion study was to select most suitable and sustainable jobs for PWD, including those with mental illness, to understand challenges faced by beneficiaries working in MGNREGS and to make recommendations for long-term employment for these individuals. Testimonials gathered from persons with mental illness by Banyan Academy of Leadership in Mental Health and The Banyan during the study showed that regular attendance at MGNREGS job site made individual with mental illness feel independent, provided a space to interact with others and increased their purchasing power. Data collected by MS Chellamuthu Trust on persons with mental illness demonstrated improvements attained in terms of quality of life and reduction in family burden after participants completed their MGNREGS work (for more details on the pilot refer to Banyan Academy of Leadership in Mental Health, 2012, Mahatma Gandhi National Rural Employment Guarantee Scheme Consolidated Pilot Study: Feasibility Report).

where the household head's annual income was less than ₹72,000, were eligible for the scheme. Family members are entitled to coverage of ₹1 lakh per year. The scheme covers 1,016 procedures in cardiology and cardiothoracic surgery, oncology, orthopaedic surgery, ophthalmology, ENT, obstetrics and gynaecology, pulmonology, nephrology and genito-urinary surgery, neurology and neurosurgery haematology, infectious diseases, critical care, dermatology, rheumatology, endocrinology, vascular surgery, general surgery, plastic surgery, medical/surgical gastroenterology, transplantation, general paediatrics, PICU, NICU and paediatric surgery. The number of beneficiaries covered as on 8 April 2014 was 6,51,185.

Conclusion and Future Directions

A review of some of the social security schemes of the GoTN establishes the state's commitment to prevent hunger and improve nutrition and health, to promote education and to protect vulnerable groups like elderly, widows, deserted women, unmarried women, children, unorganised sector workers, sexual minorities (transgender individuals), SCs, STs, minorities and

Table 7.24

District-wise Number of Total Households Worked and Total Person-days in MGNREGS in Tamil Nadu, 2013-14

S No	District	Household employed	Person days generated
1	Ariyalur	172084	9288008
2	Chennai	-	-
3	Coimbatore	96813	5428682
4	Cuddalore	427562	23233733
5	Dharmapuri	161069	8147647
6	Dindigul	186676	11485636
7	Erode	89164	5409362
8	Kancheepuram	273697	18789565
9	Kanniyakumari	32658	2161980
10	Karur	97878	5818486
11	Krishnagiri	260533	15774205
12	Madurai	244944	15190890
13	Nagapattinam	223553	10568776
14	Namakkal	146739	8899625
15	Nilgiris	31853	1099352
16	Perambalur	106120	5740508
17	Pudukottai	202840	9292165
18	Ramanathapuram	195654	12751663
19	Salem	243088	15571856
20	Sivagangai	141545	7186234
21	Thanjavur	225525	12205535
22	Theni	85336	4415492
23	Tiruvallur	197772	13541627
24	Tiruvannamalai	447181	30334776
25	Tiruvarur	138332	5584658
26	Tirunelveli	188410	11709587
27	Tiruppur	110877	7300059
28	Tiruchirapalli	247234	18808112
29	Thoothukudi	137987	8944408
30	Vellore	329634	20277874
31	Villupuram	647251	34044864
32	Virudhunagar	177695	8717219
	Tamil Nadu	6267704	367722584

Note: Chennai is a completely urban district.

Source: http://www.nrega.nic.in

PWD and in the process, attempt to break the cycle of intergenerational transmission of poverty by building human capability. However, there are some areas that need to be revisited

Enhancing Scope of Social Security Pension

Tamil Nadu has been a trendsetter for the rest of the country in terms of social security pension schemes. It could set an example for the country by revising the social security pension and index it to inflation. Tamil Nadu has already removed income ceilings for maintenance allowance for PWD. The state disability pensions insist on 60 per cent and above disability as eligibility criteria for those who are physically challenged, as well as hearing and speech impaired (Government of Tamil Nadu, 2014, Citizens' Charter of Social Welfare and Nutritious Noon Meal Department 2014-15). The eligibility criteria could be reduced to that of 40 per cent disability (the State has reduced it to 45% for those with intellectual disabilities under maintenance allowance scheme) and should include psychiatric disorders, given that GoI's PWD Act 1995 recognises blindness, low vision, leprosy cured, hearing impairment, locomotor disability, intellectual disabilities and mental illness (psychiatric disorders) as disabilities. The government could top up the pension for those with severe disability, as due to their high care needs, the carer loses access to paid employment. The government can include provisions for top ups in case of those with multiple deprivations like old age and widowhood, old age and agricultural labourer, old age and gender, old age and SC/ST, disability and old age and elderly above 70 and 80 years (referred to as old old and oldest old by demographers) . For instance, a widow who gets DWP should get a top up at 70 years of age, as women face severe economic stress during old age. Local self-government institutions can be encouraged to identify all elderly, widowed, SC, ST and PWD in their community, while being respectful of people's privacy. This would increase the coverage of schemes. Currently, the elderly, PWD, widows, etc., have to approach the government and submit several documents in order to be eligible for the pension, which imposes difficulties on them. The insistence on several documents can end up encouraging corruption and hence, this should be reduced. The government can also consider expanding coverage under the social security schemes with well-defined exclusion criteria, as the BPL criteria does not cover all the poor [refer to Dreze and Khera (2010) for a discussion on alternatives to BPL census]. The Socio-Economic Caste Census could be a useful source of identifying persons who are in need of social assistance. In India, in the bottom MPCE class, 41 per cent in rural areas and 29 per cent in urban areas had a BPL card (National Sample Survey Organisation, 2007). Further, households belonging to the top three MPCE classes in rural areas (ranging from 11-18%), 43 per cent of agricultural labourer households and 32 per cent of other labour households had BPL cards. In urban areas, only 26 per cent of casual labour households had BPL cards. In Tamil Nadu, in the bottom MPCE class, only 8.5 per cent of households in

Figure 7.4

Source of Outpatient and Hospitalised Treatment in Tamil Nadu, 2004 (as %)

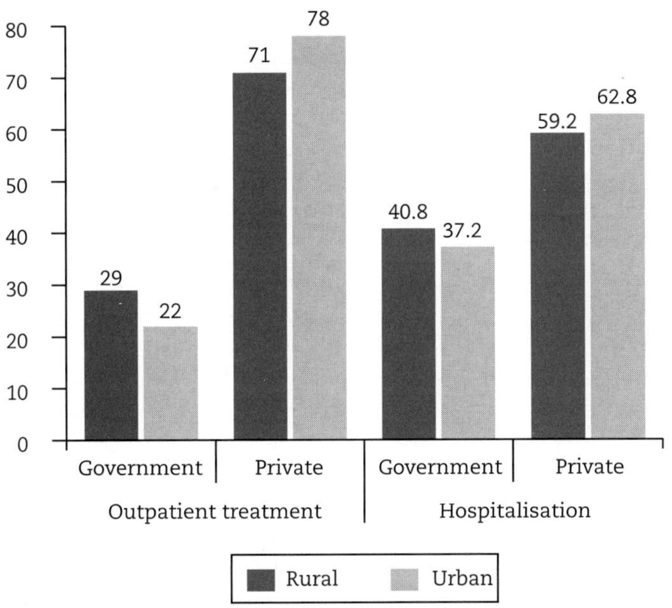

Source: NSSO (2006)

Figure 7. 5

Average Medical Expenditure on Outpatient Treatment and Hospitalisation Per Episode in Tamil Nadu, 2004 (₹)

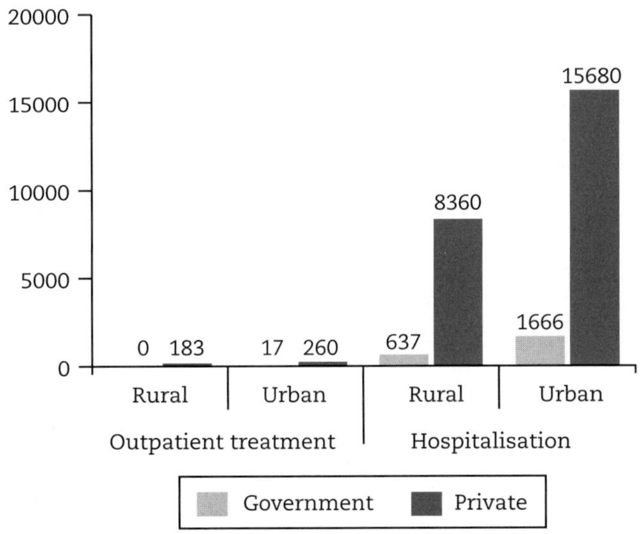

Source: NSSO (2006)

rural areas and 29.6 per cent of households in urban areas had a BPL card. The BPL criteria can thus lead to errors of exclusion and inclusion. For those sections who meet the exclusion criteria, the government can consider a contributory pension scheme. It would be worthwhile to undertake a cost-benefit analysis of administering a targeted scheme.

Mainstream Vulnerable Social Groups in Education, Livelihood and Skill Development Programmes

An area that needs urgent attention is increased enrolment of CWSN in schools, as 26.97 per cent of them aged 6-13 years were out-of-school in Tamil Nadu. In addition, CWSN should be able to access ICDS programmes so that their nutritional needs are not neglected. Further, efforts to improve access to education among SCs, STs, homeless population and third gender students need to be strengthened. Given the low work participation among women when compared to men, women should be given priority in programmes under TNSDM and livelihood programmes. Further, TNSDM and livelihood programmes need to enable access to transgender individuals, homeless persons and PWD. The case for improved participation of PWD in these programmes is important given that more than half of them lost their jobs due to the onset of disability. The GoI is committed to ensure that PWDs have barrier free access to information, transportation, physical environment, communication technology and accessibility to ervices as well as emergency services under United Nations Convention on the Rights of Persons with Disabilities (UNCRPD). It is imperative that GoTN implements barrier free access to PWDs in line with UNCRPD.

Nutrition-Diet-Women's Status-Sanitation Link

Although nutrition and food security are flagship programmes of GoTN, which has brought about a decline in the percentage of underweight children since 1992, the problem still persists, albeit to a lesser degree. As all the anthropometric indicators hover around 30 per cent, the government can choose to focus on further enhancing dietary composition in PT MGR NMP and ICDS, mass nutrition education programmes, and promotion of exclusive breastfeeding of infants till six months, encouraging timely introduction of complementary feeding for infants above six months and reduction of open defecation. Improving dietary patterns for children below five years present a challenge, given that half of the children under the age of five years are out of the ambit of ICDS services as a result of declining poverty in Tamil Nadu and the concomitant dependence on private schools. Tamil Nadu is a State where nutrition interventions have been made within the state domain and not outsourced to NGOs. It is critical to maintain State involvement, as achievement of public health goals are best undertaken by the State in partnership with the community. Research has pointed to poor sanitation, especially the practice of open defecation, as being a determinant of stunting among Indian children (Coffey *et al.*, 2013; Spears 2013). For the State to bring about substantial reduction in stunting among children, the government has to invest in improving sanitation (toilets and water supply) and creating awareness about harmful effects of open defecation. Census of India 2011 shows that 45.7 per cent of households in Tamil Nadu practiced open defecation, which was much higher in rural (73.2%) than the urban areas (16.2%). Besides, a relatively large proportion of households in Tamil Nadu did not have a proper source of drinking water and latrines in their houses. Ramalingaswami *et al.* (1996) have attributed the exceedingly high malnutrition rates in South Asia to inequality between men and women. Further, they argue that it is necessary to involve the community in the process of assessment of nutrition and to become active stakeholders in finding solutions. The State could consider using a Positive Deviance approach, which argues that there will be a few individuals or groups in a community whose strategies help in solving problems faced, despite having access to the same resources and facing the same challenges.

Custodial Care of Children

Custodial care of children needs to be re-examined by the State in the context of providing children with the means to reintegrate with society after their discharge. As there have been reports of children running away from such homes, the State must undertake an audit of and provide a child-friendly environment in these homes. There can be migrant children suspected to be in conflict with law, whose discharge is delayed due to language barriers; in this case, translation services can ensure quick repatriation. It is imperative to make sure that children get prompt legal assistance to facilitate speedy and fair disposal of their trials. Children who have been abandoned by their parents/orphaned and juveniles in conflict with law need regular support from mental health professionals and the government should appoint psychologists/social workers who have experience in working with them. This initiative is necessary to enable reintegration of the child into society and address problems of substance use among them. Vocational training provided to children has to be rendered child friendly and modernised in order to be relevant to the child's interest and ability.

Public Health Insurance and Public Health System

While the State government's health insurance scheme has provided people with options for inpatient treatment (medical and surgical) in government or private hospitals, caution must be exercised due to involvement of the private health sector, which can lead to unnecessary surgical interventions as has been shown with RSBY in Chhattisgarh. Health insurance can increase the cost of healthcare and does not address outpatient care in the existing scheme. The government should improve the quality of services in the public health sector, as people prefer private healthcare services mainly because of the perceived difference in quality and staff attitude.

Inclusion of Inter-state Migrant Workers in Unorganised Worker Welfare Board Schemes and Increased Enrolment of Unorganised Sector Workers

In the context of increased presence of inter-state migrant labour in the construction and service sector in Tamil Nadu, the government should include these workers in the Unorganised Worker Welfare Board schemes. In addition, the enrolment of unorganised sector workers in the welfare board schemes should be increased. Data from NSSO (2014) showed that among the employees in the AGEGC and non-agriculture sectors, 84.1 per cent in rural areas and 68 per cent in urban areas were not eligible for any social security benefit in Tamil Nadu. In the context of growing casualisation of employment, efforts should be made to considerably increase the numbers registered and mobilisation of resources in order to ensure comprehensive social security net for those involved in temporary or casual work.

Increase the Number of Shelters for Homeless Population and Rehabilitation Options

Currently, there are only 37 night shelters for the homeless in urban Tamil Nadu, whereas there were 50,929 homeless persons (Census of India 2011). Clearly, there is a need to increase the number of shelters, with priority to women, PWD, children and elderly homeless and to focus attention on livelihood options for the homeless in both rural and urban areas.

Monitoring and Evaluation

Although Tamil Nadu has had a long history of social security well before the GoI had initiated such schemes, very few evaluations have been done to bring about improvement. The government should get the programmes evaluated by a third party. Besides that, the government should have a proper mechanism to collect data on coverage of social security schemes. As Tamil Nadu is considered to have one of the best MIS in MGNREGS and PDS, this information system could be replicated in other social security schemes.

References

Burgess, R., and N. Stern (1991). "Social Security in Developing Countries: What, Why, Who and How?", in E. Ahmad, J. Dreze, J. Hills and A. Sen (eds.), *Social Security in Developing Countries*. Oxford: Clarendon Press.

Banyan Academy of Leadership in Mental Health (2012). *Mahatma Gandhi National Rural Employment Guarantee Scheme Consolidated Pilot Study: Feasibility Report*. Chennai: Banyan Academy of Leadership in Mental Health.

Barik, D., T. Agrawal and S. Desai (2015). After the Dividend: Caring for a Greying India, *Economic and Political Weekly* 50(24): 108-112

Census of India, (2011). *Percentage of Households to Total Households by Amenities and Assets (India & States/UTs: Village and Ward Level)*, New Delhi: Office of the Registrar General and Census Commissioner

Census of India, (2011a). *Primary Census Abstract Data for Others (India & States/UTs)*, New Delhi: Office of the Registrar General and Census Commissioner

Census of India, (2011b). *Distribution of disabled by type of disability, sex, literacy status and residence (India & States/UTs)*, New Delhi: Office of the Registrar General and Census Commissioner

Census of India, (2011c). *Disabled Population by Main Workers, Marginal Workers, Non-Workers By Type Of Disability, Age And Sex-C23Table (India & States/UTs)*, New Delhi: Office of the Registrar General and Census Commissioner

Census of India, (2011d). *Primary Census Abstract Data for Houseless (India & States/UTs - District Level) (Excel Format)*, New Delhi: Office of the Registrar General and Census Commissioner

Chambers, R. and Gregor Von Medeazza (2013). "Sanitation and Stunting in India: Undernutrition's Blind Spot", *Economic and Political Weekly* 48 (25): 15-18.

Chopra, S. and Jessica Pudussery (2014). "Social Security Pensions in India: An Assessment", *Economic and Political Weekly* 49(19): 68-74.

Citizens' Initiative for the Rights of Children Under Six (2006). *Focus on Children under Six*. New Delhi.

Coffey, D., A. Deaton, J. Drèze, D. Spears, and A.Tarozzi (2013). "Stunting among Children: Facts and Implications", *Economic and Political Weekly* 48 (34): 68-70.

Desai, S.B., A. Dubey, B.L. Joshi, M. Sen, A. Shariffand and R.Vanneman (2010). *Human Development in India: Challenges for a Society in Transition*. New Delhi: Oxford University Press.

Dreze,J. and Amartya Sen (1995). *India: Economic Development and Social Opportunity*. New Delhi: Oxford University Press.

————. (2013). *An Uncertain Glory: India and Its Contradictions*. London: Allen Lane.

Dreze, J. and Reetika Khera (2010)."The BPL Census and a Possible Alternative", *Economic and Political Weekly* 45 (9):54-63

————. (2013)."Rural Poverty and the Public Distribution System", *Economic and Political Weekly* 48 (45/46); 55-60.

Government of India (2009). *National Health Accounts–India (2004–05)–with Provisional Estimates from 2005-06 to 2008-09)*. New Delhi: Ministry of Health and Family Welfare.

Government of Goa (2014). *Welfare Schemes*. Goa: Directorate of Planning, Statistics and Evaluation.

Government of Tamil Nadu (2012).*Vision Tamil Nadu 2023: Strategic Plan for Infrastructure Development in Tamil Nadu*.

————. (2014). *Performance Budget 2014-15*. Social Welfare and Nutritious Meal Programme Department.

————. (2014a). *Policy Note 2014-15*. Social Welfare and Nutritious Meal Programme Department.

————. (2014b). *Performance budget 2014-15*.Department of Adi Dravidar and Tribal Welfare.

————. (2014c). *Performance budget 2014-15*.Department of Backward Classes, Most Backward Classes, Denotified Communities and Minority Welfare.

————. (2014d). *Performance budget 2014-15*.Labour and Employment Department.

————. (2014e). *Policy Note 2014-15*.Labour and Employment Department.

————. (2014f). *Citizens' Charter of Social Welfare and Nutritious Noon Meal Department 2014-15*.Government of Tamil Nadu.

Guhan, S. (1994). "Social Security Options for Developing Countries", *International Labour Review* 133 (1): 35-53.

Himanshu and Abhijit Sen (2013). "In Kind Food Transfers 1: Impact on Poverty", *Economic and Political Weekly* XLVIII (45&46), 46-54.

International Institute for Population Sciences (IIPS) (2014). *District level Household and Facility Survey 4, 2012-13*. Mumbai: IIPS.

International Institute for Population Sciences (IIPS) and Macro International (2007).*National Family Health Survey (NFHS-3), 2005–06: India:I*. Mumbai: IIPS.

————. (2008). *National Family Health Survey (NFHS-3), India, 2005-06*: Tamil Nadu. Mumbai: IIPS.

Mander, H. (2008).*Living Rough Surviving City Streets: A Study of Homeless Populations in Delhi, Chennai, Patna and Madurai*. New Delhi: Planning Commission.

National Crime Records Bureau (2014).*Accidental Deaths and Suicides in India*. New Delhi: Government of India.

National Nutrition Monitoring Bureau (2012).*Diet and Nutritional Status of Rural Population, Prevalence of Hypertension and Diabetes among Adults and Infant and Young Child Feeding Practices-Report of Third Repeat Survey*. Hyderabad: National Institute of Nutrition.

National Sample Survey Organisation (1998).*The Aged in India: A Socio-economic Profile, July 1995-June 1996*. 52nd Round. New Delhi: Government of India.

————. (2003). *Disabled Persons in India*. 58th Round. New Delhi: Government of India

————. (2006). *Morbidity, Health Care and the Condition of the Aged, 2004*. 60th Round. New Delhi: Government of India.

————. (2007). *Public Distribution System and Other Sources of Household Consumption, 2004-05.* , 61st Round. Vol 1. New Delhi: Government of India

————. (2010). *Education in India: Participation and expenditure 2007-08*, 64th Round, New Delhi: Government of India

————. (2012). *Nutritional Intake in India 2009-10. 66th Round*. New Delhi: Government of India

————. (2012b). *Household Consumption of Various Goods and Services in India 2009-10*. 66th Round. New Delhi: Government of India

———. (2013). *Public Distribution System and Other Sources of Household Consumption 2009-10*. 66th Round. New Delhi: Government of India

———. (2014a). *Household Consumption of Various Goods and Services in India 2011-12*. 68th Round. New Delhi: Government of India

———. (2014b). *Employment and Unemployment Situation in India 2011-12*. 68th Round. New Delhi: Government of India.

———. (2014c). *Informal Sector and Conditions of Employment in India, 2011-12*. 68th Round. New Delhi: Government of India.

Ramalingaswami, V., U. Jonssonand and J. Rohde (1996). *Commentary: The Asian Enigma*. UNICEF.

Rajivan, A.K. (2001). *History of Direct Nutrition Schemes in Tamil Nadu: An Evaluation of Central Kitchen Schemes'*, CARE 1974. December (mimeo) (updated).

Selvaraj, S. and Anup K. Karan (2012). "Why Publicly-Financed Health Insurance Schemes are Ineffective in Providing Financial Risk Protection", *Economic and Political Weekly* 47 (9): 60-68.

Spears, D. (2013). "How Much International Variation in Child Height Can Sanitation Explain?", *Policy Resaerch Working Paper* 6351. Washington DC: World Bank

Social and Rural Research Institute and EdCIL (2014). *National Sample Survey of Estimation of Out-of-School Children in the Age 6-13 in India*. Noida: Educational Consultant India Limited

UNICEF (2010).*Coverage Evaluation Survey: Tamil Nadu Fact Sheet*. New Delhi.

———. (2010a). *Coverage Evaluation Survey: All India Report*. New Delhi.

Websites:

http://www.censusindia.gov.in/

http://www.nrega.nic.in

http://www.rbi.org.in/, Handbook of Statistics on State Government Finances, 2010.

Annexure Table A-7.1

Classification of Social Security Schemes of Tamil Nadu

Type of social security	*Type of transfers*	*Name*	*Conditional/ unconditional*	*Universal/targeted*	*Target population*	*Year of inception*	*Centre/state scheme*
Nutrition	In kind transfer	PT MGR Nutritious Meal Programme	Conditional (school attendance)	Universal	School children in age group	1982	Tamil Nadu state scheme which was replicated by centre
	In kind transfer	ICDS	Conditional (attendance at anganwadi)	Universal	Children in age group 0-6 years, adolescents, pregnant and lactating women and elderly persons who have registered with social insurance schemes	1975-76	Central government
	In kind transfer	PDS	Unconditional	Quasi universal	All with PDS card are given graded entitlement for BPL and others	1951	Central government
	In kind transfer	Amma canteen	Unconditional	Universal	All	2013	Tamil Nadu state scheme
Women	Cash transfers	Dr Muthulakshmi Reddy Maternity Benefit Scheme	Conditional	Targeted	Poor women	1987	Tamil Nadu state scheme
	In kind transfer	Sathyavanaimuthu Ammaiyar Ninaivu Free Supply of Sewing Machine Scheme	Unconditional	Targeted	Destitute widows, deserted wives, physically handicapped men and women in the age group 20-40 years and Sri Lankan refugees living in camps	1979-80	Tamil Nadu state scheme
Organised Sector Workers	Cash and in kind transfers	Tami Nadu Labour welfare Board	Unconditional (conditional only in the case of educational incentives)	Targeted	Employees working in factories, plantations, motor transport undertakings, shop and catering establishment	1975	Tamil Nadu state scheme
Unorganised Sector Workers	Cash and in kind transfers	Welfare Boards for Unorganised Sector Workers in Tamil Nadu	Unconditional (conditional only in the case of educational incentives)	Targeted	17 occupations like manual workers, construction workers, tailors, artists, handloom worker, powerloom worker, handicraft worker, potters, palm tree workers, hairdressers, gold smiths, domestic workers, cooking food workers, street vending workers, tannery workers, drivers, washermen	1994	Tamil Nadu state scheme

Type of social security	*Type of transfers*	*Name*	*Conditional/ unconditional*	*Universal/targeted*	*Target population*	*Year of inception*	*Centre/state scheme*
Vulnerable groups	Cash and in kind transfers	Transgender Welfare Board	Unconditional	Targeted	Transgenders	2008	Tamil Nadu state scheme
	Cash and in kind transfers	Tamil Nadu Welfare Board for Differently-abled	Unconditional (conditional only in the case of educational incentives)	Targeted	Differently-abled	2007	Tamil Nadu state scheme
Social security pension (non contributory)	Cash transfer and in kind transfer	Old age pension scheme (OAP)	Unconditional	Targeted	Age 65 years and above, BPL	1962	Tamil Nadu state scheme
	Cash transfer and in kind transfer	Destitute Widow's Pension (DWP)	Unconditional	Targeted	Age 40 years and above, widow, BPL	1975	Tamil Nadu state scheme
	Cash transfer and in kind transfer	Destitute Agricultural Labourers Pension scheme (DALP) renamed as Chief Minister's Uzhavar Padhukappu Thittam (CMUPT)	Unconditional	Targeted	Age 60 years and above, not able to work, no means of support from children	1981	Tamil Nadu state scheme
	Cash transfer and in kind transfer	Destitute Differently abled Pension scheme (DDAP)	Unconditional	Targeted	Age 18 years and above which can be relaxed, disability 60% and above, physically challenged, hearing and speech impaired, no means of subsistence, no support from son or grandson, should not possess property of value more than ₹5000	1974	Tamil Nadu state scheme
	Cash transfer and in kind transfer	Destitute or Deserted Wives Pension Scheme (DDWP)	Unconditional	Targeted	Age 30 years and above, legally divorced for not less than 5 years, no source of subsistence, should not possess property of value more than ₹5000	1986	Tamil Nadu state scheme
	Cash transfer and in kind transfer	Unmarried Women's Pension (UWP)	Unconditional	Targeted	Age 50 years and above, no means of livelihood or income	2008	Tamil Nadu state scheme
	Cash transfer and in kind transfer	IGNOAP	Unconditional	Targeted	Age 60 years and above, BPL	1995	Central scheme
	Cash transfer and in kind transfer	IGNWPS	Unconditional	Targeted	Age 40-79 years, widow, BPL	2010	Central scheme

Type of social security	*Type of transfers*	*Name*	*Conditional/ unconditional*	*Universal/targeted*	*Target population*	*Year of inception*	*Centre/state scheme*
	Cash transfer and in kind transfer	IGNDPS	Unconditional	Targeted	Age 18-79 years, BPL, 80% and above or multiple disabilities	2010	Central scheme
	Cash transfers	Pension Scheme for Destitute Transgenders	Unconditional	Targeted	Age 40 years and above, identity card of Transgender Welfare Board, unable to work, no assistance from family members	2012-13	Tamil Nadu state scheme
Health	In kind	Chief Minister Kalaignar Insurance Scheme	Unconditional	Targeted	Members of 26 Welfare Boards in Tamil Nadu as well as those with an annual income of less than ₹72000	2009	Tamil Nadu state scheme
	In kind	Chief Minister's Comprehensive Health Insurance Scheme	Unconditional	Targeted	Families in which the head of the household's annual income was less than ₹72000 were eligible for the scheme	2011	Tamil Nadu State Scheme
Employment	In kind and Cash transfers	MNREGS	Unconditional for employment and conditional for wage	Universal in rural areas	None	2005	Central government scheme

Note: There are 17 welfare boards under the unorganised sector welfare boards which have been started at various time periods. There are 17 welfare boards for vulnerable social groups out of which information is provided for two. Some of the social security schemes have been discussed in the chapters on health and gender.

Source: Government of Tamil Nadu, various years, Citizen's Charter, policy note and performance budget

Annexure Table A-7.2

Percentage of Households Reporting Consumption of Rice from Public Distribution System across Monthly Per Capita Expenditure Class in Tamil Nadu, Andhra Pradesh (United), Karnataka, Kerala, Maharashtra, Gujarat and All-India, 2009-10

S No	State	PoR	MPCE decile class										
			0-10%	10-20%	20-30%	30-40%	40-50%	50-60%	60-70%	70-80%	80-90%	90-100%	All
1	Tamil Nadu	R	99.3	98.8	96.3	98.9	97.7	93.3	90.0	91.7	87.1	67.1	91.0
		U	95.3	89.0	91.5	87.1	80.1	82.0	55.9	51.6	45.3	24.1	67.0
2	Andhra Pradesh (United)	R	88.0	96.3	98.5	90.5	89.7	93.6	83.3	88.8	77.2	50.2	83.9
		U	81.8	80.2	79.8	71.1	65.5	46.3	30.3	13.3	12.5	3.5	42.7
3	Karnataka	R	92.3	77.7	92.5	91.5	72.8	86.1	77.9	74.5	58.8	38.3	74.6
		U	75.6	62.0	51.9	38.3	27.6	15.0	10.6	11.6	3.5	9.0	24.8
4	Kerala	R	82.4	82.7	72.1	62.3	59.0	63.8	55.3	39.1	32.9	25.5	54.3
		U	88.2	80.5	69.4	55.6	43.7	49.5	32.2	24.9	19.2	14.3	42.5
5	Maharashtra	R	73.5	72.9	56.1	47.4	47.6	47.8	46.7	40.0	32.6	24.5	46.8
		U	37.8	28.8	18.0	10.3	12.4	7.7	4.8	1.8	9.0	1.0	10.0
6	Gujarat	R	41.9	46.7	36.5	51.5	50.7	29.4	29.9	30.3	26.4	11.1	33.8
		U	31.6	13.0	24.8	13.0	10.4	5.7	7.0	4.0	1.0	0	8.3
	All-India	R	56.2	44.0	43.2	40.7	40.6	40.2	39.4	35.9	35.3	26.5	39.2
		U	38.6	35.2	34.4	31.5	27.9	23.0	16.1	13.2	8.2	3.7	20.6

Note: PoR stands for Place of Residence; R is rural and U is urban

Source: National Sample Survey Organisation, 2013, Public Distribution System and other sources of household consumption 2009-10

Annexure Table A-7.3

Details of Social Security Schemes Under Labour Welfare Boards and Tamil Nadu Scavenger Welfare Board, Tamil Nadu Puthiraivannar Welfare Board and Tribal Welfare Board Assistance Schemes

Sl. No	*Details of Assistance*	*Assistance amount (in ₹)*
1	Accident Insurance Scheme	
	a) Death on accident	100000
	b) Handicapped	10000 to 100000
	c) Loss of both legs/both hands/one hand and one leg/loss of sight in both eyes	Not applicable
	d) Loss of one hand or leg or loss of sight in one eye	Not applicable
	e) Total disablement	Not applicable
2	Assistance to natural death	15000
3	Assistance to funeral rites	2000
4	Scholarship	
	a) to study 10th Std. (for Girls alone)	1000
	b) Pass in X Std.	1000
	c) to study XI Std. (for Girls alone)	1000
	d) to study 12th Std. (for Girls alone)	1500
	e) Pass in 12th Std.	1500
	f) Regular Degree course Day Scholars	1500 per annum
	g) Regular Degree course Hostellers	1750 per annum
	h) Regular Post-Graduate Degree Day Scholars	2000 per annum
	i) Regular Post-Graduate Degree course Hostellers	3000 per annum
	j) Degree in Technical Education Day Scholars	2000 per annum
	k) Degree in Technical Education Hostellers	4000 per annum
	l) P. G Degree in Technical Education Day Scholars	4000 per annum
	m) P. G Degree in Technical Education Hostellers	6000 per annum
	n) ITI or Polytechnic Day Scholars	1000 per annum
	o) ITI or Polytechnic Hostellers	1200 per annum
5	Assistance to Marriage	2000 per annum
6	Maternity Assistance	
	a) Maternity Assistance	6000 (₹1000 per month)
	b) For Abortion	3000
7	For Reimbursement to purchase of spectacles	up to 500
8	Old Age Pension	1000 per month

Source: Tamil Nadu State Planning Commission.

8

Challenges and the Way Forward

Clearly the State has witnessed considerable advances across various domains of human development over the last decade. Economic growth and improvements in per capita incomes have been accompanied by increments in literacy levels across all districts. Access to tertiary education has improved remarkably. Significant reductions are also noticed in poverty levels during this period across all social and economic groups. Although gender and caste disparities persist, the report observes improvements in certain absolute indicators of women's well-being. However, as the introduction states, adequate policy attention is required to ensure that the gains made are secured and improved upon. The setbacks in the domain of health, detailed in chapter 5, are suggestive of possible slippages. Further, there are certain areas where the improvements could have definitely been better. In the rest of this chapter, some of the key challenges that the State faces in this regard and some relevant policy suggestions are made.

Spatial Disparities in Human Development

To begin with, inter-district disparities in terms of income and human development between the First Human Development Report and the Second Human Development Report remain. Given the different parameters used for capturing human development across the two Human Development Reports, the ranking of districts, cannot be compared between the two time points. It is however worth noting that the set of districts that registered low levels of HDI in 2003 remain largely unchanged except for a few districts such as Thiruvalur, Kancheepuran and Krishnagiri. The fact that the bulk of the big ticket productive investments by the private sector has taken place in the greater Chennai region tends to suggest a strong case for State policy efforts to redress this concentration of economic growth. Thiruvallur and Kancheepuram, the two adjoining districts of Chennai that were relatively backward earlier, have witnessed considerable improvements in some human development parameters. Krishnagiri, another district that seems to have benefitted from investments in the Bangalore agglomeration, has gained significantly. While agglomeration economies are critical to generating positive externalities in terms of learning and generating economies of scope, there is sufficient evidence globally to suggest that high concentrations of growth also generate negative externalities, such as depletion of natural resources like water and pollution of various kinds.

Recent trends in urbanisation all over India and in Tamil Nadu reveal the rise of what is referred to as census towns, i.e., spaces that are urban with regard to economic base, but still governed as rural habitations. The source of dynamism of these settlements has to be understood and used as a basis for formulation of policies that seek to decentralise urbanisation and industrial development. Similarly, there is a strong case for active promotion of regionally specific sectors. Agro-processing in districts with relatively better agricultural growth prospects, for example, can address the issue of employment generation and regional balances. While some efforts in this direction are evident, the reasons for some of them not taking off need to be analysed further and policy institutions re-oriented accordingly. The Government of Tamil Nadu has launched the State Balanced Growth Fund to address the issue of regional disparities in the state through targeted interventions in 105 most backward blocks in the State as well as wards in urban local bodies with slums. The targeted locations have been identified based on parameters such as health and education status, gender disparities, per capita income, poverty levels and unemployment. The Fund also seeks to create capacity in districts to monitor human development status at district and sub-district levels so as to ensure balanced regional development.

Gender Disparities in Human Development

Despite considerable strides that the State has made in improving women's access to education, health and incomes, inequities persist. Importantly, districts like Ariyalur and Villupuram that are backward in terms of overall human development also rank high on gender inequality, indicating multiple layers of deprivation among women in these districts. Another important issue concerns unfavourable sex ratios. Although the overall sex ratio has improved in the State, there are some districts where sex ratios have declined. While some of these adverse shifts can be attributed to migration, the fact that five districts—Ariyalur, Cuddalore, Dharmapuri, Namakkal and Perambalur—have child sex ratios lower than that of the all-India average indicates the magnitude of this phenomenon. District-level interventions to address adverse sex selection practices that were launched in other districts earlier have worked to improve child sex ratios in such districts. There is therefore a need to move beyond district-specific interventions in this regard. The fact that all the five districts also rank low in terms of human development is a cause for concern.

A related challenge concerns the persistence of gender disparities in literacy attainments. Overall literacy levels have increased significantly and the gender gap which was higher than the national average until 1991 has now fallen to lower than the all-India average. However, six districts of the State—Salem, Erode, Krishnagiri, Villupuram, Ariyalur and Dharmapuri—register female literacy rates lower than the national average. Literacy rates among women in 12 more districts are lower than the State average, but above the national average. The fact that three of the six districts exhibit dynamism in terms of income and economic development points out the absence of trickle down processes at work. The challenge is therefore to design targeted interventions in this regard. While there are differences across districts in the extent of women's participation in the labour force, the extent to which this is an actual sign of women's empowerment needs to be understood through a more disaggregated analysis that takes into account class-based divisions. This report has not been able to address gender disparities across social and economic classes, which is essential to not only understand gender inequities in access across classes, but also to identify whether there has been equitable access to programmes and schemes.

Another critical source of gender-based differences in human development concerns wage differentials between men and women in similar sectors. While there is micro-level evidence to suggest that the National Rural Employment Guarantee Act (NREGA) has led to absolute increases in women's wages in agriculture, there are striking differences in the wage rates of male and female workers in agriculture across districts. Given that women's income security is critical to both women's welfare and overall human development, interventions in the labour market to reduce wage disparities are necessary. Moreover, given the informal nature of this employment, it is indeed challenging to design appropriate interventions. Understanding the limitations to women's mobility across sectors and spaces will be important to create awareness and/or openings for increasing women's wages in rural Tamil Nadu. Importance of awareness is particularly evident in shedding social norms that guide and inform perceptions on gender inequities. The fact that a majority of women in the State perceive domestic violence as a justifiable act shows not only the importance of social institutions in conditioning behaviour, but importantly on the need to incorporate such institutional norms in designing meaningful programmes for addressing violence against women.

An important dimension of gender-based vulnerability that the HDR has sought to highlight is the pervasiveness of female-headed households in the State, which fare a lot worse in terms of access to income and assets than other households. Fourteen per cent of total households are headed by women where dependency ratios are higher than that for other households. Given that there are likely to be less number of income earners in such households, fluctuations in income will tend to be higher and hence vulnerability to economic shocks as well. The mechanisms for addressing social security requirements of such households across urban and rural Tamil Nadu will be different. The process of gender budgeting is yet to take off in the State. The classification of all programmes for women under the gamut of the Tamil Nadu Corporation for Development of Women reduces the reach of different sectoral schemes. There are several departments that do not have specific programmes to precisely address development requirements of women. A specific allocation of a certain budgetary amount under different departments, say 30 per cent, would ensure an equitable access under all schemes. There is a need to have specialised gender cells that research, document and bring to the attention of policy planners the emerging needs and issues of women. Thus, we must move away from a 'welfare' approach that confines women to being recipients of various beneficiary projects to an approach that allows women's voice and collective action to frame the contours of intervention.

In the domain of employment and poverty, the following issues emerge for policy attention.

Employment and Poverty

Despite a slight revival in the growth of the agricultural sector in the last decade, the rate of decline in poverty levels among cultivators has not been high. Further, despite a fall in poverty levels among agricultural workers, a quarter of the agricultural workforce continues to be in absolute poverty. While agricultural wage rates have increased, poverty levels among agricultural workers continue to be relatively high. While a decline in quantum of employment maybe a factor, low labour productivity and/or an inability to convert to more productive employment in some districts too are critical aspects that need to be addressed. The presence of a well-functioning public distribution system (PDS) and NREGA has served to cushion the vulnerabilities of small and marginal farmers and agricultural workers. However, a case for growth linked poverty reduction and human development for those dependent on the agricultural sector cannot be overstated in a State where 35 per cent of workers continue to rely on agriculture. While uncertainty in agricultural incomes is due to both production and price risks, production risks emanating from reduced access to assured water supply is probably the most important factor in this regard. Recent efforts by the government to support creation of farm ponds and also desilt tanks through the NREGA works need further support and expansion. The State has saturated its sources of surface water irrigation and large investments have been made in ground water recharge through various schemes. However, the drawal of ground water has exceeded its recharge in several blocks. The situation therefore highlights the need for optimal water management practices so that the need for higher agricultural productivity is addressed.

Interventions in marketing in the agricultural sector are as important as enhancing production. On the prices front, there is a need to reduce the number of intermediaries in agricultural markets but ensure that the services rendered by such intermediaries are provided efficiently through alternate mechanisms. Farmers' markets have worked well in some areas but not everywhere. Reasons for their non-functioning need to be understood and addressed. Importantly, as has often been noted, value-addition to agricultural produce continues to be low. Interventions in this area by linking up producers to processors and to larger markets are again critical. Given the mixed evidence of the benefits of contract farming in the short run, alternate models such as producers' cooperatives should be actively encouraged. Farmers' producers companies that have emerged recently in the State need to be strengthened and diffused more widely.

Simultaneously, there is a need for strengthening the real incomes of agricultural labourers through better access to social security provisions in the State and creating avenues for their transition to better employment opportunities in the non-farm sector.

Unemployment and Stagnation in Manufacturing Sector Employment

Development theory has always privileged manufacturing as a result of its higher employment and other linkage effects. However, there is a growing realisation that manufacturing has not been able to generate as much employment in recent years as in the past. Nevertheless, there are sectors that are more labour-intensive, like textiles and other light consumer goods, which must to be promoted. Importantly, efforts should be taken to ensure that firms in these sectors upgrade, i.e. move into more value-adding segments progressively with time. This will create conditions for better returns to labour. Furthermore, there is not enough emphasis on understanding the changing skill requirements in the ever expanding services sector on the one hand and the segments within services sector that are more value-adding and labour-absorbing on the other hand. The extent to which the education and health sectors, for example, can generate productive employment and other linkages, and the institutional interventions required to enhance these linkages need to be understood. Steps in this direction will inevitably facilitate employment absorption. A sectoral approach to promotion of segments in manufacturing and services is, therefore, suggested.

Micro-level studies also indicate a mismatch between supply and demand for skills in the labour market in the State, especially among the formally trained. The phenomenon of the 'educated unemployed' has to be addressed in order to ensure that the investments made in education by households are matched by adequate returns. Part of the mismatch comes from poor regulation of standards of formal education, especially with regard to private sector tertiary and vocational education. Standards in both public and private schooling too appear to be wanting. A series of initiatives have been undertaken by the State to enskill the semi-literate to improve employability of the workforce as the Pudhu Vaazhvu Thittam case illustrates. case illustrates. It is in such a context that initiatives undertaken by the Tamil Nadu Skill Development Corporation to impart and augment skills among unemployed youth become critical. Sustainability and scalability of such initiatives should be given utmost attention.

In addition to the quantum of employment, there are concerns over the quality of employment generated in recent years. Although casual wage rates are one of the highest in the country and poverty levels have declined among those employed in this category, this is a segment that has been expanding and one where poverty levels continue to be relatively high. Even in the organised sector, other studies have pointed to a growing reliance on contract employment and casualisation of work. The insecurity of such employment contracts clearly militates against the tenets of 'decent work' that is seen as critical to the idea of inclusive development. Given the large-scale out-migration and in-migration of workers from and into the State, the governance of labour market arrangements becomes crucial. Governance should focus not only on human capital formation, but also on protecting the rights of labour. A simultaneous focus on skill development and ensuring employment security will enable the State to take advantage of its demographic dividend.

The Report also reveals issues that are specific to certain districts. For instance, low agricultural productivity does not correlate completely with high levels of rural poverty, just as districts with high agricultural productivity do not necessarily have low poverty levels. Similarly, high levels of urbanisation alone do not secure better incomes for labour. The Report, therefore, makes a case for simultaneous engagement at several levels, namely sectoral, district and at the State level to tackle the problems highlighted.

Health and Nutrition

Tamil Nadu's achievements in human development are in large measure due to its accomplishments in the domain of public health care and nutrition over the last decade. Importantly, the State's pioneering efforts in using the mid-day meals scheme to address the twin issues of enhancing access to education and better nutrition has been widely acknowledged. It also goes to show how social security measures contribute to improvements in human development and also human capital. The State has witnessed improvements across most parameters of health outcomes. However, spatial disparities continue to be observed, with considerable inter- and intra-district variations in infant mortality, maternal mortality and neonatal deaths. Not surprisingly, such variations are found to be tied to differences in access to public health services. More importantly, they are also tied to differences in and poor levels of nutrition and sanitation. The district-level human development reports can shed more light on blocks even within districts with relatively high HDI that have poor access to primary and secondary care services. This is, however, not to deny the need for overall improvements in State intervention in health care. For this, there is a need to ramp up both financial and human resources. While State spending in absolute terms has gone up significantly in recent years, its share in the overall State budget has stagnated at around four per cent. Given the growing capital intensity of modern health technologies, the need for improving the share of resources for health care in the total budget cannot be overstated.

A corresponding issue is the sector's high reliance on both quantity and quality of health care professionals. This is particularly true of primary and secondary care services. Although some efforts have been made in this direction recently in the form of fresh recruitment of medical and paramedical staff, shortage of personnel is found to exist at all levels. Skill shortages too can be noticed. There is a clear need for both broad basing and improving the quality of training. (Re) opening of training institutions for Village Health Nurses (VHNs) and other functionaries is an immediate requirement. Continuing to equip staff with new skills through part-time training initiatives is important as well. Creation of new institutions needs to be backed by both adequate staffing and high quality of training by way of appropriately designed parameters for quality standards.

Another important issue that the report highlights is the decline in attention given to Health Sub-Centres (HSCs) and hence a need to focus on interventions made in spatial scales lower than that of the Primary Health Centres (PHCs). Even though the State's primary health care delivery system is held as a model for the rest of the country, intra-district variations in access can be addressed better through such scaling down of interventions. Such improvements to HSCs are also likely to generate positive spillovers in the domain of the primary health care system and further contribute to reducing the financial burden on care seekers. The State Balanced Growth Fund also seeks to improve the infrastructure of PHCs and HSCs in the most backward blocks.

Regulation of the burgeoning private health sector poses another challenge for sustaining and improving health outcomes in the State. Private investments may allow for introduction of frontier health care technologies. However, concerns of exclusion due to high costs, apart from quality issues, cannot be ignored, particularly in the context of a rapidly growing private sector and increasing costs of such health care. The introduction of a government supported health insurance scheme is noteworthy in this context. It is probably worth revisiting implementation of the Tamil Nadu Private Clinical Establishments (Regulation) Act, introduced more than 15 years ago. Alternatively, study of similar regulatory interventions in India and in other countries need to be taken up to ensure that private health delivery does not aggravate inequities in health care access. Along with such regulation, specific policy measures to ensure universal health coverage (UHC) within a decade should be initiated at the earliest.

Probably, the single most important issue with regard to the State's health and nutrition status is that of poor levels of sanitation. For a State with high levels of human development, relatively poorer access to clean drinking water and high levels of open defecation belie the State's achievements along other dimensions of human development. In fact, the State's open defecation rates are comparable with those of States with the lowest levels of human development in the country. Given sanitation's links to malnutrition and communicable diseases, the State has to give utmost importance to improving sanitation standards. While access to water maybe an issue, there is a strong degree of path dependence that needs addressing through creation of awareness.

Education and Skill Formation

As is the case with health and nutrition, even though the State has seen considerable improvements in access to education at all levels, there is definitely room for further improvement, especially in terms of quality. Among the challenges confronting this aspect of human development, increasing enrolments in secondary education is one issue that calls for attention. Given the large share of public schools in secondary education, this effort will clearly require further public resources. However, the report highlights possible avenues for a productive collaboration between the State and private and civil society actors through innovative institutional mechanisms within the ambit of the Sarva Shiksha Abhiyaan (SSA) and other such initiatives in order to address any shortfall in public resources. Apart from resource generation, community participation can also enhance awareness among households on the importance of investing in education. Moreover, such initiatives can also be very helpful in enforcing accountability of teachers and administrators of educational institutions. Although SSA seeks to provide opportunities for elementary education until the age of 14, a long-term strategy is essential to absorb extra students into higher education.

This is, however, not to deny the importance of investing more public resources into education. The parameters for evaluating quality should also go beyond mere improvements in TPR (teacher-pupil ratio) or the introduction of new information and communication based technologies for learning. Probably a key second generation reform of the education sector in the State involves designing institutions that address the accountability of the teaching community. There is also wide variation in the number of dropouts as well as in completion rates in elementary education across districts. The fact that some districts with high standards of living otherwise rank quite low in access to secondary education is a matter that demands further research and policy attention. The potential for enhancing involvement of the private sector, especially in upgrading the quality of education in government institutions, needs to be explored. The government can assume the role of a co-financier, regulator and a facilitator in the process. Standard setting and ensuring adherence of such standards is likely to constitute a key challenge for second generation reforms in the education sector. In this regard, the role of local governments, such as *panchayats*, in governance and regulation requires greater attention.

Moving to the domain of tertiary education, private actors have come to dominate in the last two decades. While excessive regulation may stifle institutional initiatives, the proliferation of a large number of colleges and universities marked by poor teaching and infrastructural standards clearly require regulatory institutions that are far more effective than those operating at present. While recent efforts to ensure a degree of autonomy to both government and private institutions of higher education for curriculum development and related activities is a positive development, establishing appropriate institutions of public accountability is equally, if not more, important. Competition and the market mechanism may ensure a degree of consumer accountability. However, despite increasing competition with the rise of a large number of private institutions dedicated to higher education, spatial monopolies and lack of information on quality and infrastructure persist. Hence, incorporating appropriate governance mechanisms to maintain the quality of higher education, even as academic autonomy is ensured for such institutions, will be critical in the years to come. Another area of intervention needed is the provision of adequate financial and non-financial incentives for those seeking to enter the teaching profession in higher education.

Social Security

It is well recognised that the State has one of the best social security nets in the country. Apart from its universal PDS and a well-functioning rural employment provisioning under the NREGA, Tamil Nadu has over the years initiated welfare measures targeted at specific population groups that are marginalised, such as the elderly, widows, deserted women, unmarried women, children, unorganised sector workers, transgender individuals, SCs (scheduled castes), STs (scheduled tribes), minorities and people with disabilities. Outcomes of such interventions are evident in the reductions made in poverty levels in the State over the last 10 years, as well as in the ability of these households to invest in education. Importantly, the contribution of such measures in dramatically reducing the incidence of child labour in the state must be recognised. The report has, however, identified a few areas that need strengthening and/or improvement.

While the State at present provides a monthly pension of ₹ 1,000 for old aged, widowed and destitute women, efforts ought to be made to increase it, as often it may not constitute a subsistence income. In the case of the disabled, the State disability pensions insist on a minimum of 60 per cent disability as eligibility criteria for those who are physically challenged, and hearing and speech impaired (Government of Tamil Nadu, 2014, Citizens' Charter of Social Welfare and Nutritious Noon Meal Department 2014-15). The eligibility criteria could be reduced to 40 per cent disability (the State has reduced it to 45 per cent for those who are developmentally challenged under the maintenance allowance scheme) and should include psychiatric disorders as well, in line with the Government of India's PWD (Persons with Disabilities) Act. The government can have provisions for top ups in case of those with multiple deprivations like old age and widowhood, old age and gender, old age and SC/ST, disability and old age.

The government could also consider including female-headed households as a category for social security pension benefits, as the chapter on gender highlights deprivations faced by such households. Local self-government institutions can be encouraged to identify all elderly, widowed, SC, ST and PWD in their community, while being respectful of people's privacy. This would increase the coverage of schemes. Currently, the elderly, PWD, widows, etc., have to approach the government and submit several documents in order to be eligible for the pension, which imposes difficulties on these people. The insistence on several documents could end up encouraging corruption and hence, this should be reduced. The government can also consider expanding coverage under the social security schemes to make it near/quasi universal with well-defined exclusion criteria, as the BPL (below poverty line) criteria does not cover all the poor. The BPL criteria can thus lead to errors of exclusion and inclusion. For those sections who meet the exclusion criteria, the government can consider a contributory pension scheme. It would be worthwhile to undertake a cost-benefit analysis of administering a targeted scheme.

Despite several programmes targeted at improving nutrition and food security, the Report has highlighted the relatively higher levels of malnutrition and anaemia among pregnant women and babies. This foregrounds the need for nutrition education, awareness programmes, improvement in the status of women and provision of nutrient rich food through the Integrated Child Development Services (ICDS) and Puratchi Thalaivar MGR Nutritious Meal Programme (PT MGR NMP). It is pertinent to observe that the average per capita per day calorie intake in rural and urban Tamil Nadu was less than norm of 2700 kcal, namely 2046 kcal in rural areas and 2135 kcal in urban areas (National Sample Survey Organisation, 2012).

Tamil Nadu is a State where nutrition interventions have been made within the State domain and not outsourced to NGOs (non-governmental organisations). It is critical to maintain State involvement, as achievement of public health goals are best undertaken by the State in partnership with the community. While the State government's health insurance scheme has provided people with options for inpatient treatment (medical and surgical) in government or private hospitals, caution must be exercised due to the involvement of the private health sector, which could lead to unnecessary surgical interventions as has been shown with RSBY in Chhattisgarh. The government should improve the quality of services in the public health sector, as people prefer private health care services mainly because of the perceived difference in quality and staff attitude.

In the context of the increased presence of inter-state migrant labour in the construction and service sectors in Tamil Nadu, the government should strengthen efforts to include these workers in the unorganised worker welfare board schemes. In addition, the enrolment of unorganised sector workers in the welfare board schemes should be increased. In the context of growing casualisation of employment, there is a clear need to considerably increase the numbers registered and mobilise resources so as to ensure comprehensive a social security net for those in temporary or casual work.

Despite its long history of provisioning social security, data collection mechanisms on coverage of various schemes ought to be improved. This can be critical not only for independent evaluations, but important also for rationalising the process. The Management Information System (MIS) that has been put in place in Tamil Nadu in the case of the Mahatma Gandhi National Rural Employment Guarantee Scheme (MGNREGS) and PDS, can serve as a model in this regard.

To sum up, the second HDR prepared by the State Planning Commission, Government of Tamil Nadu, has sought to map the improvements and achievements that the state has made in the various domains of human development and the challenges that remain. The state has emerged as one of the best performers in terms of most parameters of human development and is held as a model State in terms of poverty reduction and improvements in access to healthcare and education. In terms of the developmental goals the State through the Vision 2023 document has set high standards of human development. The present challenges are primarily in terms of sustaining and steadily improving upon the current attainments. As the first chapter points out, growing integration with global markets tend to create new vulnerabilities even as it can create new economic opportunities. Such vulnerabilities in combination with natural shocks tend to quickly erode developmental gains if not backed by sustained state action.

In terms of eliminating absolute poverty which is fundamental to the State's vision, while a strong social security net has contributed considerably, the importance of quality and quantity of jobs to be created cannot be overemphasised. With a large share of youth accessing higher education in the State which in itself is an outcome of the State's emphasis on human development, it is imperative that the State focuses on creating quality employment in the near future. This is tied to investments in appropriate skill development on the supply side and an integration of skills supply with labour market demands as the economy diversifies further into non-agricultural activities. The next important challenge to poverty reduction concerns relative poverty, especially between the rural and the urban and between those employed in agriculture and those outside agriculture. Improving agricultural productivity in a sustained manner, and backed by support in processing and marketing will be critical. Sustainable groundwater and soil management practices, and institutions that ensure such practices are to be an important component of such a strategy as the State moves into the next phase of consolidating and improving its gains. Differences in attainments across gender social groups too will have to be addressed. Relative stagnation in improvements along a few parameters in the domain of health and education too require policy attention.

List of Authors

The following resource persons prepared and finalised the contents of the specific chapters of the Human Development Report:

State Profile

Prof. L. Venkatachalam and Dr. M. Vijayabaskar, Madras Institute of Development Studies.

Status of Human Development

Dr. G.S. Ganesh Prasad, and Thiru Abdul Nazir Sab, State Institute of Rural Development, Mysore and formerly with the Madras Institute of Development Studies.

Income, Employment and Poverty

Dr. M. Vijayabaskar, Madras Institute of Development Studies.

Literacy and Education

Dr. M. Suresh Babu, Dr. Milind Brahme and Prof. Malathy Duraisamy, Department of Humanities and Social Sciences, IIT Madras.

Health & Nutrition

Prof. V.R Muraleedharan and Dr. Umakant Das, Department of Humanities and Social Sciences, IIT Madras, and Dr. Gayathri Balagopal, independent researcher and consultant, Madras Institute of Development Studies.

Gender in Human Development

Dr. R. Sujatha, independent researcher and consultant.

Social Security

Dr. Gayathri Balagopal, independent researcher and consultant.

Challenges and the Way Forward

Dr. M. Vijayabaskar, Madras Institute of Development Studies.